Hickory Tunes

—a life in school—

Hickory Tunes

—a life in school—

Brian T.W. Way

First Edition

Wet Ink Books
www.WetInkBooks.com
WetInkBooks@gmail.com

Hickory Tunes: a life in school
by Brian T. W. Way

Cover Image – Brian T. W. Way
Cover Design – Richard M. Grove
Layout and Design – Richard M. Grove

Typeset in Garamond
Printed and bound in Canada
Distributed in USA and internationally by Ingram,
— to set up an account – 1-800-937-0152

Library and Archives Canada Cataloguing in Publication

Title: Hickory tunes : a life in school / Brian T.W. Way.
Names: Way, Brian T. W. (Brian Thomas Wesley), 1951- author
Description: Includes bibliographical references.
Identifiers: Canadiana 20250207966 | ISBN 9781998324200 (softcover)
Subjects: LCSH: Way, Brian T. W. (Brian Thomas Wesley), 1951——Childhood and youth. | LCSH: Students—
   Canada—Biography. | LCSH: School environment—Canada—History—20th/21st century. | LCSH: Education—
   Canada—History—20th/21st century. | LCSH: College teachers—Canada—Biography. | LCGFT: Autobiographies.
Classification: LCC LB1774.8.C3 W39 2025 | DDC 378.1/2092—dc23

for my parents
who always read to me

Kathleen Winnifred Gaffney
1920—1980

Harry Alpheus Way
1918—1990

Time past and time future
Allow but a little consciousness.
To be conscious is not to be in time
But only in time can the moment in the rose-garden,
The moment in the arbour where the rain beat,
The moment in the draughty church at smokefall
Be remembered; involved with past and future.
Only through time time is conquered.

—T. S. Eliot "Burnt Norton" Four Quartets 1935

An aged man is but a paltry thing,
A tattered coat upon a stick, unless
Soul clap its hands and sing, and louder sing
For every tatter in its mortal dress,
Nor is there singing school but studying
Monuments of its own magnificence;
And therefore I have sailed the seas and come
To the holy city of Byzantium.

—W. B. Yeats "Sailing to Byzantium" 1928

CONTENT:

Forward:

"I'm right and you're wrong, I'm big and you're small, and there's nothing you can do about it."

—Miss Trunchbull in Roald Dahl's *Matilda*

Of all human experiences, one of the most common throughout the world, at least in the last two hundred years or so, is school. Almost everyone has gone to a school of one kind or another, the word, itself, derived from classical Greek scholē, meaning a place of philosophy, a place of leisured learning. And everyone who has gone to school has some memory of the place, of friends you had and sports you played, of subjects you took and teachers who influenced you in some manner or another; this book is filled with such memories. What follows is one of those:

A rubber sink stopper has disappeared from the Boys' Washroom in 1965 and Mrs. Martha Bates, the Principal of S.S. # 6, Ameliasburgh, is furious. She slams the door with a ferocious thrust and stomps toward the front of the room. She has kept all boys from Grades Four through Eight after school in her room and vows to do so until whoever 'stole' the stopper confesses to the crime. She is a thin, dark-haired woman with white strands starting to emerge, gaunt in the face, and always wears black boots tied with laces adorned by round leather aglets. They bob back and forth as she strides. Our Grade One/Two teacher has worn these too and I think of them, somehow, as the jackboots all teachers must wear. I am now in Grade Seven, a quiet and sensitive kid, and Mrs. Bates terrifies me, brings me to tears. She exhibits a kind of rage and power and darkness that is outside my realm of experience and I find only fear in her potentially volatile nature even on her calmest days. Her smile chills and, to this moment, an icy blade slices through the back of my neck when I remember her. She forces us to stand next to the desks, with our heads down, staring at the floor for half an hour after school and does the same the next day, while she marches up and down the aisles. And then, somehow, she forces a confession out of a boy who always seems to get blamed for every misdemeanour around the school, Red Thompson—woe to be Red became my mantra, though I always liked Red, an affable, rough and tumble rapscallion, a boy who would have fit seamlessly into the company of Tom Sawyer and Huck Finn on any of their nefarious escapades. Guilty or not, Red is forced to confess; he took the rubber stopper. Toward noon on this third day of inquisition, all the doors of the four classrooms in the school are opened by Principal's command, Red Thompson and Martha Bates in the foyer near the water fountains, and it begins, she swinging at his hands again and again and the sound of the strap echoing up the stairways, through the rooms, into the high cupola with its broken bell and down again snaking through every space of the school, Martha swinging ferocious like the high striker when Ringling Brothers rolls through town, Red holding out as long as he can, arms blushed and blistering from finger-tip toward elbow, then finally crying out like the resonant breeze must have over Dachau's dark towers, an echo raw and vibrant in the back of my skull to this very day.

Preface:
The Tune of the Hickory Stick

School days, school days
Dear old golden rule days
Readin' and 'ritin' and 'rithmetic
Taught to the tune of the hickory stick
You were my queen in calico
I was your bashful barefoot beau
And you wrote on my slate "I love you, so"
When we were a couple of kids

—Gus Edwards and Will D. Cobb, 1907

The lines of this song, at least the first four, were certainly *in the air* when I was a child and just starting school in the late-1950s. It is an early twentieth century tune bathed in nostalgia, expressing the wishful desire to return to a time of innocence and purity when life seemed less complicated and the lessons that were to be learned, straightforward and simple. That this old song somehow touched a nerve is evident; it was a standard tune in many performers' repertoires for some fifty years after its writing and its refrain continued to appear in several crusades, educational and otherwise, right up to recent time. From broad initiatives such as the influential *Excellence in Education* movement in the late 1970s or the various *Back-to-the-Basics* campaigns that have arisen over the years to the more specific *Three Rs* with emphasis on teaching children the basic skills of Reading, Writing and Mathematics, this old tune has often resonated across twentieth and twenty-first century conceptualizations about education. The Three R logo, of course, has also been adopted for a wide range of other interests including environmental sustainability (reduce, reuse, recycle), a campaign for humane animal experimentation (reduction, replacement, refinement), computer code generation (rapid, reliable, repeatable), American politics and the *New Deal* (relief, recovery, reform), Indigenous rights (resilience, reflection, relationships), cosmetic pads (reduce, reuse, rejoice), nicknames for sports' plays and players, a rock song or two and several motion pictures. A 4th R program even added the affective domain of *Respect* to the triad, the production of responsible and conscientious citizens becoming a necessary part of any learners' skill set, a dimension intrinsically inferred in the long-ago lyrics anyway—to inspire good citizenship was, after all, the purpose of the hickory stick.

While the ultimate origin of the triple "R" phrase is unclear—Saint Augustine does mention the great value of "reading and writing and arithmetic" in his *Confessions*—the popular coining of the phrase most likely comes from Sir William Curtis, a Member of British Parliament who presented the idea of the *Three Rs* in a speech in 1795, his Rs being *reading and writing* (today, the idea of literacy), *reckoning and figuring* (numeracy), and *wroughting and wrighting* (something akin to preparing students in vocational skills). (Sir William, by the way, was popularly known as Bonnie Willie and, after his death, his estate sale took more than a week to complete, among those items sold, nearly four hundred dozen bottles of wine and sherry. Bonnie, indeed!) In turn, of course, the 1907 song by Edwards and Cobb gave the phrase the mnemonic spin with which it resonates in the current-day imagination.

And, most certainly that spin has an unintentionally ironic twist, directly linking educational basics with rules and with punishment, teaching and learning to the "tune of the hickory stick." (One assumes that the contemporary advocates of the "Three Rs" did not have the beating of students in mind!) Hickory, itself, is a hard, dense wood, one of the strongest and most durable, commercially suited, originally, for use in shovel handles, baseball bats, wheel spokes, skis, ski poles and the shafts of golf clubs. And for the switches and canes used for corporal punishment in schools and prisons. That children who misbehaved, or did not learn appropriately, lived beneath the shadow of physical harm seems like a curious, archaic, even abhorrent thing to most of us now, but well into the 1970s in most North American jurisdictions, corporal punishment was still the reality. And it is a reality that continues to persist in many areas of the world often under the monikers of *caning* or *flogging*. Being taken to the woodshed, the hickory stick was the death sentence of the classroom, a point of no return where a student had pushed a teacher, or a school's sense of cultural decorum, to a breaking point. Words stopped and violence was initiated. That, by mid-twentieth century, the hickory stick was replaced by the more efficient and durable leather strap is a testament to the reality that technology always keeps pace to help enable social trends. One supposes, had the practice continued, disobedient students in our contemporary classrooms might have been brought to the front of the room, before their classmates, and tasered.

The standard British School Strap used in Ontario.

1
What is this book

Hail to thee, blithe Spirit!
Bird thou never wert,
That from Heaven, or near it,
Pourest thy full heart
In profuse strains of unpremeditated art.
Like a cloud of fire…
Like an unbodied joy whose race is just begun…
Like a star of Heaven…
Like a Poet hidden / In the light of thought…
Like a high-born maiden / In a palace-tower…
Like a glow-worm golden / In a dell of dew…
Like a rose embower'd / In its own green leaves, /
By warm winds deflower'd…

—Percy Bysshe Shelley "To a Skylark"

This book is not a memoir. Nor is it an autobiography. Neither is it a diary nor a scholarly essay, a confession or a consolation. It is not a Menippean satire. It is not entirely a personal philosophy about how teaching should be done or how teachers should be constructed or how educators should proceed about their jobs. It is not a manual. It is not a history of educational practices nor is it a diatribe concerning social trends and behaviours as they pertain to the classroom over time. It is not an exercise in cultural studies. It is not an accounting or a field notes or a scientific study or a demonstration of hyperthymesia. It is not a cock and bull story, at least not all of it.

So what is it? Well, to some extent, it is an attempt to ask that very question. It is its own question, probably the oldest learning strategy we know, dating back in time to Socrates and before; and maybe still the best methodology for sorting things out. Just ask the right question! In that regard, in the main, this book is an inquisitorial glass of memory, one person's fanciful perusal of his life and his experiences as a student, a scholar, a teacher, and a teacher of teachers in the last half of the twentieth century and a bit beyond, all to shed some light on the elusive question—*what is school?* Generally, chapters will alternate between memories of my own experiences in school and, then, brief analyses in lay-language of most of the individual trends and theories that have shaped schooling and continue to shape what happens in school to this very day; in the final chapters, recollection and analysis will blend. All of us have memories of school; perhaps my memories and analysis will help you sort through your own. As to the specific theories that have shaped the classroom, well, education is a kind of culturally philosophical palimpsest. Numerous ideas about school and educational practice always exist and linger, remaining in belief over long periods of time, layer upon layer—many never seem to go away—and part of the purpose here is to identify (to name) those strata and illustrate how they have manifested themselves in, and continue to influence the events and perception of, day-to-day teaching. If its bias is toward English, so be it; I was mostly a teacher of English Studies, assuredly a foundational subject whose development and representation, at the very least, tend to offer some insight into all, and into the trends that have beset all.

Stubbornly, this book is offered in the way it proffered itself to its author; admittedly, it includes some irregular grammar, verb tense abuse and dangling modifiers, all to better the effect and flow, I think (a colloquial timbre). And yes, I confess, in the attempt to reconstruct one's life-experiences, the ill-fated and unattainable quests of the likes of Tristram Shandy or even that Man of La Mancha come to mind—to tell one's life while living it is an impossible task. So, at times, in Huck Finn's vernacular, this is "a barrel of odds and ends." And, as will become apparent, while it is not any one of the things mentioned in the first paragraph of this chapter, it is yet all of those things. Many books have been written about teaching—treatises that offer fool-proof umbrellas under which to train and/or educate the young minds of today for the tribulations of tomorrow, brilliant academic tomes that, in scholarly and scientific ways, eviscerate even the most minute matters of human learning, journalistic accounts of young *wunderkinds* who enter schools full of tired and out-of-touch colleagues and set the world of their students ablaze. Popular culture overflows with educators and ideas—from Mark Thackeray and John Keating and Gabe Kotter to "Teach Your Children Well," "Smokin' in the Boys' Room," "School's Out," and "Teacher, leave those kids alone"—such pop representations have chimed in with dozens of variations depicting teachers as phenomenally successful and as dire failures: surely, we remember the Economics teacher, Mr. Lorensax, "Bueller … Bueller … Beuller" or John Bender confronting the woeful VP Dick Vernon (who is overseeing detentions on a Saturday): "Screws fall out all the time. The world is an imperfect place." And most of these far-reaching illuminations of the means and methods of education, from the formidable postulates of Plato to magic carpets like Zoom, have a valuable place in our understanding of what is the most complex and challenging of activities, to step into a classroom (real or virtual), encounter a group of students (no matter the age) and somehow improve their understanding of themselves and of the world that they inhabit. For surely that is what teaching is fundamentally about, what school is fundamentally about.

So, what is this book? Well, you've been to school and you know what it was like; in your reading here, you will be the one most qualified to answer that question. What is this book! For now, best perhaps to think of Epimenides' old syllogism and go forward with the simple idea that, in all probability, everything written in these pages is false. And there, let the lesson begin.

2
A Little "Pop Quiz" for You

"I know what you're thinking about," said Tweedledum; "but it isn't so, no-how." "Contrariwise," continued Tweedledee, "if it was so, it might be; and if it were so, it would be; but as it isn't, it ain't. That's logic."

—Lewis Carroll *Alice in Wonderland*

What follows is a test given to Grade Eight students in 1895 at an elementary school in Salina, Kansas. So, here is an opportunity for you to get out of Grade 8 in 1895 and advance to Grade 9 and beyond. Try it. And good luck!

GRADE 8 FINAL EXAMINATION

Grammar (Time: one hour)

1. Give nine rules for the use of capital letters.
2. Name the parts of speech and define those that have no modifications.
3. Define verse, stanza and paragraph.
4. What are the principal parts of a verb? Give principal parts of "lie," "play," and "run."

5. Define case; illustrate each case.
6. What is punctuation? Give rules for principal marks of punctuation.
7 - 10. Write a composition of about 150 words and show therein that you understand the practical use of the rules of grammar.

Arithmetic (Time: 1 hour 15 minutes)

1. Name and define the Fundamental Rules of Arithmetic.
2. A wagon box is 2 ft. deep, 10 feet long, and 3 ft. wide. How many bushels of wheat will it hold?
3. If a load of wheat weighs 3,942 lbs., what is it worth at 50cts/bushel, deducting 1,050 lbs. for tare?
4. District No 33 has a valuation of $35,000. What is the necessary levy to carry on a school for seven months at $50 per month, and have $104 for incidentals?
5. Find the cost of 6,720 lbs. coal at $6.00 per ton.
6. Find the interest of $512.60 for 8 months and 18 days at 7 percent.
7. What is the cost of 40 boards 12 inches wide and 16 ft. long at $20 per yard?
8. Find the bank discount on $300 for 90 days (no grace) at 10 percent.
9. What is the cost of a square farm at $15 per acre, the distance of which is 640 rods?
10. Write a Bank Check, a Promissory Note, and a Receipt.

U.S. History (Time: 45 minutes)

1. Give the epochs into which U.S. History is divided.
2. Give an account of the discovery of America by Columbus.
3. Relate the causes and results of the Revolutionary War.
4. Show the territorial growth of the United States.

5. Tell what you can of the history of Kansas.
6. Describe three of the most prominent battles of the Rebellion.
7. Who were the following: Morse, Whitney, Fulton, Bell, Lincoln, Penn, and Howe?
8. Name events connected with the following dates: 1607, 1620, 1800, 1849, 1865.

Orthography (Time: one hour)

1. What is meant by the following: alphabet, phonetic, orthography, etymology, syllabication?
2. What are elementary sounds? How classified?
3. What are the following, and give examples of each: trigraph, subvocals, diphthong, cognate letters, linguals.
4. Give four substitutes for caret "u."
5. Give two rules for spelling words with final "e." Name two exceptions under each rule.
6. Give two uses of silent letters in spelling. Illustrate each.
7. Define the following prefixes and use in connection with a word: bi, dis-mis, pre, semi, post, non, inter, mono, sup.
8. Mark diacritically and divide into syllables the following, and name the sign that indicates the sound: card, ball, mercy, sir, odd, cell, rise, blood, fare, last.
9. Use the following correctly in sentences: cite, site, sight, fane, fain, feign, vane, vain, vein, raze, raise, rays.
10. Write 10 words frequently mispronounced and indicate pronunciation by use of diacritical marks and by syllabication.

Geography (Time: one hour)

1. What is climate? Upon what does climate depend?
2. How do you account for the extremes of climate in Kansas?
3. Of what use are rivers? Of what use is the ocean?
4. Describe the mountains of North America.

5. Name and describe the following: Monrovia, Odessa, Denver, Manitoba, Hecla, Yukon, St. Helena, Juan Fernandez, Aspinwall and Orinoco.
6. Name and locate the principal trade centers of the U.S. Name all the republics of Europe and give the capital of each.
8. Why is the Atlantic Coast colder than the Pacific in the same latitude?
9. Describe the process by which the water of the ocean returns to the sources of rivers.
10. Describe the movements of the earth. Give the inclination of the earth.

How did you do? If you are like most of us, you would probably struggle just to pass, just to get half of the answers, just to endure the five hours of examination. Even the words or phrases themselves might pose problems. I mean, what does "case" mean or "promissory" or "principal parts" or "bushel" or "tare" or "subvocals" or "diacritical marks" and what's "orthography" anyway? Does this mean that students in the small rural community of Salina in 1895 (population approximately 6100) were smarter than we are today? Was this a town of academic brilliance, of Rhodes scholars-to-be? Well, it may have been but there are probably other conclusions, other observations, to be made.

First of all, note that almost all answers to these test-questions require specific and direct recollection of information, students must recall details that, presumably, they were required to learn by rote in prior school days. Almost all of this test asks students to regurgitate information that would have been drilled into them— dates, details, causes and effects, rules, procedures, definitions, specifics, and so on. There is no value placed on testing cognitive skills such as problem solving or critical thinking or creative processing. Students are not asked for their reasoned opinion of what the most important rules of capitalization might be but, simply, "give nine rules for the use of capitals." Somewhere "nine rules" have been decreed, "nine rules" memorized, and "nine rules" need to be re-stated. Almost all of the test is the product of memory work and, if you did not do the memorization, or if you were not able to function effectively in that way, you would not have done very well on this test. (And you would probably have exited the world of education for the world of work.)

One should also notice the arbitrary nature of the questions asked, and, of course, the cultural bias of the time. Today, there are more than a few who might question whether or not Columbus "discovered" North America. And we might point to the language section with the realization that the knowledge of the "rules" of spelling and grammar and even punctuation do not help any student become a better writer (or reader). Only a minimal request (150 words) is made requiring the student to write and, in this case, it is a composition whose emphasis is to illustrate "the practical use of grammar." Probably not a topic that inspired any great enthusiasm! The thrust here is not toward practice or good writing but toward indoctrination, grammatical and otherwise. The curriculum is a banquet set before the student who, in turn, must prove how much she or he has consumed. And regurgitation seems the primary objective! No equivocation here; the ghost of Banquo no-where to be seen at this feast. And Macbeth—well, that hell-hound may be in the details.

The tone throughout is generally authoritarian—the world is a place to be controlled, conquered, shaped, ruled, said. A base privilege and a superiority is presumed, probably a constant in Western education in all decades since such education began. Socrates asked his students question after question until the individual arrived at an acceptable answer (acceptable to Socrates and to the philosophical culture he and the student inhabited; and of course, when the ruling powers of that culture, themselves, disagreed, hemlock became part of the curricular menu). In recent times, the trend is toward using exemplars to illustrate a range of acceptable and ranked answers. In this test from 1895, though, while specific, precise answers are no doubt expected (many involving a sequence of calculations based on a recollection of skills—for instance, the student must know how many pounds are in a ton before she/he can calculate the cost of "x" many tons at six dollars per pound)—even there, sometimes the questions are slippery. Surely, then as now, there are degrees of imprecision in asking students to "tell what you can of the history of Kansas" or to indicate an event connected to a certain date. (If I were to ask you to indicate an event connected to the year 2020, most might have a similar response but, by that same token, many events happen in any single year, memory diffuses such details as time passes and 2020 would be no exception. Certainly, 2020 was the year of Covid-19, it was the year Donald Trump lost the American presidency, the year of Black Lives Matter and Every Child Matters, the year my brother died. Which cited 'event' would get the best mark?) By today's sensibilities, much of the content required in the section on Orthography would be considered irrelevant and how does one possibly answer, in any conclusive way, questions under Geography such as: "Of what use are rivers? Of what use is the ocean?" or "Describe the mountains of North America." Well, one might ask: 'of what use is a butterfly' or 'of what use is a snowflake?' Or, 'describe the moon.'

So, what is the point of perusing such an old document. Such an ostensibly dreadful and dated test? What does it tell us about schooling and education? In a word, perhaps … change. Ideas, attitudes, values, what we as a society consider to be important skills and knowledge change over time. But change is a deceptive thing. For even now, some might look at this test and say, yes, students should still be required to know certain details about Language and History and Geography, names and dates and events and parts of speech; students should still be able to calculate percentages and interest rates. Others would say there is no need to memorize such stuff when they can simply "google it" or use the calculator function on their cell or tablet. Ultimately, to understand education and the various pedagogical trends that have percolated in and around the classroom, from slate tablets to electronic ones, is to acknowledge the nature and the force of change in culture and society and technology; but while change may continually seem to flow like a stream or unfold as the seasons, there is a constant in change. One thinks of Heraclitus stepping into a river or that Yeatsian cycle of swans returning to Coole. Spring lingers in the mind even as the leaves of autumn tumble. As such, ideas and practices once implanted in the classroom rarely seem to disappear entirely as society moves on, echoes of the calliope remain long after the parade passes, I suppose. In that sense, this test is both a tombstone and a signpost and a useful reminder of the complexities inherent in that thing we call school.

3

Grade One

I've been examining half-scraps of my childhood.
They are pieces of distant life that have no form
or meaning. They are things that just happened
like lint.

—Richard Brautigan "Lint"

I had always imagined school as a quiet place. But, as my parents leave me in the custody of a stranger inside the Grade One classroom, this is the noisiest place I have ever been. While I had brothers, they were older and so most of my childhood was spent playing alone in the quiet of our front room or in the shade of the great maple that hovered over our front yard or wandering about the labyrinthine nuances of our 100-acre farm. And, with the luxury of retrospection, I also suspect that my parents had emphasized the need to be quiet at school though I was a shy kid anyway so any admonition was probably unnecessary. Although, probably, they saw me, knew me, in different decibels than I knew myself. But here in the Grade One/Two classroom, hordes of people, some my age, some older, some much older, are talking more talk and making more sound than I ever imagined could exist. Our barn full of cows and horses, pigs and chickens, feral cats and wayward pigeons, was not as restless or as loud. Adults came and left; children came and stayed—this is the first great passage in life for most of us. A shift to a daily lifestyle that will permeate the first quarter of our lives. The pattern for this first day of school was a set routine; as I later learned, for better or worse, routine is the sacred mantra of all schools and schooling. The desire for routine must be imbedded somewhere in the human DNA. Don't rock the boat; fear death by water. Here, on this first day, people come and go with train station deliberation dropping off children like the new-fangled balers in the County spit out hay. Archie Herbert, who will become one of my best early school friends and a staunch ally in many great battles of body and soul to be waged in the next couple years, arrives not so much crying as shrieking and has to be confined forcefully to one of the desks before his parents escape the building. In Grade Three, he would move away to Brighton and I would never see him again although I carried a photo he gave me in my wallet for years until it simply disintegrated. The Rossmore kids arrive, empowered with all the sophistication and suavity that living in a village that actually has a gas station and a corner store with penny candy affords, and those from far down lower Massassaga Road, the doctor's daughter and the Dutch farmer's kids and the adopted brothers, are directed to seats. The Grade Two students, confident and assured in the authority given them by twelve-month's seniority, like pros in some charity exhibition game, swagger in and seat themselves alphabetically in the rows along the east side of the room, proof that they have now risen from the lowest echelons of pedagogical stratification, and that last year's training has not slipped away entirely over two months of summer reprieve.

Mrs. Welch is our teacher for Grades One and Two; it is a four room school-house in the rural 1950s of Ontario and each teacher, all females, teaches two consecutive grades. The school is S.S. #6 Ameliasburgh—encrypted before they started giving schools the names of dead pioneers, faraway astronauts and antique politicians. S.S. #6—the name of our school rolls from the lips like some obscure stockade hidden behind enemy lines!

And Mrs. Welch is ancient, like some Great Aunt your father once introduced to you but who would only visit once again and whose name you could never quite remember. Mrs. Welch's hair is as grey as my father's Strato-Chief and held by sticks and pins like Ma Kettle's and she wears the kind of shoes that for many years I think form part of a uniform all female teachers are required to wear; those high-top black boots with laces that end in round aglets. And Mrs. Welch is relatively deaf, so in Grades One and Two we all learn to TALK LOUD. Schoolspeak—that's mostly what school means to me and my sixteen Grade One colleagues—saying every word as clearly AND AS LOUDLY as we can, without actually shouting, of course. And it takes our Grade Three teacher, Mrs. Brummel, a solid two months to get all of us to speak at a normal timbre. For us, it feels as if we are whispering in her class and we all conclude that Mrs. Brummel must have supernatural powers of hearing, for a school teacher, and we all admire her for that!

Pencils are handed out. I have never understood the teleology of elementary school pencils. In Grade One, when our hands are small, we are given giant round red pencils (no eraser) with which to learn our studies; later on, by Grade Four, inexplicably, we graduate to regular-sized yellow hexagonals, easy to hold with beautiful erasers. Perhaps by that time we have learned not to eat the rubber end or stick the slender missile in some inviting orifice. I am not sure. The red pencils of Grade One are huge—their radius at least a half an inch (two centimetres for later learners) and, as we are taught to draw circles and make lines, we almost need both hands and all the strength we can muster to hold up these delinquent pine logs. And it is only by Grade Seven that our motor skills are developed enough for us to graduate to ink. By that time, the desks contain round holes in the top-right corners filled with glass inkwells and the implements we use are fountain pens (we must supply these ourselves)—these fountain pens have levers that you pull open and bladders that contract and then slurp in the ink. They require a delicate human touch and a sensitivity between writer and written that is forever lost in the future efficacies of typewriters and keyboards. They also leave forever-stained fingers, blue or black or green. Ink cartridges have yet to appear for pens and, a new invention, the ball point, is forbidden in the school as something that will be destructive to education (similar to the arrival of calculators a decade or so later). The mythic prediction of girls' pigtails being dipped in inkwells does not materialize in my memory—perhaps the girls in my classes were wise enough not to allow their pigtails anywhere near the temptation of the well; a few ink-soaked spit balls (fired from trebuchet-rulers) were the extent of criminal behaviour. And so fat pencils, slimy mucilage, porous construction paper and Madison workbooks (Madison was the indisputable Atlas of the Canadian school system, at least until that Herculean brand named Hilroy replaced them)—these were the industrial pistons that drove our education in those early days. A curious waxy pencil, blue lead at one end, red at the other, also wandered into our daily usage but I cannot remember its specific purpose in the gradual cultivation of our randomly-fertile minds. I remember that it did have a cool paper-strip binding that you would loosen with your thumb-nail and peel off like one of those sticky fly-catcher ribbons that hung over the cows' stalls in the barn.

We do a lot of phonics in Grade One. *Buh* this, and *Puh* that. And it seems fine. It is what we do at school. When I get home, I read the newspaper and my comic books and books (what I can of them anyway), and I get read to, and I write stories or draw pictures that tell stories. Other than the farm chores, it is what I do at home. We do not have electricity yet, no indoor plumbing and, of course, most tragically, as I listen to the ravings of my classmates, no television! *Huckleberry Hound* and *Ed Sullivan*, *Superman* and *Davy Crockett* and *Leave It To Beaver* are but conjectured phantasmas of my imagination. My only 'electrified' entertainment comes from the huge battery-operated RCA Victor that sits in the rarely visited living room (mostly we lived in the kitchen in those days, where the heat was)—I can still recall *Jack Benny* and *Fibber McGee and Molly* (O the racket when Fibber opened that closet) and *The Shadow*. And we had a Victrola, too, that played those droll records from the 1930s, voices that always sounded far-away. As to school, as far as I can figure, nothing I ever do at school has any connection to life beyond the school, and that seems fine—that is an idea which sticks with me (even to the present) and I am ok with it. School is a job—a place I have to go, and while on occasion I can fake sick, or sometimes even get sick, most of the time I am forced to go by powers that are far beyond my control. In my elementary years, school is not an overly inviting, kind or pleasant place. It is dominated by biblical rules, Moses' stone tablets stored somewhere cataloguing all the things you cannot do, and it is especially aimed at the boys. The principal, Martha Bates, is a child of the blitzkrieg, commandant of concentration camp S. S. # 6. And the school in these years, still raw I suppose from the uncertain and blood-stained immediacy of World War II, is operated with a kind of regimented, militaristic mind-set. I even remember my older brothers sometimes having to wear cadet uniforms and march off to high school, BCI&VS, a school that actually had an operational rifle range in its basement (see photo of my brothers dressed as cadets, Chapter Twenty-One). And all of that was acceptable, normal, in that time. Our school yard, a page-wired square about one acre in size, is subdivided into sixteen imaginary rectangles, one rectangle for each grade divided by gender, males to the east, females to the west. The invisible lines of demarcation are made clear to us and no one crosses those boundaries. We leave the school for two recesses and lunch, follow a centre path, and turn into the designated space. No-one is allowed to stay in the school during these breaks. After each, when a hand-wrung bell sounds—the great bell in the school's cupola is unused, cracked and rusted ages ago—we line up by grade, females at the front doors, males at the rear. When the lines are straight, each of us rigid at attention, we are allowed to return to our rooms. Standing in a corner, being kept in after school, the strap—these are the punishments for all indiscretions, meted out regularly, but with a kind of existential randomness. Pushing another student one day gets you confined to a corner, another time, it gets you the strap. And most serious of all is the public thrashing, like the time Red Thompson, poor Red, got beaten because a sink plug went missing. To this day, I have often wondered how much the local mill rates were impacted by the loss of that rubber stopper. And how much was lost of our human soul!

S.S. #6 Ameliasburgh — Prince Edward County, Ontario
(the once and future Massassaga Public School)

—in 1991 (its closing year)

—illustration—circa 1900

ADDENDUM:

Kindergarten, Space and Dinosaurs

I have made no mention of kindergarten, simply, because, in the world of S. S. #6, no such *children's garden* existed. All of the local children started school in the September when they had turned six years of age according to month of birth, so some children were younger, some a bit older. And some parents and scholars have made a great deal about that, but I am not sure if it really mattered. Certainly, as classmates, we did not care—a few months older or younger did not seem to count as long as you could catch a ball or flick a marble.

While kindergarten was recognized as a viable part of public education as early as the nineteenth century in Ontario, it really only flourished in larger population centres, and often as an upper middle-class luxury—as there were regular fees to be paid for elementary school (in addition to taxes), where it was available, kindergarten generally cost quite a bit more. But supported by research, advocates for the value of a professionally-guided early childhood education system grew in number and by the 1970s, full-day junior and senior kindergartens were established even in rural districts like Prince Edward County.

Would a full kindergarten program have been better for me during ages four and five, better than wandering about the nooks and crannies of our farm or better than playing with my toy soldiers on the living room floor—building a space ship for their star-bound escapades out of cardboard cut from *Shredded Wheat* and *Corn Flakes* boxes and glued together with water and flour paste my mother made for me, partitions stuck together using a roll of that wide brown tape you needed to lick. How that stuff tasted; do you remember that flavour both repulsive and yet somehow alluring? I always thought that it must be the flavour of dead horses. Would kindergarten have taught me that?

And in 1957, just before I started school, the Soviet Union launched *Sputnik*, the first satellite to orbit the earth, and the space race was on with the dreaded Russians in the lead. Politics aside, in those days, most kids (at least most of the boys) were crazy about those temporal bookends, dinosaurs and space, so the launch of a real space craft fired imaginations. Somehow Buck Rogers and Flash Gordon and Tom Swift became a little more plausible. In education, the impact was tangible with greater attention and funding throughout and, in particular, increased concerns about Math and Science skills and lots of changes (I will discuss the impact of the *New Math* in Chapter Seventeen). Government programs were quickly initiated to provide university loans and grants to enable more people to afford higher education. Ultimately, the universal implementation of kindergarten was also a result of the space race and the perceived need to improve education, in this case by extending it. The Soviet system of education, which typically removed children from parents at a very young age, placing them in the hands of educators in boarding schools (children returned home on weekends), was phenomenally successful in the U.S.S.R., reducing illiteracy and producing a highly educated population. In Ontario, with the eventual acceptance and funding of Day-Care programs funnelling into Junior and Senior Kindergartens, the West has essentially, finally, adapted the Soviet model, educating children by getting them away from their parents as quickly as possible. And so, in spite of the fact that Apollo 11 landed on the moon in the summer of 1969, one wonders—given that the space race was really an education race—who really won?

It is interesting to note here, and it is not a coincidence, that mainstream environmental movements (*Keep America Beautiful, Pollution Probe*, and the like) also started in the same period as the race to space. In the Belleville area at that time, the city used the Bay of Quinte as its dump, simply bulldozing all of its garbage into the water and creating an island called Zwick's. The Bay was cited in the 1960s by *Pollution Probe* as one of the most polluted bodies of water in North America, biologically dead. In the summer, it stank, things of rot and decay forming a thick meniscus around its shores; fish were known to swim into the Bay from Lake Ontario and die within minutes; *American Optical*, a local factory, dumped a toxic sludge known as *rouge* directly into the waters—a stream of scarlet water bubbling with foam was nicknamed the Red River and flowed directly into the confluence of the Moira River and the Bay. The Bay actually caught fire a couple times, its flames being put out from the shore by incredulous fire-fighters. Eventually the town fathers decided to stop the dumping, dab some cosmetics on the piles of waste and call it Zwick's Park. Cancer rates around the Bay were among the highest in Canada—still are.

In rural areas, individuals more or less did the same as the city, burning trash, using refuse as fertilizer or feeding it to one's livestock. Out-dated and broken farm equipment and rusted automobiles decorated the landscape or were sometimes deposited out-of-sight in marshes or woods. Eventually, though, some habits changed. As the dinosaurs had become extinct, humans came to see that we, too, were following their fateful path. The planet was becoming used-up, a wasteland; population growth was making this world unsustainable; climate change was afoot—the space race was an education race but, ultimately, it was also the human race. First the moon; then Mars. And so, Mr. Musk, and billionaires everywhere, prepare your rocket ships to escape this planet and seek the stars; humans must do so, it seems, or risk becoming the fossilized T-rex which decorates museums and at which we stare in awe, wondering how such great beasts, who dominated this planet for a hundred and forty million years, could vanish into silence.

4

In Socrates' Sandals

Horace there by Homer stands,
Plato stands below,
And here is Tully's open page.
How many years ago
Were you and I unlettered lads
Mad as the mist and snow?

—W. B. Yeats "Mad as the Mist and Snow"

While this book is not a history of education, *per se*, a little history never hurts, especially when we understand that such a history never has an end-point. These critical thumbnails or brief sketches in every other chapter, or so, are intended to provide some insight into a few of the many individuals and/or movements which have influenced the theory and practice of education through the years. And, most important, which continue to play a role in people's thinking about school and about what education should be. These are part of the neverending story.

Indisputably, among these individuals, one casts a shadow over all, ironically one who wrote nothing on the subject or left any concrete data; that is the Athenian philosopher, Socrates (c. 470-399 BCE). Virtually all that is known of his ideas about education and his approach to teaching come through the accounts of others, of friends and students and admirers, the likes of Plato, Xenophon, Antisthenes, Aristippus and the playwright Aristophanes, among others. And yet, second-hand as they may be, the ideas of Socrates and the influence that those ideas have made on education throughout its existence in the West are virtually incalculable. And a debt is owed to Socrates for his impact on just about every other form of Western intellectual discourse as well. We all walk in Socrates' sandals. Now, how many of those ideas actually belonged to the individual Socrates, or how much is simply attributed to him, laid on him like oils over a base, is impossible to ascertain in the absolute. Most certainly Socrates becomes Plato's protagonist in somewhat the same way, perhaps, as Julius Caesar or Macbeth might be Shakespeare's, although Socrates did exist in Plato's time. (In Plato's *The Republic*, of course, Socrates is a central character who coaxes numerous acquaintances into disparate expositions, all for the purpose of sorting through the various philosophical exigencies of living a just versus an unjust life.) While Plato's ideas and Plato's philosophies, then, are certainly an extension, perhaps on occasion a modification, of Socrates' thinking, like the eponymous debate over who wrote Shakespeare's plays other than that whittawer's son from Stratford, the issue of who the *real* Socrates was seems irrelevant—call him Socrates/Plato or Socrates/Xenophon if you wish. The important fact is that, like the writings of Shakespeare or the epics of Homer, the collective of ideas under the name Socrates has had a substantial influence on education and thinking in the West, essentially, right up to and including present day. (And, I might add, whenever one thinks oneself to be overly clever or intelligent, just read a few random paragraphs of Plato and, humbly, one will be reminded that there is still much to learn.)

So, essentially, what is the shadow that Socrates has cast over education? Well, first of all, Socrates was a moral philosopher, focussed on human values, concepts such as ethics and goodness and justice, all with the goal of creating better citizens and, thus, a better society; he was interested in getting his fellow citizens to enter into a journey of self-discovery, a journey to find the just or principled self within. Socrates felt that there were essentially two different kinds of knowledge, an ordinary knowledge and a higher kind. While the ordinary knowledge of how to build a fire or construct a chair was useful, it was not a kind of knowledge that gave the individual any wisdom. More important was the acquisition of a higher knowledge, a kind of definitional, conceptual knowledge which could bring the individual to a condition of knowing how best to live. Most are familiar with Plato's "Allegory of the Cave" in which the majority of humans are chained in a cave, staring back at a blank wall and seeing only the shadows cast by things that cross in front of a fire at the cave's opening. These individuals know only the shadows of reality and only a few struggle to free themselves, to break their chains and perceive the truth—these are the philosophers who come to understand the higher levels of reality, to see in the real light of the sun concepts such as natural science, mathematics, deductive logic and illuminating ideas. Socrates dwelt in a time when Athenian democracy was under pressure and in decline and his ideas, in seeking to bring individual citizens to a purer, deeper understanding of the self, were generally in conflict with those in power who wished to maintain a firm hold on the *status-quo* (as most in power always do), eventually leading to Socrates' infamous death-by-hemlock execution, always characterized as a noble act. Socrates felt that Athenians were too concerned about their jobs, their families, and their politics, the ordinary things of their lives, and not concerned enough with what he called the "welfare of their souls." Society, simply put, was too materialistic. (One thinks here of our own *amazon*-world and Alphonse Karr's observation—*plus ça change, plus c'est la même chose.*")

The most critical aspect of Socrates' influence on the world that followed, of course, was not just his ideas about the function of a best society, a utopia, but his logical approach to problem solving, his dialectic method of inquiry (classically known as *elenchus*). In this tactic, a series of questions is asked in an attempt to enable an individual, response by response, to come to an understanding of the fundamental (and divine) tenets of her or his own knowledge or beliefs. Under the skilled questioning of the teacher, the student directs her/him-self to a profound revelation. Socrates' approach was not intended so much to impart his own knowledge as it was to empower students to arrive at their own understanding of what they could, of what they did not know. (Even toward the end of his life, Socrates was noted as saying: "I only know that I know nothing.") The student discovers truth over falsehood, virtue over ignorance. For Socrates, human beings contained within the divine spark of the gods. By their very nature, humans were rational beings (*animal rationis*), imbued with an illimitable potential and a will for intellectual pursuits. Ignorance, as such, was the root of all moral evil but humans, always capable of reasoning, could always know good. And for Socrates, no human being who truly knows good will follow the path of evil. (The eighteenth-century satirist Jonathan Swift would re-define human-beings as *animal capax rationis*—animals capable of reason—capable of, but not always practicing it!). Fundamentally, Socrates established a dialectical method which used critical inquiry to examine all popular opinions and assumed fact, to explore the nature of epistemological conceits. One can understand why the politicians and other authority figures of the day were at odds with him and accused him of corrupting the youth of Athens. Few politicians ever really want a population of thinkers—as a recent example, in our own time, the Conservative government in Ontario rejected and ejected the phrase *critical thinking* from Curriculum Guidelines. *Problem solving* was acceptable and included—that might help keep the assembly lines running—but not *critical thinking*, where a worker might start to ask questions about the nature of her/his job or rate of pay. It is interesting to note, after the Covid 19 pandemic forced many office workers to work at home and gave them some time to think about their lives outside those boxy office towers, large percentages of workers resisted a return to the cubicles of their former working lives.

As the process became refined (and distilled) over time, Socrates' model became adopted as the model for instruction—the teacher asking the student one question after another to the point where knowledge was attained (and demonstrated)—and the Socratic method was born. Ideally, the purpose of the Socratic method was never to retrieve an answer, as such, but to provide enough questions to enable the students' own understanding; more on this in Chapter Sixteen. And it has existed as the central methodology of teaching for the last 2400 years. It is probably also the primary blanket of intellectual exploration laid over almost every other aspect of human endeavour since. The lawyer cross-examines the witness. The doctor questions the patient. The police officer interrogates the suspect. And the traditional methodology of the teacher, from kindergarten to graduate school, is pretty much locked into place.

Beside Socrates (and/or Plato), one other classical figure predominantly shares in the intellectual nascence at the heart of the evolution of education—that man from Stagira, Aristotle bar Nicomachus (383-322 BCE). Socrates and Aristotle—like 'love and marriage' in the old song, I suppose, you can't have one without the other. And like Socrates,

Aristotle's philosophical interrogations have also influenced almost every intellectual discourse in the West. His writings at various times consider music, theatre, rhetoric, poetry, physics, biology, zoology, language, politics, economics, and a host of other subjects, so on that basis alone, one can understand his influence on education. In many ways, he was the great brander and compartmentalizer. The subjects we study, the subjects we teach are Aristotle's subjects.

So in general it might be said that while Plato idealistically looked to the heavens, Aristotle's focus was materialistically toward the earth—Raphael's famous fresco *The School of Athens* (1509) depicts them thus, Plato pointing up, Aristotle motioning down. Much of Aristotle's thought involves the analysis, classification and definition of the things of his world; like Adam in the Garden naming things, Aristotle demarcated what subjects required study and, in that vein, directly influenced educational curricula, in lower and higher institutions of learning, well into the eighteenth century, and beyond. Apocryphally, as Aristotle broached and added his spin to Plato's ideas, Plato once said of his former pupil that he was 'like the foal who kicked his mother after draining her dry.'

Aristotle was a champion of education for the masses and insisted that teachers should be the best educated of all, delivering not just their own knowledge but information that was confirmed by their research. Teachers needed to be informed scholars; they needed to understand ethics and politics and have a clear philosophy of life. And the education they imparted should not involve the mind alone but it should extend to activities that invigorated the body (to help boost bravery but also to allow for enhanced leisure)—music, dance, play, debate, theatre, physical activity—determined by the age-appropriateness of the student (importantly, Aristotle felt that education needed to be offered in stages (essentially the idea of *grades*) congruent to the growth and development of the individual). And as Aristotle notes in Book VIII of *Politics*, there are four practical purposes of education: reading and writing, physical training, music, and drawing. Learning comes from involvement with life; one learns to do things by doing them. To become the illuminated individual who frees oneself from Plato's cave, the individual thus needs both *phronesis* and *sophia*, both practical wisdom and theoretical wisdom. The student needs to learn causes and reasoning and such (the theoretical or philosophical disciplines), but the student best learns how to be just or brave by doing things that are just or brave (the practical and technical disciplines). That clarification of the nature of understanding and that progressive analytical, scientific mindset are perhaps Aristotle's greatest influence on education through the centuries and, in some ways, the other side of the coin from Plato/Socrates's transcendental idealism. For Plato, the purpose of education was to free the visionary soul and, by so doing, illuminate virtue (or truth); for Aristotle, the purpose of education was to attain happiness through the acquisition of knowledge (and in such happiness, virtue is attained). Simply, for Aristotle schooling enabled students to develop and practise habits of reason that would enable them to lead an active better life.

5
Grade Two

About suffering they were never wrong,
The old Masters: how well they understood
Its human position: how it takes place
While someone else is eating or opening
a window or just walking dully along;...

—W. H. Auden *Musee des Beaux Arts*

Now no matter, child, the name:
Sórrow's spríngs áre the same.
Nor mouth had, no nor mind, expressed
What heart heard of, ghost guessed:
It ís the blight man was born for,
It is Margaret you mourn for.

—Gerard Manley Hopkins *Spring and Fall*

For many contemporary students, knowing that most of us in our school days wear the same clothes to school all week would be an horrific thought; clothes and style are of little concern in the time and place and relative rural poverty of S. S. #6 in the late 1950s and early 1960s. Choice of clothes alternates week to week, a second wardrobe worn while the first is washed and ironed by our mothers, an ingrown part of the weekly drudgery of that role, I suppose. I still remember my mother at the old wooden ironing board on Tuesdays (Monday was wash-day; Tuesdays for ironing), delicately flicking drops of water from a bowl over shirts and pants like a holy sacrament before she swept the hot iron to eliminate the evil of wrinkles. Of course, you always changed into work and play clothes as soon as you got home each day—that helped to keep the world of school separate from the real world. One stiff and shiny pair of leather shoes is purchased in August; I recall breaking these blister-mongers in around the farm during the final days of summer freedom and on our yearly excursion to the Belleville Fair where they are coated by the fine dust of the bauble-laden midway. The yearly fair arrived with an exotic mystique, a panache and colour that transfixed the dull world of our lives. Like the fruit of Tantalus, giant prizes, stuffed animals and transistor radios, hovered just overhead in the booths of all those esoteric games and all you had to do was fire a dart to bust a balloon (the one with the gold star beneath) or toss a nickel into a jar. The shining lure of candied apples, the aroma of fried onions, the gleam of caramel corn or the mystery of pink cotton candy were only surpassed by the temptation of fat or bearded ladies and monkey boys with long tales and scantily-dressed snake charmers and other wondrous enchantments, all advertised on giant posters and to be found just off the midway's main thoroughfare—but my parents never took me there. We toured the farm displays and animal buildings instead; as if I hadn't seen a cow or a tractor before. My mother always prepared a picnic; we parked in the infield encircled by the race-track and we ate sandwiches and drank Freshie in our car, the five-cent drinks and ten-cent burgers of the fair being too expensive; if the price of admission included the early Grandstand Show, we stayed to see Gordie Tapp and his Cousin Clem, or local stars like *The Singing Post Family*, or maybe Chuckwagon races imported from the famous Calgary Stampede or Yvonne Duhamel, imported from Quebec, sparks flying from the metal cleats of his boots, as he bent into the corners and ripped like a man gone mad around the dirt-track on his flying Yamaha. Somehow as darkness settled, the circling lights of the Ferris wheel intensify and the discomfort of hard new shoes drifts away like a quietening storm moving off over the lake and, now, at summer's end, I am ready for school to begin again.

The strong students and the weak ones have emerged, and no-one really knows why. Why arithmetic or spelling or phonics or art comes easier to one student than another remains one of those great mysteries of the cosmos like the big bang or cancer or why the dinosaurs died. Why some become Shakespeares and Mozarts and Einsteins and most become you and me. At S.S. #6 Ameliasburgh, all of us come from mostly the same homes, with the same meals, the same chores, the same lawn games (like *Red Rover* and *Hide and Seek* and croquet), the same radio and television programmes (those that have TVs), and yet differences have emerged. Some students get it, others do not, others are somewhere in between. And so the world takes shape in our small room and, across the universe, I suppose. And at the end of June, when all of the pupils' names and averages are published in our local newspaper, the *Ontario Intelligencer*—a newspaper once owned, arguably, by Canada's worst Prime Minister, Mackenzie Bowell—the entire community will know who the intellectual haves and have-nots are and there is always a slight sense of that ancient Greek bop, of hubris and nemesis strutting the floor to a rock 'n roll rhythm, when the son or daughter of the local big shots; the ones who lord it over the community in their respective roles as Doctor with the five acre lawn or Head Trustee and Caretaker of the local United Church; when their son's or daughter's grade is lower than that Dutch farmer's kid down the road, son of the man who was captured and forced to collaborate with the Nazis before escaping Europe with his family to farm for many years and die from cancer in the 1980s. And, on occasion, the local MPP's daughter, thick as soured cream, fails a grade and those iterated procla-mations, 'I told you so's,' are the whispered *hors d'oeuvres* of local euchre parties. For these are the days when failure means a child must repeat an entire grade with new classmates; these are the days before self-esteem has taken the wheel and no child is left behind, before 'every child matters', a time when failure is made as public as telephone party-lines shared across the County, when The Sprague Telephone Company is as mighty as Ma Bell, and frail, old bird-like women in their dimly lit parlours lift the receiver delicately after every ring, no matter the declaration; whether two short, one long, or one short and two longs, they keep themselves informed of all the news not theirs to know. Ahh,

Mrs Hillman, we know you are there as your oh-so-familiar grandfather clock ticks away in the background—yes, everyone knows you're listening but we keep on talking anyway.

There is a dead cow in the vacant field to the east of the school. We discover it first thing in the morning, still and peaceful, painted in wet dew before the heat of the sun rises. It has escaped from Valleau's farm next door, gorged itself on fresh alfalfa that must have seemed like those irresistible apples of Eden, and died from bloat. It is enormous as it lies on its side near the school fence. And nearly all of us second-graders rush to see this day-changing thing. This kind of scene, the road-kill-happenstance of rural farm-life, fascinates us like marsh fires and spring's flooded creeks and skittish deer wandering across the back yard. From what we have been taught, if not from our own farm erudition, we know that it is a Holstein, a milk-cow, black and white splotches separating it from the cinnamon Jersey or black Angus or red Hereford or rare cream-white Charolais. Pictures of livestock were tacked to school walls, lessons were taught and memory tests given; 'Name the four types of work horses' (Belgian, Percheron, Clydesdale and Canadian, in case you have forgotten!). Bloat was a common occurrence among farm cows; I recall my father on numerous occasions mixing family size coke bottles with a solution of detergent and warm water and forcing the mixture down a cow's throat to make it burp or fart and save its life. Once I saw a vet in our stable pierce a cow's left side to let the gases out spraying a fine rain of blood over his white overalls. And the cow instantly calm, breathing normally, chewing its cud (whatever that was) and returning to being like all of the other cows. *Let Gryll be Gryll*, I suppose. Our bloated cow-next-door, as our class thought of it, remains in the field for a couple more days before it vanishes, taken away after the school is dismissed one day. The hay field is cut, windrowed, and then transformed into rectangular bales. They dry brown in the sun like lonely tombstones.

A tale of bloated cattle—I recall one of the few tales of the Second World War my father ever told. Dad never said much about the war that used up nearly six years of his life—at the age that I went off to university, he went off to war, and 'O' the difference in education between those two. He always said that those who never went to war were the ones who talked about it most, and they were also the ones who crawled out of the woodwork to strut in the Legions' parades when the war was over. My father signed on in 1940 once telling me that he did so simply because everyone else did—he held no illusions of flag or glory although his schooling had steeped him in all that Kiplingesque patriotism. He tried to become a paratrooper but had flat feet and so was disallowed. (Given the perilous nature of that profession, had he succeeded, I probably would not be writing this today!). Attached to the First Division, he (C34482) was a part of the 11th Canadian Army Field Regiment, 11th Light Aid Detachment. They travelled with the artillery unit that followed the infantry into war, leaving their stationing in Aldershot and the Battle of Britain, sailing past Gibraltar (where they were strafed by the Luftwaffe, their first "action") to campaigns in Sicily, Italy, Belgium, Holland and, finally, by war's end, Germany. Basically, my father was trained as an army mechanic and, with his band of brothers (Sandy and Frenchie and the rest), drove a vehicle called a Breakdown to tow and service other trucks and tanks that needed help, especially in the rainy seasons when the terrain became a muddy soup. But war stories were rare. Once, as they drove up a steep hill, they heard a distinctive whining noise and both he and Sandy jumped to the ditch as a Stuka rose above the rise and strafed the front seat of the Breakdown. One summer's day in Italy, Dad and a couple buddies were standing near a dusty crossroads when a jeep pulled up; the man in the backseat flashed a "V for Victory" salute with the stub of a cigar wedged between his fingers and said "Keep up the good work, boys" before the vehicle sped off. It was Winston Churchill much closer to the front than he probably should have been. On another day, after the German troops had moved on in retreat, my father and his buddies stopped and explored a farm where, in the stable, they found an Italian family bound and executed, their bodies bloated in the tremendous heat of the Italian sun so that flesh protruded even through the eyelets of their shoes. As they left, there were fields full of dead animals, starved to death and bloated in the sun, or killed by shrapnel. My father described soldiers, hardened in mind and body by that point, using the dead beasts as target practice, gas and blood bursting into the steaming air. One can only

"Somewhere in Italy, 1944"—Sandy, Frenchie, Clem, et al (Dad, second from left, back row, in the photo left, and in suspenders above; a farm-boy, so "Clem" was his wartime identity as anointed by this Band of Brothers. Everyone had a nickname—I've often wondered if such mock-identities were somehow a protective buffer against the ever-present possibility of loss although I realize nicknames were a common custom in the era). As well, most are smoking— cigarettes were probably as vital to the war effort as bullets although Dad said he learned when not to smoke after a new and pompous Captain, out for a smoke one evening, was shot at (uncertain by whom); after dark, lit cigarettes were great targets for snipers; an alternative, *Copenhagen Snuff*, became a kind of chewing tobacco my father used all his life, a pinch under his tongue.

wonder at the impact all of this must have had on a young farm boy from Prince Edward County. His university! After the war, my father was offered free training to become an engineer on Great Lakes' freighters but he said that he was tired of the military rank and file of such things and simply wanted to return to the independence of the farming life. And poor though it was, that was what he did.

Santa Claus always visited in mid-December, always surprising us, ho-hoing his way suddenly into the classroom, asking us, with a nod to the teacher, if we had all been 'good little students' this year and then handing out candy canes and small paper books to each of us. Sometimes he arrived early enough in December to bring a Christmas tree into the classroom which somehow changed the entire ambience of the place, aroma and magic and all, and we will spend much of the next couple weeks making paper decorations for it. He tells a couple corny reindeer jokes; I actually remember: 'What do reindeer hang on their Christmas trees"; 'hornaments' he says with a laugh. And then he hurries on; he has other business to attend to including visits to the other classes. With his great girth swaddled in red, outlined by a snowy ruffle and magnificent beard, wrinkled face and soft blue eyes peering through delicate spectacles, he is truly Santa and remains so in my memory to this day, even though I am told later in the know-it-all cynicism of Grade Eight that it is really Mrs. Welch's husband making his yearly visit. But I have always doubted that and even now during the mid-December days as the world turns cold and bleak, I can look up quickly from the labour of my desk and behold this larger-than-life fellow barging through the door and breaking down the routine of our days with kindness and a gift and his mighty "Ho! Ho! Ho!"

It is an early spring Thursday and Cathy Tomlinson is dead. She is one of our Grade Two classmates and her house, near the end of lower Massassaga Road, has burned down. Instead of running from the burning house, Cathy, with her dark page-boy hair-cut, hid underneath her bed, probably a place of sanctuary all her life from things malevolent. Her burned remains are discovered in the late night and the news delivered early next day to the school. There is silence and whispering, a quiet murmur across the schoolyard that somehow seems appropriate in a place where first human death has come, much sharing of rumours, of how the fire started, of what was found, a vicarious thrill of somehow being a collective part of something that will be canonized in tonight's local newspaper. The school's flag is lowered to half-mast. But mostly, the usual routine continues. Bells ring and we line up in gender-divided rows at the doors. "God Save the Queen" is sung and "The Lord's Prayer" mumbled and the day unfolds. I suppose in Grade Two we do not really understand what the empty seat really means, what the final signification is of the teacher collecting up Cathy's print-book and pencils from her desk or un-tacking her artwork from the wall; what seems to be the wild portrait of a large brown horse with a great white forelock and blue eyes in a crayon sea of green; farm animals were last week's motif in art. In the distant future, when such events occur in a school, there will be an avalanche of crisis teams and school psychologists and social workers of various hues and fragrance, a grim pack of these poseurs of the heart, but here there is none of that. Sad, truly, but this event is a kind of thing that has happened before and will happen again. We do arithmetic for what seems like hours and then our weekly spelling test and then recess and the day spins out as all the days before and after. And, as it seemed to me then and still does now, perhaps that is as it should be. There is no need to speak of a sorrow we do not understand to strangers who pretend to care, who follow manuals about what to say. We do not need some other's prompting about how we are supposed to feel. In our own way, as individuals and as a class, as humans, we did what had to be done. We pushed on. We chanted the morning rituals that our society dictated to us. We added and subtracted. We filled blank paper with ten new words that we had to memorize; and some of us did. It is, as I later learned from living and from the great poets like W. H. Auden and w. c. williams, what we must do; whether Icarus plunges or tall buildings fall to earth or little girls with page boy haircuts perish in flame; we scratch our itchy butts, we turn to our ragged lives and push on. And by Monday, the empty desk has been removed from the row and stored in the foyer beneath the stairs and as the days and weeks pass on, in summer thunder and autumn winds and wintry short-cuts across the frozen marsh to and from school, that empty desk becomes unremembered, only reappearing if some new student arrives, which is a rare occurrence in this rural wilderness, and even by then it would just be another wooden thing. Like the answers to the arithmetic problems or the esoteric words of a Grade Two spelling test, in time it came to seem as though it had never been at all. But that is not exactly true, and can never be so. For here, for now, Cathy, with this sleight of my memory, at the very least, I remember you and a degree of sadness is lodged in my soul for who you were and for what might have been. And that is, I think, the way it should be, must be. Always.

ADDENDUM:

Farm and Family

In the late 1950s, Upper Massassaga Road is part of the main highway between Belleville and Picton, stretching through some ten family-operated farms, each approximately 100 acres in size, the standard allotment to Loyalists as migration to the Canadas began in the late eighteenth century. Farms spread across relatively flat sandy loam and clay terrain, just large enough to sustain the livestock and crops, the women and men that nestle here and small enough to be maintained by the family's manual labour.

I grow up in such a farming household, my grandfather Wesley (after whom I am named), my mother and father (Winnifred and Harry), and two older brothers (Robert and William). I spend my childhood exploring the territory that extends between marshy boundaries, the north fed by the Bay of Quinte, the south, indirectly connected to Lake Ontario. Our house is a fairly-standard two-story frame farm-house owned by Wes, an entrepreneur-of-sorts in the early part of the century when he serviced farms near and far with the power of his George White steam-powered tractor and threshing machine. As with many, the arrival of the Great Depression had a severe impact leaving Wes quite poor and sometimes embittered; simply put, no-one could pay for the services he rendered. Although relatively unacknowledged in that we were all the same, a tangible kind of poverty blanketed the community in which I grew up well into the 1960s; it was a shared reality, put on each day and worn like an old coat by almost everyone. In fact, home-made and used clothes were the norm and survival on the meagre produce of the farms, an accepted reality—potatoes, carrots and other root crops filling cellar bins with their heavy earthy aroma along with jars of every preserve imaginable, young and old taking on jobs in seasonal industries as they materialized. I remember my mother's cut and scarred hands from peeling tomatoes on the assembly line in Sprague's canning factory. I remember the pelts of muskrat hides stretching and drying in our basement as my father became a farmer-turned-trapper through the winter to supplement the family income.

As an aside, from the margins of my muskrat memory (the marshes in those days seemed full of their reed-humped houses), we had a great shaggy dog named Ted who, through the year, used to kill a dozen or more of those marshy creatures and lay them on the front stoop; I recall my dad noting that Ted always seemed to dispatch them in a way not to ruin the pelt, easily paying for his keep in that manner. (Note: Ted was not a cuddly or cute beast; he had his place to lay in the kitchen and, while he was a good farm dog, he was not one that, as a child, I ever ventured near—he never harmed me but his demeanor, his casual guttural utterances, were defined enough that it was clear his life was complete without my comradeship. When his final muskrat days were done, he was buried beside the cherry tree that grew in our side yard. His predecessor was Rex, a part-wolf mongrel who, I am told, would simply lay on the stoop and by his growly snarl would stop travelling salesmen in their tracks—no barking was ever necessary, and none set more than a footstep in the yard. After repeated scraps, Rex finally killed Grass's neighbouring bulldog who insisted on returning to our farm to battle time and again; the final deed was done in silence. Yipping and yapping came later with my dogs, a pair of cute and furry miniature collies whom I adored and christened Lassie and Fluffy, not particularly imaginative nomenclatures but dear playmates and the closest of beloved friends throughout my growing years on the farm. To my memory, though, they never caught a muskrat!)

When people talk today of the proliferation of technological change, computerization, AI, AGI, ChatGPT and the like, I often think of my grandfather Wesley. Born in 1878, one of his earliest memories from childhood was of troops mounting the train in Belleville to go west and 'put down' the Riel Rebellion in 1885. The arrival and development of the train was a relatively new 'invention' at that time, especially in Canada, replacing the stage-coach and certainly increasing the efficiency of military deployment (a rude awakening to Riel and his followers, as well as to anyone used to stage coaches which would leisurely wait for all passengers to arrive before departing—not so much the train with schedules to keep and tracks to share, the allegiance of technology forever shifting from human to machine.) In his lifetime, Grampa Way saw the arrival of train, automobile, telegraph (wired and wireless), telephone, radio, television, co-axial cable, giant ocean liners (six days to cross the Atlantic give or take an iceberg), airplane (eight hours, no icebergs), electricity, transatlantic cables, indoor lighting and plumbing, super-highways, space exploration, the electric toaster, and a host of other everyday gadgets and inventions and medicines and procedures (as well as a couple world wars, the atom bomb, nuclear weapons, ICBMs, cruise missiles, *etc.*). One is reminded, I suppose, that technology is always changing, developing, and my grandfather, in his life, certainly experienced change every bit as dramatic as today's electronic whirlwind. I remember him loading me as a three-or-four-year-old into his car, a Terraplane (it looked like a Model-T), and driving over to the Brants' corner store to buy some penny-candy; then he would cruise around some of the County's back-roads and reminisce about people he'd known and the stories of their lives ("lattimir", a poem in my collection *magic birds*, recounts one such tale of an old farmer who decided to go back in time and live in a cabin in the woods; he was institutionalized for his decision). Wes told me many such stories: I recall another about wolves bringing down a horse-drawn sleigh in a blizzard and another of a 'gravedigger business' in which, after the graveside service, the body was dumped out of the coffin which was sold back to the funeral parlour which, of course, resold it to another 'customer'—one coffin was used three times in one week, he claimed with a smile. And I recall him repeatedly conquering me at checkers and crokinole (he loved those games) and endlessly playing solitaire (from time to time, 'accidentally' dropping his cards to the floor to improve his odds at winning). Grampa Wes died too early in my life for me to remember all his tales well but he always resides in my memory, teller of stories, endlessly rocking in his chair by the kitchen window where the summer's geraniums sat, chewing from a plug of tobacco, occasionally hitting the spittoon, and always twirling a strand of snow-white hair. I am reminded, at the very least I suppose, that we should all listen to the stories our grandparents tell just a little bit more.

(My other grandfather, after whom I am also named, Thomas, died in a housefire before I was born. I know him only through a few fleeting details recounted by others, single frames from an old film flickering. He was a bear hunter—I saw the great, spiked traps one time in my grandmother's cellar—he owned a remarkable six-sided rifle, he always wore his hat, a large fedora, indoors and out, he spoke seldom, often sitting to the side and making occasional quasi-philosophical comments when the conversation in the room lessened, and once, having skinned and stretched a bear-skin in the woods, he awoke to see its outline high among the trees, thought it looked 'human' and was 'bushed,' running terrified all the way home; then, as the sun rose, he regained his composure and, a practical man, returned and retrieved the hide—a good bear fur was worth far more than a waking night terror.)

My mother was a kind and loving soul—I never recall her saying one bad word about another (she probably did, but not to my ears). She grew up in L'Amable, south of Bancroft, came south to Belleville for work at a young age (sending her wages north to support her family) and, for much of her life, wore the label of farm-housewife taking on all the continual labours of that occupation, including the raising of three boys; in the latter years, she worked at Weese's and Barber's Flowers, assembling all the complex decorative arrangements required of that profession. My poem "beautiful sacrifice" in *redirection* is a stark recollection of the cancer that ended her life far too soon.

My father grew up on the farm in the County, although as a young man he worked on the Great Lakes canaller, the Glen Allan, and then volunteered as a soldier with the outbreak of World War II. In a Light-armored division attached to the second regiment, he served in the battles of England, Sicily, Italy, Belgium, Holland and into Germany at war's end and, as I have written elsewhere, must have experienced things no young farm-boy (or anyone else) should ever have experienced. Having been offered a free ride and the opportunity to advance through the sea-faring ranks on Great Lakes' freighters after the war, he chose to return to the poor albeit egalitarian regimen of the farm, a world sans rank and file. He was always a good father to me; he treated me fairly and we could talk endlessly about almost any topic you could imagine and, when I helped him on the mail-route (Dad took on R.R. #7 Belleville, providing a far more stable income as small farms struggled under new agricultural regulations in the 1960s), we would argue for or against the opinions of radio phone-in callers (that show still exists on CJBQ) or sing along together with the various popular tunes of the day. At Christmas, I remember us belting out "Felix-nabi-dab" with all the comic bravado we could muster. While age and alcohol took their toll, that spirit remained to the end—I can still hear him boldly recite those old patriotic poems like "Sergeant of the Buffs" and, always, I will recall with fondness our seamless and poignant conversations.

I always admired and respected my older brothers. They certainly played with me when time permitted in my developing years as 'the baby brother' but they were also in their teens by the time I started to be cognizant. At ten and nine years older, they were both of a different generation and a different culture—they were Elvis and Haley, I was Dylan and the Beatles; they were coal-oil light and farm labour, I was electricity and the mail route; they were ducktail and brush-cut, I was long hair and beard. Robert graduated high school to find a life-time job in Kingston at DuPont; Bill opted for the married life with Susan and eventually, some four children later (Debbie, Jeff, Robbie and Steve) secured a job at Moore's Printing. While our choices in life took us in different directions, we always connected through the years and maintained a friendly, laughing and loving rapport.

Along Upper Massassaga Road now, there are no farms at all— some of the land is still worked, one small patch grows grapes, but most has returned to bush. There are a few new homes but the road, itself, which was once a busy thoroughfare you had to wait to cross, now has crumbling, weed-riven shoulders, the guardrails along the marsh rotted away—passage seems perilous, the road about to dissolve into time. So, we are reminded, things change, such is the nature of living, but recollection remains and in that, at the very least, I think, sense resides and what is human prevails, lasts and is nourished. Our memory is the library of life. So let the roads return to bush, let technology thrive and claw anew the future, and tell your tales, too, Grampa, and twirl your hair by the geranium window as a young lad listens; for someday, he will tell his own.

Wesley Way and his George White Steam-driven Thresher

[My piblings: Irene, Francis, Ethel, Jim, Joan, Clifford, Michael; first cousins: Wanda, Mervin, Patsy; Pauline, Karen, Pam, Kathleen, Julie, Michael; and niblings: Debbie, Jeff, Darlene, Rob, Aleina, Steve.]

6
Nomads and Farmers and Factories, O My!

Love goes toward love as schoolboys from their books,
But love from love, toward school with heavy looks.

—William Shakespeare *Romeo and Juliet* 2.2 167-168

Long before Socrates or his fellows ever posed a question, the human species rose up out of the sweltering climes, navigated ice ages and began to meander about the planet in small groups hunting and gathering the substances necessary for survival. The living was no doubt difficult (but when isn't living difficult)! Education involved continual exploration, each new dawn calling for human invention, adaptation, skill and courage. One imagines much of the time being spent in a kind of investigative play for adults and children alike, with practise and search and discovery forming the way of living successfully, and an exciting way of life it probably was, at least when you weren't being chased by some prehistoric long-toothed tiger. And, as such, the instinct for search and discovery probably represented the most remarkable traits of these nomads as a species, in some way being the quintessence of what it meant to be human. Out of such inquisitive play, habits developed that enhanced reasoning and pattern recognition; add to that, opposable thumbs and the rest is, as one might say, human history.

About twelve to fifteen thousand years ago as the current ice age retreated, these nomadic peoples discovered a way to capture and control the kernel of their food (literally) and agriculture was born.

Crops were grown and tended and the domestication of certain animals followed. And education changed. While the hunter-gatherer life certainly demanded the acquisition of certain skills and knowledge for survival, the agricultural life offered security and stability but it demanded … work. It was labour intensive, most days farmers rose at dawn and worked until sunset. And while villages and cities and politics were born and populations expanded significantly, education for the child was redirected from hunter-gatherer play and exploration to agrarian sweat and labour. As more children could be supported and fed, so more children could be employed in the work force to support that family and its village—in some ways, this remains the mantra of the farm in most of the world to this day. While population growth and survival were enhanced, for children the focus of daily education became mostly the drudgery of essentially unskilled and repetitive labour. Each new dawn brought more of the same—gone was the thrill, the excitement of the search and the discovery of what might lie beyond that next hill or through the dark forest. Now it was milk the cow, tend the field, and tomorrow, do the same things all over again.

The coming of agriculture also meant that the idea of property and ownership emerged. One is reminded of Jean-Jacques Rousseau in *Du contrat social*:

> "The first man who, having fenced in a piece of land, said "This is mine," and found people naïve enough to believe him, that man was the true founder of civil society. From how many crimes, wars, and murders, from how many horrors and misfortunes might not any one have saved mankind, by pulling up the stakes, or filling up the ditch, and crying to his fellows: *Beware of listening to this impostor; you are undone if you once forget that the fruits of the earth belong to us all, and the earth itself to nobody.*"

As certain individuals accrued more land, using others to work those lands made sense and those others often had no choice in the matter. It was often a case of work or starve. Various forms of servitude and slavery developed and, by Medieval Times, as these feudal systems congealed, the drudgery of the agricultural life for children intensified. Records of brutality to child labourers are numerous; children were trained to be obedient and reverent to their lords and masters or face time in the stocks, beatings or worse. Corporal punishment was the currency breathed.

As the feudal systems faded with the rise of industry and the yeoman (or middle) class appeared, not much really improved by way of education for most children. Instead of employment in the fields, young children were herded into workshops and *dark, satanic mills* to use William Blake's imagery. A few youths who were fortunate enough to be born into families with wealth or status may have had governesses or access to Grammar Schools and were apprenticed out of those schools into select trades, usually around age thirteen, the standard canonical age. Shakespeare, the son of Stratford's mayor, as an example, attended the King's New School in Stratford-upon-Avon. Latin was the core subject; students were required to speak Latin, even at recess, write compositions in Latin and undertake the study of classical authors such as Ovid, Virgil, Horace, Seneca and Cicero. Consequently, references to and use of the poems and stories of those writers occur frequently throughout Shakespeare's adult works. At school, around his neck, young Shakespeare would have carried a horn-book, inscribed with the alphabet (upper and lower case) and the Lord's Prayer—not many of these horn-books survive in that they made good school-yard weapons and, in later decades, they were constructed of cardboard which, in weather, had a limited neck-life. At thirteen, Shakespeare and his classmates would have started apprenticeships, in William's case, in his father's business of glove-making and leather goods. But, as we know, the magical theatres of London soon beckoned, although before he left Stratford, he did marry Anne Hathaway in 1582 (she was eight years his senior and, apparently, three months pregnant but such circumstances were not that unusual in Shakespeare's time, or, one supposes, in any before or since!). For his time, then, Shakespeare was a well-educated young man with plenty of experience, it seems, in and out of school; the education and training he'd received was certainly very serious and very classical and there are many moments where such knowledge can be seen informing the content and imagery of his plays. *Titus Andronicus* and *A Midsummer Night's Dream* are heavily influenced by Ovid, *Hamlet*, *Macbeth* and *The Tempest* owe much to Virgil, *Julius Caesar* to Cicero, and so on, and images of education never seem far from characters' thoughts and ideas:

> If to do were as easy as to know what were good to do, chapels had been churches, and poor men's cottages princes' palaces. It is a good divine that follows his own instructions: I can easier teach twenty what were good to be done, than be one of the twenty to follow mine own teaching.

—Portia *The Merchant of Venice* 1.2 13-17

Shakespeare and like males of his economic standing were the exception, of course, not the rule. In their employment in cities and factories, thousands of children died through disease, malnutrition and fatigue. Females, from a time when they could stand and walk, were mostly interned in matters of the household—learning to clean and cook and take care of younger siblings. How many might have grown up to be great poets or playwrights or leaders in other capacities, we can never know. And while conditions did improve marginally through the nineteenth century, even the laws that were passed seemed minimal by today's standards. For instance, by the 1880s textile manufacturers were forbidden by law from employing children under nine and had to limit the work-week of ten to twelve-year-olds to 48 hours per week, for thirteen to seventeen-year-olds, 69 hours. And while chimney sweeps may dance and sing in Disney's *Mary Poppins,* most coughed and asphyxiated in the coffin-like environments in which they laboured—few lived to age forty. William Blake's imagery is haunting:

> When my mother died I was very young,
> And my father sold me while yet my tongue
> Could scarcely cry "'weep! 'weep! 'weep! 'weep!"
> So your chimneys I sweep & in soot I slee

—"The Chimney Sweeper" 1789

In so many ways, Blake's *Songs of Innocence and Experience* captures the essence of childhood in the late eighteenth and early nineteenth centuries, the contrast and tension between the natural inclination of childlike delight and discovery on the "Ecchoing Green" in opposition to the grown-up world of servitude and labour, the world of the industrial blast furnace which dares to forge that fierce "Tyger Tyger, burning bright." As time passed, attitudes changed, political powers shifted, and technology progressed. The gradual automation of industry improved its efficiency and the need for child labour declined—the novel idea arose that childhood was an ideal time for learning. Besides, more educated children might create more efficient workers, although most owners of industry did not want their labourers to be too educated for obvious reasons. On the side of those labourers, a central tenet of Marx and Engels in *The Communist Manifesto* (1848) is for universal public education. Among other considerations, one supposes that educated workers are more likely to be revolutionaries. Essentially, really from the time of Shakespeare on, the idea of compulsory public education gained more widespread appreciation. Martin Luther, and the Reformation he inspired (with a nod to Henry VIII and Anne Boleyn in England, of course), was one of the major forces of change behind that thinking. For Luther and Calvin and Wesley, and the myriad of religious groups that broke with the Roman Catholic church, direct connection to God was the road to salvation. For that, individuals needed to be able to experience *The Bible* for themselves without an intermediary and, to do that, of course, individuals needed to be able to read. Beyond learning to read, part of that meant that church proceedings, if there were any, needed to be conducted in contemporary languages and the Bible needed to be translated and printed in the same manner. That happened all across Europe, perhaps the most impactful being the King James' version in early seventeenth century in England—urban legend even claims that Shakespeare, himself, may have contributed to its writing. The Roman Catholic Church, of course, maintained its spiritual cloak of mystery, using Latin services well into the 1960s—so did medicine (prescriptions still use Latin codes such as *bid* and *q6h* and *qod*). And as details about the unjust horrors of the Residential School system unfold in Canada at this writing, one is reminded that the ascetically conservative Roman Catholic church has never been very kind to children, or to women. Across Europe, from hundreds of years of persecution, the stench of witch-fire smoke still remains in the air.

One of the best examples of the Reformation in educational matters can be seen in the Puritans who felt persecuted in England, and so, many moved to Holland, then to North America. Although strict in their theocratic practices, the Puritans formed a learned culture that prized education. The head of each household was required by law to educate his (her) children and, after settling in Massachusetts in 1630, within ten years they had established the first university in the so-called New World, Harvard. Young students learned from the *New England Primer* which, along the lines of the horn book, became a foundational pedagogical concept for the teaching of reading and, in some sense, for the idea of the educational textbook in general, establishing a motif which exists to this day. (Just ask any current college or university student what the price of such textbooks are!) For the Puritans, of course, the goal of education was the goal of their religious society, to create individuals who would worship and fear the arbitrary might of "an angry God" to use Jonathan Edwards' phrase. Famously, the Primer that children read contained images of martyrs being burned alive, many instructive stories and cautionary passages from the *King James' Bible* and an alphabet of rhymes designed to help students learn to read (often emphasizing dire moral consequences of failure) beginning with "In **A**dam's fall, we sinned all. / Thy life to mend, this **B**ook attend. / The **C**at doth play, and after slay. / A **D**og will bite, a thief at night." and ending (finally) with a hopeful image of potential salvation, "**Z**acchaeus did climb the tree, his Lord to see."

And so the pattern of public education was more or less established. Students collected in one place for a period of time, usually about six hours per day, and were paced through a curriculum decided upon, essentially, by whomever ruled the region or the country (aristocracy, democracy, theocracy, whatever). That inculcation or curriculum, what is to be learned, how much and how quickly, has always been a political construct, not an educational one. If labour and the world of field and factory rules, then education will be determined by what needs to be done in the fields or the factories. If Latin is the language of the church and the church controls the land, Latin will be taught. If the winds of change favour other ideas, be they *critical race theory* or *feminism* or *social justice* or *nationalism*, then whatever is taught in school will shift allegiance to tat. Curriculum rides a one-eyed horse; it is always a politically-fickled mount—in the end, a society does not teach students how to make Molotov cocktails if that society does not expect students to use them. And so, always, the dictate to society is be aware, and beware, the lessons taught.

Example of a Horn Book, so-named because the tacked-on protective cover was made from cow/oxen horn or hoof.

7

Grade Three

But never met this Fellow
Attended or alone
Without a tighter Breathing
Or Zero at the Bone

—Emily Dickinson "A narrow Fellow in the Grass" 1096

Holidays appear as manna-from-the-gods in the elementary school classroom, the gasoline that fires the engine; as I rummage through my far-off memories it seems to me that most of our class time was spent in preparation for one holiday and, when that one passed, the teacher tore down the decorations and we were instantly engaged in planning for the next. Even to this day holidays provide the *raison d'être* for a multitude of elementary events and activities. And in the contemporary multicultural world, the landscape is even broader. As once Hallowe'en, Thanksgiving, Remembrance Day, Christmas, Valentine's Day, Easter and Victoria Day were pillars of the public school curriculum, now multicultural observances (diversity holidays, if you will), from Hanukkah to Ramadan, Diwali to Mahayana, QingMing to Juneteenth, impact hours of school with their music and art and traditions, and decorations. And dare one forget Robbie Burns Day and Groundhog Day and, more recently, Family Day and Black History Month and, I almost wrote Sir John A. Macdonald Day, but, so I am told, that one is currently under scrutiny. Small blunt scissors (I only ever saw these in school; at home I'd use long, sharp scythe-like implements of destruction), and, as noted before, sheets of something called construction paper, and endless jars of mucilage, with their slanted and slitted rubber tops, fuel our directed creativity. For Hallowe'en, paper lunch bags would be decorated with images of jack-o-lanterns and witches and taped to each of our desks as repositories for spooky cards, pressed from perforated sheets and secretly deposited by our classmates. I often felt that, after the cards were punched out, the perforated sheets that remained seemed more interesting than the cards that had been, like beautiful and bewitching pieces of art, their existential holes the ghosts of ephemeral spirits of the season, destined to a quick passage from this earthly plane to another, namely, the trash bin (recycling yet to be conjured). As different holidays came and went, I remember drawing, painting and/or cutting out witches and pumpkins and pilgrims and candy canes and Christmas trees and wreaths and red hearts and white crosses and a host of other apt icons. What magic it was to fold a large piece of paper, sketch a shape and then cut and unfold it to reveal a unique snowflake or an arc of joined angels—the music of heaven seemed to fill the air. These snowflakes and angels were carefully displayed across the windows, filtering the winter sun as it weakened in the sky to cast arcane shadows across the room. And cutting, curling and gluing small rectangles of construction paper into cylinders, linked together to make long multi-coloured chains to be hung all around the room.

I recall now a memory that has haunted me down through the years for some inexplicable reason (perhaps simply being human). A large garter snake has slithered into the school-yard at recess and is surrounded by all of us, prodding it with sticks, tossing pebbles, the girls in the style of the day squealing and jumping back each time it moved to escape. I remind everyone of some folk legend I have heard, *that a dying snake's tail will twitch until after sundown*. Then in a brutal moment, without thinking, I step on the snake's head. It leaps and twists itself around my shoe and then turns into a ball and coils away and my classmates grimace and shout in dismay and turn away as the bell to end recess rings. Why did I do that, I have often wondered ever since? To impress the girls with an act of bravado, perhaps. It didn't. And that memory, that act, has stayed with me all these years so much so that there are still moments when I wake in the middle of the night filled with guilt at the senselessness of my act. Can I say of this encounter, as Emily Dickinson did, that I was overwhelmed with that sudden chill of "Zero at the Bone" or like D. H. Lawrence as that yellow snake arrived ahead of him at a water trough and he threw a stone at it, that some cultural fear drilled into him by a "voice of education" took over? Perhaps. Similar to Lawrence, I have regretted my act ever since:

> I thought how paltry, how vulgar, what a mean act!
> I despised myself and the voices of my accursed human education.
> And I thought of the albatross,
> And I wished he would come back, my snake.
> For he seemed to me again like a king,
> Like a king in exile, uncrowned in the underworld,
> Now due to be crowned again.
> And so, I missed my chance with one of the lords
> Of life.
> And I have something to expiate:
> A pettiness.

—D. H. Lawrence "Snake" 1923

So I have always carried an unabsolved shame for that action. Perhaps everyone has one of those moments in life, I don't know—perhaps that is simply a part of this complex thing called being human. But somehow, in that memory, a curse resides with me and casts a reductive shadow over all that I have ever done. Sins run deep, I suppose, and embarrassment and regret are requisite cancers that abide in each of us gathered like dark flowers from the sides of the road where car wrecks happen. Could we have treated someone better than we did; did we do all that we could have in some moment of crisis; could we have avoided some instant of shame and humiliation? The old Christian myth reminds us that there is a fierce angel who waves a sword at the gates of

Eden forbidding re-entrance, but, of course, the true curse is not that we cannot re-enter the garden but that we cannot forget what its eternal innocence must have been like. What a pure, ageless possibility of joy was there!

After the recess bell one day, David doesn't line up at attention. David is a new kid in school and is clearly different. He wanders between the Grade Three queue and the Grade Four. When reminded to line up, he says what none of us would ever imagine saying to a teacher: "Why? That's stupid!" It is an amazing revelation for which the teacher in charge that day has no reply; her only ontological response is to grab David by the arm and force him into our line. It is the kind of observation for which five years of secondary school and six weeks of teacher training have not prepared her. Another day, during art, when the subject is Hallowe'en, David dips his brush into some yellow paint and stabs yellow blobs on a large piece of white construction paper until all of the surface is an irregular vista of yellow. Yellow suns and yellow mountains and yellow valleys and yellow shadows; uneven yellow rivers running past uneven yellow houses into uneven yellow seas. Yellow people sinking into yellow quicksand. Yellow three-legged monsters and yellow aliens in low-flying yellow saucers. It is bright and dark all at once. But, though Seurat or Van Gogh might have approved, such post-impressionism seems underappreciated in this time and this place—at the end of the day when the rest of our pumpkin-laden, witch-and black-cat-infested landscapes cover the bulletin board, I see David's masterwork curled in the corner garbage can. And a few days shortly after, David does not show up at school and we never see him again. There is no explanation and, in some strange way, none of us is surprised. He was not really one of us, we knew that. One, he was a newcomer; in Prince Edward County, if your family pedigree does not date back at least six generations, you are forever a newcomer. And two, we all knew that he was strange, probably nuts, a twirling finger about the ear, retarded, cuckoo, cranked, rattled, buggy, a looney, a weirdo, a goof—and all the other cruel epithets of the day, and he certainly didn't fit the daily harmonies of S. S. #6 or the County for that matter. Maybe the world. And yet, we did not forget him; his memory became a kind of callous urban myth for our class. We'd threaten to "do a David" or declare "that's stupid" when we found out about another numbing routine to be affixed to our daily lives (and everyone would smile) or, some other day when the system seemed to be grinding us down, we'd plan in our next art class, *en masse*, to fill our canvases with yellow blobs of paint. But we never did of course. No-one ever really does those kinds of things. Except David, who did not fit in and who understood something we did not; who looked at our world all those years ago, and summed it up—"That's stupid" he said and, on some level, he was right. He had touched the sky and found that the world was hollow—and then he disappeared to some other place like a single yellow blob dissolving into a vast yellow landscape.

Many things have changed for the better over time—attitudes toward women and immigrants and minorities and sexual preferences and physical and intellectual disabilities among them. Not that things are perfect, or ever will be, but things have changed. And so, in thinking of David and in the revitalizing knowledge of how different such views generally are today, I recall my brief encounters with another citizen of my world, Donald Hillman who, in the vernacular of the day, was considered *simple*. He walked with a distinct limp and spoke with a heavy slur and a slobber. Donald was in his early-thirties and lived at home. He had never attended school. The only alternative place for the Donalds of the day was being locked behind high walls in the asylum in Kingston, *The Bug House* as it was called. Instead his parents protected him in an upstairs room, taught him what they could, and put him to work in the community's stables shovelling out manure and, on summer farms, loading bales of hay or pitching sheaves of grain on wagons. 'Go, Donald, go,' the men would shout and Donald would fling those heavy bales up onto the wagon, one after another, loading twice what the others did and joining in the misunderstood laughter all the men shared. And maybe that made him feel a part of their world, I don't know. For lunch, he carried an old pillowcase and he pulled from it, every day, a baloney sandwich wrapped in waxed paper, leaves of lettuce sprinkled with sugar, and an apple; he would quench his thirst by drinking from a pump at the well or the cow's water trough. As a young kid, I was always fascinated by the stories of his strength and his routines, but slightly scared of Donald as well—one day, as he came walking by with his uneven gait on his way home, he flashed black and greasy hands near my face. I recoiled in terror and he laughed as he ambled on. Another time for no reason as he passed, he suddenly placed his thumbs in his ears, wriggled his fingers at me and brayed—what, I later learned, the British call *cock-a-snook*. And so Donald was an uncertain, unknown entity to me and he lived just up our road. I went to sleep on many nights imagining him peering through the window of my bedroom, tapping it for entrance, even though I slept on the second floor. But unlike Heathcliff on the Heights, about whom I read many years later, I did not invite the spectre in. I think of Faulkner's Benji or Steinbeck's Lennie or even Harper Lee's Boo. I had always been taught to be wary of strange acting animals—rabies was a scourge among foxes and raccoons and groundhogs at that time. And to me, Donald had the unpredictable demeanour of such a creature, and I am now ashamed to admit, I was afraid. And in the end, I also regret to say, I do not know what happened to Donald. During the years I was away at university, his parents died and he disappeared from our road. And that was that. Such are the haunting vagaries of that time and of that place.

ADDENDUM:

Next Door at the Revills

I spent many hours growing up next door at the Revills. The Revills owned the farm next to ours on Upper Massassaga Road and while I had many neighbourhood friends—Randy Kerr, Rick Goulah, Doug Dainard, the Roseberry and Hart clans—my best friend through all the years of my growing up is Alan Revill. In my memory, since before memory began, Al is always by my side through those years, always. Al and I walked to school together in grades one and two, later rode our bikes (Al was one year older so we were in the same classroom every other year, at S. S. #6 and later at BCI); we played with puppies and stray barn cats, explored the edges of our farms becoming familiar with every shadowy corner in both barns and every wild apple or plum or hickory tree in and around the back woodlots. We played around the pond next to Simon's old cemetery (which sat on Revills farm), watched foxes play in their dens in front of the woods, rode our bikes to Ameliasburgh to explore the dilapidated remains of Roblin's Mill and even borrowed some apples from time to time from Norm Salisbury's orchard next-door. I helped Al as he built a log-cabin in their woods—even Thoreau would have been impressed (maybe!—we started with a hatchet cutting small logs, then gravitated to large ones as the walls climbed higher, but it worked). We played catch, baseball and football, and shot baskets endlessly and, somewhere, Al came up with real fencing equipment and we donned the mesh masks, raised the untipped épées and proceeded in the manner of the best Zorros we could. It is a wonder that either of us survived to tell the gallant tale. But we had fun, always. Eventually, we both attended Western (albeit, at different times, Al for his BA, I for my MA) and as I pursued a teacher's life, Al became involved in environmental and political spheres.

Al's parents were Eleanor and Al (generally referred to as "Big Al"); Barbara and Patricia were his two sisters (each a couple years older). It must be said that Al's parents were a bit different. While the majority of people up and down the road was working class, employed on farms or in various moderately-skilled jobs in and around Belleville and Trenton, Mr. and Mrs. Revill were both university-educated and that set them apart. In their world, I was in a different kind of school. Big Al was an engineer who operated his own company and Eleanor, from the Ottawa area, kept a barn full of English jumping horses. Their origins and their education meant that they spoke with a tone and an accent and a thoughtfulness different from that of others in the County, their phraseology and expressions sounded different, delivered in complete and deliberate and reasoned ways. Not that they were ever condescending or superior in attitude; they were good neighbours and fit in their own way into our community. On occasions too numerous to mention, as I played around the house with Al, Mrs. Revill would have me in for lunch, usually a peanut butter sandwich and a glass of Kool-Aid. And on many occasions, she invited me along as she took Al and his sisters across the County, parking on a side road next to a quiet access to a stony beach and Lake Ontario. There, I wandered up and down the shore collecting shells while the others swam; then a picnic lunch was served. Big Al gave me my first paying job in the summer after Grade Eleven, cleaning out the stalls and feeding and caring for the horses first thing in the morning, then putting up rail fences through the rest of the day. One of the horses had become tangled in a page wire fence a year before and had to be destroyed so the project was to replace all farm fences with rails—I built some of the most crooked rail fences ever constructed. I also remember helping the Revills set up and monitor jumps at a Belleville Fair competition. When all is said and done, I cannot explain how influential Al's parents were on me overtly and subconsciously and on my pursuit of my own education; simply they showed me a world that was nowhere else to be seen in my growing years; they gave me a gift, I think, never knowing what they gave. But, still, their ways were a bit different. They had a Pavlovian system of whistle blowing to call their children back to the house; Mrs. Revill would step out their door and blow one for Barbara, two for Trisha and three for Al. Whenever you heard the whistles in the wind, you knew who was being called home to the Revills.

The Revills house was perfect, like something out of a television sitcom. There was an oversized two car garage, paved drive and basketball backboard and net, a large rec-room in the basement that had a ping-pong table (later it held Al's race car set) and a workroom where tools hung on a peg-board with an outline drawn around each so you would always know what went where (or what was missing). Their backyard contained a couple swing sets, a glider with benches and a standard "A-frame" with wooden seats. I remember cranking that swing up and up, one rear leg lifting on each swing forward as the clouds rose and the earth fell. And Al would push this daring act even farther than I.

The Revills and my parents were good neighbours to one another; without request, my father cleared snow from their drive on several occasions and jars of preserves were often exchanged. Dad helped Big

Al when he experimented with raising sheep and, when the Revills house burned and needed to be rebuilt, our garage served as a storage space for what furniture was saved. It was simply a reciprocal world back then where community compelled such acts of kindness without a second thought.

While there is undoubtedly much beyond recollection, some memories seem fixed. I recall one Firecracker Day, as we always called Queen Victoria's birthday (now generally known as the May Two-Four holiday), when Al and I decided to pool our fireworks and have a grand show—we had Roman candles, pinwheels, spinners, red bombs, cone fountains, sparklers and a burning schoolhouse (basically a small cardboard replica of a brick schoolhouse with a candle inside; when lit, the school house simply caught fire and burned to ashes—while not very exciting, it was mostly, I suppose, a firework of the psyche, a symbol of the way school was typically thought of in the popular imagination). We set up in a patch of dirt that we had had hoed out at the bottom of our lawn and waited patiently for darkness to fall, or tried to, but then catastrophe struck. The very first firecracker we lit, a Roman candle, tipped over, fired along the ground and set all of our firecrackers ablaze—we had placed our stockpile too close to the firing pit and everything was lost in a brief flash of glory. A brief, loud bonfire. We were pretty disappointed, of course, having looked forward to this event for some time, searching out and preparing the perfect site but, we learned our lesson the hard way, like most lessons worth learning, I suppose. But then, the very next day, Al showed up at my place with a couple boxes of new fireworks and, that night, we were able to celebrate good old Queen Victoria after all, albeit the day after her birthday, this time making sure not to make the mistake of the previous night. Al's father, Big Al, had heard of our fireworks' disaster and, in an act of kindness and generosity, probably with a quiet smile when he heard of our misadventure, had come to the rescue.

Another warm summer evening, Al and I are playing around my house when we decide to light out. No reason is ever really discussed that I can recall; there is no cause for rebellion or cessation or adventure, we just start walking west along the road, zig-zagging in and out of the ditch as we go, keeping on and on even as the home whistle blows thrice for Al. And it will blow again and again. We walk and walk and the darkness begins to fall and we have nearly reached the new highway that has just been built, the one that cuts through the marsh past the new sub-division named Fenwood Gardens and near Weatherhead's, probably a couple kilometres up our road, when a familiar station wagon pulls up beside us. Big Al just looks at us and calmly says, "Get in." (It turns out that neighbours along the road have spotted us and turned us in.) We are quickly transported back to my place where I am dropped off. My parents say very little—I just watch whatever's on TV before I go to bed but I do notice that I don't see Al again for a week or so, and his whistle call is silent. For some reason, this is an event that I have always remembered, the night Al and I lit out like a pair of Huckleberry Finns; I suppose, maybe, at some point everybody needs to do the same in life, just turn west and start walking. Light out for the territories! Al and I did that when we were young and, I must admit, I have probably done that several times since. Instilled with an inquisitive nature, in some way, perhaps, I've never stopped lighting out. Moving on from one thing to another, leaving one situation to seek another, 'cause, as Huck Finn says, "I been there before." If nothing else, such was the legacy bestowed in the years of my growing up next door at the Revills.

Al (right), Lassie and her pups, and me in my old straw hat that I wore into oblivion.

8

The Victorian House

To build a house and live the changing years
Like flesh for the soul; the walls are an hourglass
For our motes of time, that drops them grain by grain
Until the last mote falls and the house is void
And we go out—wherever we must go:

—Philip Child "The Victorian House"

The impact of the Victorian Age shook the planet. Like no era before, its pervasive legacy has inspired supporters and detractors, defenders and deniers ever since. From medical breakthroughs in the identification of diseases such as scarlet fever, typhoid and pneumonia to pharmacological developments in drugs as varied as morphine, quinine, codeine and iodine, from explorations leading Europeans to a greater understanding, and invasive colonization, of the African continent and beyond to mapping the frozen tundras, north and south, to political and social theories aimed at balancing taxation and easing penury to sterilizing the poor and assimilating Indigenous children *via* residential schools—ostensibly with the intent of improving the world, the reach of the Age extended to every arena of human thought and endeavour (sometimes for good; often not so much, especially in today's thinking). And the theory and practice of education was certainly a part of the mix, the influence of many of the era's pedagogical ideals continuing in the air well into our present time.

> … we are here as on a darkling plain
> Swept with confused alarms of struggle and flight,
> Where ignorant armies clash by night.

Matthew Arnold is probably best known for his most anthologized poem, "Dover Beach," a profound dramatic monologue that addresses one of the great Victorian ordeals of doubt, the fading of the Christian certainty of belief under a Modernist onslaught and its scientific way of looking at the world. Like waves on the pebbled beach, for Arnold, this inexorable tide of insecurity brings "the eternal note of sadness in."

Arnold was not only a respected poet, ranked in the Victorian Age in such company as Tennyson and Browning, but, for thirty-five years, he was employed as one of Her Majesty's Inspectors of Schools across the central region of England. Living in the Lake District, he was a close friend of Wordsworth and of Clough (the elegiac subject of one of Arnold's greatest poems, *Thyrsis*: "Why faintest thou? I wander'd till I died. / Roam on! The light we sought is shining still."). He studied under his father (who was Headmaster of Rugby School, a classical scholar, a Christian soldier, and a liberal Protestant who evangelically supported the necessity of moral virtue and one's duty to work for the good of society); Arnold also attended to the sermons of John Henry Newman at University Church—Cardinal Newman became a colleague and friend. And Arnold absorbed the various contemporary sentiments espoused in that intellectual age: eighteenth century rationalism influenced by the ideas of John Locke, transcendentalism from Germany and America, new scientific theories in geology and evolution and the ideas of the Chartists, Benthamites and, of course, his own father's and Newman's thinking as well. He earned the appointment to become a School Inspector in 1851, a position Arnold often described as *drudgery* but a financially-secure position which allowed him to marry, raise a family and otherwise earn his way in the world. He travelled extensively back and forth across central England viewing classrooms, watching students perform their lessons and listening to the comments of parents (more or less, what School Inspectors do to this day). And, by all reports, he loved fishing. One supposes, the many hours spent on the platforms of railway stations, on trains and in hotels, and possibly on the banks of streams, gave him time for thinking and writing about what he observed, the provincial matters and manners and the education that he witnessed, and time for his poetry, too. He was honoured in being named Professor of Poetry at Oxford for two terms and presented lectures there in which he developed the theories that would become *Culture and Anarchy* (1869) and the basis for much of his other social and literary criticism, writings which provide an illuminating snapshot of the time. With his pronounced mutton chops, his ever-present walking stick, his frequent caricatures in *Punch*, and the upright, moralistic dimension of his work, next to the Queen herself, Arnold seems the archetypical Victorian.

In "Memorial Verses" (an elegy on the death of Wordsworth), Arnold imaged the contemporary society in which he lived as an "iron time of doubts, disputes, distractions, fears" and characterized the "benumbed" world of Victorian England as one that lacked moral or spiritual substance, a world hostile to intellectual pursuits. For Arnold, change was needed and that would be instituted by universally educating the public—all children needed to be schooled. In "Culture and Anarchy," Arnold famously identifies the purpose of that education as "the pursuit of perfection," establishing a clear path along which to bolster and maintain the best heritage of the culture and "to perfect" humankind:

> The pursuit of perfection then is the pursuit of sweetness and light. He who works for sweetness and light, works to make reason and the will of God prevail. He who works for machinery, he who works for hatred, works only for confusion. Culture looks beyond machinery, culture hates hatred; culture has one great passion, the passion for sweetness and light. It has one even yet greater!—the passion for making them *prevail*. It is not satisfied till we *all* come to a perfect man; it knows that the sweetness and light of the few must be imperfect until the raw and unkindled masses of humanity are touched with sweetness and light. If I have not shrunk from saying that we must work for sweetness and light, so neither have I shrunk from saying that we must have a broad basis, must have sweetness and light for as many as possible.

In accord, John Henry Cardinal Newman, Arnold's teacher and friend, presents the theory this way: "I am asked what is the end of University Education, and of the Liberal or Philosophical Knowledge which I conceive it to impart: I answer, that what I have already said has been sufficient to show that it has a very tangible, real and sufficient end, though the end cannot be divided from that knowledge itself. Knowledge is capable of being its own end. Such is the constitution of the human mind, that any kind of knowledge, if it be really such, is its own reward" (*The Idea of a University* 1852). From Newman and Arnold, then, the central Victorian purpose of schooling is the delivery of knowledge for the sake of knowledge, for the sake of culture, for the development of morally educated ideas. Simply, through schooling all youngsters in the land are imbued with society's finest ideas and ideals and, inherent in that process, all that is best in the history and the culture of the empire is preserved.

As a specific example to clarify, one of the most tangible examples of the propagation of these ideas occurs in textbooks that were produced during the time, and following, for use by teachers and students in England *and* in the "colonies". For example, I have in hand *The Ontario Readers* (*Second Book* 1924), an anthology for students which begins with the text of "God Save the King," followed with "The Arab and the Camel," that story in which a camel, on a cold night in the desert, negotiates its way into the tent bit by bit until "the Arab" (racism noted) finds himself outside in the chill, the final sentence, and moral, reading: "It is a wise rule to resist the beginnings of evil." (Now, personally, I am uncertain if the camel is actually evil or simply more intelligent than its master but I will leave that debate for another time!) At any rate, after that in the textbook, there is a short prayer to God by Thomas Moore ("This Wondrous World"), Stevenson's "My Shadow," "The Pail of Gold," a fairy tale about greed, and so on—the rest of the anthology filled with short fables and poems and stories and Biblical "Psalms" and parables for the most part offering cautionary tales and moral messages. I pick up a copy of another book from this era, meant to underscore lessons extracted from the various *Readers, The Ontario Teachers' Manuals: The Golden Rule Books* (1915)—subtitled "a graded system of moral instruction." According to its *Preface*, this text is intended to be a manual for teachers guiding their instruction of students in "the aims and methods of moral training, … with the virtues that should be practised in the different relationships of life." The *Preface* adds to this sentiment:

> …there are some lessons that exhibit several classes of virtues and some that exhibit those more spiritual elements of character which cannot be definitely classified under any of the headings without risk of giving rise to misunderstanding.

Can *sweetness and light* be far behind! The "Table of Contents" speaks volumes. "Form I" begins with the following outline of study or curriculum:

The Bodily Life:

1. Cleanliness of person, clothing, food, and surroundings.
2. Self-control in eating, drinking, breathing and sleeping.

The Social Life:

1. Manners in the home and the school: behaviour at table; politeness in greetings and in questions and answers; punctuality and promptness; tidiness in the home, school, and street.
2. Obedience to parents and teachers—prompt, unquestioning.
3. Truthfulness in speech and action; honesty in work and play.

The Intellectual Life:

Industry, accuracy, thoroughness.

This outline continues through "Forms II, III and IV," adding categories along the way that include **The Economic Life, The Civic Life** and **The Aesthetic Life.** Some examples of the goals to be reached include:

Exercise:
Regularity, Temperance.

– Courage to endure little pains and discomforts
cheerfully; to follow good example and resist bad
example; to confess faults or accidents.
– Modesty in the home and the school; at meals; in
speech; in bearing—quietness, humility; respect for the
aged and women.
– Love of parents, brothers, sisters; of home, school,
country.
– Courage—physical, of the soldier, the bully, the
bravo, the angry man, the man who takes useless risks.
– Generosity or charity for the poor, the deformed, the
unfortunate, the erring.
– Truthfulness—kindness and sympathy.
– Patriotism—love of home, and country and its
national emblems and songs, of institutions; pride in
the great men and great deeds that have helped to
make our Empire.
– Political duties; the vote—the nature and responsibility; zealous support of good measures and good
men; tax paying; serving the municipality, city or nation
as a privilege and a duty.
– Love of the beautiful in nature, art, conduct, and
character.
– Taste as revealed in dress, choice of friends,
literature, and amusements.

The modern-day teacher, and students and parents, too, may smile at
some of the content here—exactly what "the exercise of self-control"
might be while one is sleeping does give pause for thought, as does the
requirement of giving respect to "the aged and women"—and most
certainly the emphasis on "men" is quaint and dated, but the
overarching theme behind all of this is the shaping of children to
become model citizens of the society in which they exist and to accept
the values which that society holds at that moment in time. And, in this
case, those include those classic Victorian sensibilities of duty and

patriotism and obedience and belief according to one's place in the familial or social order. Rebels need not apply.

Today, while this cultural heritage approach to education seems elitist, prescriptive, patriarchal and certainly outdated in a multicultural context, there are still many who will read the expectations above and nod their head in the affirmative, who will look back fondly to an assumed time of obedience, structure and definitive values, when kids respected their elders and did what they were told to do, to those *good old golden rule days*. In the end, once again we are reminded that contemporary education dons a jacket of many layers, a palimpsest of disparate ideas, many with feasible theoretical underpinnings and historic exemplars, but also with certain ideas that are extraordinarily out-of-touch with present-day thinking and current realities. At the very least, the conclusion: from teachers and administrators to parents and caregivers, for all those involved in or trying to understand contemporary education, it is a complex and labyrinthine tapestry. For better and for worse, the "golden rules" of the Victorian yesteryear have never entirely disappeared.

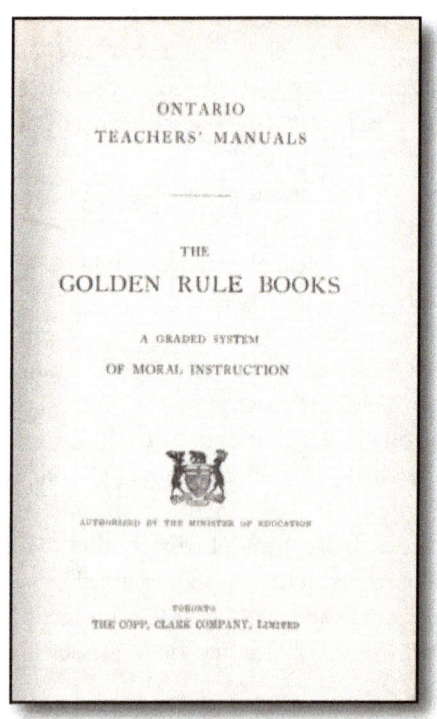

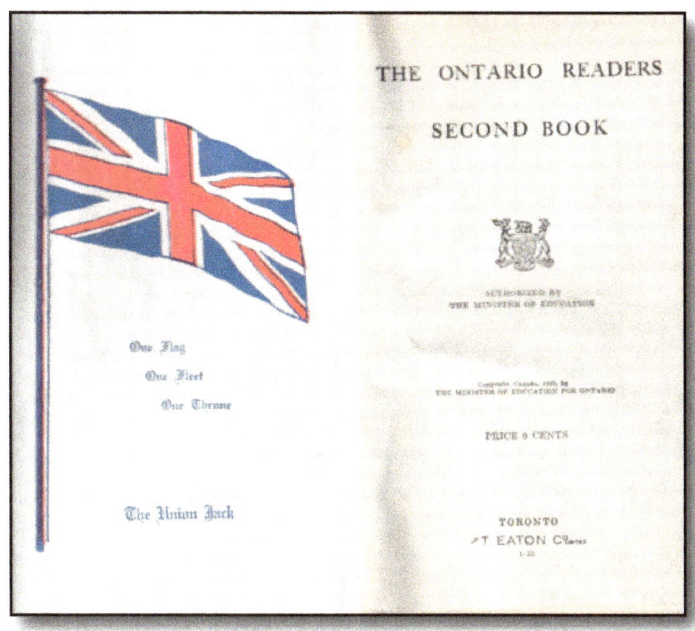

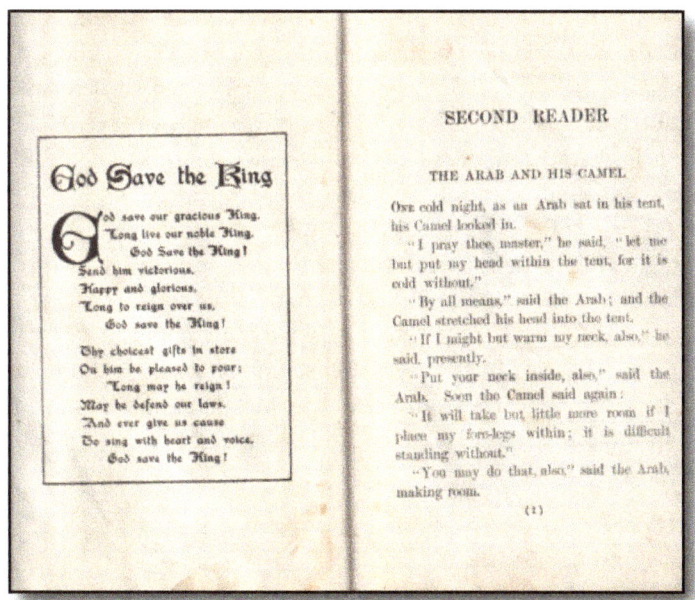

9

Grade Four

Ah, for just one time I would take the Northwest Passage
To find the hand of Franklin reaching for the Beaufort Sea
Tracing one warm line through a land so wild and savage
And make a Northwest Passage to the sea

—Stan Rogers "Northwest Passage"

Upstairs in one of the two small rooms, Mrs. Iola Brummel is our Grade
Three/Four teacher. While the other teachers live in Belleville or deeper
in the County, Mrs. Brummel lives just down the road. We like her. She
is one of us, a kind and gentle person who gets us to lower the volume
of our classroom voices (after the influence of hearing-challenged Mrs.
Welch) and leads us deeper into the world in which we live. Her son,
Bradley, is in the next grade. I like Brad who will be ahead of me all the
way, through high school at Belleville Collegiate and on into
university—our final encounter is on his return from university on
Thanksgiving of his first year, flashing a peace sign to all of us through
the classroom window (most of us did that encore tour—Thanksgiving
would be our first visit home, and vainly parading about in our leather
college jackets, we visit the teachers we liked one last time basking in our
superiority over former friends still trapped in the confines of high
school, and then the auguries of circumstance and distance will take us
far away forever).

For Bradley, I often wondered how strange it must have been to
have your mother as a teacher, the authority of school and the love of
home ever-overlapping like some cosmic eclipse, rounding a corner to
hear some ill-informed student say something about your mom and her

classes as if some uniformed sports commentator were analysing the Bolshoi ballet. And I never think of Bradley but that the image of Mrs Conroy rises to mind. A widow, she lived in the large house at the east end of upper Massassaga Road, the house that the Thompsons sold when they moved to Tweed to open their butcher shop and before the Goulahs moved in and Ricky became one of my all-time best friends and his older sister, Sherilynn, became the goddess of our elementary school. Mrs. Conroy, a tall woman with pure white hair, frequently hosted community gatherings and card parties where euchre was played, tea was served and prizes were won—I still have a small vase in the shape of a pair of menacing sharks swimming side by side. And it still amuses me, two of the universe's deadliest creatures knifing through the airy seas of our house with meek African violets growing from their backs. As part of her ritual, Mrs Conroy would hand out candies and small toys

to the younger set who attended with their parents. I was a kid from a poor family (I suppose by today's standards, all of the neighborhood families were) so any kind of candy or gift was a rare treat but, on one occasion, Bradley informed her that he did not like the particular candy she had given him. "Oh," was all she said. I remember that response and how, from then on, she would secretly find me at these gatherings and, like some beneficent Artful Dodger to innocent Oliver, slip clandestine treats and treasures into my hands. 'From London with Love,' I guess, or wherever Mrs. Conroy was from. By the way, I have never said 'no' to candy before or after. Once she gave me two tiny plastic toys, like the kind you'd find in *Crackerjacks*; they resembled the scrimshaw that bored sailors would carve from scraps of whale-bone between hunts, one, a majestic schooner in full sail, flags

flying, and, the second, more mysterious, a sailor holding the arm of an ape who stands on a box, both with a steadfast look, gazing out to some ocean I imagine they see. They still occupy a distinct place on my mantel next to two small metal Herefords-on-wheels, the few enigmatic detrita of my childhood that remain, items that will no doubt be tossed without heed into the trash when I am done.

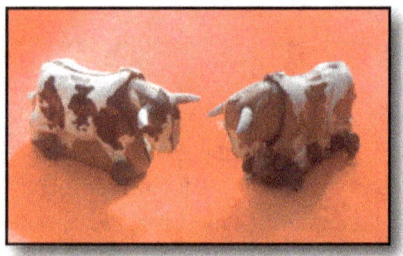 

By Grade Four, we read intriguing accounts about the great European explorers (at least, considered "great" in those days)—Henry the Navigator, Vasco da Gama, Ferdinand Magellan, Christopher Columbus, Sir Francis Drake, Hernan Cortéz and Francisco Pizarro, leading us toward the stories of North America's earliest European voyageurs—Champlain, Cartier, La Salle, La Vérendrye, Hudson, Brulé and the rest. They are the erstwhile scraps that will be forged into what will become our understanding of the origins of Canada. But mostly, they are good stories and I enjoy them—and I am fascinated by the notion that two of these famous explorers, Champlain and Brulé, actually set foot in the County, my homeplace, and somehow that makes these accounts seem real and unreal at the same time. Of course, in our History and Geography classes, there is no mention of colonization or the negative aspects of empire-building or of the diaspora; no recognition of Indigenous leaders or heroes, or their rights; that kind of thinking was yet to develop. Along with "God Save the Queen," we sing "Rule Britannia" and "The Maple Leaf Forever.' Canadian nationalism, Quebec liberation, protests against the war in Viet Nam and various other culture wars of the 1960s had not yet stirred to life. While portraits of the young Queen Elizabeth and Prince (not King) Philip hang above the blackboard, the stern and determined Queen Victoria still peers across the room. The spectre of World War II casts a dark shadow. Convoys of army vehicles regularly pass my home and, as a little kid, I charge to the side of the road and salute. Conversely, when a German family named Brauer moves into a house along the Marsh Road, for people in the community, they are outsiders, not invited to local card parties and gatherings. For a long time, Germans are perceived as the enemy and represented everywhere as such in comic books and films and even pro-wrestling, Fritz von Erich goose-stepping across the ring. Most students had relatives who had served, some who had perished—Steven Sharpe, a classmate, had lost an uncle—and everyone had parents who had suffered under the at-home shortages and restrictions. I recall my mother showing me these strange partly-used coupons that allowed her, she told me, to go to a store to purchase designated foods and

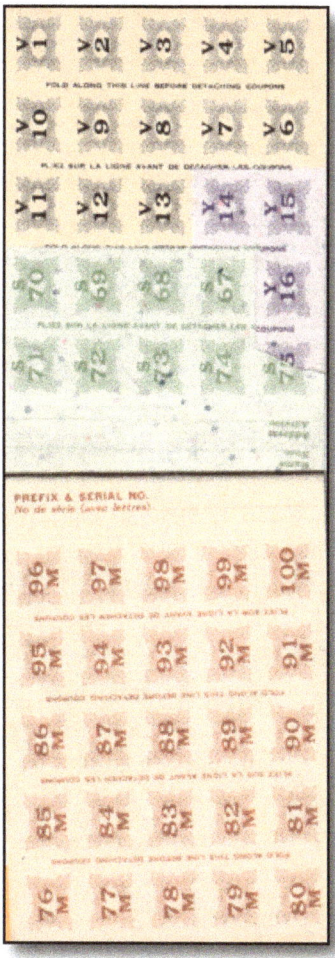

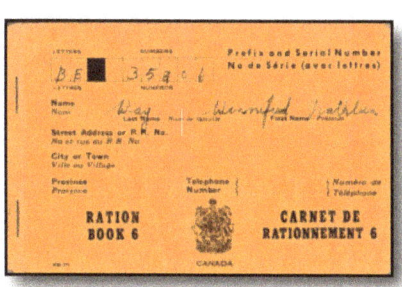

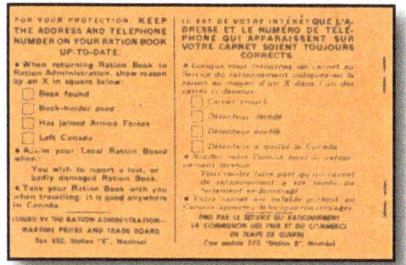

milk. In this vein, I suppose, I always took very good care of any toys I received; at school, supplies were always distributed in a carefully rationed manner and a strict military mindset governed many aspects for a long time.

Marbles. We all carried a pocket full of marbles, the boys, at least. And in the Spring and Fall before and after class we gather under the small "Royal Oak" tree on the north-west corner of the school just before the playground-grid starts—in 1937 acorns had been sent from Windsor, England to schools across Canada to honour King George VI's coronation and the tree grew and is still there today. We would heel an indentation in the soft ground, establish a circular perimeter or taw line and begin the game. I no longer recall all the rules but I do remember portentous decrees regularly issued from the powers-that-were to senior students not to take advantage of younger students who often had poorer skills, both motor and negotiation. Cats-eyes, bonkers, aggies, steelies, boulders, alleys, tigers, pearls, bumbles, swirlys and red devils became the language of the marble wars as did keepsies, quitsies, shooter and knuckle down. And in the end, senior students almost always won the younger students' cache and the younger students were trained not to complain to anyone, that was a rule of the game. And besides, next year or the one after, their time would come to win all the gleaming cats-eyes of the world.

Beyond marbles, collecting and trading for collectibles was also a major clandestine activity. We traded hockey and baseball cards, of course, and once I traded a fishing net to Randy Kerr for a couple lacrosse sticks—it was a sport that was just being reintroduced in the area. I became a decent lacrosse player, Captain of our high school team and a defenceman and Assistant Captain for a couple years on Belleville's semi-pro squad (we were paid a small honorarium to cover travelling and meal costs so, in my mind, that made us "semi-pro"). We also collected a series of so-named *Jello* coins, a set of 200 plastic coins available in Hostess, Shirriff and other Jello products, one year, planes, the next, cars—round images on shiny paper set inside a coloured plastic circle stamped with a propeller for the planes, a wheel for the automobiles. I managed to complete both sets through some wild trades, one time swapping five discs for the number one *Cugnot*, the rarest car of them all (at least in my collection). In terms of education,

I suppose we learned skills in negotiation, research and just plain-old dickering, and later we came to realize one of marketing's most clever sleights, offering one thing while selling another. A lot of potato chips and Jello were negotiated on the trading floor (*aka*, weekly grocery trips). But in spite of that there was a satisfaction and some knowledge gained too in seeking out and amassing this collection of planes and cars.

Every other week on Tuesdays Mrs. Hannah arrives bringing with her a flannel board to tell us Bible stories. Jesus mounts the board with his white gown and blue sash, the crowd gathers below him and he begins: "Blessed are the pure in heart;" another week Noah floats his great ship in and all the pairs of animals, giraffes and chickens and cows and lions, dutifully board the boat; and then there is heroic Joshua and enduring Jonah and mighty Samson and David and Goliath and Daniel—*mene, mene, tekel, upharsin'*—and the pageant of Christmas where a new star rises in the heavens (this story was so good it often took two visits to tell) and the sorrow and joy of Easter where three dark crosses line a hill. Today this approach would be applauded as 'Storytelling' but the content, of course, would have to be changed. The public educational powers-that-be have become nervous around the issue of religion, at least (maybe especially) Christian religion—long gone are "The Lord's Prayer" and the Bible readings that would have started every day throughout my school years. And we understand the reasons, how society and culture have changed. It is a multicultural planet just beginning its birth-pains and no-one wants somebody's single version of religion or spirituality foisted down their throats and, while I certainly understand that argument, I also think that something has been lost. When Santiago in *The Old Man and the Sea* struggles with bleeding hands to carry his ship's mast up the beach, while Luke Skywalker hangs upside down on the crossed antennae at the bottom of Cloud City, when replicant Roy Batty delivers his magnificent final elegy in *Blade Runner* or Harry Potter dies and is resurrected, contemporary youngsters do not recognize nor are they moved by the depths of the Christic symbolism. The absence of experiencing the emblematic meaning and impact of those moments is an unfortunate fortfeiture. And so much literature, music, art and other aspects of Western culture, at least well into the twentieth century before postmodernism emerged, have been infused with those Christian themes and iconographics that some exposure, call it *Biblical imagery* if you wish, some exposure to the Hebrew hero-stories and their mythology seems valuable, at the very least, to provide a deeper sensibility of the rich heritage of Western culture, of the human condition as citizens of the West. Our current students have little, most often, none. They are poorer for that. And, arguably, immigrants to our country from various non-Christian areas of the world are poorer, too, for that to which they are never exposed. Along those lines, many aspects of the mythologies of the world (Greek and Roman and Norse and Celt and Asian and Indigenous and the rest) form a platform, like Yggdrasil, itself, in which our current culture has deep roots—from *The Game of Thrones* to *The Lord of the Rings* to *Harry Potter* and all the blockbusters of the *DC/Marvel* universes, understanding the origins and formulae of such stories, and their relation to religion and myth, is to understand oneself and humanity (at least in the West). And, mostly, they are good stories, too. Recently I had one group of senior secondary students, as a small research project in the context of reading Eliot's *The Waste Land*, spend some time researching allusions including the Biblical name "Lazurus" to try to suss out the meaning of the reference—after three days, they discovered the wrong Lazurus. In that context, one might say, "Jesus wept" (but there are many, of course, who would not recognize that reference either). All that aside, we enjoyed Mrs. Hannah's Bible visits. She told us good stories illustrated by her felt art. And we remembered them, at least, bits and pieces. There was probably a bit of sermonizing underneath but that vanished like sweat after recess on a hot day and, from what I can ascertain, did us no terminal harm. At the very least, there were no tests. And, at least I remember who Lazurus was and understand the inexplicable power inherent in the brilliant story of the Nazarene Jesus (just as a remarkable story, if nothing else) on his journey from Bethlehem to Calvary, and that story is worthwhile knowing, whether one believes in some religious context or not. It is a good story!

From the current teacher's side of this ledger, of course, at an elementary or secondary level, dealing with the stories of any contemporary religion can be a delicate challenge. Teaching Greek mythology to adolescents or teenagers is one thing, but teaching Christianity or Islamism or Judaism is something else. Ironically, Religion is often the course in separate Catholic Schools that teachers strive to avoid teaching; it just comes with too many challenging pitfalls that defy the party line. Even beyond that, it is often very difficult to present stories embedded in a contemporary religion to those children who may still have a belief system wrapped around them, or beliefs in some other. It is often very challenging for students to engage with stories of David or Adam or Abraham or Jesus and disconnect from their own fundamental religious belief, in effect, to separate the dancer from the dance; in fact, it may be impossible. Even some adults find that difficult. So, for teachers, I suppose, *caveat emptor*. Or *Jesu Maria* as the good but meddling Friar in *Romeo and Juliet* exclaims.

ADDENDUM:

Where is He Now?

For some, the gods appear often and with ease. I am not one of those. Perhaps it's because I was never baptised but, in all of my days, I have never seen one sign, one *iota*, if you will, that suggests some otherworldly or omniscient divinity watches over the universe. A decade or so after World War II ended, I was born and my mother wept, or so I was always told. By the time of my birth, my Mom, who was of Irish descent and Roman Catholic (vestiges of that always filled the fringes of our lives), had already had two boys and desperately wanted a girl so I did not exactly fill the bill. It was then that the doctor told her that I was the most beautiful baby he had ever seen which, she always claimed, made her feel better; me too, I suppose. It's the story I'm sticking with, anyway! My father named me (the name just occurred to him for no particular reason, he always said); Dad rarely reasoned out his actions, in the same manner as he almost never spoke of the war, or of religion. Those areas that must have filled so much of his life were left a blank to me. I suspect that the war-ravaged fields of Sicily, Italy, Belgium, Holland and, in the end, Germany were no place for a farm-boy and left no room for God or His like, and so, it naturally followed, I think, I have never been a believer, at least a Christian. I inherited a blankness in that realm. Now, over time, I have read the sacred texts and tried to understand most of the world's religions—probably liked Hinduism the most; transcendentalism was a central concern for many of the writers I've admired from T. S. Eliot to Hawthorne, Emerson, Whitman and Melville (surely one of the abiding themes of *Moby-Dick* has its source in the *Katha Upanishads*: "Who sees the variety and not the unity wanders on from death to death"—doomed Ahab never comes to that understanding; Ishmael, the survivor of that tale, does). So I admire certain religious texts at the very least on the literary level, but, other than that, I have no religious motive, *per se*, in wishing that our contemporary students were exposed to a bit more understanding of the basic themes, patterns and stories of the *Holy Bible*, and other religions, too—mythic and cultural motives trump any religious. But when it comes to formal religion and the way most are worshipped and twist human behaviour, well, I think I'm with John Lennon there (you know how it goes):

> Imagine there's no countries
> It isn't hard to do
> Nothing to kill or die for
> And no religion too
> Imagine all the people
> Living life in peace

Now I am not denying the capacity within all of us for that sensation we may call spirit, which we may cite as a divine spark—I have read the Romantic poets and have seen a spiritual essence lifted up by poetry and song and puppies but that is an ideo-centred thing; our own ability to be inspired, to be god-like, however we define what such creativity may be. Such sensations are remarkable but not evidence to suggest the existence of some external divinity. Prometheus, old boy, the fire you stole, you lit yourself! Even Shelley, atheist that he was, would have known that. As my wheel-chair bound big brother, once groomed for the church by a local minister named Neadows, confined in long-term care at a place called Hastings Manor, isolated from the world in those years of *Covid-19* madness, as my big brother Bill would exclaim emphatically in his final years, "So, where is He now? Where is He now?"

10

From Bleak House to Bauhaus

riverrun, past Eve and Adam's, from swerve of shore to bend of bay, brings us by a commodious vicus of recirculation back to Howth Castle and Environs.

Sir Tristram, violer d'amores, fr'over the short sea, had passencore rearrived from North Armorica on this side the scraggy isthmus of Europe Minor to wielderfight his penisolate war: nor had topsawyer's rocks by the stream Oconee exaggerated themselse to Laurens County's gorgios while they went doublin their mumper all the time: nor avoice from afire bellowsed mishe mishe to tauftauf thuartpeatrick: not yet, though venissoon after, had a kidscad buttended a bland old isaac: not yet, though all's fair in vanessy, were sosie sesthers wroth with twone nathandjoe. Rot a peck of pa's malt had Jhem or Shen brewed by arclight and rory end to the regginbrow was to be seen ringsome on the aquaface.

—James Joyce *Finnegans Wake* 1939

In the 1890s, when Mr. Hyde emerged from Dr. Jekyll's shadow and Charles Marlow journeyed to meet Mistah Kurtz deep in the heart of darkness or, for that matter, when Jack the Ripper stalked the *Penny Dreadfuls*, it was a sign that the human perception of things was changing. As Malcolm Bradbury and James McFarlane say in their seminal collection, *Modernism* (1976):

The Modern movement in the arts transformed conscious and artistic form just as the energies of modernity—scientific, technological, philosophical, political—

transformed forever the nature, the speed, the sensation of human life. The experience of modernity and modernization was not obscure. It happened in the streets, the homes, the factories, in the political and economic system, on the battlefield and in the world order.

As always, as one cultural age fades into the next, enacting and flaunting difference are necessary criteria—you cannot write Dickensian novels or bow before Turner's landscapes forever and you probably need to let your audience (or clientele) know. So, Modernism moved in and its ways of thinking and its methods of doing replaced the Victorian mindset in most things, including ideas about educating children, much the same as, before it, the sensibilities of gothic Romantism had replaced eighteenth century rationalism or the racy comedies of the Restoration had reopened stages and boldly disrupted Cromwell's stern Puritanism. A critical part of Modernism was a conscious awareness of its own modernity—as fine art and decorative art were intentionally blended in the brushstrokes and designs of *Art Nouveau* and Stravinsky's harmonies and melodies idiosyncratically broke all the rules, modernity drew out its own cognisant blueprint. Part of that was in reaction to and retreat from the Great War which blew the world apart—a generation and its idealism brutally lost in muddy trenches and pointless conflict. That war, in particular, of course, cast a metaphysical twilight over the lost generation of the twentieth century, at least until the Great Depression and World War II and the Holocaust and the nuclear-shrouded Cold War and, in the new century, the coming of Trump and *Covid-19* made that twilight darker.

In 1899 Sigmund Freud published *The Interpretation of Dreams*; purposefully he re-dated it to 1900 to cement it like a keystone at the beginning of the century. In that seminal work, Freud explored the workings of the human mind and the meaning of its dreams and nightmares by using a diagnostic, scientific approach, the same way a regular doctor might in diagnosing some bodily ache or as a mechanic might if a cylinder were misfiring in one of those relatively new inventions, the auto-mobile. Picasso and Duchamp painted, Giacometti and Ernst sculpted, Gropius, Meyer and Rohe (along with the likes of Klee and Kandinsky) formulated the Bauhaus concept of design to amalgamate aesthetics and mass production—science and psychology evolved as the true touchstones of the twentieth century. As Virginia Woolf commented: "Everything is the proper stuff of fiction," but "for the moderns ... the point of interest lies very likely in the dark places of psychology" (*The Common Reader* 1925). In fact, a technique called *stream of consciousness* became a widespread style of writing adopted by most of the significant prose writers of the twentieth century, the likes of Joyce and Hemingway, Faulkner and Lawrence, and Woolf, herself, and it came directly from a synthesis of the fragmented events of modern times and Freud's thinking, his resonant image of the oceanic *id*, origin of the deepest impulses of human personality and behaviour. Modernist theories and writings replace Victorian dogma with their own—in particular, with the intentional disruption of the linear flow of narrative, often altering any sense of unity or coherence in plot and character and appearance. Modernist fiction uses irony ubiquitously as a motif to question the moral and philosophical meaning of culture, to place inward consciousness in opposition to rational, objective discourse and to foreground the alienated role of the artist in society. Language and technique were often given preference over plot or content—anyone who has tried to read Joyce's *Ulysses* or *Finnegans Wake* will understand— just peruse the text quoted at the beginning of this chapter (most of the 500-page novel is composed entirely using this arcane dialogue and style—a stunning achievement that often stuns the reader, like a corpse rising at a wake).

In collusion with these radical practises, modernists presented a formidable theoretical design for literature, and the analytics known as *New Criticism* were born. New Criticism was elitist, hard, cold and intellectual in its commensuration of literary merit; we owe much to it for its toughness, its practicality, and its attempt to focus with clarity on specific texts, on close analysis, and on tough questions—it was an attempt to approach literature with a scientific impartiality. As an example, in *Aspects of the Novel* (1927), E. M. Forster clinically prescribes precisely what a novel should be, listing the *aspects* it must contain— story, people, plot, fantasy, prophecy, pattern and rhythm. Without those aspects, the fiction will fail as, say, Gertrude Stein's novels did for Forster. James Joyce once claimed *The Waste Land* ended the idea of poetry for ladies (from Ellman's *Golden Codgers*). In "Tradition and the Individual Talent" (1919), T. S. Eliot, himself, emphasizes his view of the need for a distinct and depersonalized literature: "The progress of an artist is a continual self-sacrifice, a continual extinction of personality" (*The Sacred Wood*). Modernism is a literature that tries to erase its author, aspiring to be "dry, hard, classical verse" (T. E. Hulme "Romanticism and Classicism" 1913). For Joyce, the artist was a distant god paring his fingernails. Conservatively, modernism looked back, admired, and borrowed from the invaluable though fragmented and depleted ancient mythologies and traditions of the classical past while trying, in Pound's sense, to charge the starkly contemporary images of its own art and language with meaning. Its emphasis was on the immediate and the internal. Literature through its precise and sparse and fragmented imagism should reveal those moments that most reify life's greatest mysteries. revealing the patterned energies of life itself (to use Kenner's phrase for Pound's Vortex—*The Pound Era* 1971).

A stern era demanded a stern education and an ascetic, rigorous teacher. Modernism defined the persona of that teacher as the all-knowing high priest at the centre of the classroom, distanced from the students, a new-age austere Socrates competent in her/his knowledge-base and asking questions of students until they arrived at the correct answer, and testing or examining them afterwards just to make sure. The teacher had to know the answers, of course, and, for the most part, the answers were what the teacher knew. It is a philosophy that dominated teaching through much of the twentieth century and beyond. Originating in the ideas, if not always the practises, of the likes of Ezra Pound, T. S. Eliot and E. M. Forster and, after them, scholars such as Bill Wimsatt, Cleanth Brooks, Allan Tate, and I. A. Richards (*Practical Criticism*), teaching was to be done in a scientific way. The text was the repository of meaning (anthologies with their collection of bits and pieces were the holy bibles of modernist education)—to be able to regurgitate that text, whatever it was, through repetition and memory and testing was the job of the student. Context, personal response, sentiment, attitudes or feelings were irrelevant in the classroom much as they would be in a scientific experiment. You cannot form an emotional attachment to the cute rat you are about to dissect.

In English teaching, probably one of the most influential Modern theorists was A.C. Bradley, through his lectures and, especially, his critical publication, *Shakespearean Tragedy*. For years, perhaps even to this day, the plays of Shakespeare were taught using Bradley's psychoana-lytical considerations of the protagonists; for instance, the idea that the tragic hero has some kind of flaw that precipitates his downfall (Macbeth is too ambitious, Othello, too jealous, Hamlet, too thoughtful, Lear, too old?) or that the plays have a rising action which, in Act III, undergoes a climax, then a falling action, catastrophe and resolution (Gustav Freytag's dramatic pyramid worked along these same lines.) While the fact that Shakespeare's characters are all remarkably different and much more complex than any simple "flaw" and that his plays never quite followed set structural patterns (actually, Shakespeare never wrote his plays with scene and act divisions at all) did not seem to prevent the teaching of the plays using such preconceived tools. Given the challenging nature of the plays, perhaps, for students and for teachers alike, any help was better than no help at all. And a Modernist mindset prevailed; a scientific approach was desired and a scientific approach used; namely, Bradley's.

Ultimately, teaching owes much to Modernism for its clinical, no-nonsense, scientific approach. A lot of information was delivered and drilled into students. However, many students were also drilled out of school altogether by this "dry, hard" approach. For its frequent insistence that a single meaning exists, for its absolute attempt to isolate text and classroom from context, for its over-indulgence on terminology and its intellectual elitism, for its elevation of teacher into master, an elitism emerged that made the instructor the irrefutable sage on the classroom stage (this was a difficult role for some teachers to play, but it was the expectation of School Boards, Superintendents and Principals everywhere) and it made the learner dependent on that teacher's ability (or opinion)—there was pressure on the teacher to know or appear to know *all the answers* and never to tolerate any challenge to that knowing—for its de-emphasis of genuine, immediate response (gut reaction, surface reaction was never sufficient or acceptable), for its insistence on secondary sources (Eliot's great poem, *The Waste Land*, was even published with foot-notes; *Cole's/Cliff's Notes* were born), this firm approach to education is sometimes found lacking at least to our contemporary sensibility. It was an Age that banned sentiment and emotion; and it was a deceptive and dark time, too. With its suffragette sensibility and Jazz Age flair, its innovative free verse and daring Cubist experimentation, Modernism always appeared far more progressive and liberal than it ever was. Eliot and Pound often spoke of the primal rhythm of the tom-tom sounding beneath all of their works (Eliot punned that with his own name), but that rhythm was also the sound of SS troops marching through Europe's streets, the pounding of *Sturmabteiling* fists on doors in the Jewish ghettoes. At the same time as the movement tended to reject all stuffy things Victorian, Modernists also conservatively sought to retain the best of cultures past, to shore those fragments against their ruins. G. K. Chesterton, C. S. Lewis, Evelyn Waugh and T. S. Eliot, among others, all converted to Roman Catholicism and Ezra Pound could be found broadcasting pro-Mussolini and anti-Semitic propaganda on Italian radio. Jim Crow laws were being enforced in America, the voting rights of Doukhobors and the freedom of Asian-Canadians were being denied in Canada where residential schools also continued to smother Indigenous children and bury them without grave-markers, and the dark forces of Fascism slowly turned to war across Europe; and often, it seemed, those dark sensibilities weren't far away in schools. One thinks of the many grim reminiscences of school in popular culture, such as Pink Floyd's *The Wall* or Tony Richardson's *The Loneliness of the Long Distance Runner*.

In English classes, the "lit-crit" game came into being—as a student in a class, the first text you needed to read was the teacher. Understand that text and you would probably get a good mark. I recall in senior high school a great debate arising one day in our English class over the meaning of Robert Frost's "After Apple Picking":

> My long two-pointed ladder's sticking through a tree
> Toward heaven still,
> And there's a barrel that I didn't fill
> Beside it, and there may be two or three
> Apples I didn't pick upon some bough.
> But I am done with apple-picking now. …

Several classmates argued that this was a poem in which the speaker was contemplating death and the afterlife, while the teacher insisted that it was simply a poem about work and harvest. Although I actually thought that the death and spiritual themes were relevant, I remember raising my hand and agreeing with the teacher which I felt to be more prudent at the time. (In retrospect, years later, I came to the thought that, perhaps, the teacher was just taking his position as a means to generate discussion, which was an excellent strategy if that was what was happening. Not sure to this day!) On another occasion, in university, I had a likeable professor for a course in eighteenth century literature and, through his lectures and discussion, came to find out that he had completed his M.A. in Medieval Studies. Essentially, for every paper I wrote whether it was on Swift or Sterne or Pope, I included some reference to Chaucer or the Gawain-poet and I always received a positive response on my papers and decent grades to boot. Shameful, probably, but also the characteristic of one who was a successful student, one who had learned to be good at the lit-crit game. George Bowering's "A Poem for High School Anthologies" is spot on:

> This will be serious, literature,
> & Canadian, you'll have to look out for
> the author's intentions, & also
> his tricks, his puns, his jokes, the things
> he is doing to make it difficult
> & hence worthwhile. Right?
>
> Pay attention. You might be asked:
> what is the most vivid figure of speech
> in this selection? Just remember this:
> The ivory wings of the white bird
> fell off & woke the sleeping maiden
> who gently lifted her feet
> from the oven, piping hot!
>
> Now you may ask yourself, what
> does that symbolize, & as a matter of fact
> why does the author say what
> at the end of the line?
>
> Oh, I forgot,
> George Bowering was born in
> Princeton, British Columbia,

December 1st, 1939, the son of
a high school Latin teacher. ...

—excerpt: George Bowering
"A Poem for High
School Anthologies" 1979

Somehow, I always think of the line in Dylan Thomas's wistful "A Child's Christmas in Wales" in which the speaker lists all of his "useful presents" concluding with:

> And pictureless books in which small boys, though warned with quotations not to, *would* skate on Farmer Giles's pond and did and drowned; and books that told me everything about the wasp, except why.

Often, trapped as I was in this "dry, hard" form of modernist education, from totalitarian teacher to ringing bell to swinging strap, this was the way I felt, learning "everything about the wasp, except why." Maybe that's why I write this book.

11
Grade Five

This little light of mine, I'm goin' to let it shine
This little light of mine, I'm goin' to let it shine
This little light of mine, I'm goin' to let it shine
Let it shine, let it shine, let it shine

—Harry D. Loes "This Little Light"

Our Grade Five and Six teacher is Mrs. (Hessie) Giles who also lives down in the County—in fact, her father's house is on our road not far from the school and he delivers the R. R. 7 mail out of Belleville until that job is taken over by my own father in his fortunate escape from the debilitative poverty of the small farm. Mrs. Giles is a large woman in girth and in spirit; she treats us with a warm sense of humour and kindness and direction—she will later be a Principal in the County. At a school reunion when S. S. #6 was being closed, she remembers me as a sensitive kid, one day finding me, she says, sitting at my desk with tears in my eyes. I tell her that I still am a sensitive kid—those tears have stayed in my eyes all my life. Mrs. Giles nods and smiles knowingly.

During the regular lessons of the class, Mrs. Giles plays many games with us like "I Spy"—whose purpose, of course, was to reinforce the concepts of Phonics and rehearse procedures such as raising one's hand, then standing to answer, but for us it was fun, just a game. And she loves singing, or so it appears. She leads us in many tunes that, I suppose, come from some curriculum-stamped song-book but, to us, constitute the standard greatest hits of the elementary world. One day she soothes us through the melancholy of *A Scottish Soldier*, on another she rocks the room by belting out *This Little Light of Mine*—"Hide it under a bushel, / NO, I'm going to let it shine! / Let it shine! Let it shine! Let it shine!"— her joy energizing our spirits before lunch (though, I admit, enthusiasm aside, none of this ever made me a better singer).

Each day after lunch, Mrs. Giles reads a chapter from a novel, usually ending with some kind of cliff-hanger finish that leaves many of us wanting more, groaning our displeasure at the abrupt closing. It is again a skilful act of misdirection on her part—we are captivated by the entertainment but also calmed and quieted after our raucous hour at play, and so readied for the afternoon lessons. Mrs. Giles could probably have been an adept magician held in high esteem at Hogwarts. The novels, as such, are often the *Hardy Boys*- or *Nancy Drew*-type and we are encouraged to find like books and read them on our own. By Grade Six I have read all the books in the school, even getting permission to enter the Grade Seven/Eight classroom and borrow books from its bookshelf. From the *Peter Rabbit* of Beatrix Potter to the tales of Thornton Burgess and through series like *Tom Swift* and *Doctor Doolittle* and even the occasional *Trixie Beldon*, I read them all. There is no library, as such, in our school nor in our community and few suitable books at home so one must do the best one can in such quests. But books were important and had their impact. As noted, my parents often read to me—my father read aloud the books that he liked when my bedtime arrived. My drowsy moments before sleep were filled with the marvellous escapades of *Tarzan* or the *Musketeers* or *Sir Nigel* or *The White Company* or rollicking poems that Dad had once been forced to memorize in his school days like "The Destruction of Sennacherib" (Byron) or "The Private of the Buffs"—I can still hear Dad's rousing recitation:

> Last night, among his fellow roughs,
> He jested, quaff'd, and swore;
> A drunken private of the Buffs,
> Who never look'd before.
> To-day, beneath the foeman's frown,
> He stands in Elgin's place,

Ambassador from Britain's crown,
And type of all her race.

—Sir Francis Hastings Doyle, alt.
"The British Soldier in China" 1860

He would orate these with a drama and bravado that stirred some facet in his psyche planted long before in the early days of the century (a time when empire-building and "taking up the white man's burden" were still in vogue, I suppose). And at these words I felt some stirring, too, and I asked him once what "Elgin's place" meant but he didn't know; it was memory and rhythm and romantic gallantry that mattered. My mother read stories from the *Golden Books* series and *Black Beauty* and *Jo's Boys* and once read one of her favourites to me, *Anne of Green Gables*. She bought me a couple comic books each week, usually one featured a popular cartoon or TV character (from Bugs Bunny to Huckleberry Hound to *The Three Stooges* to *Bonanza* and *Have Gun Will Travel*) and one involved the fantastic (Batman or *The Justice League of America* or *The Twilight Zone*)—like so many kids in those times of *Sputnik* and rocket launches, I was crazy about outer space. Sometimes one of the comics would be from a series called *Classics Illustrated* and there I first read many of those dense pieces of world literature made easier, *Moby-Dick*, *The Count of Monte Cristo*, *Wuthering Heights*, *Robinson Crusoe* and *Ivanhoe*. (My brothers in high school bought the *Classics Illustrated* of *Hamlet*, *Julius Caesar* and *Macbeth* as alternatives to reading the originals and it was there that I first read the Bard.) I also recall to this day Mrs. Giles reading a new book to us entitled *The Cat in the Hat* and the class was so mesmerized by it we requested that it be read again and again until finally it had to be returned to the Corby Library in Belleville (at least that's what Mrs. G. said probably worn out by reading the same text over and over). But kids are like that with such things—repetition is often fire stolen from the gods. And that Dr. Seuss text enthralled and fascinated us, a magic act that conjured a latent rebelliousness in us to which the Cat's antics spoke; and it reinforces for me the remarkable power that words and story can have and compelled me in my own fascination as a kid with reading and writing, a fixation which continues to this day. And, through the years, I have seen that same magic ignited over and over for children and young readers in series like *Goosebumps* and the S. E. Hinton novels and *Harry Potter* and *Twilight*. *The Cat in the Hat*, of course, tapped into a common motif in children's literature, the rebellious child—all of the 'conduct' or 'bad girl/boy' books, novels like *Peter Pan*, *Anne of Green Gables*, *Oliver Twist*, *Tom Sawyer*, *Little Men*, *Where the Wild Things Are*, *Mulan*, *The Northern Lights* and later film franchises such as *Minions*, *Angry Birds*, *Moana*, *Home Alone* and such.

I should reiterate that the Grade Three/Four and Five/Six rooms are upstairs in the old school building—it's a funny thing but this building is always old in my memory, in the same way, I suppose, these teachers are always old. Actually, most were probably in their forties or late thirties, maybe less, but we were young and they were not us and, therefore, they had to be old, didn't they! They were like grandmothers to us. By the time I attended S.S. #6, two new rooms had been added, low and sleek on the western side of the school and probably each one twice the size of the upper rooms. Polished hardwood floors and wooden walls are replaced with terrazzo and painted drywall. When my father attended this school, it was two rooms only, and I always recall the one vivid memory he used to tell (when I was old enough to understand). Around 1930, Mr. Collins was the Principal and taught Grades 5 to 8; Miss Harvey was the new teacher and she taught Grades 1 to 4. It was lunch hour and a beautiful spring day and the students had all gone out, in particular, to play some baseball. But in their haste they had forgotten to bring along the ball so my father went back into the school, climbed the stairs and pushed open his classroom door. And there, on the floor of the Principal's classroom, there were Mr Collins and Miss Harvey, shall we say, romantically entwined, her dress up and his pants down. *In flagrante delicto.* My father, a farm-boy, had seen enough around the pastures to understand what was transpiring. Dad said that, in his state of amazement, he simply stepped around them, picked the ball out of a box marked "sports" at the back of the room, said 'thank you' and returned outside where his classmates were waiting to play their ball game. Nothing else was ever said for the rest of the year, according to my dad, but his marks improved in all of his subjects, even the ones in which he was not very good.

At one point in Grade Five, all of the yardsticks disappear along with the maps that hang over the blackboards of S.S. #6. I figure, at first, that it must be some cartographic alien abduction; then all are returned in a week or so, but in a changed condition. The yardsticks and maps at this time had all been donated by companies like Neilson and Borden and all contained images of different chocolate bars and milk products. But some guardian angel in local education (or at the provincial level) has decided that these advertisements should not be allowed in schools and so all of the yardsticks have had the ads sanded off and all of the maps have had the border ads on the bottoms removed, or painted over. It is the kind of sentiment that erupts in schools from time to time—getting rid of Coke and Pepsi machines or trying to cover the brand names on computers. But it is a futile crusade—we live in a commercial world and, like so many things, banning or sanding off a name is not the answer. Beyond the classroom lies a jungle of billboards and TV commercials. Teaching students about commercialism and the nature of the advertising world would have been a lot more productive, then and now. And, tangential to this anyway, by 1975 Canada adopts the *International System of Units* (*SI* or the metric system)—metre sticks and Celsius measurements arrive and the maps are all replaced as metres and kilometres take over the roads and milk cartons evolve from quarts into litres. Those old Elsie the Cow maps and Jersey Milk chocolate bar rulers were doomed anyway.

Ray O'Coin joins our class part-way through Grade Five. He is a couple years older than most of us, shaggy dark hair and hardened features that make him seem even older than he is. But he has an infectious smile and a gentle demeanour and he and I naturally become friends. He tells some great stories about the various places he has lived and characters he has known and heartily joins Mrs. Giles in her robust musical sing-alongs, although much of his class time seems spent in inhabiting his own world. I always recall one day in Grade Seven, smiling at some moment of his own invention and appearing not to pay any particular attention to what was going on, he irritates the Grade Seven teacher, Mrs. Bates, and is called to the front of the room to get the strap. He extends his large callous-rough hands and grins throughout the punishment, still smiling as he returns to his desk—O Che Guevera, revolutionary extraordinaire, you should pay attention, for this is truly the way totalitarian regimes are conquered, I thought (well, at least, so I am thinking now). And one day, not long before Ray turned eighteen and disappeared forever from our world, he invited a friend and I to bicycle down to his house in Rossmore and, while by today's standards all of us would be considered poor, in entering Ray's home-world I came face to face with real poverty. He and his mother lived in what, at best, could be described as a shack on the edge of the Bay of Quinte; the house actually had a condemned sign nailed to its door (Ray pointed at that as we entered and laughed) and one of its four small rooms had its floorboards broken revealing the grey dirt beneath. To the side of the dwelling, an outdoor toilet sat perilously over the lapping waters of the toxic Bay. Probably not by choice but it was the place where Ray and his mother could afford to live.

Ray invited us into his room, an eight-by-eight-foot space occupied by two small beds. My friend and I sat on one and Ray, sitting on the edge of the other, lifted up a large acoustic guitar and began to strum, his rough hands taking on what seemed to be an impossibly nimble task. "Would you like to hear a song?" he asked; we both nodded and he began:

> Love is a burning thing
> And it makes a fiery ring
> Bound by wild desire
> I fell into a ring of fire.

And Ray bent over his guitar and poured himself into the Johnny Cash hit. It was my first concert, I suppose, and I was blown away by it and immediately understood, I guess, how one survives living in a shack in the 1960s by a polluted Bay in a barren village called Rossmore. And I have thought about Ray and wondered what became of him many times throughout my life and I have been to concerts by the Stones and Springsteen and Dylan and McLachlan and the Hip and Crow and Foo Fighters and Simon and Pavarotti and Blood, Sweat & Tears and The Dead and Petty and Great Big Sea and Buffett and Cohen and Prine and the London Philharmonic and Johnny Cash, too, and many more, and none seemed better than the moment Ray leaned over his old guitar and sang out his wild desire. Not Elvis or Chuck Berry or The Beatles, no, but Ray—Ray O'Coin was my first hero of rock. Still is! And whatever may have become of him ... well, as you know, the vaults of time and tide hold many dear secrets and he is one; but to this day, I can see him cradling his old axe in that dilapidated shack, and his voice resonates through my deep heart's core:

I fell into a burning ring of fire
I went down, down, down and the flames went higher
And it burns, burns, burns
The ring of fire, the ring of fire.

Our Grade Five class (Mrs. Giles in the back) having just received, it would seem, gift copies of *The New Testament*, which in my memory was a fairly regular event—we were given a lot of *New Testaments*. To my surprise, over fifty years later, I can still remember the names of all of my classmates in this photo (of course, most of us were together for thirteen years in a row, elementary then high school). As to where the *New Testaments* went, that is a matter less clear.

[Note: on the walls behind us, pictures of animals—for some reason, pictures of animals always seemed to fill the walls of public school.]

12

The Thieves of Tomorrow

"If we teach today's students as we taught yesterday's, we rob them of tomorrow."

—John Dewey *Democracy and Education*

The Socratic teaching method that Modernism evoked was not exactly what Socrates would have embraced. For the Athenian philosopher the answer was never the key (although Socrates, as Plato recreates him, has plenty); instead, the process of questioning was designed to produce an affable argument or dialogue which, in turn, motivated critical thinking and illuminated the fundamental suppositions and ideas in the thought-processes of the individuals involved. Socrates, as such, was not an answer guy; he was not the person in the room who knew everything (although, in truth, he probably was) but the goal of his questions was to enable his students to direct themselves toward a clearer understanding of the matters at hand and, thus, of themselves.

Like that mythic Colossus at Rhodes, the American John Dewey stands over the early twentieth century as one of its most remarkable psychologists, philosophers, humanists and educational theorists. A long-time professor at Columbia, he was a staunch advocate for liberal democracy: "Democracy and the one, ultimate ethical ideal of humanity are to my mind synonymous" (*Early Works* V.I) and, accordingly, he became involved in many of the social causes of his time including union rights, women's rights and the suffragette movement— notably, he writes: "You think too much of women in terms of sex. Think of them as human individuals for a while, dropping out the sex qualification, and you won't be so sure of some of your generalizations about what they should and shouldn't do" (*Middle Works* V.VI). He was a pragmatic philosopher and felt that the best path to attaining a civil democratic ideal lay not only in giving people the right to vote but, also, in reforming the education they received. In this way public ideas and debate would be informed through intelligent communication among the public, the politicians and the academic experts. Probably Modernism's greatest impact on Dewey's functional psychology was its rational scientific nature which spurred Dewey's insistence on precision in language and terminology. But like Aristotle, he felt that enabling people and not just informing them was the true goal of education.

In his enlightened ideas about educational reform, Dewey has been labelled a progressivist. He saw schools as social institutions and believed that education was the key in improving the moral and social development of a culture and that the traditional classrooms, as he saw them at the beginning of the twentieth century, were not achieving that. He felt that children needed to be engaged in their learning; education needed to be an experiential process, akin to the natural process of living, and not simply the filling up of an empty vessel. Or as he claims: "Education is not preparation for life; it is life itself." His was a learner-active approach; children learned by doing, by discussion and debate and problem-solving and play among themselves (one thinks back to the early hunter-gatherers and how daily discovery marked the evolution and survival of their culture). While Dewey did envision a kind of balanced approach in terms of content—there did need to be some middle ground between the curriculum and the student—ultimately, he felt that children learned best when the curriculum was in some way linked to their previous experiences and knowledge. Students did not just need to learn stuff but they were served best when they learned *how to learn*. In that way, like training an individual how to farm or fish instead of just giving her/him food, the potential of a future would be ensured. So, in that regard, teachers needed to take on the role of guide or facilitator, not sage or fount. In a Dewey world, one might say that good teachers needed to be good children—to enjoy working with children and to have the capacity to want to learn themselves. Activities such as science experiments and physical education and field trips were a part of the Dewey classroom. And so was egalitarianism; the classroom was a space that enfolded all students regardless of race, religion, gender, class. At the end of school, Dewey felt that children should emerge, regardless of the role or the job or the profession they entered, as thoughtful and wise citizens. As he hypothesizes in *Democracy and Education*: "Were all instructors to realize that the quality of mental process, not the production of correct answers, is the measure of educative growth, something hardly less than a revolution in teaching would be worked."

Playing in the same league as Dewey, Maria Montessori was an Italian physician, psychologist and anthropologist who spent a lifetime in the study of children and how they learned socially, intellectually and physically. She described her *Montessori Method* of teaching as a scientific pedagogy designed to modify and improve the individual. She believed in the creative potential of children and their natural spontaneous desire to learn—she also believed in each child's right to be treated as an individual. Montessori felt that the potential of children was being stifled in the traditional classroom which she once described as a place where "children, like butterflies mounted on pins, are fastened each to his place" (*The Montessori Method* 1912) The Montessori classroom is a child-shaped space, where children learn individually by responding to materials provided (beads, blocks and/or cylinders of wood could be the textbooks students used); group activity tended to be more in a random vein and the teacher ideally remained in the background. Children moved freely in this environment and, when and where necessary, the teacher provided materials and mediated and demonstrated the desired skills and manners of behaviour. Self initiative and self-education led to a student-centred, self-regulating classroom in which discovery, independence, collaboration and imagination were the hallmarks of learning. Students mastered the basic skills of everyday life, then moved on to more academic pursuits. Grades and tests were secondary concerns, at best.

Among Dewey and Montessori and other proponents of Progressive education, certain common precepts and practices emerged. All were based in modernist scientific beliefs arising, fundamentally, out of the ideas of Psychology. Common to all, education is not something that should be imposed on the child from the outside but, rather, in content and methods and individuation, education should foster and draw out the possibilities from within the child. Education should always recognize and demonstrate the democratic value of the individual and activity-based school programs should be shaped and centred for the child, not the other way around. These ideas sifted themselves into educational practices throughout the twentieth century, some in totality (as in Montessori Schools), some in the inclusion of active methods in school programs such as P.T. or in-class scientific experiments or the extensive use of field trips (getting the kids outside of the school); some were implemented more in claim than reality, more said than done. But generally, today, these progressive philosophies hover over the classroom like *Nearly Headless Nick* at a Hogwarts' banquet, their influence forcing a shift in educational practices from a regimented worship of the past to an active apotheosis of the present and future. When you see a classroom with students up and moving around, chatting to one another and being active in their own education, the spirit of John Dewey cannot be far away. Socrates, too!

13
Grade Six

Ah well I bless my soul
What's wrong with me?
I'm itching like a man on a fuzzy tree
My friends say I'm actin' wild as a bug
I'm in love I'm all shook up
Mm mm oh, oh, yeah, yeah, yeah!

—Elvis Presley / Otis Blackwell "All Shook Up"

Johnny has kissed Heather at recess—the word spreads around the playground like the annual spring wildfire across the Massassaga marsh. In Grade Six, Heather is the prettiest girl in our class but no-one had ever thought of actually kissing her. And then came Johnny. All stories have their heroes, or villains, I suppose, and so it was with the world of S. S. #6 Ameliasburgh. Johnny is a member of the Salisbury clan, a notorious band of local shady-doers. Gutsy and gritty, yes, but also willing to forgo the ethical border that most in the community abide. And so, rightly or wrongly, whenever something is stolen, whenever an abandoned barn is set on fire, whenever a Heather is kissed, the Salisbury name rises up. My father even shot at one once, at least according to family lore. After my grandmother died in 1937 and before he met my Mom, Dad and his father would go out to the barn to do the late afternoon chores—the barn was located across the main road, about 300 metres away—but on several days when they returned to prepare their supper, they noticed that things were missing, bags of flour and salt one day, a new shovel another. So my father took the household shotgun with him and, using the culvert underneath the road, he snuck back to the house as dusk came on and, sure enough, saw a figure coming around the back corner of the house. It was Elden Salisbury (Johnny's grandfather). Instinctively, my father raised the gun and shot. He missed Elden, fortunately for Elden and for Dad, I think, but not so much for the old shithouse; buckshot holes remained in the door of that outhouse until it was taken down five decades later. As to Elden, he took off, running like a wise rabbit, and nothing went missing from the house during chores thereafter.

And so, Johnny has kissed Heather. He has taken that one giant leap toward the future that most of us, truth be told, had not really even thought about at this point. Johnny wore his hair slicked back in an Elvis Presley style and was a cocky little soul, tough and mean, frequently lording himself over others and pushing others around. In today's vernacular, I suppose, he was a bully. I remember him swatting Archie one day on the way home from school and pushing him down toward the swamp and once I caught him, for no reason, snapping the multi-coloured plastic streamers from the new handlebar grips I had just received for my bike. Then one day in Grade Six something happened; I do not remember what exactly, but Johnny and I fought. I was an introspective, shy kid and generally terrified of the school's system of crime and punishment but, nevertheless, on this occasion I waded into Johnny and wailed away on him punch for punch knocking him across the school yard—I was a bigger kid and had a distinct advantage by sheer size. In that regard it was not a fair fight. And I was out-of-control angry. A predictable mob of students encircled us like celebratory Romans until a teacher intervened and led the two of us back to the school where we stood along either ends of a wall until lunch hour ended a few minutes later. Then...nothing! We go back to class where we sit a couple desks apart and the afternoon continues as usual. I suspect the teachers knew what the situation was; my reputation as a good kid, and Johnny's alternate rep, played a part. In the zero-tolerance attitudes of today, of course, suspensions from school would probably have been the result. But not then. And, of course, it should be pointed out that both of us carried knives—I think all boys in those days carried the ubiquitous pocket-knife. I had two—my step-grandfather Phil Green gave me a sleek grey one and, a week or so after that, my grandfather Wesley gave me one too, a shimmering multi-coloured beauty. I still have those knives today although I do not carry them anymore. As students, the main difference between then and now, I think, is that we would never have thought of using a knife against someone else—they were simply tools of our time and age and served many purposes but weaponizing them was not something we would do. Following our battle, things went on as usual, Johnny and I even worked as partners on a science experiment in Grade Eight and then through the separation that high school brings, we rarely saw one another again.

The saga of the Salisbury clan in our community was a complex one. It was often a love-hate scenario. Adults along the road gossiped about their nefarious escapades but made business deals with them as well. We had rock fights with them as kids, then played as team-mates on the Massassaga Junior fastball team where Jimmy Salisbury (a cousin of Johnny's) was our coach and appointed me Captain. His older brother, Roger, was a solid member of what my two elder brothers called their "gang of five" (along with two Thompson brothers). My own parents were best friends with Norm and Jean Salisbury and double-dated with them in the early days. Norm was a successful businessman, a carpenter by trade, for years building houses throughout the community and, also, running a farm-market business. He had a quick temper as well; once I saw him throw Jimmy against a wall at a community card party and, from a fence-line beside his apple orchard, Al Revill and I watched as he knocked his wife down and beat her as she lay on the ground. And then, one day in the 1970s, Jean lay herself down on a pile of wood in their back yard and fatally set herself on fire; within a couple years Norm remarried and then, shortly after, shot his new wife and killed himself. It was a dark time for everyone for, whatever their reputation, the Salisburys were a part of our community and theirs was a cruel fate. No-one deserved that—I remember Roger showing up at our place and talking with my Dad for hours about what he should do. And then, years later, I do not know how or why, old highway 62, the central road through upper Massassaga, got rechristened Salisbury Road—it is the ironic stuff of fiction, I think, the kind of thing William Faulkner might have dreamed to life in his gothic vision of the decaying south.

A County Road sign with a dark legacy.

One day in Grade Six, Mrs. Giles sees me squinting at the board; the nurse (who visits the school every Wednesday) phones my mother who arranges an eye test with Dr. Rose about whom I remember nothing but his name; and glasses are prescribed for me for the rest of my life, although for many years, at best, they are *broken glasses*. I was an active kid, football and fastball and lacrosse and low hanging branches in our woods and everything else; on a continual basis the lenses or the side pieces or both seemed unable to withstand what I deemed were things that needed to be done. In a time before plastic lenses and safety glass and protective goggles, I think that I wore broken glasses more than I wore whole ones. Playing football in high school, the helmets fit so tightly, I had to play without glasses and, not being able to see those running backs or wide receivers rushing past, that was surely the reason why I missed so many tackles! At the very least, as they say, that's my story and I am sticking to it.

On another day in Grade Six, after morning recess, Judy, who sits right in front of me and forever wears her hair in a ponytail, suddenly has blood on her leg though she did not seem to be cut or wounded or in any great pain. The nurse, in school that day, is summoned and Judy is carefully, quickly, removed from the classroom. She returns the next day and seems fine, with no visible scars or bandages. Nothing is said; no word is ever spoken of the incident and I am too shy to ask, wisely I suppose, but I come to the realization that the universe holds secrets that in Grade Six I have yet to fathom. And in many ways that realization still holds true today—mystery abounds and the more I know, in fact, the more I realize I do not know. And there is Judy with her ponytail, still with blood on her leg and never a reason why. And the universe spins on.

As Mrs Hannah brings her flannel-Bible-board to us every other week, in the alternative times a music teacher arrives and tries to train us in the singing of songs and in understanding the enigma of musical notation. Just as we have conquered the squiggles of the alphabet, another set of squiggles confronts us. It is almost too much. While I cannot remember her name, I do know that she took on her task with sincerity and effort—I suppose, as I think about it now, she probably drove here and there about the townships every day of the week but in those insular days of being a child one thinks of her but in one single moment and place, as if she conveniently popped into existence only on those days when felt-Jesus was off somewhere fishing and music was needed to fill the void. Music is actually a subject for which a grade is entered on our report card so her presence is not just a lark but serious minstrelsy. She has no instrument but, like everyone I have ever known in a school setting, she possesses this round plastic device, like a hunchback harmonica, and she blows into that before she can sing. Squeaky sound emerges. To me, it is as if this pitch-pipe contains the genii of song and must be given human breath, like some mystic *open sesame*, before the music can resound. Sometimes, she will sing an entire song, and that is a pleasant diversion, before she asks us as a class to follow along. She has booklets of songs; she has us put away our pencils, pens and crayons, then she hands the songbooks out, collecting them again as she is about to leave. They contain the classics of the elementary musical pantheon in that time—in my memory "Froggy Would A-Wooing Go," "My Bonnie," "The Minstrel Boy," "A Scottish Soldier," "This Old Man," "Molly Malone," "Row your Boat," "Old

Smokey," "My Wild Irish Rose," "Greensleeves" and "La Cucaracha" and a host of holiday ditties such as "Silent Night," "Jingle Bells," "Easter Parade" ('though I never did find out what a "rotogravure" was) and "Good King Wenceslaus." And hymns (or near-hymns) too, like "Rock of Ages," "How Great Thou Art," "Jesus Loves Me," "Michael Rowed the Boat Ashore," and "Onward Christian Soldiers." For our report card mark, each of us has to stand beside our desks and sing a verse or two of some song. Before each of us begins, the music teacher diligently blows on her pitch-pipe although, to my tone-challenged soul, she could probably have paraded John Philip Sousa's marching band through the room and I would have been no better off. From the pointers that she always stressed repeatedly, though, some of us have discovered that as long as you held a note, or a noise, at the end of each line, she would sense improvement in your singing, or at least your effort, and give you a good grade. (First rule of being a good student, right, know the teacher!) I remember yelling out the lines of "Green Grow the Rushes Oh," stretching out that "Oh" at the end of each line like a blood-hound on the scent of a fleeing con, and I got my "A" in Music. The true horror for us was being forced to listen to the entire class, one student after another, doing the same thing, and in retrospect I cannot imagine what it must have been like for the Music Teacher…enduring that endless caterwaul, the cacophony of dissonance we called Music. And that poor Music Teacher, having to survive that day after day, school after school, class after class. Sisyphus embracing his stone. A living nightmare incarnate. I think of the old country saying: "I have seen old dogs, and I have seen bold dogs, but I have never seen an old bold dog." So, I suspect, one might say of Music Teachers. And inherent in this memory, throbbing to mind like a friendly toothache, I recall that bizarre ditty we tone-cursed-many were forced to sing year after year like the manic march of lemmings to a cliff:

> Row, row, row your boat
> Gently down the stream
> Merrily merrily, merrily, merrily
> Life is but a dream.
>
> Ah yes, perchance to dream…

14

Invasion of the Brain Snatchers

We almost always have choices, and the better the choice, the more we will be in control of our lives.

—William Glasser *Control Theory in the Classroom*

Education is the process in which we discover that learning adds quality to our lives. Learning must be experienced.

—William Glasser *The Quality School*

Ring a bell and the dog salivates. We all know that Pavlovian parable! Behaviourism or behavioural psychology, arising out of those familiar pseudo-scientific twins, psychology and sociology, made many significant inroads into educational and pedagogical theory in the twentieth century and beyond. Some critics claimed that it enabled many to achieve success who would have been abandoned by previous approaches; conversely, others argued that behavioural practises destroyed the ability to read and think properly for an entire generation. Essentially, using techniques of systematic observation (hence, it seemed scientific), this theory of learning advanced the idea that all behaviours were acquired through conditioning. And that conditioning, classical or operant, occurring in the individual's response to environmental provocations, and enhanced by rewards and punishments, shaped the individual's personality. In this climate, from a child learning to raise a hand to a spy being triggered to be an assassin, any individual can be trained to do any task. We are all Manchurian candidates. One might recall the old empirical philosophy of John Locke but, more to the era, John Watson and his oft-quoted passage: "Give me a dozen healthy infants, well-formed, and my own specified world to bring them up in and I'll guarantee to take any one at random and train him to become any type of specialist I might select—doctor, lawyer, artist, merchant-chief and, yes, even beggar-man and thief, regardless of his talents, penchants, tendencies, abilities, vocations, and race of his ancestors" (*Behavior: An Introduction to Comparative Psychology* 1914). Certainly, an optimistic claim and one that any parent or caregiver would embrace as a provision of hope for her/his child.

Watson, in company with Ivan Pavlov, B. F. Skinner, Jean Piaget, Leon Festinger, Erik Erikson, Abraham Maslow, Lev Vygotsky and others, with theories involving the melodious likes of behavior modification, stimulus response, cognitive development, social learning, cognitive dissonance, psychosocial development, self-actualization, mechanistic measurement, and more, the twentieth century was flooded with behavioristic approaches. And no Noah in sight! These theories carried the weight of science and the prestige of psychology and were sifted into educational theory and practice in huge doses. One controls the variables, one breaks the task into several small stages and then tracks the progress of the students as they work through those stages one step at a time. In general, in this approach, the student learns bit-sized pieces of stuff, working from the part to the whole. Eventually, the bits become the whole. And on some level this approach works. For instance, I had two Australian Cattle dogs and, instead of scratching at the door or howling and barking, both dogs learned to ring bells posted inside and outside to gain entrance or exit. This system of behavioural modification made a lot of sense, and generally allowed me to avoid having to clean up certain unwanted consequences. However, in the world of the classroom, this approach tended toward a reliance on exercises, small activities and tests, BUT not all subject matter could be broken easily into small bits—one is tempted to think of the old parable where blind men examine an elephant and each logically arrives at a different conclusion as to the nature of the beast. Additionally, sub-skills can sometimes be harder to learn than whole skills, and often lack purpose or meaning; nevertheless, behavioural approaches came to dominate pedagogy through most of the middle of the twentieth century. For many students, they seemed to work.

Perhaps the classic example, which spurred decades of controversy, was the implementation of a new and foundational approach to teach children how to read called the sight method (or "look-say" or "whole word"). This approach replaced the method of Phonics which had been in practise since the Victorian era, an approach in which students learned the sounds of English and sounded out the words of the language—*buh ... ahh ... tuh* sounds out *bat*; *kuh ... ahh ... tuh* becomes *cat*; and so on. Phonics came with many issues, of course, such as the complications caused by regional dialects, and there was a long list of debilitating rules and exceptions that needed to be learned; for example, consider the following (and there are many similar examples):

> "G" followed by "e, i or y" usually has the soft sound of "j." Example: "gem, gym, and gist." (Elsewhere "G" usually has a hard sound. Example, "got, gun and gate.")

> When a syllable has two vowels together, the first vowel is usually long and the second is silent. Examples: "pain, eat, boat, rescue, say, grow." NOTE: Diphthongs don't follow this rule; in a diphthong, the vowels blend together to create a single new sound. The diphthongs are: "oi, oy, ou, ow, au, aw, oo" and many others.

I find myself confused just typing out these rules—and the weasel word in each is *usually*. And just consider trying, phonically, to sound out words like *island* or *queue* or *gunwale* and all of the different ways that the combination "ough" can be sounded phonically in English: through, though, bough, enough, cough, hiccough [hic'cup'], trough, tough, borough, lough ['lock'], thought. And the old comic example, how do you spell the word FISH using Phonics; well, it might be GHOTI: Gh as in tou*gh*; o as in w*o*men; ti as in na*ti*on? GH-O-TI = Fish! And have a look at Dan Ackroyd's classic "Decabet" skit from *Saturday Night Live* for an imaginative and satiric spin. His well-meaning and earnest bureaucrat is priceless.

The new behaviourist *sight method* had students recognize (and "say" or "read") a word next to an image or object; the first reading primers often had one word per page, with only five new words per sequence or story. The basal primers that became most popular, really from the 1920s well into the 1960s, were the infamous *Fun with Dick and Jane* readers; with only two or three words per page, regularly repeated, and accompanied with soft and inviting watercolour paintings of the characters and objects (often pets). Each line in the following example represents a new page:

Come, Baby.
Run, run.
Run and see.
Look up, Baby.
Look up and see Puff.
Look up, Baby.
Look up and see Dick.
See Dick go up.
See Dick go up, up, u
Oh, Jane.
See Dick come down.
See Puff come down.
Down, down, down.
Oh, oh, oh.
See Puff come down.
Go, go, go.
Go, Dick, go.
Go, go, go.
Help, help!"

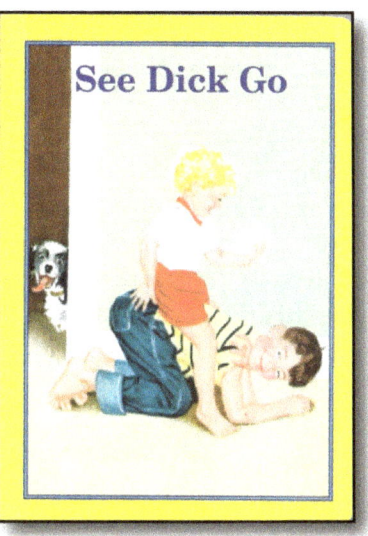

In reading this repetitive text (one resists Freud here), students would learn certain words and meanings, for the most part, words that would have some conceptual sense in their own lives or perhaps in a previous story they had read—up, down, look, go, run. But one question that arises: are you compelled by what you've read here, are you feeling that you just must read on to chapter two? The probable answer is 'no.' Meaning, sense and interest were typically non-existent in these sorts of stories—as I have mentioned elsewhere, I experienced this stuff at school, and pure Phonics instruction, too, then went home and read my books and comics, which were of interest to me. School and life never seemed to cross paths. For years, though, these "Dick and Jane-style" texts drove the reading curriculum, and most other subjects of study as well; today certain web-based programs continue to do the same. Of course, publishers have also often had a huge influence on such educational initiatives, sometimes for educational good, sometimes just for profit. And has that changed at all as we embrace this brave new technological world and its online pedagogies; well, to be kind, let's just say conclusions have yet to be made?

Issues accumulated around this new reading approach. Some argued that the "look-say" method would lead to reading disabilities as students inevitably encountered a grander world-stage with an illimitable range of different words. Reading development could be limited by memory (typically, an adult uses 50,000 words but memory can be limited to about 2,000.) Robert Flesch's *Why Johnny Can't Read* (1955) criticized the simple stories used and the techniques of Phonics not used; others argued that this approach did not teach students necessary reading skills (decoding, fluency, prediction, vocabulary, construction, inference, cohesion, skimming, scanning, *etc.*) And, of course, much was made of the stereotypical biases of books such as the *Dick and Jane* readers, that standardized white, chauvinistic, middle-class world—Father wore a suit and worked in an office, while Mother cleaned the home and took care of the children; and even the pets, Spot and Puff, seemed pretty much middle-class Caucasian.

Of all the theories and trends that besiege education, Behaviourism is perhaps the one that has held its grip firmest for the longest, even beyond the turn of the millennium. When I moved from Oxford County in Ontario to teach at Clarke Road Secondary School in the London District, during the summer a copy of Bill Glasser's *Control Theory in the Classroom* arrived in the mail from the school. Glasser had given a talk the previous year at a local Professional Development Conference and, collegially, the school had decided to adopt Glasser's approach to pedagogy school-wide, requiring each teacher to read this book and apply Glasser's Behaviourist strategies in their classrooms. One of my favourite places I've ever taught, Clarke Road Secondary School was a tough, proud school, located in the east-side of London, a working-class, multi-ethnic area with a fair bit of poverty and some gang violence too. The Glasser approach essentially placed the emphasis for choice, responsibility and transformation in the hands of the students, trying to make students understand that they had the power to control the consequences of their lives. Issues such as attendance, civil behaviour in class, appropriate language, timely submission of assignments, and so on, were up to them to solve. Ownership of their success was their own responsibility; they controlled it. Glasser later changed the name of his theory from "control" to "choice theory" to avoid confusion with other earlier concepts and, I think, to lessen the pejorative sense of the approach. Did the theory work? Well, I always felt that it was a good attempt at giving the school a research-based, informed, uniform approach to teaching and discipline, if nothing else; and I was impressed with and applauded the effort. And, at the very least, it did get the teaching staff thinking about the craft of teaching. As with so many things though, discrepancies appeared. One V.P. at the Road, a friend with whom I shared many a good laugh and had the utmost respect, placed the phrase "Teamwork Wins" at the bottom of every memo she sent out, simpático with the Glasser theory. The notion, of course, was that all staff should work toward the same goals, march to the same drummer, but in time it became evident that 'teamwork' really meant doing what the Administration wanted. In my sense, Control Theory aside, a lot of the students at 'the Road' came from challenging situations at home, if they had a home at all; they were often children of the streets and a bit of kindness and flexibility on the part of teachers went a lot farther than any umbrella theory.

A couple years after I arrived at Clarke Road, I was asked by Ted McTavish, another V.P., to help him give a P.D. presentation to the staff on *The Quality School*, another book by Glasser. I remember reading it, making notes, and passing those on to Ted, who then gave the presentation using my notes. I am not sure if Ted ever did get around to reading the book himself, but he did get promoted to a Principalship shortly thereafter. He became a good friend and a golfing buddy of mine (we played courses across the south-west and Michigan, too) but, tongue-in-cheek, I never let him forget that Glasser moment and what a wonderful presentation he made, how he took ownership of the instant. He would always just smile that impish grin of his and say: "yes, it was wonderful, wasn't it!"

15
Grade Seven

Anybody here seen my old friend John?
Can you tell me where he's gone?
He freed a lotta people but it seems the good they die young
I just looked around and he's gone

—Dick Holler "Abraham, Martin and John" (1968)

Our Grade Seven and Eight teacher is Mrs. (Martha) Bates, the principal of the school. She towers over our world and terrifies me, and many others too (I think). In some ways she is an effective teacher, she gets her lessons across, but often she descends into a kind of hysterical monomania that would have made Ahab quake. She slams doors and yells at classes and keeps entire quadrants (most often, the boys) in after school and, no matter the weather, forces everyone out at recess and lunch. Before class she slurps oranges like a vampire and her punitive strap seems ever at the ready, any minor act on any given day can bring on corporal punishment delivered with an exuberant fury. I do not wish to be too unkind but, for a shy and sensitive kid as I always was, this was a horrible environment and it cast a shadow over all of my elementary school years. I came to hate school, and fear it—education was life in a concentration camp. In my recollection, many times I feigned illness, simply, so I would not have to go to that terrible place (part of that, I suppose, was also that I was a fairly gifted student and not much of what we did at school challenged or interested me). As well, as later years spent studying and working in education brought me to understand, given the relatively gentle rural nature of this school, set in a civil and respectful community, most students with solid nuclear family backgrounds, such a heavy hand was not needed, and did far more harm than good. In many ways, it was an opportunity lost. But Mrs. Bates was a child of her time, a paranoid and defensive post-WWII world under the newly-born blossom of atomic annihilation where definitive, rigid rules piled one on top of the other and aggressive, violent reaction was the norm. For me, the iron-ambiance forged by the leadership of S. S. #6 etched a bad blueprint for schooling.

Nevertheless, can you still recall the following—maybe you had to memorize it as I did?

> I wandered lonely as a cloud
> That floats on high o'er vales and hills,
> When all at once I saw a crowd,
> A host, of golden daffodils... (Wordsworth)

Or maybe, "I think that I shall never see/A poem lovely as a tree" ("Trees" Joyce Kilmer). I still recall a long (and prosaically charming) passage from the *King James Bible* which we had to commit to memory in Grade Seven:

> And it came to pass in those days, that there went out a decree from Caesar Augustus, that all the world should be taxed. And all went to be taxed, every one into his own city. And Joseph also went up from Galilee, out of the city of Nazareth, into Judaea, unto the city of David, which is called Bethlehem; To be taxed with Mary his espoused wife, being great with child. And so it was, that, while they were there, the days were accomplished that she should be delivered. And she brought forth her firstborn son, and wrapped him in swaddling clothes, and laid him in a manger; because there was no room for them in the inn.

Regardless of content or context, that methodology continued on into high school where the memory work often included darker literary pieces like Old English ballads or war poetry such as Owen's "Anthem for Doomed Youth" or select speeches from Shakespeare. I still recall

King Lear's impassioned plea "O, reason not the need! Our basest beggars/Are in the poorest thing superfluous..." or Macbeth's dire summing up: "Life's but a walking shadow, a poor player,/ That struts and frets his hour upon the stage, / And then is heard no more. It is a tale / Told by an idiot, full of sound and fury, / Signifying nothing." This was a time and place before computers and other electronics filled the vacant spaces of the classroom and our minds. Memory work, rote learning, spelling tests, and examinations that valued and rewarded recollected information were the order of the day. One only has to look at that sample examination from Salina (1895) that I included earlier in this book. Modernism valued the preservation of these selected fragments of our culture; these decontextualized bits and pieces, selected and collected and anthologized—this was the grease on which the gears of education ran. "Sumachs have turned their green to red" we chanted, "wild birds are flying south." As our parents and grandparents had memorized and could bring a selection of galloping rhythms to conversation, so too, we were asked to commit to memory a range of lyrics and prose, and many of these bits and pieces still stay with me in random ways, as I am sure they do to others of this generation:

> There is something in the autumn that is native to my blood
> Touch of manner, hint of mood
> And my heart is like a rhyme
> With the yellow and the purple and the crimson keeping time

We rarely discussed or debated or analyzed these lyrics. How is a heart like a rhyme, or what quality exists in the autumn that might impact our feelings? We never wrote our own personal responses to the message given by any of these poems. Such was not important. We were never asked to question what we were reading, to examine or interrogate the poet and how her/his historical time might have influenced what was written. In fact, in our study of *The Merchant of Venice* in Grade Nine, the Hebrew religion was never mentioned—we never learned what a Jew was, let alone consider what seems to me to be a central issue of prejudice or intolerance in that play. We were simply told to memorize parts of it, answer questions about other parts, and that was that. We would then move on to the next required piece; in Grade Nine, that happened to be J. Meade Falkner's novel, *Moonfleet*. In part, this was a post-war, nebulously militaristic culture where orders were given and actions required—thinking was not a part of that equation. A good memory was. Education was knowing when to duck, and being able to recall the parts of a gun (as in Henry Reed's sober "Naming of Parts," which we also memorized). And for those of us who were effective at the task, that part of schooling meant for good marks. And while education in general has now shifted on to value different skills and methods, on occasion, for me, certain lines from these long-ago pieces still slip into my head and, somehow, strangely perhaps, bring a comfort—they are old friends:

> Along the line of smoky hills
> The crimson forest stands,
> And all the day the blue-jay calls
> Throughout the autumn lands.

Two or three times during the year in Grade Seven the 16mm projector would be borrowed from the United Church next door and we would be shown a film of some sort, usually exotic locations with African villages and images of small children of the Maasai with far-off blurry figures that we were told were lions and giraffes. Then a pamphlet was handed out with a picture of this African veldt and an invitation for all to come to the church basement on Thursday night where a pair of missionaries, like Paul's offspring, would talk about their experiences and show a longer film about their adventures on the 'dark continent,' a phrase still used in that time. This was the only electronic media that we received and, while it may pale in an age where digital images flood the classroom, we ate it up. It was so different, so rare and weirdly entertaining, so much like those scarce Saturday afternoons when I got to the Belle or the Park movie theatres in Belleville only, here, right in our classroom, the experience, *sans* popcorn and that bad Elvis movie, was always a thrill. At the end of it all, however, I'm afraid we were not very good messengers for these evangelicals—as I walked home, I recall the ditches of our gravel road randomly littered with discarded pamphlets, the lions and giraffes of Africa confused by their plight, abandoned to roam the inclement marshlands of upper Massassaga instead of the tropical plains of the Serengeti.

An encounter with the forbidden—the following is part of an

excerpted passage that was included in our *Grade Seven Reader*—and it is a passage that we were prohibited from reading. Students would be asked to stand and read aloud but, when they came to this paragraph, Mrs. Bates would stop them and have them skip to the next. The passage, too offensive for our mid-1960's ears, is that which follows, from *Gulliver's Travel* (Part II, Ch. 5), the account of tiny Gulliver among the giants of Brobdingnag being kidnapped by a court monkey:

> After some time spent in peeping, grinning, and chattering, he at last espied me; and reaching one of his paws in at the door, as a cat does when she plays with a mouse, although I often shifted place to avoid him, he at length seized the lappet of my coat (which being made of that country silk, was very thick and strong), and dragged me out. He took me up in his right fore-foot and held me as a nurse does a child she is going to suckle, just as I have seen the same sort of creature do with a kitten in Europe; and when I offered to struggle he squeezed me so hard, that I thought it more prudent to submit. I have good reason to believe, that he took me for a young one of his own species, by his often stroking my face very gently with his other paw. In these diversions he was interrupted by a noise at the closet door, as if somebody were opening it: whereupon he suddenly leaped up to the window at which he had come in, and thence upon the leads and gutters, walking upon three legs, and holding me in the fourth, till he clambered up to a roof that was next to ours.

While it seems so quaint today, especially in this age of the worldly internet, that this language, this image, would be considered inappropriate for us to experience at age thirteen or fourteen may seem odd, but such was the ethos of that time, at least in that place. Of course, our friends in Grade Eight had already told us about this notorious passage and this equally peculiar pedagogy, so all of us anticipated this moment as if it were Christmas morning, and we quickly read the illicit passage anyway (several times in fact). Add to that, of course, many of us came from farms where the suckling of animals was a common experience—in fact, many of us had helped calves wean themselves by coating fingers in a pail of milk, then sticking them in their mouths. But… reading about it, well, that was something else, I guess. Of course, when all is said and done, while the *Grade Seven Reader* contained many stories and excerpts, that forbidden passage from *Gulliver's Travels* is the only one I remember all these years later!

Mr. Dunsmore was the local Inspector of Schools and came upon us twice a year in the ominous role of the invader Hannibal descending with elephants and mercenaries and all. Although I have been told later by his colleagues that he was actually a pleasant person, on visits to the school he was stern and methodical and never cracked a smile. Principals and the like, of course, were trained in that manner, serious and sombre figures of authority and command, dictators-in-training. In those days, Inspectors had the power to fire teachers on the spot if they detected flaws in the local educational domain. As rumours of his coming to the school spread, a wave of efficiency and urgency executed a *coup d'etat* over our habitual routines—classrooms were tidied, hallways swept and cleared, new artwork pinned up, proper procedures and behaviours edified, certain subject lessons rehearsed. First, Mr. Dunsmore was a male, a macho authority-figure who entered this female cloister with all of the swagger of Valentino in a harem. The teachers who lorded it over us were now lorded over themselves, diminished in a masculine shadow, cowing through files and desk drawers to grant Lord Dunsmore anything he wanted. This was a time, of course, when all positions of power, in education and most of society, were granted to males, no questions asked! Father knew best, you know, just like Jim and Ward and Ozzie and all the rest in that patriarchal world of black and white TV!

Second, not only was Mr. Dunsmore a feared masculine invader but he was also a master of academics, Socrates incarnate, or so it seemed. One day I recall him having the Grade Seven/Eight class stand and, row by row, he would ask a question. A question—out of nowhere that had any relevance to anything we had been taught; our row got asked: "What is a bungalow?" If we knew the answer, we were to sit down, so I sat—I didn't want to look stupid. But there must have been an uncertain quality in my sitting for, sure enough, he asked me for the answer. And I said "a boat" which seemed like a logical guess to me (perhaps I had been thinking of a "bowrider" or a "catamaran") but my answer was wrong and I was told to stand again and remained so, along with a few others in the room, until all the rows were finished. I have often recalled this incident and the more I became informed with the effective practices and theories of education, from Socrates to Goodlad, Frye and beyond, a worse practice I cannot imagine. And I still flinch every time I drive by one of those small post-war houses. And cannot help but wonder how well one of those bungalows would float in a flood.

Mr. Dunsmore's invasion of the school would cease by day's end and, I suppose like the breath of relief in the bunker when the shelling stops, things would return to normal. Teachers would relax to their regular posture, the calmer pace of the hours would return, welcome dust would rise to settle again over the rooms, and most of us would now resume, at this safe distance, our habit of calling the Inspector of schools, Mr. Dunce-more (I mean, what would you expect of a name like that in the juvenile realms of the era!).

It was a damp and blustery day in late November; raw grey showers skimmed across the landscape like shivering foxes on the run. And it was the first time I had ever seen an adult cry. Mrs. Giles had tears in her eyes as she stood at the door to Mrs. Bates' classroom. Mrs. G. had gone out at lunch to visit her parents who lived only a couple minutes away and returned with the most improbable news. "Mr. Kennedy's been shot" I heard her say and, unsteady, she turned away and went upstairs to her classroom. Mrs. Bates showed no response, stoically proceeding with the afternoon lessons like any other day—what else could one do, I suppose. I remember walking home quickly, and alone. The world seemed quiet, freezing, and I wanted to see what the television was saying. And when I got there, the old seventeen-inch Admiral was on and Walter Cronkite was talking and talking and talking. He was very good at that even though there was really very little to say, very little information to give. John Fitzgerald Kennedy was dead and a suspect had been arrested in Dallas, Texas. I think, for any who were of a cognizant age, that day remains as the most memorable, perhaps most stunning, moment of our lives. No-one really had an explanation; I mean, that kind of thing was the relic of history, or the stuff of other countries. But not in modern time, not in America. And while we came to understand later that JFK had his warts (don't we all), at that moment

Camelot seemed palpable and he was the shining, young king bound to lead the world where it had never gone before with the beautiful Queen Guinevere (aka Jackie) at his side. What was almost worse, as usual I got up early on Saturday morning to watch my litany of cartoons, but everything was pre-empted. No Popeye or Quick Draw McGraw or Yogi Bear. Nothing—just men in black suits saying the same thing over and over for hours, in fact, for days. And somehow, even though it was an American event, that dreary Friday marked a time when the world seemed to change, when a line was drawn for most of us between what was and what was to come. From Viet Nam and the British music invasion and the rise of Canadian nationalism (including a new flag and Expo '67 and the methodical creation of a Canadian literature) and the hippie movement and shows of social conscience on TV and civil rights and women's liberation and all the rest. It was the moment that gave birth to conspiracy theories, a cultural concept that has vacillated since then from the inane to the violent. Yes, even though we were not really aware at the time, the times they were a-changin'. JFK was dead and for the first time in my life (though not the last), I had seen an adult cry. (I include a poem I wrote about that time at the end of this chapter.)

The winters then seemed colder than the winters now, more wintry, if you will. Snow arrived by late November and stayed intact until the middle of March and we adopted to the season like moths to the flame. The path from my house to the road was a crevice over eight feet high. We guided sleighs and toboggans down the great hill behind Roseberry's house next-door; as the toboggans slickened the paths, we shot out over the ledge and crashed with joy into the crunchiness of the winter marsh. The newly invented aluminium saucers swirled even farther, and one had to be careful to avoid the metal runners of the Flexible Flyers slicing past. We kept snow cleared from the perfect oval pond behind Robinson's house and many were the Stanley Cups won and lost in that frozen arena. In the school yard we rolled up half a dozen large snowballs, six feet in radius, and pushed them together to form a huge rectangular fortress. We dug holes in it and smoothed its top and defended it like Spartacus at Vesuvious. And one glorious day an ice-storm coated all the world with a sheen that glittered like diamonds in a crown. As I walked past the Goulah's house, where Mrs. Convoy lived before her stroke, Sherilynn appeared in a pink winter coat with matching mittens. By then, Sherilynn Goulah had emerged as the goddess of Grade Seven, attractive in a Laura Petrie kind-of way with that practiced Marilyn lisp and charming coyness. She had become the carnal focus of every boy in the school, although, I realized, well beyond the awkward farm boy that was I. But she was always pleasant to me— her younger brother Rick and I were great friends. And we walked to school together on this shining winter day. The convex gravel road was coated with an inch and a half of ice, slick and treacherous and sloping to each side. And Sherilynn and I walked down the middle of that crystal way, one on each side of its apogee, holding hands to keep from sliding apart, to keep from falling. Holding hands with Sherilynn Goulah and the crisp blue world shimmering all about us. Grade Seven and the glistening future stretching out before us. And then Sherilynn's pink mitten slipped off and she and I started to slide slowly toward opposite ditches and we turned and watched each other slip away and waved a cold farewell, her mitten in my hand. And we laughed, the most genuine laugh I think I have ever had, at the silliness of our predicament, our lives, our future. And Sherilynn came to be 'in the family way' in high school and disappeared from the visible world in accord with the social morays of the time. But in that era and that galaxy, no tears need be shed, frozen or not—for one time she was Queen of the World and, me, well, once in that far time and place, I held her hand and we walked a shining path toward the future.

The King of our class was undoubtedly Steven Sharpe, from Rossmore. Steve was fit and handsome and an excellent athlete, playing on an elite hockey team in a league in Belleville—I later taught Karen, a niece of Steve's who was a delightful young woman although, sadly, eventually descended to a career in local politics. Steve was a good friend, one of the most gifted students in our class; we played in the schoolyard all the time and he was the shortstop to my third base on our school softball team; I'd like to say we were a sure-fire double-play combination but I'm not quite sure, at that age, we ever exactly got around to turning double plays—a single toss in time to first was miracle enough. Sad to say, we did get in one fight once, over what, I can't remember? We were playing catch with a baseball he had brought to school and a brawl broke out between us over something and he certainly beat me in that fight; but then, nothing came of it. We cleaned up, the teachers ignored it and we carried on our relationship as normal. Strange things, sometimes, those events in the hormonal lives of young teens (older ones, too, I suppose). In the years after school, I only saw Steve a few times—he became a police officer on the Belleville force and served out what I surmise to have been a very successful career.

There was a serious side to the snowfalls of these times. In this era Russia and China and the United States all regularly conducted tests of their atomic and nuclear weapons, blowing away small atolls in the far Pacific or blasting craters deep within the Kazakhstan steppes and the frozen Gobi desert. The radiation from those tests rose, drifted to the east on the prevailing winds and fell as snow all across Canada. Children, in particular, were warned never to taste these deadly snowflakes, never to let them sit on your skin. And, as a reminder, every Saturday morning at eight o'clock, in the middle of the weekend ration of cartoons— *Huckleberry Hound* and *Ruff 'n Ready* and *The Roadrunner* and *Rocky and Bullwinkle*—television screens would freeze for a full minute and a high-pitched horn would sound—this was the Conelrad warning system (*Control of Electromagnetic Radiation*) which broadcast across North America to warn that, if nuclear war was imminent, this system would tell us what to do. Indeed, we paused and wondered. I always remember an early comedy routine by the brilliant George Carlin in which he played Al Sleet, your hippie-dippy weather man, who concluded his weather report: "…rain and sleet throughout the day, however, the radar is also picking up a squadron of Russian ICBMs, so I wouldn't sweat the thunder showers, man." Sometimes today, when I hear of the traumatic fears children must be suffering in the wake of 9/11 or from the isolation of *Covid-19* or some other such calamity, I understand, but I also think back to the days of my youth when the snow that fell was certain poison and the sky held the promise of imminent annihilation. Truly, some things never seem to change even as they do. At the very least, it is good to reflect, but then, just push on and don't sweat the thunder showers, man. For, as Barry McGuire in that time starkly forewarned:

The Eastern world, it is explodin'
Violence flarin', bullets loadin'
You're old enough to kill but not for votin'
You don't believe in war, but what's that gun you're totin'?
And even the Jordan river has bodies floatin'
But you tell me
Over and over and over again, my friend
How you don't believe
We're on the eve of destruction

Or as Dylan prophesied: "Yonder stands your orphan with his gun /
Crying like a fire in the sun / Look out, the saints are comin' through /
And it's all over now, baby blue..."

It was a cold winter, but the routine was firm. Any flexibility that a
sane humanity would have enacted did not exist in the heart or soul of
S. S. #6. Three times each day, two recesses and lunch, students were
evacuated from the school moving to the wintry yard and swirling
winds. On one cold day, with temperatures dipping below minus twenty
on the old Fahrenheit scale, several students were frostbitten, earlobes
and fingertips and the like, and the writing was imbedded on a wall of
ice. A petition went about the neighbourhood like the wild fires of the
spring marsh and, at the end of it all, before the next year began, Martha
Bates was fired.

ADDENDUM:

the day they took my cartoons away

the day after they took my cartoons away
there was nothing to show
still they showed nothing all day
the day before
a dull friday in the late fall
it was goin to be a hard winter
that was the first time i seen a grown-up cry

though not the last
the grade six teacher
a large woman shall i say
came into the principals room after lunch
the principal was my teacher
said somethin quiet all of us heard
'mr kennedys been shot'
and she brushed back a tear and swayed unsteady
the principal just nodded
she was a cold thing with laced up leather boots
she carried on with the day
arithmetic after lunch
then art where we cut coloured angels
from folded paper
cause christmas was a-comin
and you needed somethin to put in the windows
and i walked home that afternoon alone
it was grey and wanted to rain
i hurried
no birds were singin
at least none that i could hear
it was a thing that didnt seem possible in our time
is what i remember
the 17-inch admiral was on
but no friendly armchair for two to curl up in
no michelle or howard the turtle
who said corny things like
where is the red sea
its on my report card
only the grey man in a white shirt and black tie talking
fiddling with his dark glasses
different from this grey man
when the mercury rockets went up
he talked all night said nothing over and over
he was very good at that
but no fred or barney no twilight zone
though it felt like twilight zone
and on saturday morning i got up as usual early

but where was ruff n ready
huckleberry and quick-draw
no popeye or rocky and bullwinkle
there was nothing a human could watch
no stooges
in a world where the stooges had taken over
a world full of men in black suits
but empty it was empty
and i was mad
and it was too crappy to play outside
sure things happen bad things
but where were my cartoons
i needed them didnt everyone need them
more this morning than any other
and over sixty years later
while i dont remember much else
i remember that
the empty tv world emptied
the grey man talking about nothing for days
nothing was all there was
and dark splatters on that light grey dress
later it was made pink in life magazine
there were plenty of cowboy hats
parade-fit white stetsons
but not those of roy or dale or the lone ranger
there was that bent-over man
in a crazy sunday hallway
and horses strutting and a kid saluting
and the silence of the birds
that day after i saw an adult cry and sway
that was the day
they took my cartoons away

(published in *magic birds* SurePrint&Design 2024)

16
Resurrection of the Truth

But you who seek to give and merit fame,
And justly bear a Critic's noble name,
Be sure yourself and your own reach to know,
How far your genius, taste, and learning go;
Launch not beyond your depth, but be discreet,
And mark that point where sense and dullness meet. …
A little learning is a dangerous thing;
Drink deep, or taste not the Pierian spring:
There shallow draughts intoxicate the brain,
And drinking largely sobers us again.

—Alexander Pope "Essay on Criticism: Part I, II"

Under the influence of Modernism, but often echoing the old Victorian ideal of keeping the 'cultural heritage' alive, the approach called Socratic teaching (or the Socratic Method) emerged to dominate mainstream pedagogical tactics throughout the twentieth century. The *case* of Ontario's Bert Case Diltz provides a striking example. Diltz, a veteran of World War One, graduated from Queen's University with his Honours B.A., took an M.A. from Columbia and then went on to teach for decades at the University of Toronto where he became Dean of the Ontario College of Education from 1958 to 1963. In that time, everyone who became a teacher in the province was required to attend and acquire her/his qualification at O.C.E. in a six-week summer course; in the subject of English, in particular, all were trained in Diltz's methods—the Diltzian way was the highway. Then, by the late 1960s, Teachers' Colleges and Faculties of Education were created and a full-year Bachelor of Education degree became a requirement to teach in the province. Typically, the instructors hired at these institutions were disciples of Diltz so the Diltzian method was spread like the gospel and continued to have an enormous influence for a long time. As part of that process, Diltz published several theoretical books outlining his theories of teaching—*Pierian Spring* (1946), *The Sense of Wonder* (1953), *Patterns of Surmise* (1962), *Sense or Nonsense* (1972)—and edited numerous anthologies of poems and short stories, grammar and language texts, to provide school classrooms with the materials on which to practise his approach: *New Horizons* (1955), *Poetic Experience* (1955), *Word Magic* (1957), *Many Minds* (1963), *Frontiers of Wonder* (1968), among others. Like many others, I studied from several of these anthologies as a high school student and then, after being trained in the Diltzian method while earning my B.Ed., I taught from those same anthologies in my first years teaching in this province.

Worth noting by way of example, in his "Introduction" to *New Horizons*, a child of his time, Diltz affirms an elitist New Critical or Formalist attitude; the mission of the teacher is to resurrect the truth of the past for the sake of the present:

> Every poem included is a work of art in which the content and the form complement each other, and every poem opens a clear way for the apprehension of poetic experience. Not only is each poem representative of some of the best effort of its author, but it reflects in some degree the artistic temper and tempo of the time in which it was written. Popularity alone is no proof of excellence in poetry. This anthology sets a standard of achievement for senior students in this branch of study.

Pierian Spring (1946) provides a good example of Diltz's fundamental method, his ideology. Here Diltz reveals a blended pedagogical philosophy, melding a quest for the student to unveil the self, as Socrates had envisioned so long ago, into the Modernist desire for a rediscovery and reclamation of values scattered in the fragmented remains of the culture, and all under the guidance of the refined "art and craft of teaching":

The urgent need in education today is the resurrection of the truth of sound values as revealed and recorded through the ages rather than the indiscriminate following of the "trends" of modern socialistic opinion. *Pierian Springs* advocates the study of *subjects*, the materials of language and mathematics, history and science, rather than the discussion of the popular side of controversial "issues". It recommends that pupils be taught to read and interpret literature rather than to watch the movie director's conjuring with its reducible images or to listen to the radio narrator mouthing its most affecting sounds. It recommends that one of the chief aims of education is to transmit our heritage through our experiencing of it rather than to subscribe to descriptions of contemporary society as conceived by theorists and explained by those who naïvely suppose that what appears to be practical today will perforce be practical tomorrow.

If one of the chief aims of education is to help boys and girls to discover the best that is within them, to find themselves, and to clarify their own characters, the precedence must be given to the calling and charging of teachers rather than to the unleashing of educational moochers to prowl for what they can get. The art and craft of teaching must again take precedence over the cult of administration and the pseudo-science of education. The awakening of an inquisitive spirit must receive more attention than the fostering of an acquisitive attitude. Exact scholarship must replace maudlin impressionism in education.

Within those theoretical publications, Diltz included specific poems or passages and then offered diagrammatic schemes to illustrate how the "exact scholarship" might proceed. For example, in *Pierian Spring*, Diltz imagines "Pupils" (his word, always) reading Wordsworth's "It is Not to be Thought Of" and then shows how a teacher ("T") might design the lesson:

T: Why do you think Wordsworth contributed this poem to a daily
newspaper at that particular time?

P: England was in danger of invasion by Napoleon.

T: The following excerpts from Green's *A Short History of the
English People* may suggest a little of the tension in public
feeling to which Wordsworth hoped to give direction.
*"It was plain that a struggle was inevitable; and in May 1803 the
armaments preparing in the French ports hastened the formal declaration
of war.*
*England was now the one country where freedom in any sense remained alive.
A camp of one hundred thousand men was formed at Boulogne, and a host
of flat-bottomed boats gathered for their conveyance across the Channel.*
*The invasion seemed imminent when Napoleon, who had assumed the title
of Emperor, appeared in the camp at Boulogne. 'Let us be masters of the
Channel for six hours,' he is reported to have said, 'and we are masters of
the world.'"*

Why is this poem particularly significant for us today?

P: In recent years Hitler, seeking world domination, tried the same
thing.

T: He, too, would have tried to subjugate England even as
Napoleon subjugated Switzerland and other neighbouring states
[T. re-reads the poem]:

> It is not to be thought of that the Flood
> Of British freedom, which, to the open sea
> Of the world's praise, from dark antiquity
> Hath flowed, "with pomp of waters, unwithstood,"
> Roused though it be full often to a mood
> Which spurns the check of salutary bands,
> That this most famous Stream in bogs and sands
> Should perish; and to evil and to good
> Be lost forever. [In our halls is hung
> Armoury of the invincible Knights of old:
> We must be free or die, who speak the tongue
> That Shakespeare spake; the faith and morals hold

Which Milton held.—In everything we are sprung
Of Earth's first blood, have titles manifold.]

To what does Wordsworth compare freedom?

P: Freedom is compared to a mighty river.
T: How far in the poem does the comparison extend?
P: To the word ever, and the first period, in the ninth line.
T: What purposes does the comparison serve?
P: It supplies the framework for the continuous flow of thought
and emotion down to the final period.
T: Whence comes this river?
P: From "dark antiquity."
T: Where is that on the map?
P: It is not a place but a time in history.
T: What is the significance of "dark"?
P: It suggests that freedom's source is prehistoric.
P: No record of its origin exists.
P: The spirit of freedom is very old.
T: Whither is the river flowing?
P: To "the open sea of the world's praise."
T: Where is that? ... [and so on].

This *question-and-answer* sequence, then, is the ideal Socratic method of teaching as envisioned and promulgated by Diltz; and, as noted, it had an impact for years across the province of Ontario and, in like kind, in most other jurisdictions. It's how teachers were taught to teach, to some extent in all subjects and levels, but particularly in English and Language Arts. More than just a practical method, the approach took on a psychic dimension—it became what teaching was thought to be. And while this representation in *Pierian Spring* is an idealization (I can't imagine any teacher, then or now, actually using "whither" or "whence" in a question), questioning technique, the refined skill involved in asking the precise question at the precise time, probably remains the most invaluable skill any teacher can ever have and still remains as a central tenet of any teacher's skill set. Ask the right question and I have seen a flurry of hands go up in a class that was previously asleep. And for many other professions, from doctor to lawyer to police officer, skilful questioning is a vital skill to possess. Also evident in this sequence, of course, is the given that "T", the teacher, has full academic command of the material at hand, knowing exactly what questions to ask and in what order—hierarchical schema such as Bloom's *Taxonomy* underpinned this approach—as well as knowing what extraneous or background materials might be useful to introduce (such as, in the example above, topical information about the publication of the poem in a daily newspaper and/or Green's *History*). The teacher understands exactly what she or he wants the 'pupils' to learn from reading this poem and, through precise questions and timely exposure to certain external sources, guides the pupils to the light. (It is worth noting, appropriately, that Diltz's *Patterns of Surmise* is constructed almost entirely of these 'Q&A' sequences.)

Through today's lens, of course, this approach may seem lacking, authoritarian and somewhat stifling—personal response and engagement seem missing and the central theme of the poem, itself, which praises Britain's supreme right of empire, passed down it seems from the "first blood" of Eden through the words of Shakespeare and Milton, never comes under question. That is not to say, of course, that it is not a fine poem, an experimental Petrarchan sonnet and a good example of one of the greatest Romantic poets near the height of his powers expounding his conservative radicalism; in another way, as well, *Pierian Spring* is a text that reveals a great deal about attitudes in the immediate aftermath of World War II. And, however one sees it today, this *new critical* approach projected the spirit of its time—teaching was to be a clinical, no-nonsense, scientific procedure aimed at training students in how to dissect and understand what the text, from word to comma (in this case Wordsworth's poem), seems to be saying. First you eviscerate the text; then the world. There is no fooling around here. It was an era of the sage on the stage and the Diltzian Socratic method sang the song. (For interest's sake and much greater detail, Don Gutteridge's *Stubborn Pilgrimage* (2017) gives an extensive account of Diltz—well worth a read for any interested in the history of this approach.) One actual flaw that emerged in this modern Socratic adaptation is simply that, very often, the teacher did most of the talking, asking questions, but then elaborating on the questions and challenging the students' answers, preaching more than teaching. Surveys (for example see Deosaran/Wright) actually showed that, in many of these classrooms, the teacher dominated the discussion, talking 80 to 90 per cent of the time. And many teachers, especially new teachers learning the craft, fear silence, asking a question, then re-posing it, often again and again, in effect, eventually supplying 'the answer.' In such instances, clever (or lazy) students often learned to wait long enough and their work would be done for them. (As a counter-measure in teaching, I used to enjoy asking a question and then waiting … and waiting … and waiting. Silence puts a powerful pressure on a class especially if it knows that it must respond, that the teacher is not going to do the work for them. My fall-back strategy, if no answer was forthcoming after a couple minutes, was to have each student write down a response, then start again, having them read what they wrote if all else failed. At the very least, this got students talking and shut me up!) As the era began to shift, in many ways Diltz's final theoretical text, *Sense or Nonsense* (1972), is a cry of desperation, of defiance, against the inevitable change that he felt was coming:

> The psychologists and sociologists may classify and corral the less talented and encourage them to accept their lot, but they cannot make students of those who have little aptitude for learning. Must the whole system of education be modified in order to accommodate their whims or unstructured tantrums? Without restraining banks a river loses its identity. Whether the student works with language or with lathe, he is in school to organize and develop his mental faculties. The theorist, on the other hand, would drive him along the road to chaos without a creed.
>
> Whatever else is lost in the morass of experimenters, the study of literature must be preserved. It is time for those who believe in real education to stand fast together. The Scots have a lovely lilting word for it: *craigélachié.*

Although Diltz feared that "real education," as he labelled it, was disappearing, times do change, and no era seemed to change faster (at least on the surface) than the 1960s. Dylan went electric. Hair got longer, skirts shorter, and television hit its stride—the electronic Age of

Aquarius flowered, and the Global Village made all of us next-door neighbours. Initiatives in curricula such as the *Hall-Dennis Living and Learning Report* in Ontario (1968) were designed to give students a wide range of options and freedoms, introduce new courses such as film study and Theatre Arts and encourage the practice of team teaching and a rotary system of education for Grades Seven and Eight. Questions asked by teachers were intended to be less specific and more open-ended. Even the school buildings themselves seemed caught up in this psychedelic whirlwind—in the span of a decade, they went from multi-floored edifices to one-floor structures where classrooms had no windows to open concept formations (classrooms without walls, often encircling a library or activity centre), and then, to being closed-in again by the 1980s. Students' schedules changed as well. Semestering and the credit system evolved (no longer did failing one subject mean that you failed the entire year, forced to redo everything). The concept of Middle School was also developed in which cohorts of students, generally age twelve to fifteen, were concentrated—kids without models of leadership on either extreme some argued; others applauded the focus given to a developmental age set that never seemed to fit previous groupings. One casualty in secondary school was the thirty-five-minute class which had been a long-time standard, where:

— students typically took eight classes per day all year long

— eight classes of Mathematics and English per week (three days had 'double' classes)

— five of Science, Physical Education, French

— three of History, Geography

— one option: a double-period juggling act of Music, Visual Arts, Drama, Typing, Commerce, Home Economics, or Shops—Auto, Drafting, Metal and Woodworking; maybe Agriculture.

With the arrival of the credit system and the semester format, this menu changed dramatically:

— students now took four classes per day, typically seventy to seventy-five minutes in length

— a mid-year break near the end of January with a slate of examinations

— a new set of four courses

— all courses were now weighted equally (while time spent in English or Mathematics declined, more time could be devoted to the other subjects—students may not have been given as much time practicing writing or Algebra but they were better at basketball or typing.

— somewhere between twenty-five and thirty credits needed to earn a diploma.

As often happens with change of any kind, there were great debates over the pros and cons of the new credit/semester systems and of Middle School, but as the age of information and computers cemented the presumed need for speed and greater efficiency, the changes settled down like autumn frost on a bed of flowers. Change was here to stay; the acoustic guitar, even Dylan himself, may have been relegated to the side-lines in a cast. And for scholars like Diltz, it truly must have seemed as if "real education" was doomed. The Diltzian method, an exacting, demanding formula fit for an authoritarian Age, no longer quite fit a culture of flower power and tie-dye. Culture is a rough beast, always shifting and changing whether we like it or not. And while some knowledge of Diltz may still offer a signpost that is useful to us—he was certainly a major influence for a long time and symbolic of the system *status quo* for a long time—we are reminded that education is always part of a fluid stream, a moving reflection and explication of the time in which it is alive, or at the very least trying to represent that time. But it must always be alive, always inquisitive and flexible, measured and seeking, directed with an informed cultural presence, trying to catch up to the world in which it lives and predict that which lies before. One recalls those lines of Alexander Pope: "A little learning is a dangerous thing; / Drink deep, or taste not the Pierian spring…"

ADDENDUM:

More Excellence and More Of It

Bert Case Diltz was not alone in his concern about a decline in educational methods and standards after the 1960s. Concerns were expressed and significant changes to education began to be implemented across the United States and Canada under the impetus of something generally labelled the *Excellence in Education* movement. By the late 1970s and beyond several *doom and gloom* documents such as *A Nation at Risk* and *The Paideia Proposal* emerged; enhanced by the likes of Goodlad's *A Place Called School,* Sizer's *Horace's Compromise,* Bloom's *The Closing of the American Mind,* Boyer's *High School,* Slezak's *Odyssey to Excellence* and Rutter's *Fifteen Thousand Hours* (in England), the *Excellence in Education* movement cried out for higher standards in educational institutions; conservative times ruled (Mulroney in Canada; Reagan in the U.S.; Thatcher in the U.K.) and demanded longer school days, more course structure and fewer options for students. Schools needed to be more challenging, more academic, more tightly closed in. So, for students, more Science, more Physical Education, more languages (French, Spanish or German) and fewer optional (*i.e.: interest*) courses. On first glance for many, these strategies may have made sense but, as we know, there is always some danger in removing *interest* from a place like school—at the very least, it may mean that what remains in school needs to be made more interesting, and that is not always an easy task, or a desired one. (As an example, and for its own survival, History (a subject imbedded in the past, not the future) caught on to this, generally shifting from a 'causes and effects' ideology to a cultural studies approach, what the Romans ate for lunch becoming more important than when the Gallic wars were fought.) Incidentally, this was also the era in which what had been the most common *other* language taught in schools, Latin, began to fade away—the Second Vatican Council in 1959 had decreed that Catholic Mass could be spoken in other dialects and, by the late 1960s, universities in general, and Medical Schools in particular, began to abandon its use—Classics Departments struggled to garner enrolments and many universities let them dissolve utterly. Utility took the wheel, and Business and Commerce Faculties were born and thrived. (I do recall that, by my Grade Ten year I was still required to take French *and* Latin, then, in following years, I could choose one or the other, or both.)

Then into this mix of curricular upheaval, like the cat in the hat, along came the concept of cultural literacy and the birth of what came to be called the culture wars. At the centre of this, E. D. Hirsch with his small but evocative text, *Cultural Literacy* (1987), in which he says "… all educated people share common knowledge; we must identify the core of that knowledge and teach it to all children." The central theory seems simple—each nation has a common cultural history and vocabulary and schools should adopt that as its curricula and teach that to its citizens; in some ways it seems to be an echo of Victorian and early Modernist sentiments, to keep "the heritage" alive or, at least, shore up its ruins. Hirsch subtitled his book, "what every American needs to know" and even appended a list of 'names' and/or 'things' people should know; the following is an excerpt:

…
eviction
evolution
ex cathedra
exchange rate
excise tax
exclamation point
executive branch
exeunt
existentialism
Exodus, the Book of
ex officio
expanding universe
expatriation
expense account
Experience is the best teacher
expletive
exponential growth
export quotax post facto
expressionism … *and so on*

While interesting, perhaps, such lists are fundamentally absurd—*exeunt* and *existentialism* are placed side by side but surely, conceptually, the idea of a group of characters exiting the stage (*exeunt*, the Latin plural of *exit*) and *existentialism* (for example, Heidegger's conceptual *Das Man* vs. *Dasein* or Sartre's *The Myth of Sisyphus* or Kierkegaardian *subjectivity*) are intellectually far apart. Hirsch includes the word "potato" but leaves out "tomato." Now what kind of civilisation can exist without tomatoes! It follows, I suppose, that words like 'pizza' or 'bruschetta' are nowhere to be found. And if problems arise in producing stepping stones to cultural literacy in the so-called melting pot of America, how impossible would such notation be in a multicultural or regional nation such as Canada. From *frazil* to *Coho* to *scree* to *bluffs* to *kayak* to *streetcars* to *Tabarnack* to *Blue Nose* to *Screech* to *Yes b'y*, Canadians have no uniform national vocabulary and that is probably not a bad thing. In fact, it helps define the richness of our culture, of who we are—our regional diversity.

Fundamental, at the very least, among the problems in advocating cultural literacy are two questions: one, whose culture represents the core; and two, what do we need to know about the items in such a curriculum (how do we account for change). If Christopher Columbus is on the list, as he is on Hirsch's, why is he there and how is his representation to be analysed. Then, and now! Our contemporary "woke" or "cancel culture" would simply have him erased, eliminated along with hundreds of other people and statues and stories and paintings of the past that do not measure up to contemporary attitudes and values, but that's not good enough; that's not an informed or intelligent way to deal with such things. Who was Columbus? What did he do? Why did he do it? Explain the *Zeitgeist* of his time. Why has he been celebrated as he has? Why is he no longer seen as the explorer-hero? Should we remember him? Why? Why not? (By the way, in contemporary Canada, at this writing, Sir John A. Macdonald's name could be inserted here.) Hirsch's selection, as many critics have pointed out, seems to be filled with a lot of dead white males (a sign of his time … perhaps?) and leaves out as much as it includes (such as 'tomatoes'); especially as our post-modern world becomes more multi-cultural, and multi-oriented, such lists are not only problematical to compile but often ridiculous and probably undesirable; in some ironic way, of course, Hirsch's cultural literacy actually sparked a challenge (unintentionally, in some ways) to the traditional curriculum and to the traditional canon of topics and books and authors. Should students read Hemingway and Fitzgerald or Gilman and Morrison, Callaghan and Leacock or Atwood and Munro, and Ricci and Kogawa and Bissoondath and King (Thomas or Stephen)? (The answer, by the way—all of them!) While I will return to the issue of curriculum later, it seems to me that a curriculum based on any notion of cultural literacy is undesirable, absurd (but as I will suggest, that may be exactly what transpired, and continues to do so, in the twist of the millennium). Beyond that, it is probably useful to note, undesirable as this theory may be, I have taught in and visited many schools where what might be called an 'unofficial cultural literacy' seemed resolutely in place, where *To Kill a Mockingbird* and *Lord of the Flies* and *The Stone Angel* were endlessly taught and I never saw an English Department that did not include Shakespeare, usually several of his plays across the grades. Once, that was true of Shaw, as well. Arguably, of course, a good book is a good book, a *teachable* book is a *teachable* book and some are more appropriate in that regard than others. Age appropriateness comes into play, as does budget—usually a school can't simply throw out everything to start anew every few years, though gradual change is healthy.

As an aside, books used and stories read in school always paint an interesting portrait of the beliefs held in the culture at large at any particular point in time and place; texts are replaced as values and the understanding of those values shift in society—from Science to History, this is probably true for all subjects. Sometimes change is inspired directly by world events and beliefs and social movements, sometimes by the timidity of publishers, sometimes influence comes by way of random sources such as film. (I've taught many relatively obscure books placed on courses because of the popular success of a film—*One Flew Over the Cuckoo's Nest*, *The Loneliness of the Long-Distance Runner*, *Shane*, *Forrest Gump* and *The Princess Bride* come to mind. Humorously (to me anyway), I recall a Department Head who saw the film *Ordinary People* and loved it; he ordered two class sets (about 75 books) only to discover a couple swear words on the very first page ("fuck" and "shit," I think)—those books were shelved in his room, and never used, in his mind language far too risqué for his community-at-large. He was probably right.) Try reading any of the following, all texts widely taught across Ontario at various times since the 1940s, and see what shifts in beliefs and attitudes you will find: *Priester John*, "Gunga Din", *Moonfleet*,

Cue for Treason, "The Most Dangerous Game", "Leiningen versus the Ants", *Silas Marner, Boss of the Namko Drive, The Giver,* "The Lottery", *The Catcher in the Rye, Of Mice and Men, Lord of the Flies, The Stone Angel.*

When it comes to Hirsch and his *Cultural Literacy,* I am reminded of Ezra Pound's *The ABCs of Reading,* published a hundred years or so ago, in pure Modernist style, an arrogant and elitist text that laid out a fairly snobbish list of required pedagogy. As influential and brilliant as Pound was—*The Cantos* is a modern epic—he did end up in prison as a Fascist anti-Semite, on charges of treason and facing a death sentence; ultimately, he spent much of the rest of his life confined to St. Elizabeth's Asylum for the insane. E. D. Hirsch, on the other hand, retired from the University of Virginia as a Professor Emeritus.

17
Grade Eight

She bathed in her still garden, while
The red-eyed elders, watching, felt
The basses of their beings throb
In witching chords, and their thin blood
Pulse pizzicati of Hosanna.

—Wallace Stevens "Peter Quince at the Clavier"

Around 1960, the future Nobel laureate, singer/songwriter Bob Dylan arrived in New York City from Hibbing, Minnesota, near the Canadian border, to write and record that song which became a pop-anthem for the era, "The Times They Are A-Changing" and so it was for our little school in rural Massassaga. The earth spun on a new axis. Mr. (Fred) Holmes arrived from Northern Ontario to be the new principal of S. S. #6. He is our first male teacher and brought an entirely different ambience to the classroom, a new attitude to the school at large. The imaginary divisions of the playground are removed and we are free to wander from side to side, front to back. We are allowed to stay in classrooms at recess and lunch if we so choose and, as the year progresses, many of us do to talk and argue with Mr. Holmes about everything from what the best hockey team is (he was a huge fan of the *Toronto Maple Leafs*) to modern trends in music, and hairstyles—*The Beatles* had just arrived in North America to play *The Ed Sullivan Show* so such crazes and fashions marked the cusp of change. One day in early September Mr. Holmes notices that we are playing soccer with a sponge rubber ball (the old tri-colour kind)—for us soccer, like almost every sport, is really hockey without the skates and sticks. We body-check and 'foot-handle' through the other team's players and celebrate our goals like the Golden Jet (Bobby Hull was born and lived locally and was adored by most before the domestic abuse aura descended); I remember deking the ball through Bobby Mitchell one time for a goal and raising my hands, feeling like the Rocket bursting off the wing (I was a Canadiens' fan) just as Bobby crunched me into the fence. Seeing us playing with a rubber ball, Mr. Holmes tossed a real soccer ball to us. We barely know what to do—but we quickly adapt, the goaltending improves and the ball loses its sheen quickly—this is the bright yellow-brown soccer ball that has rested atop a shelf at the back of Mrs. Bates' room for years like some sacred fruit in a garden. Mr. Holmes delivers it like some mythic hero of song and story.

And suddenly, instead of just reading about experiments in our Science textbook we are doing them. Johnny Salisbury and I are paired to light a flame beneath a one gallon can into which we have placed a cup of water (something like that anyway) and, when the water boils and we screw the cap on the can, it crushes into itself like magic. On another occasion I actually go out during class to find a grasshopper—it is during the fall when the grain fields are golden and 'hoppers' are plentiful. I observe the creature, then draw and label one, an effort that later wins me a first-place red ribbon at the Belleville Fair. It seems a quaint recollection these days when students in Senior Elementary are building and firing rockets and completing projects in Quantum Physics, but this was a time of grasshoppers, I guess, and rockets and quanta were still the propriety of world governments racing to the moon. Mr. Holmes organizes a County-wide athletic competition among all the Public Schools where I medal (ribbon, actually) in high and long jumps and in the softball throw. Exhibition fastball games are set up with the closest schools—O the glory days! During practices, Mr. Holmes competes with us like a kid and, later, will join the local men's team in the North Shore league. I remember in our first game against the Public School in Rednersville, I was placed fifth in the batting line-up though I knew I was the best hitter on the team and, boosting my vanity, I hit probably the longest home run I ever hit in my life. The bat struck the ball as if the two were one (you know the feeling) and, like a missile, the thing arced far over the centre fielder's head, hit a down slope, torpedoed through the parking lot and disappeared into the far ditch across the road. I could have walked around the bases, but I didn't. In the next game, a week later against Albury, having learned his lesson (I always thought) Mr. Holmes batted me clean-up; ironically, of course, I did not repeat my hitting heroics but did make one of those plays at third that was pure instinct, not skill. A ball was clocked over my head; I leaped as high as I could and, by the will of the gods of flight, the ball stuck. I also made three or four plays on regular ground balls and my buddy Bob Mitchell caught every one of my throws to first. My team congratulated me each time as I came off the field and I saw Mr. Holmes smile. After all, I had been an all-star for a couple seasons in the area junior league.

At the start of each day, the Grade Seven and Eight students were invited to provide some information about current events in the world—this was a voluntary exercise but also the first time in my school experience that the classroom connected to something real, something beyond itself. So Ham the Chimp, Yuri Gagarin and John Glenn orbiting the earth became part of our schooling; China taking its place in the United Nations is an issue; so too, a war on the rise involving the U.S. in some faraway Asian country named Viet Nam; Marilyn Monroe dies; so too Dag Hammarskjöld and Albert Schweitzer; after a long debate with many alternatives, Canada adopts a new flag. The best current event ever occurs when Ricky Goulah raises his hand one Spring day to announce that the *Montreal Canadiens* have defeated Chicago to win the Stanley Cup. As mentioned, Mr. Holmes was an ardent fan of the *Toronto Maple Leafs* and I was a Habs' fan—one Christmas I had been given a table top hockey game and, my brothers, being Maple Leaf fans and older, commandeered the Leaf side while the Canadiens fell to me, and so I became a fan by default and have been ever since. Mr. Holmes and I argued all year long about the respective players and abilities and statistics (Frank Mahovlich was his favourite Leaf player; Boom Boom Geoffrion and Jean Béliveau of the *Bleu, Blanc, Rouge*, mine) but Chicago ousted the defending-champion Leafs in the semi-finals, and in the finals Claude Provost shut down Bobby Hull and Jean Béliveau won the first ever Conn Smythe trophy. It was a good day in current events and I sat smugly silent in my seat. Ultimately, of course, Mr Holmes coyly got the last laugh—on my final Report Card for Grade Eight he wrote: "Brian should participate more in class discussions and be willing to accept the ideas of others and to use them to his advantage." While he was probably right, my father chuckled at this, memorized it and repeated it back to me at various times throughout the rest of his life.

Our classes were victims, or so it seemed, of something called the New Math. In many ways, as noted, this curricular change was a reaction to the success of the Soviet's *Sputnik* and the space race and the feeling that scientific and mathematical skill levels needed to be raised in the West in order to compete with a portentous threat from beyond the iron curtain. Physics and Chemistry and Biology were changed in secondary schools, so it was felt that elementary school Mathematics needed to be changed as well. The Grade Seven textbooks arrived the year before, shiny and orange; instead of multiplication tables and exercises in changing pecks to bushels or rods to acres, I recall being introduced to bases other than 10, matrices, algebraic inequalities, Boolean algebra, set theory and modular Arithmetic. My Dad was always very good at Arithmetic and he couldn't make heads or tails of this. There were many complaints from the general public and, truth be told, I think a lot of teachers had problems, too. Luckily for us, there was some kind of printer back-log at the Ministry of Education and the Grade Eight textbooks never got printed (at least, none ever arrived at S.S #6); when it came time to study Math, the Grade Sevens simply handed the texts they were using over to us and we did the same chapters and exercises over again that we had done the year before. And I can tell you, second time around, it still did not make much sense to me; in fact, I often wonder if that was part of the turning point that made me embrace Language and English studies as my vocation and not choose a career in the Maths and Sciences. At least, a story or a poem entertains before it confuses... usually!

And so, the year unfolded; and Mr. Holmes was a light for me (and most of the rest of our class, I think)! We were given a much more active and involved education by a teacher who seemed engaged in our lives and the world about us; mostly he seemed relaxed, real and human. He had a genuine sense of humour and, it seemed, he cared. And what curious recollections fill the memory; I recall one day he asked the class if anyone knew how to spell the word "gunwale" and I put up my hand, spelled it correctly as he printed it on the board. "How did you know that, he asked?" and shook his head with a smile. And that human quality was his undoing—one day in our classroom Red Thompson said or did something to get under Mr. Holmes' skin and a fight erupted, fists flying and desks being knocked over. And at the end of the year, as we graduated so did Mr. Holmes, fired from his short-lived stint as principal of S. S. #6. We only find that out later in the summer. And while what he did was a grievous error in temper and judgement, I still cannot but marvel at the way our world changed and grew under his spell. Perhaps it was just that he was the first male teaching-role-model in my life, I don't know! What I do know, Mr. Fred Holmes remains, probably, the greatest teaching influence on my life. And I was sad to hear of his departure though I knew the reasons why. I think of the words of Melville: 'Ahh, Bartleby! Ahh, humanity!'

Students in our senior classes are also subjected for the first time to a series of province-wide standardized aptitude assessments that generally come to be known as IQ tests. These quizzes are quite different from anything that we have ever done both in content (they are abstract and very American) and in method (using scantron sheets for our answers), but where some students flail away at the disengagement from regular routine, I recall finding the tests interesting, generally quite easy and a refreshing break from daily routine. The questions are mostly multiple choice and test for skills in Arithmetic, Reading and Logic. For instance:

1. given 2 8 32, logically, what would be the next number in the sequence:
    A) 32   B) 128   C) 256   D) 512
2. Book is to Reading, as Fork is to:
    A) drawing   B) writing   C) stirring   D) eating
3. A palindrome is a word or phrase that is spelled with the same letters forward or backward:
    A) True   B) False
4. If you rearrange the letters of "ahret," you would have the name of:
    A) Ventricle   B) Fish   C) River   D) Planet

Although we never see our scores and I am not sure what these tests test, if anything, I do quite well (I gather around 150) and go forward to secondary school with an asterisk next to my name meaning, in the code of the day, that I am "a student to watch."

It is the third week of June. Hot. Humidity on the rise. The previous year, the County has dredged a channel through the marsh just behind the schoolyard connecting the storm culvert under Highway 62 to the Bay of Quinte. Better drainage, one supposes. And one day during afternoon recess several classmates collect around the back fence. Curious, I wander over and stand to the side. A small pontoon-style raft is drifting along the channel with two young women on board. High school is out, final exams finished, and these girls, probably in Grade Ten or Eleven, are from down the road and a couple guys know them. They are laying on their stomachs on bright beach towels, bikini-clad with the top strings undone, white lines across their backs still visible, trying to take in all the sun they can and generate a deep, ubiquitous tan. These are the days when bodies tanned dark and lustrous are considered a healthy thing; these are the days of *Coppertone* and *Tahitian Tan*. The boys and the young women, one sits up, one hand precariously holding her bikini in place, natter away at one another as they drift pass. Light banter. Flirting. And like those elders in that poem by Wallace Stevens, I suppose, "the basses" of our being awake. And the bell rings to end recess; we turn away, and the raft drifts on. Certain as the heat of the season, it is a suggestive moment of passage, an instant suspended, between what is and what surely will be. The warm current is slow but inexorable. There is no turning back nor would our deep desire will such a turning anyway.

There is no Prom, no gowns or mortar boards, no stage with flowers or banners or filigreed diplomas. No yearbooks to sign. No hugs or even handshakes—I have never seen anyone hugged in all my time at school. It is simply not a part of that time and place. Simply, school closes fifteen minutes early on a late June afternoon as it has always done every June in my schooling experience; we are given our threefold Report Cards and, happily, we scamper away to the joys of summer (or for labour in the farm harvest for which this agricultural model of schooling was implemented in the first place). We are fine with that; school is a place from which to escape—it is how things have always been and the excessive idea of tuxes and gowns and Proms for kids in Grade Eight (or even in grades younger) will not materialize for many years. Changes in demographics mean that our Grade Eight cohort is enrolled in a new high school for the fall, Moira Secondary School, and not Belleville Collegiate which older friends and siblings and parents and grandparents have always attended. This is a terrible decision—Grade Nine at Moira, buried far away in a sterile edifice north-east of town, does not fit us. It is too new and too shiny. These are not the hallways of our ancestors—like the lyrics of "The Scottish Soldier" that we have sung so often: "These are not the hills of home." And certainly not the legendary instructors about whom we have been told endless stories—Red Townsend and Sparky Heard and Father Buckley and Shotgun Kelly the Librarian. Our psychic spirits seem far away and, when the decision is reversed next year for Grade Ten, most of us opt to go to BCI and things seem better for us in its old and worn and sturdy brick walls. Simply, Grade Nine is a year stolen from us by some anonymous number-crunchers, a year which can never be restored.

ADDENDUM:

Reports

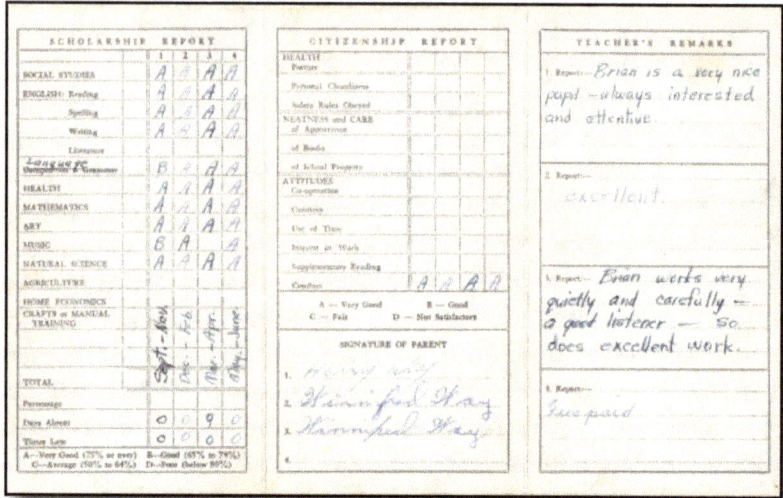

1. Example of the long-standard tri-fold Report Card (Grade 4)
2. My infamous Grade 8 Report; *touché* Mr. Holmes

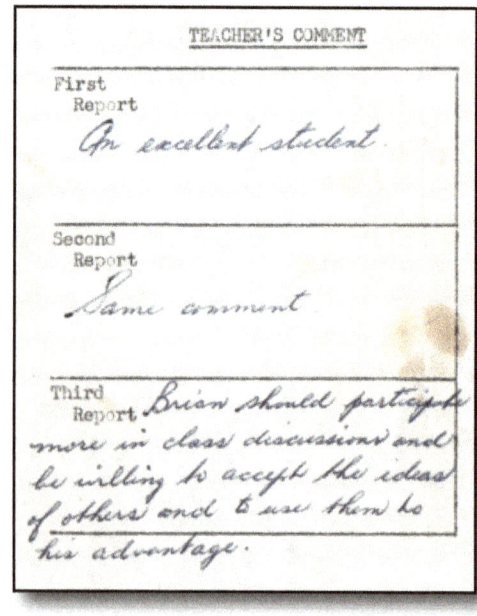

18

The Rose-Coloured Roller Coaster

We live in a political world
Turning and a-thrashing about
As soon as you're awake, you're trained to take
What looks like the easy way out

—Bob Dylan "Political World" 1989

If real estate has to do with location, location, location, then the Ministry of Education and its various policies and documents have to do with politics, politics, politics! Curriculum is always more about politics than education, new Math, whole language, critical race theory and all the rest. Even sex education! Every document ever produced is driven by one political agenda or another. In a broad sense, this is understandable—the body politic that trains its young to be Molotov-throwing revolutionaries will not last long. But there is also a ludicrous element to this as well, at least in practice. The chart which follows offers a thumbnail sketch of the various curricula that have been put in place in Ontario in the last few decades—what a whirlwind of change and, I suspect, most other jurisdictions in North America have followed a similar pattern! While explaining the details of these years would require more time than I have left on this planet, perhaps the key component illustrated by this chart, once again, is the idea of change, itself. The fly in this ointment wears a political button. The word for curriculum derives from the Latin *currere,* meaning *to run the course*; ideally, an educational curriculum is intended to identify and represent a citizen's course, a nation's course, those most critical aspects that a society sees necessary for the growth and development of each individual—social, emotional, cognitive, physical, linguistic, moral. In looking at this chart, though, it becomes apparent that the *currere* is mostly just run from election to election. How such expectations can change so radically all within such a relatively short time—the answer, the simple side of politics, not some grand political theory but frequently the petty attitudes of the petty moment. The Conservative government initiated its Common Curriculum in the early 1990s, the NDP was elected and replaced those documents with their own and, just two years later, the Liberal government did the same. Such modifications are neither economical nor smart, just a political game. And, from Junior Kindergarten to secondary school graduation, teachers are caught in the middle, students at the bottom—it is little wonder that many teachers pay little real heed to the guidelines on a day-to-day basis. I knew one Superintendent who actually expected teachers to write a curricular expectation on the board each day and strive to achieve it—not likely to happen! Teachers tend to hunker down and teach their classes as they have always done—*plus ça change, plus c'est la même chose*. But that, too, may not always be a good thing.

And so, how do you create a curriculum? From an overarching theory to the nuts and bolts of what a child needs to learn from day to day, the idea is immense. And while it is beyond my scope here, let me suggest an example for clarification. Let's choose Grade Three and let's pick Geography (*Social Studies* as it is currently called). What should a child know by the end of Grade Three in *Social Studies*? Should she/he/… know the names of all of Canada's provinces? Yes? The territories, too? Ok! And should she/he/… know the names of all of the capital cities of Canada's provinces and territories? Fair enough! Now should she/he have to know one hundred percent of those names? What if she/he/… only knows eleven of the thirteen capitals (that New Brunswick capital is always so tricky and how do you even spell the capital of Nunavut?) Does this mean that the student fails Grade Three *Social Studies* and must repeat it next year? Or repeat the entire grade (which is what used to happen in Ontario—fail one course and fail the entire year.) And what if that student is your child? Is eighty per cent enough? Or fifty? And so it goes. Once you establish the required expectations of the curriculum (the province's names and the capital cities, for instance), you then need to establish performance standards (how much knowledge is acceptable for a child to pass). And

A Sketch of Educational Change in Ontario Since 1950

1950 Hope Report	-reorganized teacher training (possibility of dual certification) -grade divisions: 1-6; 7-10; 11-13 (proposed junior colleges)
	new curriculum guidelines
1962 Robarts Plan	-three new secondary streams (four-, five-, and two-year); -three career-oriented programs (Academic; Business and Commerce; Science, Technology and Trades) -end of Province-wide examinations (1967)
	new curriculum guidelines
1968 Hall-Dennis: Living and Learning	-4000 school boards reduced to 100 or so -credit system ("semestering" is initiated) -many new subject options (such as Dramatic Arts, Screen Arts) -absolute parental choice as to placement of child re stream, program -Intermediate Division given some status -emphasis on learning curricular Aims and Objectives
	new curriculum guidelines

1981 Review Project
Report on Secondary
Education
	-Grades 7, 8, 9 and 10 aligned (Intermediate Div.); Grades 11, 12
	  (Senior Div.); Special Education emphasized
	-Ontario Academic Credits (OACs) replace Grade 13 (compulsory
	  exams; ISPs initiated)
	-compulsory French; more credits, fewer options
	-Whole Language; reduction of instruction in phonics, grammar

	new curriculum guidelines
1990+ Royal Commission: For the Love of Learning *and* The Common Curriculum	-Grades 1 to 6 aligned as Formative Years -Grades 7, 8, 9 aligned as Transition Years -Grades 10, 11, 12, OAC as Specialization Years (never happens) -emphasis on Science and Technology, Media Education -emphasis on Outcomes, Skills and Provincial Standards
	new curriculum guidelines
1997 The Ontario Curriculum	-Grades 9, 10, 11, 12 aligned; OAC eliminated -new emphasis on Co-operative Education and Testing
	new curriculum guidelines
2010+ Ontario Review and Revision Guide	-Kindergarten, Elementary (1-8), Secondary (9-12) -de-streaming; ongoing revisions to courses and expectations

this is the place where grades enter the picture (percentages or letter grades or numbered levels of achievement or simply Pass/Fail, or whatever demarcation is used). And, in recent years, rubric charts are generated to describe each given level of achievement, such assessment often supported by exemplars, typically using a 4-point scale. So a child may get 4 in one assessment, 2 in another, and so on, and detailed descriptive information is available for each. At the end of the unit, or semester or year, a grade-point average is achieved. In theory, from east to west and north to south, every child (every parent/caregiver) knows exactly what the grade/level is and what it means. Standardized tests are developed—in Ontario, these have typically been issued for Grades Three, Six and Nine, with certain tests for specific subject areas, such as Language and Mathematics, at other grades. A standard province-wide Report Card is now sent out and, in following the dictates of formal curriculum development, the system-wide results of student achievement are calculated and reported and changes, if needed, are implemented in the system and/or in the standardized curriculum. If students do not do well, 'fire the teacher' may be the battle cry! In the USA, in general, where students have often not achieved well against the standards, the solution has often been a simple one, lower the standards and then test again. With our current electronic wizardry, it is easy to see that happening in Ontario. (As an aside, there is big money in the business of generating and administering such tests and in all the corelative materials such a system seems to require; at times, testing seems to drive education far more than it should. That is surely the dark side of curriculum implementation. When a teacher is spending more time on testing and tracking and evaluation than she/he is spending on prepping and delivery of lessons, and interacting with students, then something is rotten in the state.)

In simplified chart form, curriculum development usually looks like the following:

Curriculum Development
1. **Educational Standard**—What needs to be known in each subject (age/grade dependent)
2. **Performance Standard**—How much (at least 50% is the norm)
3. **Test**—Province-wide (at least in some subjects, some grades)
4. **Report**—Use a common report card/system; publish results (easily done in our electronic environs)
5. **Analyses/Corrections/Revisions**

Additional issues need consideration. Should a curriculum be standard across an area as large as the province of Ontario? Does a child in Pickle Lake need to know the same things as a child who lives on Yonge and Bloor? The answer, of course, is complicated and can initiate great debate. There are few black bears on Yonge and Bloor, few bears of any kind in fact, so knowing about their habits and behaviours might be a waste of time; not so in Pickle Lake where that knowledge could save your life. The same is true in reverse about traffic lights and shady strangers in High Park (a different kind of bear, I suppose). On the other hand, the child of Pickle Lake might not stay in Pickle Lake forever and, it could be argued, deserves to have the same education, the same chance, as the child of a metropolis.

Related to this and a long-standing aspect of the Ontario curriculum which can be a topic of divisive discussion, streaming. The *Addendum* which follows offers a more detailed discussion; for years in this province, when students enter secondary school, they are placed in a 'pre-determined division' of classes for which there is a defined destination—label them as you wish, one stream is directed toward university education, a second stream toward college, and a third toward work. (And while not labelled as such, children in Elementary schools tend to be sorted into certain groups as well, the prolepses of later paths they will follow.) In fact, for many years in Ontario, one stream actually graduated students at the end of Grade Ten, but, of course, the state of the world has shifted since and that practice has been phased out (one recalls that there used to be a three year B.A., too, but that has pretty much vanished; in fact, it is not uncommon now to hear that an M.A. is the new B.A.). There are many, particularly in the USA, of course, who would decry streaming and insist that all individuals should be given the same chance, the same education, to enable them to be president (although they rarely mention the role a bank account plays). Many in Ontario have now come to look at that middle stream, in particular, and see it as a dead zone which leads nowhere (I think Stephen King wrote the book). However, I have also seen individuals that were flailing in an academic or work stream and blossom in the middle. I remember genial Dan, who was Bubba to his friends, whose Dad had been killed in a horrible snowmobile accident when Dan was very young; Dan, who had been labelled as one who would never be more than barely literate—I remember Dan in the 'middle' level working hard, coming to recognize his weaknesses, learning to read and write and conquer the appropriate and reasonable challenges of that stream with pride, getting into College and earning a welding diploma and securing a certification in Scuba diving. I remember Dan engaging in a remarkable life and career, challenging and interesting and successful, doing underwater welding across Canada and around the world. I remember Dan, years after graduation, a successful citizen, taking me to speedboat races on Fanshawe Lake. I remember Dan, who was Bubba to his friends. I remember Bubba.

ADDENDUM:

To Stream or Not to Stream

At this writing, the system of streaming in Ontario is on the verge of extinction. Streaming students in high school—that is, having students choose and be separated into different tracks as they begin Grade Nine and proceed with their education—was a practice that extended back through most of the twentieth century and forward into the twenty-first. Usually the choice, based on the student's grades and interests, was made by the student with advice from caregivers and help from some authority in the elementary school. In this way, the student was placed on a particular assembly line of courses aimed at a specific destination. At this writing, in Ontario, those lines are labelled Academic, Applied and Essential (or Locally Developed); the first aimed at university, the second, at college, and the third toward some occupation. (Previously, they were Advanced / General / Basic; before that, Arts and Science / Science, Technology and Trades / Business and Commerce, and so on.) Within the streams, students could sometimes choose certain options. As noted, though in an academic stream, I took a 'Shops option' (when I probably should have taken Art and Music) but at the end I did learn some Woodworking and Agricultural and Automotive skills—though perhaps learning to play the violin or paint like Cezanne would have served me better?. In more recent iterations of the system, students have the opportunity, especially early on in Grades Nine or Ten, to switch from one stream to another if so desired.

There are positives to streaming. Students are enrolled in classes that provide practical or academic materials suited more closely to their interests and abilities; self-esteem is enhanced by the successes they can achieve; preparation toward the desired endpoint, practical or academic, can be set at an appropriate standard without leaving students behind. Students coming out of de-streamed Elementary classes, especially in the Advanced levels, will tell you that they are pleased to be able to work in a like-community, with fellows as capable and interested as they. As a teacher, I confess, I liked streaming, having a grouping of students whose abilities and interests were more closely aligned. Teaching Grade Eleven or Twelve in the middle stream was always my first choice; I enjoyed those classes. The students always seemed genuine to me, a like-minded cohort, and appropriate materials and methods were easier to isolate and deliver. As to teaching the university-bound streams, well, no matter the grade, that was always a pleasure, too—often, mostly, you just needed to avoid standing in the path of their success. And I once worked with a school dedicated to the workplace stream and saw students, provided with all the resources they needed, achieve resounding success in practical destinations, learning to be Chefs and Auto Mechanics and Hair Stylists and such. In a non-streamed environment, such students would more than likely have been lost in the crowd, and to the streets.

There are negatives, too. Streaming sometimes seemed like the segregation of education. Statistics showed that, of those who started Grade Nine in the middle stream, on average only four per cent actually went on to College, the supposed goal for which that stream was intended. That middle track was a dead end. And not to generalize too much, but if you have ever taught a Grade Ten middle stream class (perhaps on a Friday afternoon), or seen one, you know where teachers' nightmares come to life. Many students on the verge of freedom-16, with the knowledge that the authority of school posed no threat to them and offered little promise, were hell-on-wheels. While the university- and occupational-streamed classes had a distinct goal, were engaged with meaningful tasks and often filled with like-minded and motivated individuals, the middle stream, while interesting, was sometimes chaos personified. Attitudes, study habits, civil behaviour and attendance were often a significant challenge, and many students went missing-in-action. And in particular, following the *Black Lives Matter* explosion after 2020, the concept of streaming has become racialized—many caregivers-of-colour, generally in urban centres, have found their children grouped among the aimless living dead. And when Toronto screams, government in Ontario hears.

So, streaming, at least for Grade Nine, is about to disappear in Ontario, as it has disappeared across all the provinces of Canada. But it probably won't, not really. Strategies have already emerged—*De-streamed, Academic* and *Open* labels are being affixed to courses, and understandably so! Mathematics and Science and the various conceptual densities of English and History and French and such, even in Grade Nine, can be academically challenging. Elementary schools, which supposedly have no streams, always seem to have students arranged in groups or clusters where abilities are isolated, where academically gifted students are often assigned to help less capable classmates. While groups labelled the Blue Birds and the Vultures may no longer exist, other internalized labels do. In some sense, right or wrong, that's the way of the world. Streams and divisions exist. Doctors dine with doctors and construction workers with construction workers. Factory workers and university professors rarely meet at Starbuck's to discuss the philosophic (or practical) nature of things. Hopefully ethnicity or religion or race is not a factor, but it probably is. Take a look at most college or university cafeterias and see who sits with whom. Streaming is how we live as a species, how most species live. Wolves and bears do not feast together although they do co-exist in the same terrain. It is the natural way of things, ostensibly, the way species survive. Will that change in a hundred or a thousand years? Idealistic as we strive to be, and we must always be that, schooling still remains a part of the naturalistic world. Streaming in some form will probably never disappear.

19

Grade Nine

When I think back on all the crap I learned in high school
It's a wonder I can think at all
And though my lack of education hasn't hurt me none
I can read the writing on the wall

—Paul Simon "Kodachrome" 1973

For Grade Nine, our school class from S.S.#6 was shipped to Moira Secondary School—it was a fine example of how bureaucratic thinking can mess with human lives. My older brothers, my father, my grandfather and every other person native to our community had traditionally gone to Belleville Collegiate Institute and Vocational School in downtown Belleville (originally called Belleville High School, its school colours aligning with its initials, Black, Heliotrope, Scarlet—isn't Heliotrope a lovely colour? By contrast, Moira was grey and maroon— I always wondered who dreamed those "wow" colours; I mean, what in hell is maroon, anyway? And grey? Yikes!). BCI, over fifty years old, was a unique place with a sports field too small for soccer or football, a baseball diamond where flies to left field soared into downtown streets. There was never a team name and, though a shaft had been constructed on the north side of the school, no elevator had ever been inserted. In a clever correction, the yearbook for BCI was entitled *The Elevator*, giving the school what the builders did not. The stories, the myths, the memories of high school and our expectations for that experience were all centred around BCI—the legendary Sparky Heard, Red Townsend and Shotgun Kelly the Librarian awaited but never materialized—so being enrolled at Moira was a culture shock to be sure. Moira was Belleville's third High School: BCI was the first, Quinte, second. Centennial would soon arrive in the West End, then Bayside, an open concept school half-way out-of-town toward the air base and Trenton. (It was the end of the baby boom years so the post-war progeny was now of age to invade high schools and expansion was in order). So Moira was a relatively new school, with its Trojans (these valiant warriors were a popular school moniker, at least, up until the name became mostly associated with a method of birth control) and up-to-date Technology and fine Physical Education facilities and rotary system and all the rest, but my memories of my year are slight, in part, I suppose, because I did not want to be there in the first place and did little to foster an attachment—it was the only school year, for which they were available, that I never ordered a yearbook. Psychologists would be able to tell you something based on that alone. It was the first year I rode a bus—I was the last stop on the route in the morning and the first drop after school, so that was good. In the mornings, though, the bus would temptingly stop at BCI to let those students off and then journey on for fifteen minutes to the north-east side of town and Moira. Its feeder schools included students from the east-end of town and north toward Tweed and the Tyendinega Reservation (now, *Mohawks of the Bay of Quinte*) and, as it turned out, for one year only, the northern townships of Prince Edward County.

My parents, with my blessing I guess, had enrolled me in the Arts and Technology program which had the Shops option, not Arts and Science which had Art and Music. This was a curious choice in that, throughout my childhood, I had drawn and written stories and poems and was quite artistically inclined. But, I suppose, coming from a farm background and with my father having trained in the army as a mechanic, that was not too surprising. And the Shop that I took at Moira was Agriculture. Mr. Mabee was the teacher and we spent a lot of time in the fall hoeing and digging in the flower beds around the school (slave labour for the School Board, I think in recollection); we grew Narcissus and Daffodils in the greenhouse and we planted those projects as they began to sprout in the spring. Agriculture was a double class, about seventy minutes in length, but Mr. Mabee was an army vet who loved to tell stories of the war. During sessions in class as the year went on, students would ask something about the war intentionally and Mr. Mabee would get talking and talking and, before you knew it, the bell rang and class was over. No work got done, no homework got assigned; it was a classic example of students reading the teacher and acting accordingly. But still, after all these years, that is what I remember most of this singular class; Mr. Mabee and his war stories which were interesting and heartfelt and the Nazis were always defeated as the Narcissus and Daffodils quietly marched toward Spring.

Probably the single most important class I ever took in all my life in school was Mrs. Raney's Grade Nine Typing class. It is a skill that I have never stopped using, even here today as I tap out these words. Mrs. Raney, a slight, be-speckled woman who reminded us that her name was easy to remember—just think of the weather—operated her class with a business-like precision. Typing from bell to bell amid the steady bells. But typing did not come easy to me. While I could swat a baseball through a gap in the infield or cradle a lacrosse ball past another team's defense, pecking out the keys in any sort of rhythmic manner was a challenge. The goal was twenty-five words per minute (timed, number of words minus errors) but the massive old typewriters had no lettering on their keys and we were trained never to look at the keys anyway. Sit up straight we were reminded; posture was somehow important to typing, one foot behind the other, knees together. (In reflection, of course, this was probably an echo of the days when pools of typists formed female ghettoes in office buildings across the land.) And keep your eyes on the paper, never look at those keys or at the large poster above the blackboard that illustrated the curious QWERTY system, which dated back a hundred years or more, a system actually designed to slow typists down. Sometimes music played and the class typed to its rhythms like a mechanical orchestra. And we learned to push the keys firm and straight but with a rhythm that would avoid a cluster of key-rods grinched in place—to this day, as we use computer keyboards, you can spot most of us who learned in this era by how unnecessarily hard our fingers hammer the keyboard. In Mrs. Raney's class, no feathery touch would get the job done; a firm straight pressure on those heavy keys was needed and, when the platen bell rang, a sure push on the carriage lever to start the line anew—electric typewriters were yet to breech the horizon in schools. I was amazed at how quickly some students managed the skill, their movements a blur, their typewriters sounding like the tommy guns in Mr. Mabee's war—my guess, some of the wealthier kids had typewriters at home on which they clandestinely practiced. (The first typewriter I had, a used manual Underwood that my parents bought for me for second-year university, and it was manna to me.) As to Mrs. Raney's class, by the end of the year I was over thirty words per minute on a regular basis and, while my speed has declined, I have used that means ever since. And beyond being a mere skill, as a writer I was always fascinated at the magic of typing, how the meaning of words seemed to shift when they were translated from cursive writing into type, how typing, using space and form on the page, could alter the very essence of a piece of writing. That transmigration fascinates me to this day.

Science was delivered to us by a man who terrified the class, Mr. Luscher. We nicknamed him *Luger*, of course. He was a no-nonsense man from Germany, tall and stern, hair combed straight back, and he spoke with a distinct clipped-accent. Part of our post-war cultural prejudices were probably at work; nevertheless, Science class unfolded as a serious and ordered place of study; we motored through the textbook, made our notes and conducted such experiments as Grade Nines were permitted to do. We tried not to tip back on our stools and lose balance or get caught cranking those mysterious gas valves open. Mr. Luscher showed us many cool experiments from the front of the room—his experiments always seemed to work for him—and once, he even showed us a large snake (he always kept one in a glass tank on the side of his desk) devour a mouse. By the end of the year, we came to like this man from Germany; he was organized and methodical in his teaching but he was also sincere and it felt like he wanted us to learn and we came to like him for that. A lot of his stern demeanor had subsided during the year, or maybe our prejudices had melted. I even remember his final advice to us: "Travel," he said, "Try to travel the world and learn from what you see."

Like a lot of teachers at Moira, our French teacher was young and, I suppose, a modern child of her time. She was an attractive woman and not afraid to flaunt that flamboyantly; she wore short skirts and tight sweaters and, in my memory, shimmied around the classroom always emitting a sensual vibe. In today's vernacular, she was 'hot.' French, though, as a subject, was not. It was frightening. On the first day, I remember the wave going up and down each row, having to say "Je m'appelle" and then our name. I mean who knew to what we were confessing! And then later being asked "Quelle heur fait il?" What in hell did that mean? But once again we survived the travails of learning. The mademoiselle spoke only French for the first couple weeks; what a relief it was finally to hear her speak in English and know that she could! I was never very good at French but I tried and kept on at it for the rest of high school—it was, after all, Canada's other official language, which I always thought was a cool thing and I always wanted to learn it. But, I think, like dancing or singing or being a virtuoso on the violin, so many qualities people possess are inherent skills, and for me fluency in spoken French was akin to one of those and I did not have it. Fortunately, I suppose, most of our work in French was not of the speaking kind; language and grammar captained *le bateau* and so we learned to write a bit of *la langue* and I could pass. Probably, most memorable about the year, and probably for the wrong reasons—*la sojourn* our class made to the stage during the Christmas assembly. Sister Jeanne Decker from Belgium came to be promoted as *The Singing Nun* after she recorded a catchy hit tune, "Dominique"; she had made an appearance on *The Ed Sullivan Show* and our teacher had purchased her album and played the song in class a lot, having us sing along. The idea then came to her, as Christmas approached, that we enjoyed the song so much, we should perform it for the school. I suppose she was a young teacher trying to make a mark and show her support for all-things-Moira and perhaps she was trying to expose this barren culture of eastern Ontario to *un peu de culture française*, I don't know. But there we were, a reluctant squadron of Grade Nine prisoners-of-patois herded onto the stage in front of a packed auditorium. Luckily, our teacher brought along the record player and allowed *The Singing Nun* to join us in the background and, to their credit, several of my classmates warbled away to their best:

> Dominique, nique, nique
> S'en allait tout simplement
> Routier pauvre et chantant
> En tous chemins, en tous lieux,
> Il ne parle que du bon Dieu,
> Il ne parle que du bon Dieu.

Me, well as you know by now from what I said of my elementary school experience with Music, I can't sing and, true to form on this occasion, did so to the best of my ability. I moved my lips a bit—my buddies in the audience made fun of me for months—but in the annals of history, I suppose, I was probably a part of the first *ever* performance of *karaoke*. I guess someone just forgot to contact the *Guinness Book of World Records*! *C'est la vie.*

(As an aside, at the very least in a media-studies context, *The Singing Nun's* appearance on *Ed Sullivan* pretty much ended her rising career; while the song was pretty, Jeanne was not—her appearance did not match the audience expectations—a pop culture nun should look like Sally Fields or Julie Andrews, Ingrid Bergman or Audrey Hepburn, right! Eventually, *The Singing Nun* was expelled from the church (to which she had donated almost all of her royalty and performance income), and she and her partner, Annie Pécher, lived in near poverty in Belgium until, in 1985, they committed double-suicide, Jeanne, in death, holding her guitar in hand. *Dominique*, indeed!)

In many ways, high school French, arrived too late for me and most of my class-mates. What linguistic and other scientific studies have come to show is that humans learn language most fluently prior to puberty—thereafter, the *dura mater* of the brain begins to harden and the best most adults can do is learn to speak a second language with a discernible accent, if at all; young children only need exposure to become fluent in any language in a relatively brief time, but that exposure needs to happen whey they are young. And so, today, most second-language learning begins early in schools which is exactly where it should. For my generation, sadly, *c'était trop tard*!

My English teacher was Mr. Greig, actually an Art teacher, and he was a bit on the different side. He always pushed a tea cart from class to class and around the room, and I have seen him throw a kid out of class if a door was open in the room's cupboards, even though we had just arrived in that room, and he'd eject anyone who mispronounced a word like *bade*—it had to be said to rhyme with *sad* or you were gone! But I enjoyed the reading and writing that we did. We read a bunch of old English ballads like "The Twa Corbies," "Sir Patrick Spense," "Edward," "Thomas Rhymer," and "The Daemon Lover." Often we memorized these; I still recall the wonderful and chilling refrain from "Lord Randal:"

"O where ha you been, Lord Randal, my son?
And where ha you been, my handsome young man?"
"I ha been at the greenwood; mother, mak my bed soon,
For I'm sick at the heart, and fain wad lie down."

These ballads all seemed to be about macabre and gruesome topics—
murder, betrayal, love, loss and crows feasting on corpses—and were
right down my alley, once you got past the archaic language, at least. And
we studied Mythology and I adored the arcane stories of gods and
heroes doing fantastic things on valiant quests—they reminded me so
much of many of the movies I had been taken to by my parents, *Hercules*
and *Sinbad* and *Sleeping Beauty* and such, and of the fantastic comic book
stories I had read. And they were written in such dramatic, romantic ways:

The good ship Argo heard him, and longed to be away
and out to sea; till she stirred in every timber, and
heaved from stem to stern. She leapt up from the sand
upon the pine trunk rollers the heroes had laid before
her, and plunged onward like a gallant horse, till she
rushed into the whispering sea.

—excerpt "The Quest of the Golden Fleece" *Classical
Mythology* King/McKechnie

What we did not read in class from the King and McKechnie text, I read
on my own, even finding *Part One* of the text in a bookcase at the back
of the classroom and reading it, a volume that focussed on the origin
stories of the Greek pantheon.

I also encountered my first Shakespeare in Grade Nine English, *The
Merchant of Venice*, and how strange, how foreign and far away was that,
but somehow how wonderful and magical, too. After all these years I
still remember:

The quality of mercy is not strained;
It droppeth as the gentle rain from heaven
Upon the place beneath. It is twice blessed;
It blesseth him that gives and him that takes: ...

Just as wondrous, perhaps, we read that play aloud in class, sometimes following an LP recording—I loved it, just like story-time after lunch with Mrs. Giles. And, ever since, in my own classes in English, from Elementary to Graduate school, I have always tried to read aloud when the opportunity arose—there is no better thing in a Language Arts/English class than for poems and stories and plays to be heard in an effective manner and context. I should also say that we read *The Merchant of Venice* without one mention of Jews or prejudice—how far away were my Grade Nine days, I suppose, from our current state of social justice or being *Woke* where the issue of racism would probably be front and centre. We also read *Moonfleet* and *The Eagle of the Ninth*. We drew the family crest from *Moonfleet*—all children in the history of education did that, didn't they—and along with *The Eagle of the Ninth*, Mr. Greig had us write our own novel, in class, chapter by chapter. Inspired by the Sutcliffe novel, I wrote about a lost Roman legion in its quest to return home. So English became a comfortable space for me, in spite of Mr. Greig's unpredictability and the persistent study of grammar (a continuation of the illimitable parsing and parts-of-speech-and-sentence identification of earlier grades). Grammar aside, I came to look forward to English class.

Frontispiece from King/McKechnie *Classical Mythology in Song and Story Part II* 1939 (my older brother's copy)—I love(d) this book.

Mr. LeBaron was our Geography teacher, a kind, gentle and witty man, the teacher in the school (and almost every school has one or two of these) for whom all students have respect and admiration, the teacher whose class everyone wants to be in—Mr. LeBaron, a teacher-god of Moira. For these gods, reputation, alone, often takes care of discipline, students in the class commanding others to behave. Mr. Sneddon, our Mathematics teacher, sat on the same Olympian heights as Mr. Lebaron, efficient and crystal clear in his explications of the labyrinthine depths of his chosen subject. He cared for his students and they returned the favour. (When I transferred to BCI, I met Mr. Lebaron's son Mike who was made of the same kindly metal as his dad, and a helluva basketball player, too.)

In Physical Education, we had to buy the Moira uniform—yes, a grey T-shirt and maroon shorts and a cloth jock whose purpose, to this day, I do not comprehend except perhaps to keep all the parts together for purposes of identification after some catastrophic accident. Certain memories haunt me from those days: one, we were required to buy some deodorant, the spray-on kind and my Mom and Dad thought that was pretty funny for this rough and tumble rural kid to be wearing such perfume. As well, in the seven minutes between the cessation of whatever we were doing in class and the shuffling off to our next, we were required to take a shower and the teacher would often stand in the change-room to make sure everyone complied. I suppose, collectively, Grade Nines could stink pretty good but I never thought that these two-second showers did much good except to be an exercise in embarrassment for most (being caught in a crowd of naked males is a phobia I still embrace) and the pretense of a shower did nothing to dissuade any odour; it simply made most of us damp for the next hour or so. The other great humbling of mind and body in Physical Education was dropped on us like a bomb; with no warning—for a two-week session in mid-winter, some curricular genius decided that Dance should be part of the grand scheme of Physical Education. (A movement had started in the discipline to include activities other than football and gymnastics, activities that some students might actually continue to include in their daily lives after school ended—some classes learned how to bowl, some to play golf). So we kept our regular class clothes on, the great bifold door that divided the gendered gyms rolled open like the Red Sea and there, on the other side, stood the girls of our class. Familiar expectations were jarringly altered in this unfamiliar situation, the girls appearing like a group of intimidating strangers, though we had been mingling with them in another class just five minutes before. And we were frightened of what lay before, nervous as summer bugs on a hot griddle. The teachers, male and female seen together for the first time ever, demonstrated what we were supposed to do. The dances were all distant and ancient, not actually hops or bops that anyone under the age of eighty would do; mostly we had to engage in various types of folk and square dances. The highlight for me (I suppose) came during the Mexican Hat Dance when my partner, by chance, was the prettiest girl in our class, bright and blonde, and we cavorted around a sombrero tossed on the floor, awkwardly kicking up our heels in a three-step and lightly touching hands as we circled the lid, then reversed our direction. And the two weeks of Dance ended and none of us wound up in Emergency or the Asylum and life moved on. Although other treacherous moments in Physical Education lay ahead—the Symplegades of gymnastics (vaulting split-legged over the Pommel or the Trapezoid) and the mad horrors of the impetuous Trampoline or merciless Parallel Bars and the creepiness of grasping a friend's sweaty torso in wrestling—I never danced again in Physical Education and, rarely, anywhere else. My loss, I suppose. Maybe! Probably the world's gain.

Belleville is a town without any bookstores so the arrival of a large van called the Book Mobile was a treat. For me it began a lifetime of scouring towns and cities in search of various kinds of Book Stores, specialized and antiquarian, used and unique. I used to travel to Toronto regularly to visit the SCM Book Store in the bottom of what used to be Rochdale College and The World's Biggest Book Store near the Eaton's Centre was amazing. Now, of course, Amazon and ABE and Indigo have taken over and, while you can find almost anything you seek, somehow, the anticipation, the mystery and thrill of entering some newly discovered book shop has gone away. All the books from Amazon smell the same. As to the Book Mobile in Grade Nine, beyond the library, I don't think that I ever saw as many books in one place, and all kinds from literature to history, even books in French. And I purchase the first book I have ever bought, a small softcover copy of Roget's *Thesaurus*, a book (*volume, tome, manuscript, brochure, edition, tract, manual, paperback*) I still have to this day.

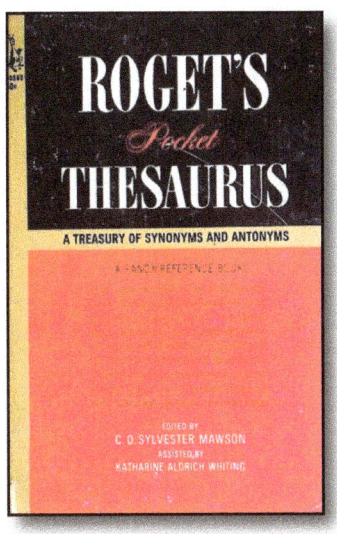

Mr. Linton Reid was principal of Moira when I was there; in all the time I saw him, I don't think he ever cracked a smile—that old stoic code of being a principal, you know. (Later, I met his daughter Jain at BCI—as buttoned-down and conservative as Mr. Reid was, Jain was a burgeoning child of the sixties, a gloriously wild and rebellious hippie spirit, always pushing the boundaries of the decorum of the day, it seemed, even inventing the spelling of her own name.) At the end of our year, those of us from the County were given an option, continue on at Moira, or enroll at BCI next year. A few chose to stay—my good friend, Randy Kerr, was one. He had been very successful on the school wrestling team; he loved it and I think that influenced him (and there may have been a girl, too?). Most of the rest of us from S. S. #6, though, opted for BCI to reinstate our cultural heritage. I recall that Mr. Reid, who was also being shuffled on to another school, gave a final speech of farewell upon his leaving. He was an intellectual kind of man who had edited some school literature anthologies, and he used an analogy in saying his good-bye that I have always remembered. He said: "Put your hand in a bucket of water and remove it; the hole that remains is how much you will be missed." And so with those words in my heart, classes ended, I was exempt from all my final examinations, and I rode the bus home, leaving Moira forever. And I never regretted that decision. Moira had been fair to me, treated me well, but it was not the hills of home.

20
WORK!

Dobie Gillis:	"It's all right, Mom, I have to go upstairs anyhow and start my homework."
Maynard G. Krebs:	"WORK!"
Dobie Gillis:	"Maynard, it's the kind of thing we do at school, not the other kind."
Maynard G. Krebs:	"The other kind of what?"
Dobie Gillis:	"Work."
Maynard G. Krebs:	"WORK!"

—*The Many Loves of Dobie Gillis* TV Sitcom 1959-1963

Underneath all that we may say and do regarding the education we receive, or impart, lies one seminal question: what is the purpose of education? Why do we require most humans to attend this institution called school for nearly twenty per cent of their lives? What do we gain from that experience? What should teachers be trying to instil? What is the point of it all?

Well, one *common sense* answer, always—the purpose of schools is to prepare students for work, to prepare citizens to do jobs that will enable them to survive by supporting themselves with the daily necessities. So whether the subject is English or Mathematics or Art or Music or Physical Education, or whatever, school must prepare citizens for some kind of job that will put bread on the table (or rice and beans, soy milk and tofu)? And if that is not the primary goal of school, what is?

Given the idea that schools produce the citizens of a nation, there are, of course, many factions in society that want to answer that question, many who wish to determine exactly what happens in schools: governments, politicians, churches, parents and other caretakers, students themselves, school boards and administrators, teacher regulatory boards, teachers, teacher federations, corporate and business and professional groups, labour unions, colleges, universities, tax-payers in general, and probably others, as well. The pressure for accountability and competency among teachers continues to build as does the pressure to ramp up standards for students with pre- and post-secondary testing, including literacy testing, all increasing expectations at the curricular level province-wide. Attempts by various factions to influence core materials and values taught are quite common. Should either *Harry Potter* (with its witch-craftian content) or *Adventures of Huckleberry Finn* (with its disobedient hero and its use of the "N-word") be allowed in the school library and should the topic of masturbation be included in the Grade Six *Sex Education* course of study, or should *Sex Education* be included at all? Issues of censorship are probably the most visible examples of attempts to control what happens in school. The essential fallacy in censorship, of course, is the belief that a piece of literature or a film, or even any particular lesson, will have a certain effect on the person who experiences it. That is the folly of the censor. Most of us (I hope) do not really think that relevant exposure to certain knowledge or new ideas is going to harm a child (in fact, some of us think that such exposure may be one of the central purposes of education). Sex education is not going to create depraved carnal maniacs, reading *Hamlet* is not going to tempt a child to commit suicide and *To Kill a Mockingbird* does not create racists—while various questions might be raised by those texts, raising such dormant issues may be a good thing. If problems exist, root causes lie in deeper streams—the sooner addressed the better. For teachers, of course, the issue of age appropriateness trumps that of censorship. *Hamlet* in Grade Three, unlikely; in Grade Twelve, why not! *Finnegans Wake*, anywhere—no (as grand a book as it is)! And in the educational realm, of course, the issue of censorship is complicated by ideas of parents' rights and students' rights, and by the context of the school and the community. Cultural standards and customs will play a role. Separate schools and private schools march to the sounds of their own regulated drummers. And home schooling— well, really, is there any such thing?

So while there are many forces at play when it comes to ascertaining the purpose of education, the question remains: is a capacity for productive work the central goal? Well, that famous scene from *Twelfth Night* comes to mind. Malvolio, the taciturn Puritan, disturbed from his slumber by the late night "uncivil rule" and "caterwauling" of Toby and his drunken friends, commands them to silence or be thrown out of the house. Famously, Sir Toby replies:

> Out o' tune, sir: ye lie. Art any more than a steward?
> Dost thou think, because thou art virtuous, there shall
> be no more cakes and ale? (II iii)

If work is the goal, does this then mean that school must be the place where "there shall be no more cakes and ale." To a great extent, the counter argument can be made that education should be a place that is all "cakes and ale."

First of all, regarding the purpose of education, beware of any who claim that we must educate students for the future, for the jobs of tomorrow. In fact, of those people, "weave a circle round them thrice!" Educating for the future is impossible. Simply put, no-one can know the future. Astrology is not a science; fortune cookies never accurately predict anything. In a practical sense, at best, schools should try to exist and teach in the present, and strange as it may seem, that is not an easy thing. Step into many shops in any number of schools and you will feel as if you have entered the Waverider or Tardis, a time portal to the past. Old cast iron machines covered in layers of glossy green or grey paint give the space the aura of some late Victorian work-house. Contemporary classrooms full of computers may disguise the time warp a bit but the programs tell the tale and many schools can barely afford to keep moderately up-to-date. (The key to computer technology is often hidden like some Easter Egg in a video game: the hardware is cheap to acquire; the program costs are exorbitant.) And while there are those who would say, but look at Bill Gates or Jeff Bezos or Elon Musk, surely they must have been educated for the future, or educated themselves in that orientation. Not sure; I suspect that, mostly, they capitalized on the present and were intelligent (and fortunate). Right time, right idea, a bit of good luck—billions in the bank! And for every one of those successful entrepreneurs, there are a million others with boxes of nowhere-widgets piled in their garages (or in the garages of others because they were bankrupted and lost their homes along with their investments and inventions).

So the very best we can do is educate students for the present, or what approximates the present. In fact, a traditional argument exists that the real intention of schools should be to educate for the past, to maintain and re-enforce the *status quo*. Even businesses that support school enterprises or offer prizes at graduation really do not want the product of a school to be their replacement. Societies do not want to graduate revolutionaries. And of those I have encountered who are fiercely advocating the need to produce students who will change the world, the social justice crowd, invariably most want to change the world in a way that suits them, to reinforce the status of their world-view, to re-gild their own crown.

So, with work in mind, what role should business play in school, as a guiding force if nothing else? Since the 1980s, at least, representative business leaders and practitioners have regularly been a part of the planning processes set out by educational boards and districts; employability charts are commonplace in matters of curricula and school divisions; Departments (even Art and Music) are regularly required to create lists of jobs and/or relevant skills that might be earned by enrolment in that particular subject. Much of the *Excellence in Education* movement was based on business models such as that of Peters and Waterman (*In Pursuit of Excellence*), TAP programmes (*technology advantage*) are up and running everywhere, 40 hours of community service or more are often a requirement for graduation and, since the late 1960s, an entire labyrinth of Community Colleges has been established in Ontario and elsewhere, ostensibly with the purpose of offering specific job-oriented programs in a range of fields from nursing to construction to bio-chemistry to esthetics and spa management to para-legal practices to culinary skills, and more. As well, recently, phrases such as *critical thinking* have been pushed aside in documents in favour of phrases such as *problem solving*—presumably the latter assists in production, the former might cause problems. The word *culture* (implying class, I think) has also generally been suppressed in many recent documents here in Ontario. So, business has certainly influenced the direction of education in recent decades, but the question remains—to what extent should business guide education? Well, possibly, not at all. One might argue that no person of business or industry should ever be allowed anywhere near a school. In many ways business and education are worlds apart. You can't fire a student, at least not in the twenty-first century. And success in school is rarely determinable, and certainly not in any year-end transcript (marks in any true educational sense are always meaningless). And the pay for being a responsible student is often intangible at best … a piece of paper, often without any concrete dividends until many years in the far future, if at all. Teaching a subject in elementary or high school with a job in mind seems to me to trivialize education. Among other things, business and the women and men of business have no moral or ethical compass. Ostensibly, by its very nature to use Tennyson, business is "red in tooth and claw." Sure, at the end of the quarter a business may help out some welfare charity for a tax exemption, but it was likely the cut-throat operation of business that destroyed some other enterprise and created the need in the first place. And in such a world, why teach poetry or Shakespeare or Art or Music. Or ideas of any kind. In a world that feeds on the bottom line, what need is there for cakes and ale? But without such frostings, what a dull and sterile thing education would be! What a dull and pointless world this would be.

Most students these days, from senior elementary through higher education, seem to work at part-time employment—this also means that their education is part-time. Part-time work, especially if it rises to over twenty hours per week, has been shown to have a negative impact on students' educatable lives (interest in school declines, attendance drops, study habits dissolve, as do hours of sleep, and drug and alcohol use increase). Several reports on education, including Radwansky's as early as 1987, suggested that governments should discourage part-time employment but that is simply too much of a hot potato for any government to handle. For many businesses (fast food chains come to mind) part-time labour has become their backbone (low wages, no benefits, free from union hassles, limitless workforce, easy replacement, rigid rules and regulations) and for many families, working children have once again become a necessary source of income to support the household. For students, having some cash provides a degree of independence and certainly helps pay the cell phone bill; however, the rise of part-time employment has become one of the challenges to contemporary schooling. We seem to have returned to an earlier time, that of the hunter-gatherers or the agricultural society in which the need for formal academic education was minimal and work was a seamless part of the living, simply being part of a family and its way in the world. But in the fast-food milieu, those human elements are missing; employment involves a raw descent into a hellish environment that is both sterile and draconian, everything shaped like a patty and deep-fried in fat.

So, when all is said and done, should work be a primary goal of education? My response is 'no.' There will be time for work when a time for work is needed. And the fundamental skills of any workplace are always taught at that workplace anyway and cannot be predicted or presumed years earlier in a school setting. Even in highly skilled occupations, maybe especially so, the skills of surgery or litigation will be taught at an appropriate time, not in Grade Three. Childhood is brief and we only get one chance at it. Let education speak to and reveal all the useless joys it can. Whether it's kicking a soccer ball or blowing badly across a flute, firing up a Bunsen burner or meeting with a mischievous cat in a hat for the first time, let be. Besides, there are plenty of fundamentals that need to be learned, reading and writing and learning to behave in a social setting, colouring in and outside of the lines and all those wonder-filled journeys into the beautifully useless realms of art and music and poetry, and calculus and physics. Let the use-filled requirements of work and business remain as future shadows; let the world of cakes and ale be centre stage with its glimmer of light and hope and humour at least briefly to illuminate students' lives in every way possible. There will be plenty of time for the mind-forg'd manacles of labour. For now, let's give Maynard G. Krebs and his paranoia about 'WORK' its due. His days of taking a three-hour tour to become stranded on a desert island with the Professor, the Movie Star, the Skipper, and the rest, are yet to come—there working continuously, building a hot air balloon from raincoats, a battery charger from coconuts, a telephone from a conch shell, and countless other things.

21
Grade Ten

When humour goes, there goes civilization.

—Erma Bombeck *If Life is a Bowl of Cherries What am I doing in the Pits*

Laugh as much as possible, always laugh. It's the sweetest thing one can do for oneself and one's fellow human beings.

—Maya Angelou *Rainbow in the Cloud*

The bird a nest, the spider a web, man friendship.

—William Blake *The Marriage of Heaven and Hell* 1789

Bob Mitchell is the funniest human being I have ever known. Bob and I were classmates throughout Elementary School, attended Moira in that heartless one-year experiment by the local Poohbahs of Ed, and then returned to BCI for the rest of our high school. Bob's natural sense of humour is quick and witty, cutting and cunning. He is the son of, you might have guessed it, Bob Mitchell, the owner of the corner store in Rossmore. Mr. Mitchell was a war vet, a sailor whose forearm sported the first genuine tattoo I had ever seen, a sailing ship inked beneath his skin while he was on shore-leave on some exotic Pacific island, I think. (Nowadays, of course, everyone has tatts but none of them, it seems, have any real meaning; they're all hearts and horseshit.) The other tattoo I recall seeing in that time was Ray Clarke's, another man my father knew; Dad asked Ray to roll up his arm one day and he showed me his tatt, etched on the underbelly of his left forearm, five numbers, deep and blue. It was a different kind of tattoo. Ray had been a paratrooper in the war, caught behind enemy lines, imprisoned in a concentration camp and given his tatt by the Nazi SS. It still burns a deep blue-fire in my mind's eye. As to Bob's Dad, both being vets, Mr. Mitchell and my Dad seemed to be able to talk for hours, though I never heard them talk much about war. Real vets never do, I guess, though all seem to have the enduring bond that the wail of shells invokes. My Dad ran the local mail route (R.R. 7) and the group boxes for Rossmore were placed next to the corner store—probably good for business—so he and Mr. Mitchell met and talked often. On those days, sales were a bit slower and the mail for the rest of the route was always delivered a little bit later.

Bob Jr. and I probably drew our humour from similar sources. He had access to plenty of comic books in his Dad's store, of course, and always showed up at school with the latest copy of *Mad* magazine. Its satire was clever and risqué, hilarious to us, and we were not alone. Alfred E. Neuman's catchphrase, "What, me worry?" was echoed by young teens everywhere throughout the fifties and sixties—the "E" in Alfred's name by the way stood for *Enigma*. Pink elephant and Newfie jokes and *The Three Stooges'* revival on TV came and went, but *Mad* endured for decades. And from television, on CBC, the gentle *Friendly Giant* and the punchy afternoon comedy of *Razzle Dazzle* made its mark, "the show for kids and turtles" with Howard the Turtle and non-stop, self-deprecating puns and bad jokes (and who wasn't in love with Michele Finney). Wayne and Schuster, the Canadian comedy team, had specials on CBC and regularly showed up on *The Ed Sullivan Show* spurring a kind of national pride. And Sullivan always had on those old-time Borscht Belt comics like Myron Cohen, Shecky Greene, Jack E. Leonard and Henny Youngman—sometimes their jokes would stab with instantaneous one-liners, sometimes they offered long drawn-out stories for which you had to wait an eternity for the slick punch-line at the end of the tale. And Bob Hope and Jack Benny and Lucille Ball and Jackie Gleason and Red Skeleton and Carol Burnett all had an influence. And there was the inventiveness of *Rowan and Martin's Laugh In* and the edgy *Smothers Brothers*. While by no means pristine—stereotypes and difference and human frailties were often exploited—the humour usually seemed kind and gentle, not as abrasive as in recent years. And television's purest creation, the sit-com, probably reached its zenith in the early 1960s with the flawlessness of *The Dick Van Dyke Show*, polished and refined and consistently funny.

**Belleville Collegiate Institute and Vocational School
1928-1992**

For much of our time at BCI, Bob and I would meet after lunch in the mezzanine catwalk which surrounded the gyms, lean against the rail and chat away about this and that and the other. Sometimes a third friend, Cliff Parcells, who was from Jamaica, pure and gentle and soft-spoken, would join us and share his unique views of the world as it unfolded about us in Grade Ten and beyond. I remember Cliff's droll entry beside his photo in the Grad yearbook, next to *Probable Lifetime Activity*, Cliff wrote: "Waiting to die." While that may seem odd or even morbid, if you knew Cliff, you would understand that sense of humour immediately, especially entombed as his summation was destined to become among all of the yearbook's other pretty fantasies and inanely optimistic predictions. As to Bob, when my father died many years later and I had returned from far away for the funeral, Bob showed up and sat with me in the funeral chapel throughout the evening and we met again, in better times, at the celebratory closing of S. S. #6. At that event, one of our most successful classmates came by to shake our hands clearly flaunting his Rolex (he was a local wheeler and dealer in real estate); after he moved on, Bob casually commented: "Yeah, but he has all the personality of a toaster;" I laughed out loud. Bob still had it! He stood next to me and had his son snap our photo and we have not seen each other since. His father's corner store is closed now in Rossmore (it's recently reopened as some kind of vegan pet spa) and BCI is long since rubble; the last I heard, Bob lives somewhere in Toronto. But I can still see us, leaning against that railing, exchanging witticisms, sorting out our lives and giving shape to the future of the world as it inexorably stretched out before us.

At BCI, in many ways we are interlopers, outcasts. The year in Grade Nine for which we were absent means that we have missed out on all of the typical bonds that are born in that year, friendships, shared class experiences, club- and team-mates, connections with teachers, even intimacy with the spaces of the school, itself. BCI is a huge building in comparison to our elementary school, four stories in height, classrooms around the outside, gyms taking up the inner space of the first two floors, the classic proscenium-arched auditorium occupying the top two. The cafeteria is in the basement with a senior lunch room now occupying a separate space around the side, the long narrow room that used to be the rifle range when my brothers went there. A program known as Cadets thrived in many schools for twenty years or so after the war, a requirement existed for all male students, on certain days of the year, to dress in military uniforms and march about while the girls watched; cultural changes in the 1960s, among other things, meant the disbanding of that program in most schools. As Charlie don't surf, so hippies didn't march. The rifle range at BCI became the Senior lunch room. Adding to our role as exiles at BCI, we are also kids from the country, from outside the feeder schools that all our new Grade Ten classmates attended. We are not city kids. We are different, many are the daughters and sons of farmers not the offspring of doctors and lawyers—BCI draws many of its students from old and affluent inner-city neighbourhoods. That country-city division remains ingrown throughout our years at BCI; we are subtlety excluded on many occasions, not appointed to be Prefects or published in the yearbook or involved in the School Council or its committees. Part of that, simply, is the physical reality of distance as well; I played football one year and getting home after practise and games was a nuisance. It was about twenty kilometres; sometimes I walked or hitchhiked and, often, a neighbouring family whose son, Rodney, played Junior ball, gave me a ride (many thanks to the Wyatts). And, of course, I must admit, that I have often been an outcast of myself anyway; as I was in Elementary school, so I remained as a teen, shy and introspective, often discovering in my isolation and imagination and desolation, delusion or no, a natural sense of peace. Outcast was the place where I truly belonged. And to this day, not much has changed in that regard.

(As I mention the Wyatts, who operated the Mountain View Cheese Factory, many kudos to them—they sponsored a team in the North Shore Fastball League year after year, spending far more on uniforms and equipment I think than any return they ever could have received, except perhaps to watch their sons play ball. Such was true of many small businesses in many small communities at that time, I suppose, and individuals, too. Such as Ralph Ackerman, who freely donated a large parcel of his farmland for the Massassaga ball diamond to be built. In part, it was what made communities, communities.)

Although distance made it difficult for me to be involved in high school sports of the varsity kind, something called intra-mural sports was huge at the time. These would be held during the common lunch hour when gyms and playing fields were devoid of classes. Sometimes *Home Forms* created a team but, most often, sheets were posted, we would sign up, be assigned to a squad, and *let the games begin*. Remarkably, we played full-contact football (we would rush to the change rooms, don the old pads and helmets thrown away by previous school teams, play a mad game for forty minutes, then reverse the procedure to return to classes), and there was also softball, basketball, volleyball and lacrosse. Forbidden from playing because of their expertise, team members of the varsity teams would act as organizers and referees, probably a valuable training experience for them. For some students, it has been said that being on a varsity sports team was their *raison d'etre* for attending school and, I do know, after football season there were a few students who seemed to disappear. But for most, I think, playing a sport is, primarily, just that…playing. Whether intra-mural or varsity! Transporting oneself, transforming oneself into an activity for the fun of it. The desire to win, to achieve some elusive goal, sure! But mostly, sports were a journey back in time to that carefree childhood when any activity became a game and the world was a place where pleasure reigned. To become a child again, as Blake reminds us:

> To see a World in a Grain of Sand
> And a Heaven in a Wild Flower,
> Hold Infinity in the palm of your hand
> And Eternity in an hour.

—William Blake *Auguries of Innocence* 1803

As the semester system took over under the earnest ethos of the excellence in education movement, intramural sports declined. Practically, most schools had five periods per day, blending lunch hours into the schedule—gyms and sports fields were used all the time. And more of a business-like urgency seemed to descend on the educational scene. And besides, varsity sports reigned; sports like hockey and soccer and rugby came on the scene and not without expense either. In today's dollars, it costs nearly a half million dollars to equip a junior boys' football team, and even more to run the hockey squad or swimming team and rent the necessary venues. And I have no doubt that today those concerned with safety would cringe to see the equipment we donned to play our forty-minute rag-tag lunch hour contests. But it was a time when we were boys and boys love the rough and tumble, don't they! Now, like those Cadet uniforms or the carefree echo of childhood's laughter, those intra-mural pads and helmets reside in that fading space that shapes the depths of time and memory.

My brothers, Bob and Bill, in Grades 11/10, off to a day of Cadets at BCI, *circa* 1955. An interloper has invaded their photograph, taken with the Brownie camera pictured below.

ADDENDUM:

Expo

Summer 1967. In all of our lives there are certain moments that act as signposts marking one distinct passage or another; some are personal—graduation, marriage, births, deaths—and some are public—for me, the assassination of JFK, the moon landing, Henderson's goal, the fall of the twin towers. And one of the most significant signposts was certainly Expo '67, the extraordinary, officially-sanctioned World's Fair held in Montreal.

Canada turned one hundred years of age in 1967 and festivities were extensive. School children received pins and posters and booklets. One-hundred-year family farms were honoured with roadside plaques. Pioneer cemeteries were rehabilitated. Both John Diefenbaker and Lester Pearson resigned to make way for a delightfully unpredictable storm called Trudeaumania. Yorkville put some flowers in its hair and Gordon Lightfoot (by commission) wrote the "Canadian Railroad Trilogy," Al Purdy, *North of Summer*, and Margaret Atwood, *The Circle Game*. Literature, music and art flourished, Jewison's *In the Heat of the Night* premiered, the Order of Canada was created, homosexuality, decriminalized, the Armed Forces Tattoo exuberantly toured the country and the Toronto Maple Leafs won the Stanley Cup. But the undeniable hub of the centennial celebration was Expo '67, the officially sanctioned World's Fair running from April to October on islands reformed in the St. Lawrence just south of downtown Montreal. It was a sparkling event; a tangible signal that Canada had arrived as a nation...Canadians as a people.

Relatively inexpensive school trips by bus were available at the end of June, four of us staying per room in a dire pressboard "motel" haphazardly constructed on land south of the site. I went with classmates Jake Vos, John Top and John McKilliken; the accommodations were spartan but we didn't care and made the most of the day-and-a-half we had. The Fair's site was huge but we visited as many of the ninety international and corporate pavilions and dozen or so thematic areas as we could. And sampled as many different kinds of food as we could; John Top even managed to get served a beer at one restaurant but he didn't like the taste and threw most of it away.

Overall, words really cannot describe the sensation that was in the air. Surfaces shimmered. Lights shone. Everything was new. From the Geodesic Dome sparkling like a jewel on Île Sainte-Héléne to the cave-like dwellings of Habitat 67 to the never-ending midway of La Ronde, and all the tent-shaped and inverted pyramids in between, the pavilions and structures of Expo were architecturally remarkable, strange and postmodern, like something from another planet or a different dimension. Everything experimental—possibility was alive, tomorrow personified.

A hundred different accents could be heard in a single day from visitors and hosts. Monorails glided, sidewalks moved, grates underfoot vibrated and vacuumed to remove the dust from your shoes, hand-held calculators and computers and video-telephones seemed the stuff of comic book sci-fi come-to-life, multi-screen films were projected in 'circle-vision' (in Canada's pavilion, the Mounties performed their thrilling *Musical Ride,* climactically charging, lances down, directly at everyone) and, echoing inside me ever since, the mesmerizing images, fragmented and moving, of Ontario's celebratory film: "...a place to stand, a place to grow, Ontar...iar...iar...io."

It was Expo '67.
It was magic.
The world born anew.
Possibility alive.
The future at hand.

22
Common Sense is not so Common

"Le sens commun n'est pas si commun."
—Voltaire *Dictionnaire philosophique portatif 1764*

"Common sense is something that everyone needs, few have, and none think they lack."
—Ben Franklin

"I've found that common sense ain't so common."
—Mark Twain

"Common sense ain't common."
—Will Rogers

"Common sense is what tells us the earth is flat."
—Stuart Chase

"Le bon sens est le bien le plus largement partagé au monde, car tout homme est convaincu qu'il en soit bien pourvu. [Common sense is the most widely shared commodity in the world, for every man is convinced that he is well supplied.]"
—René Descartes

"Horse sense is the thing a horse has which keeps it from betting on people."
—W.C. Fields

"The cradle rocks above an abyss, and common sense tells us that our existence is but a brief crack of light between two eternities of darkness."
—Vladimir Nabokov

Common sense! When it comes to challenges facing education, there is almost always the temptation to call on some simple folk wisdom to fix the problem, to call for some *common sense* solution. Historically in North America, at least, the tendency toward this sensibility has a long history, dating back to the Puritan William Bradford's call for "a plain style, with singular regard to the simple truth in all things" (*Of Plymouth Plantation* c.1620) to the street-wise advice given by Ben Franklin in *Poor Richard's Almanac* to Thomas Paine's arguments for American independence in his pamphlet *Common Sense* to "Honest" Abe Lincoln to Will Roger's proclamation that he "never met a man he didn't like" to person-in-the-street interviews in the modern media to the explosion of unqualified personal opinion on all the social media platforms, and programs like *The View, The Talk, TMZ,* and *The Real,* as well as all those quick-answer sound-bite-celebs endlessly consulted on the news-entertainment channels like *CNN* and *FoxNews.* Random opinions now seem to be broadcast everywhere in the *Twitterverse* (now the *Xverse,* I guess)— concepts like Q-Anon and a myriad of other conspiracy theories have emerged. UFOs and Sasquatch swarm our neighbourhoods. In a Comtean sense, I suppose, it is a positivist search for the absolute. Remember *MuchMusic's* "Speaker's Corner" where everyone got to be on TV or recall, in Ontario, the Mike Harris Conservatives trying to instigate what they called a "common sense revolution," a philosophy reborn in Donald Trump's monomaniacal mission to "make America great again."

This heightened tendency is, in part, a peculiar by-product of our contemporary media democracy, driven by the gargantuan appetite for programming as much as anything else. Along with a general human distrust of professionals, of intellectualism and science, a firm but sentimental belief in plain, simple, down-to-earth folk wisdom abides—overly-educated eggheads may know stuff, but, but really…! There is a staunch belief that "common sense" will solve all the complex problems of education and the world—thus, a blanket approval tends to be given recent revisionist policies: loads of grammar returning to contemporary curriculum guidelines; 40 hours of mandatory volunteer service for students; regular testing; literacy testing; teacher testing; and even the return of spelling tests and cursive writing. For the most part, of course, this reflects a naive point of view which is entirely inadequate for complex educational problems. To think of it another way, most of us would hope that, when our surgeon is standing over us in an operating room, scalpel in hand, she or he is relying on more than *common sense* when the cutting begins. During the Coronavirus-19 plague, of course, the outcome of this denial of science sadly led to many deaths.

The back-to-the-basics movement plays in the same ballpark. This is the nostalgic idea that once, back in the *good old days*, things were better everywhere, especially in education. You know, where we began: *school days, school days, good old golden rule days*. This is the myth of the garden. Of returning to paradise, but it is a desire to return to a place that never existed. Or even if it did, even if we could find Eden, from what I've read, there's a huge dude with wings and a fiery sword guarding it. No. We cannot go back-to-the-basics. We can't go back to anything—you can't go home again, Thomas Wolfe reminds us. It is impossible, and furthermore, a first question which arises, would we really want to? Would we want to return to some earlier place and time, schools where students learned in rows (desks bolted to the floor), stood at attention to answer questions and cowered under the shadow of corporal punishment, a world with no vaccines and no electricity, no dentists and no deodorant, where females were banned from medical schools and Indigenous children shipped off to residential schools? And the inherent question follows, whose basics? Do we return to a time of rote learning and memorized multiplication tables, of push-ups and jumping jacks, of ink-wells and cursive script? And whose basics? Liberal, conservative, communist, Catholic? To a great extent, the back-to-the-basics ideology is more about the issue of control than it is about issues of education, often boiling down like some kind of sour maple syrup as a means to measure curriculum, to rate teacher competency and to force measures of accountability. As noted in Chapter Twenty, from parents and people in the street to businesses and governments, and all the special interest groups in between, there are many forces at work in our society who wish to control education for their own purposes. The pressure for accountability and competency never lessens on teachers and on students through the likes of province-wide testing, literacy testing, higher education testing, international testing, teacher testing, and more. And, in the end, all of this has far more to do with a desire for control and power than it does with educational achievement or purpose.

In the end, common sense may be no sense at all.

23

Grade Eleven

Do you remember an Inn, Miranda?
Do you remember an Inn?
And the tedding and the spreading
Of the straw for a bedding,
And the fleas that tease in the High Pyrenees,
And the wine that tasted of tar?
And the cheers and the jeers of the young muleteers
(Under the vine of the dark verandah)?
Do you remember an Inn, Miranda,
Do you remember an Inn?

—Hilaire Belloc "Tarantella"

In our contemporary cookie-cutter world, where every teacher must have a uniform Bachelor of Education degree and, often, other pertinent certifications, too, and in which teaching jobs are typically as scarce as blood donors at a sharks' convention, gone are the days of the eccentric, those teachers that were unique, truly odd or different in method and behaviour. While I understand, generally, this is probably not a bad thing, still, there lingers the indisputable sense that something marvellous has been lost from the world of education. Although an extreme example, I often think of something like Key and Peele's "Substitute Teacher" sketch (*"Ya done messed up A.-A.-Ron!"*) and smile at what has been lost. For there was a time in the fresh post-World War II baby-boom years when school boards were desperate to fill their faculties. High school graduates only needed a six-week summer course to become a teacher, military veterans (especially officers) were automatically cast in Administrative positions, full sections of *The Globe and Mail* were crammed with advertisements for jobs (especially the Tuesday *Globe*) and, on a select winter weekend, most Boards would be found on the same floor of a Toronto hotel where they would sign teachers on the spot, often pulling applicants at random into rooms as they wandered down the corridors. That meant, as the more preferred positions in the major population centres became filled, often with the best paper-qualified candidates, Boards deemed less desirable, often in fringe areas, hired almost anyone they could get. And in many cases, somewhat eccentric individuals became the formidable mainstay of these schools. Private institutions (with lower pay and no benefits or job security) collected hordes of these unique barbarians. But ask any grandparent about her or his teachers and, most likely, the names and deeds of some of these marvellous individuals will sprout like beautiful thistles from the ditches of their scholastic memory.

For me, Sparky Heard was one of those eccentrics. He was a large man, always wore a light grey suit, and his sparse hair eternally looked as if it had been caught just as a windy front moved through; usually he sat at his desk and grunted his lessons using a pointer and gesturing to chalk calculations he had previously etched on the board; sometimes he just read aloud and explained the examples from the text. Only on rare occasions did he perambulate the room, his instructions often made in guttural bursts like *Highway Patrol's* Broderick Crawford on speed. Lesson given, the textbook's even numbers would be assigned from the current chapter for homework; I did not mind this—if I had time, I usually finished the assignment before the thirty-five-minute period ended. Thus, no homework … a good thing! Next day, Sparky would randomly designate students to put our answers on the board, proof as to whether we had done the work. The answers would be taken up, then the odd numbers of the exercise would be given as homework for the next day and the universe would unfold. Sparky sat at his desk, often shoving the eraser-end of a pencil in his ear, examining the contents and repeating the procedure with the other ear. Once, I remember for some reason I don't remember, he got angry with the class and called us all "a bunch of mods." But I always liked Sparky in some odd way, perhaps just because of his oddness. Math class reminded me somehow of the culvert that ran under our busy road—sometimes as a kid I would journey through that place safely below the helter-skelter world above, finding random refuse and the tiny skeletons of creatures that had crawled under there to die in peace—it was a dark, damp place, yes, but, enough light filtered in from each end and it seemed far away from the outer world, a momentary respite of magic and mystery. Thus it was with Sparky's Math class—it was, as if, instead of crossing the bridge, you journeyed under it to meet with the ogre face to face and there to learn of cabbages and kings. And, so often to me, thus it was with all of the classes of the eccentrics.

Red Townsend was another, once a star athlete now turned Physical Education and Science instructor. Red was a larger-than-life personality with an infectious sense of humour, always called us by elaborate nicknames he made up (mine was *hi ho silver a-way*) and filled our Health classes with lessons on the rules of various sports and on the organizational schema used to set up athletic tournaments. He also taught us to list and memorize stereotypical traits that characterized Caucasoid, Negroid, Mongoloid and Australoid races. To this day, I remember being taught that Mongoloid peoples were not individually creative but good at copying the ideas of others. Red was a product of his time and, while his educational directives may seem to have misfired a few times, especially by today's standards, he emanated a magnetism; he was a teacher you wanted to call yours.

There was Mr. Morrison, a young Geography teacher who always wore a cowboy hat and, down on hands and knees, desks pushed back, drew maps in chalk on the brown linoleum of his classroom floor. And Ralph Cook of Tillsonburg, the Math teacher who sometimes showed up to teach with his suit hastily pulled on over his pyjamas; Ralph played the bag pipes, had a huge collection of bag-pipe LPs, drove a thirty-year old Land Rover and had been to England seventeen years in a row the year I first met him. He loved local history and warm Guinness. And there was Mr. Lambert, the wood shop teacher at BCI who always wore a paisley ascot and played flute in the school band, who knocked on the door to the Staff Room door looking for Mr. Heard some ten years after that room had been converted from a class room and Sparky long-since retired. And I have already mentioned Messieurs Mabee and Greig and there were many more; now, while I understand the value of academic qualifications and homogeneous professional behaviour in our contemporary school systems, something has been lost in the quirky individualism that many of these eccentrics brought to the educational banquet.

I also recall Miss Mosser who taught us History. She was a first-year teacher and a fragile soul who tried her best but often seemed overwhelmed by the rancour of the random assembly she faced daily. This was a time when the fates decreed different combinations of classes based on the options you chose, and certain cohorts collected malevolent reputations. So 10A and 10B were typically the most responsive, best-behaved classes but reputation descended from there; usually, I seemed to end up in 10D or E, scowls already on teachers' faces when we entered the room. I never liked being condemned into one of these groups because reputations spread like plagues and these classes, which I generally found dull enough anyway, tended to be dire; teachers prejudicially unleashed the heavy-handed dogs of discipline at the least provocation, and that usually made things worse, not better, and never deterred the core disrupters anyway (most of these were border-liners, students nearing that magic age of freedom-sixteen after which school would be but a tale of unlearned lessons and outlaw escapades). So whistling bombs dropped at the back of Miss Mosser's room and spit balls flew like catapulted missiles in the ancient wars she talked about in class. The Bic Company made a ballpoint pen from which the cap and cartridge could be removed easily leaving a near-perfect pea-shooter. At one point, inevitably, Miss Mosser turned from the board and was hit in the forehead by a spitball and she began to cry and left the room. Some of us felt bad about that but it did not really faze most, I think. Shortly after, a VP arrived and things were quiet. Miss Mosser returned and things were better for awhile but, like the endless snows of deepest winter, chaos soon started to amp up again. After Christmas, she did not come back, lost in time and place, I suppose, like most of those we encounter in our lives, and always a reminder to me that, while I think teaching to be the greatest job on the planet, in certain times and places, for some, it can be the worst. After the holiday break, a permanent substitute was brought in and marshalled the group through the rest of the year; and as spring approached, several of the border-liners predictably drifted away like the seeds of dandelions obeying the winds of change. In that teeming baby boomer ethos, retention was not the incantation of education, as it is now. In those days, all children did not seem to matter as much and lots were left behind; in fact, some were cast aside as a good riddance. The gas pumps and greasy spoons of the world awaited.

I also had and/or knew many teachers who were not of the errant or eccentric clan but of the excellent variety. I have already mentioned a few and include a "hall of fame" following this chapter. It is not always easy to say what makes the best teacher. Certainly, the best teachers are friendly, but never friends (in particular, often not friendly at the start of a term). Usually, the very best teachers are simply recognized as such by everyone in a school, even the malcontents; they are the teacher gods. Sometimes they exhibit some idiosyncratic quirk or quality that speaks to the personality of individual students; sometimes they just contain an irresistible cool that talks to all. They have a unique and earnest gem in their soul. At the very least, to me, excellence in teaching is always characterised by three aspects:

> 1) expertise in the subject (such depth allows the teacher to fill in the margins, to paint the subject matter in a variety of ways to make it interesting and relevant, to make it something more than just a subject; to link it to the relatable and the germane; to make it magic and alive; in this regard, having subject specialists is vital in any school setting from Kindergarten to Graduate School);
>
> 2) an innate ability to connect with students and the desire to do so (whether speaking in class or nattering away when met in the halls or elaborating lucidly on some tactic while coaching a team, close but distant at the same time);
>
> 3) command of the classroom (as much as most teachers dislike discipline, enforcing the rules and boundaries is vital; for the teacher it may be boring and get in the way of the lesson at hand but, without this regimen, the centre cannot hold).

When those elements are in place, all teachers can be excellent and the classroom becomes a sacred space, the true centre of education.

Frank Buckley (English) and Bruce Retallick (History) were probably the high school teachers who most exemplified these behaviours and most influenced me to pursue higher education in the disciplines I did. Each one had the knack to engage us as students in the courses they taught, rousing debates and discussions often filled the rooms spilling into the halls as bells rang, although in both cases these teachers presented their classes using traditional Socratic methods. Sometimes there were surprises—I remember a senior History class, after I had completed a research project on the causes and effects of the American Civil War, Mr. Retallick asked me to teach that material to the class, which I did, essentially mimicking his style. And, discouraged that the yearbook editors had not included any of the writings I submitted, Mr. Buckley was undoubtedly the force behind my being chosen as Valedictorian for our class and delivering the speech in that divisive and turbulent time in Canadian history, a nation both celebrating its centennial and searching for an identity while Quebec nationalists, with kidnappings and violence, sought independence amid cries of *"vivre le Québec libre."*

Beyond Mr. Buckley and Retallick, Ron Green comes to mind. Mr. Green was a well-respected and admired Math teacher, of Mohawk heritage. He taught with precision and kindness and a fine sense of humour; most everyone enjoyed his classes (even though it was Math!). I recall an incident one day, unusual to say the least, a student in our class exploded in anger toward Mr. Green, calling him every racist epithet you could imagine; Mr. Green simply asked the student to leave. And to this day, I always remember him turning from the classroom door, with a smile, and saying to us: "You know, I never let anyone else ruin my day." I have always remembered that and, though never as wise or as gifted as Mr. Green, I have tried to follow his advice and, I will say, it has helped me through many a challenging situation, many a difficult day. Never let anyone ruin your day.

I also remember a moment in another Mathematics class, a senior class taught by Mr. Hildebrandt—in some way Mr. H. was the archetypal Math teacher, trim, clean-cut, precise and crystal clear in the manner in which he could explain arcane concepts (he actually left the classroom to go into Administration and was my first Vice Principal, probably the reason I got hired for that job in the first place—he was part of the

Interview Team.) In one moment of one of his classes, everyone was working on a particularly tricky Calculus problem and, all those years ago, I distinctly remember sitting back in my desk and watching three of my classmates huddled over the problem as they pried at decoding its stubborn enigma. I remember the delight and joy in their faces and I realized that was also the same delight and joy I felt, not in Math, but in English when I beheld the Beggar, the Madman and the Fool intersect on the wasted moors in *King Lear* or revel in understanding the monumental irony of Gregor Samsa awakening as a bug or Willie Loman's tragic misunderstanding of what comes with the territory. I was good enough at Math and at Physics—Queen's actually offered me entrance into a program called Pre-Meds—but while I understood those disciplines, for better or for worse there was, one might say, poetry in my blood and fiction in my bones. I knew at that moment in Mr Hildebrandt's class that English (or maybe History) was the path that I would pursue. And ultimately, while I taught English in many places, English was never a subject I ended up teaching; it was a life I ended up living.

ADDENDUM:

My Teacher Hall of Fame

The list which follows will mean nothing to you, nor should it. It is a personal list, the greatest teachers in my life, my Teacher Hall of Fame; I include it as an invitation to you to make your own. Among other things, such an activity will get you thinking about those teachers who most influenced you on your life's journey and who most deserve a moment of reflection and honour from you. In that regard, I am not convinced about a lot of the nonsense that has been said and written over the years about the best teachers, teachers as heroes or leaders or role models or cheerleaders or rebels with a cause or fighters for social justice or mentors who were your friends or saints who set the world on fire. No! Those are the things often said by those fringe players, like Deans and Directors, who never really seem to understand what an effective teacher is. Let the celluloid ghosts of Mark Thackeray and John Keating and Gabe Kotter rest in their fictive graves. Key to all, as I have mentioned before, good teachers always teach a subject and teach that subject with a degree of passion but also with a great degree of sincerity and hard work and comprehension for the subject, with compassion for their students, yes, but mostly with care that the lessons get delivered effectively and their students' understanding and awareness is enabled and elevated. It is through the teacher's handling of the subject that no child is left behind, that the world is changed for the better.

The inductees into my **Teacher Hall of Fame** include the following:

Elementary:	Ms H. Giles; Mr. F. Holmes
Secondary:	Mr. F. Buckley; Mr. B. Retallick; Mr. R. Green
Undergraduate:	Professor A. Alpers; Dr. A. C. Hamilton; Dr. C. Pullen; Dr. K. McSweeney
Graduate:	Dr. A. Gedalof; Dr. J. Zezulka; Dr. J. Reaney
Colleagues:	A. Tait; N. Basacco; B. Charlton; Dr. D. Allison; Dr. M. MacCormack
Students:	A. Caulfield; S. Ross; D. *Bubba* Demeester; F. Pelletier; O. Gutauskas; R. Venga

Note: I have not included relatives or many friends; their contributions were extensive but, for the purposes of this list, I exclude them as teachers—it goes without saying, I think, I learned a great deal from all of them.

Now, I invite you to make your own **Teacher Hall of Fame**:

My Teacher Hall of Fame

Kindergarten/ Elementary	
Secondary	
Post-Secondary	
Friends, Colleagues and Others	

24

Opening Pandora's Boxcar

Poetry & prose had for a long time fallen into the false hands of the false. These new poets confess forth the sheer joy of confession. They are CHILDREN. They are also childlike greybeard Homers singing in the street. They SING, they SWING. It is diametrically opposed to the Eliot shot, who so dismally advises his dreary negative rules like the objective correlative, *etc.*, which is just a lot of constipation and ultimately emasculation of the pure masculine urge to freely sing.

—Jack Kerouac *Scattered Poems*

With the naissance of the Baby-Boom generation in the years after World War II came a significant paradigm shift in the culture at large— art, architecture, popular music, habits of entertainment, philosophy, poetry, novels, theatre, critical perspectives, social norms, medical diagnoses, the foods we ate, the clothes we wore, the political *Zeitgeist*, all changed. Adequately or not, this cultural shift away from the template of Modernism came to be labelled Postmodernism and the impact on our culture, on education and on the practice of teaching has been pervasive. At the core, the perception of students; in effect, the very essence of what it was to be a student changed. The student now became the centre, the heart, the text of education. The phrase, *student- centred learning*, resounded. In the Modernist classroom, with teacher-as- director, the student unveiled the text to understand the self; but now, in the Postmodernist world, with teacher-as-observer, the student unveils the self to understand the text.

The impact of this remarkable shift (which happened gradually, of course, in the decades leading toward and through the millennium) even altered the way schools looked, buildings now had skeletal entranceways, open ceilings and visible conduits, allowing the inhabitant to see beneath the skin of the construction itself, to open up and play in what were once the hidden recesses of the world. In some ways, that is the essence of postmodernism, the compulsive tendency to pull back the curtain to reveal the previously unrevealed thing itself, to deconstruct the very space in which we reside. And on the beneficial side of that strip-tease, issues once hidden, such as the treatment and role of females and persons of colour and Indigenous peoples and the elderly and the disabled and those with different sexual orientation, among many other representations, have all been cast under the spotlight, their curtain pulled back. And this movement translated itself from the world of high art and culture to the everyday and the local, from the sacred to the banal—Jesus Christ became a Superstar and soup cans became Art, the once-discarded mistakes of film became outtakes attached to the credits, often as entertaining as the movie itself; instant replays altered sporting events even as they were played and everything, it seemed, became carrion to feed tabloids and *TMZ* and the omni-present Paparazzi. The wide world became a web of information saturated with technology, cell phone intractably in hand—and it is with some trepidation that we recall webs are not only beautiful and intricate architectural creations but also designs that serve as engines of slaughter.

By way of example, I grew up in a community where, up and down the road, everyone knew you and if you dared commit any misdemeanour you would be rebuffed all the way along the road and twice again when you arrived home (whatever that "rebuffing" might mean!). On Sundays, almost everyone went to church—all the stores and movie theatres were closed anyway. My grandfather Wesley, a farmer all his life, whether he went to church or not (he rarely did), always donned his favourite suit on Sunday, spats buttoned over his shoes, striped elastic garters on his shirtsleeves. (That suit, dark blue with wide pinstripes, a fashion from decades earlier, was the suit in which he was buried and, somehow, it looked fine.) Hallowe'en was not a simple event, a knock on the door to receive some candy, but rather an evening-long odyssey through the community during which you and your friends would be invited inside each house while the adults talked to you and tried to guess your identity; then you would move on to the same interrogation next door. Community card parties, engagement and baby showers, even *shivarees* were regular occurrences. But as the twentieth century transformed into the twenty-first, the magic of the deconstructive tendency took hold, the means and will of place and transportation changed, urbanity expanded, neighbours were supplanted by Facebook friends and local community disappeared, paranoia and theories of conspiracy abounded; churches, ministering to a diminished handful, closed and the world of information streamed in to fill the empty gaps. Our lives were expanded and contracted at the same time, enhanced and devalued as downtowns starved and malls, then big box corporations ate the planet. Much was gained in the postmodern transformation, of course, from access to a universe of information and a thousand sources of entertainment and human footprints on Mars, but from parenting to driving to self-defence to physical and mental health, schools inherited responsibility for all that was left behind when church and community vanished. And so, postmodernism moved across the waters of our consciousness and took over the pedagogical podium, call it Smart-Phone or Streaming or Zoom or TikTok or X or what you will.

In the realm of English and teaching, after WWII, literary fiction began to take on a shape of its own with various major divergences— the Beat movement (Kerouac, Ginsberg, Ferlinghetti, Snyder, Patchen, McClure, Whelan, Burroughs, Cassidy, Kesey), the Confessional poets (Plath, Lowell, Sexton, Bukowski, Purdy and Layton) and the Counter-culture writers (Borges, Calvino, Brautigan, Barthelme, Barth, Gass, Vonnegut, Johnson, Coover, Sukenick, Robbe-Grillet). The literature which emerged was quite different from what existed before—self-reflective and self-reflexive texts that continually questioned or even deconstructed themselves and saw themselves as part of the larger process of things, involving author and reader and other texts, sometimes including drawings and photographs and other extra-textual materials. As Ron Sukenick said of the previous Modernist novel: "the form of the traditional novel is a metaphor for a society that no longer exists" (quoted in Jerome Klinkowitz, *Life of Fiction*). There was a widely-felt sense among these writers, and the prominent literary critics of the era (such as Fiedler, Hassan, Klinkowitz, Barth, Derrida, deMan, Fish) that literature had taken a new turn, that the old literature and critical approaches had, in John Barth's phrase, become exhausted or "used-up" (Barth's *The Friday Book*, 1967, which is, in many ways, a manifesto of Postmodernism). Many writers began to produce a self-conscious, playful type of fiction variously labelled surfiction or midfiction, avant-garde or transfiction, or metafiction. In the novel, *The Abortion: An Historical Romance 1966* by Richard Brautigan, Brautigan, himself, shows up to deposit a book in a fictional library. Vonnegut in *Slaughterhouse Five* draws a picture of Montana Wildhack's breasts, ostensibly, because words are woefully inadequate to describe her anatomy. Barthelme, two-thirds of the way through *Snow White*, includes a questionnaire asking the reader to rate the book so far. Calvino's *If on a winter's night a traveller* begins on the front cover, each succeeding chapter of Abish's alliterative *Alphabetical Africa* adds one more letter in sequence to the text, and Johnson's *Albert Angelo* has holes cut in the pages so the reader can glimpse future events, always to the confessed fictive mantra: "Telling stories is telling lies." The Beats write accounts of their own lives making themselves the protagonists and the Confessionals speak in their actual voices, crafting themselves and their specific experiences as fiction (including very personal details about occurrences such as mental illness and attempts at suicide). Modernist writers like Eliot and Joyce would have been thunderstruck at such content, and probably quite dismissive.

In education since World War II, signs of postmodernist ideas and trends are everywhere. Before Postmodernism's influence took hold, when I was in high school, our English teacher would put a question on the board and we would spend the rest of the period writing an essay-style answer. A week or so later, we would get a graded paper back with a mark, usually no comments, and, a week or so thereafter, repeat the exercise responding to a new question. Following are actual examples from my senior English notebooks (from a term in which we studied drama):

- Discuss blindness as an important theme in *King Lear*.
- Explain the significance of justice and trial in the tragedy that befalls King Lear.
- What meaning does the phrase "the call of the absolute" impart to Ibsen's *The Wild Duck*.
- Drama of the Restoration abandoned Puritan morality through its use of farce. Discuss with regard to *The Beaux Stratagem*.

– Analyse the importance of the "fifth character" in
   The Glass Menagerie.
– Explain *The Glass Menagerie* as an allegory.
– Who is the greatest victim in *Death of a Salesman.*

Bottom line, most of us became quite proficient at writing on our feet, so to speak, and it set us up fairly well for the examination cycles which were to follow at university. But, we never, ever thought of writing as a process, of doing a rough draft and then editing and revising until we reached a final polished production. Education happened in the moment; learning was not a process but an event. In some sense, that instantaneousness was the purpose of education. All of that changed with the rise of Postmodernism. And excessively so, for now the pervading idea seems to be that education is a process, that the treadmill of learning never stops. Is it then logical to conclude that, if one never stops learning, one never truly learns anything? Ever? And perhaps, as foundations continually shift like tectonic plates beneath our feet, as technology changes rapidly even on a daily basis, it seems, that is as it must be.

The following list highlights some of the educational trends and beliefs that emerged as Postmodern sensibilities took over. I will elaborate on some of these in the chapters which follow but, it must be emphasized that, before 1950, none of these trends or strategies would have existed in any institutional context or been given any widespread consideration or acceptance.

– learning as a process (including the idea of life-long
   learning)
– writing as a process (writing folders; portfolio
   assessments; exemplars; Atwell; Graves...)
– expressive language (Britton; the personal growth
   model; journals, journals, journals...)
– whole language (unhooked from phonics;
   Goodman; Smith; Rich...)
– linguistics (descriptive grammar; sentence
   combining; common errors)

- world as classroom/text (educational courses or units in
  sexual orientation and gender identity; parenting;
  technology; bullying and violence prevention; drug abuse;
  equity; personal and home finance; critical race theory;
  social justice issues; martial arts; driver education...)
- de-streaming
- broad-based education
- student-centred education
- media education / reading popular culture / film studies
- theatre arts education
- computer education
- multicultural education
- collaborative education
- independent learning/independent study
- personal growth and self-esteem
- reader response theory (Rosenblatt; Bleich; Fish; Iser...)
- authentic assessment
- common standardized curricula
- standardized assessments / outcomes-based assessments
  / expectations / exemplars

...and more.

However one reads it, the conceptual shift that has occurred in the last half century in education and elsewhere is remarkable, and dramatic. In pedagogy across all disciplines, text has become TEXT, which is to say, the borderlands of most studies have been broken down. Marshall McLuhan's Global Village has come to fruition across our planet and in our classrooms, and in the very ways we think; as McLuhan once wrote: "The automobile is an extension of your feet, clothing an extension of your skin, glasses an extension of your eyes, the internet an extension of your nervous system" (*War and Peace in the Global Village* 1968). "We will wear ourselves," McLuhan once said: "Now man is beginning to wear his brain outside his skull and his nerves." As an aside, a few years ago I remember writing *Print Preview*, an undergraduate research and writing text, where in sample exercises and such the editors insisted that every proper name reflect multi-cultural diversity—Mary became Komalpreet, John, Ichiro, and so on. Global Village, indeed!

Not only are they studied but, just as notably, theatre arts, film, television, advertisement, popular music, Zoom and streaming platforms, Google-search, and so on, infuse teaching today. Non-literary or non-traditional texts are common and popular culture is often taught where, once, only an elite culture was considered. The study of History now seems almost as much about popular life as once it was about names and dates, causes and effects. How the Jacobins dressed and what they ate has become as important as what they believed in during the French Revolution or when it began, and why. Lines have blurred—in university studies, in particular, subject boundaries are often abolished as students take such courses as: "Botany in the Poetry of Shelley," "The Geography of Harry Potter's England," "The Physics of *Star Trek*," "Wasting Time on the Internet," "Politicizing Beyoncé," "Bagpiping and Burns," "Taylor Swift and Her World" and "Comic Art" (all actual course offerings in various North American universities at the time of this writing).

And so, relentlessly, Postmodernism imprinted its dramatic paradigm shift on education and on culture, at large. And in many aspects, often linked to the digital age and our multiverse, the change seemed all-encompassing. This time Pandora had pried open, not a box, but a boxcar. Most mythologies, as we know, offer stories of individuals driven by pride and greed, cunning or curiosity, and Pandora's tale is one of those. She was the first human female (an Eve-figure whose name literally means 'all-gifted'), created by Hephaestus upon Zeus's order and part of the Olympian god's plan to punish humans for accepting and using Prometheus's gift of stolen fire. Pandora's story is a theodicy, essentially intended to explain how evil and other discomforts came into the world. And thus, although warned not to, Pandora succumbs to her curiosity and opens a *pithos* (a jar—(mis)translated in most versions as a box or chest) and, from biting insects to pandemic plagues, all sorts of irritations and dangers are released into the world. According to Hesiod's version of the tale, only a butterfly remains, symbolic of *Hope*, always providing for humans the possibility that something positive may be found no matter how much suffering must be endured. For traditionalists, in education and elsewhere, much of the widespread impact of Pandora's Postmodern boxcar seemed dire. While change is inevitable, and there always seems to be a cost to be paid, real or perceived, the extent of changes wrought by Postmodernism seemed cataclysmic—cell phones and vaping and opioids and the rest. But, however one sees the situation, while dangers may have been unleashed, the boxcar is also full of wonders. Hope is alive; Hope is afoot. For education, for our students. And surely, Pan-dora, symbolic red boots and purple backpack and all, has become an exalted explorer and no longer just a bored and neglected housewife in ancient Greece.

So, Modernism presented one scientific, formalistic, determined way to interpret the world; Postmodernism insists on diversity in the world and in the education therein; thus, new angles of perception and inquiry are encouraged, necessitated (psychological, sociological, linguistic, historical, racial, ethnic, gendered, economic) and always changing like the universe itself. The teaching process has become recursive—one never stops asking questions, not only of the text and the students and the society but of the questions themselves and, ideally, of the questioner, too. All the Klieg lights are turned on, the cave is enlightened, deconstructed, and, without a shadow in sight, Plato now interrogates his own interrogation. And in such light, across such space, it is sometimes hard to know the teacher from the student, and that may be a good thing.

25
Grade Twelve

How far away the stars seem, and how far
Is our first kiss, and ah, how old my heart!

—W. B. Yeats "Ephemera" 1884

Well people I've been here before
I know this room and I've walked this floor
You see I used to live alone before I knew ya
And I've seen your flag on the marble arch
But listen love, love is not some kind of victory march, no
It's a cold and it's a broken Hallelujah

—Leonard Cohen "Hallelujah"

Al Purdy! As we reflect on our lives, each one of us surely recognizes certain moments when some distinct change occurred, when a path divided and the route we took changed us forever. Perhaps we met a true love or experienced some tragedy. And in aging, it is our reflection on those moments that informs and enriches our understanding of where we've been and who we are and why. T. S. Eliot says it proficiently and beautifully:

We shall not cease from exploration
And the end of all our exploring
Will be to arrive where we started
And know the place for the first time.

—T. S. Eliot "Little Gidding" *Four Quartets*

Surely all of us have those life-shaping moments—those spots of time
as Wordsworth called them; Eliot labelled those moments, incarnations;
for Joyce, they were epiphanies; for James and Gide, moments of
germination.

One afternoon in the spring of Grade 12, such a moment happened
to me. The Senior students were called to an Assembly; Mr. Richardson,
the new English Department Head, came onstage, gave an introduction,
and Al Purdy stepped to the podium. Purdy was the first living writer I
had ever encountered; he had won a couple national awards for his work
and, most remarkable, he lived in Ameliasburgh, only a few kilometres
from my home. Purdy read in the afternoon, comic and poignant and
irrepressible, then returned in the evening for any interested students. I
had just got my driver's license and Dad offered the car, the first time
that I had ever driven at night. I picked up our neighbours, the Harts,
and sat in a classroom at BCI and listened as Purdy read poems,
answered questions and told stories, in particular about a recent trip to
Cuba where he had met Che Guevara and, also, Pierre Elliot Trudeau,
who had just swept to power as Canada's newest Prime Minister.
Trudeaumania, and all of that! Needless to say, we were very impressed.
And for me, it was a moment that I have never forgotten. I always
dabbled at writing as a kid and here was Al Purdy—a living writer, and
a person who made his living as a poet, and a person who only lived a
few minutes away in the village that was once called Way's Mills. In
retrospect, who knows exactly how that moment impacted my life but I
do know that I have never forgotten meeting and living under the
influence of Al Purdy, one of the best Canadian poets ever, a man who
wrote about the world in which we actually lived, both near and far,
refined and rowdy, and who in some way spoke to the undistilled spirits
of my soul. Throughout my life, I grew and was charged and changed
by his words:

The black millpond
holds them
movings and reachings and fragments
the gear and tackle of living
under the water eye
> all things laid aside
discarded
forgotten
but they had their being once
and left a place to stand on

—Al Purdy "Roblin's Mills (2)" 1965

That "black millpond" to which Purdy refers was created by my own ancestor, John B. Way, when he built the first gristmill in Ameliasburgh before he traded it to Owen Roblin, a subject that Purdy was then researching and would turn into his *magnus opus*, *In Search of Owen Roblin*. In later years I would continue to read Purdy's works as they came out, met him a few times at readings and, after his death, had the honour of serving on the Board of Governors' organization responsible for maintaining his A-Frame cottage for a "writer-in-residence" program. I also had tea and lunch several times with his widow, Eurithe; and she showed me her awesome collection of rare and special Art books based on Al's work (I used those to set up a display at the cottage).

As I have suggested before, every class has a student or two who rises above the ranks of the mere mortals and takes on the monarchical role of Queen or King, and our high school class was no different. Our King was probably David Wright, tall and handsome and popular, a star of various sports' fields, king of the year-end Prom and son of a local Dean in the Anglican church. His future path was surely one of gold and trumpets. And our Queen was Carole Lennox. Attractive, long auburn hair, a cheerleader and active in numerous other school organizations, and one of the three or four most intellectually gifted students in the school. Both were friendly but diffident to me in my role as a marginal subaltern of their demesne. But Carole's true apotheosis as the goddess of our world was confirmed, of course, by the fact that she began to go out with a boy from an upper-year class. Beyond that, for me, Carole initiated what was one of those moments of illumination in my life. This was an era of sweaters, Perry Como cardigans were everywhere and those school cardigans, you know the style, three stripes on the sleeve and a letter on the front. Carole wore one of those but not on this day. I was standing near the door of a second-floor corner room waiting for afternoon classes to begin and, across the hall at her locker, Carole finished putting on some lip gloss, flipped her hair back, turned and tugged down on the sweater she was wearing, an act that emphasized the nubile contours of her body. Along the wall near the door to the adjacent classroom, I noticed three young male teachers, their gaze on Carole and, as she tugged, they privately turned to one another with percipient nods and smiles, then moved off to teach their respective classes. I realized in that moment, curiously, I suppose (I had not thought of this before), that an instinctive connection existed between the grown-up world, the world of the teachers, and our world of being young. That clandestine world of adults, who up to that point had not seemed quite human like us, was suddenly not some far-off land of secret concerns and serious things but simply a world just a step away and paths and points of intersection were already in place. What impacted us, impacted them. Our worlds overlapped or, maybe, were just one-and-the-same. In that moment, I felt a surprise, an exhilaration, a smugness and a sadness, too, a kind of burden of realization I suppose which I have carried with me ever since—was it for this the clay grew tall? And to this day I remember Carole's sweater, a comfortable fuzzy mohair, a rich and earthy burnt umber in colour.

The best friend I met at high school was the big Dutchman, as he called himself, Jake Vos. I had grown up knowing various Dutch families along our road, the Bosmas and Keirkes and Tops, most refugees from Hitler's invasion of the Netherlands. John Top, in particular, was a school-long class-mate and friend, his mom and dad hard-working farmers who owned a property near the end of Lower Massassaga Road. And his younger sister, Linda, was one of those who "skipped" a grade in the early years, a practise fairly common in those days because of a student's brilliance, and sometimes, I think, to balance out the class numbers (cheaper to skip a student than buy a new desk). Jake Vos and I became almost instant friends; he had an infectious sense of humour—to this day I can still see him smile and hear him utter phrases about things in life that fell into or out of favour: "You can't beat it with a stick" or more adamantly, "He ought to be shot and pissed on"—and we both took an Arts Program with a Shops' option so we were in all the same classes.

During the spare period we had in our senior year, we would often walk downtown (about five minutes away from BCI) to the *Cozy Grill* where we would have coffee and a piece of pie. This was a time before *Tim Hortons* and other fast-food restaurants took over the psyche of the world. *The Quinte Hotel* was also on the way, offering four drafts for a dollar at the time, and I knew some classmates who used to partake, but that was never for Jake and me. Pie and candy were more our fare. Jake had relatives in Holland and they would sometimes send over these salty licorice candies which, I always felt, were disgusting, but Jake liked them, or so he said. And sometimes serendipity had its role to play. It was at the *Cozy Grill* one time with Jake that I read a paper placemat set down in our booth; I actually took it home and taped it to my bedroom wall and, much later, made specific use of it in my novel, *The Prince of Leroy*. That placemat expressed a Zen-sentiment that I carried with me into what was to become a lifetime in teaching, a mantra to this day that I hold in memory and which I think aptly describes the teaching life in particular:

> *You only begin to understand the true meaning of life*
>
> *when you plant a tree under whose shade*
>
> *you know you will never sit*

It was Jake who convinced me to try out for the senior football squad in our Grade Twelve year even though neither of us had played Junior. We were never very good but the team was worse—I think we only won one game that year, against woeful Picton, some of whose players only had old leather helmets to wear, the kind without faceguards. On the other side, we played Quinte who was a powerhouse; two of their running backs (Wellesley and Townsend) actually made it to the CFL for brief pro careers. I played middle linebacker and mostly rushed the seams; on one occasion, the stars collided and one of their star backs and I mistakenly met; I ducked and he tripped over me, gaining only minimal yardage and no touchdown on that play. It was a defensive victory and, although a matter of happenstance, probably the highlight of my football career. Against Quinte, mostly, my blitzing strategy was to avoid the seams where those monsters were running. I also played offensive guard although I never did figure out those complicated blocking assignments; I just tried to stop the player in front of me and, most often, that seemed good enough (to me, anyway). The Cheerleaders hailed and chanted—"Hey Hey BCI / Go Fight Win / Hey Hey BCI / It's time to send *David* in"—they never inserted my name into that cheer of theirs. And to be honest, in spite of the eternal Cheerleaders' optimism and energy, given the skill of our team, Coach Beevor could have sent Jesus in and it wouldn't have made any difference! Jake was probably a bit better football player than I but, with the tough Grade Thirteen academic year ahead, we both decided to hang up our cleats after one season. I'm sure General Managers in CFL offices across the country wept a tear.

Jake sang in the school choir, pretty much the only male to do so, but he didn't care. He started dating a fellow chorister and, at one point, tried to get me to ask her best friend to the school Prom but I declined for various reasons, mostly shyness and some inner fear, I suppose, that I might actually be called upon to dance. I guess, at heart, I didn't really want to go although, I admit, I have thought about that decision ever since, long after the streamers and the music have faded away.

After he got his driver's license (he only failed the test once which was a common occurrence for almost everyone in those days), Jake used to drive out to our place in the County and we would go, where else, to the *Cozy Grill* for pie and a coffee! Jake went to Brock University and did very well there but after meeting up once or twice after first year our paths went in different directions and we never saw one another again. But I will always remember the Big Dutchman, his broad smile and slap on the back and the taste of that salty licorice from a place so far away.

Elizabeth Anne Louise Marie Vardy! Over fifty years later and I still recall her full Catholic name. O sweet Anne! I had an enormous crush on Anne Vardy. I guess she was the first great love of my life. She was slim with long auburn hair and her locker was next to mine. She had a casual self-confident manner, offering wily matter-of-fact comments on the state of our world, candid and witty. I adored her direct, blunt charm! Always wishing me a good morning, sometimes with an ironic tone, and telling me to have a good weekend when those occasions arose. She had no airs, brushing her hair, snapping up her undergarments through her dress with aplomb, spilling her ongoing observations to me with humour and candor. I used to help her carry her books to class, remembering meeting Mr. Buckley on those black back stairs and the knowing spring smile he gave us. But I was always too shy and lived out-of-town and Anne always had a boyfriend of one sort or another. She went off to one of the universities in Ottawa and, like virtually all of those I knew in high school, I never saw her again. Several years later, when I returned to BCI to teach, I read her marriage announcement in the local paper and smiled, I think, pleased to know she was well and saddened too at the empty twist of things. But I remember the true gut feeling of that first love—how it hums through your being like hydro wires in the heat of summer and all things are warm and possible, firm and sensual, in the palpable present and simple future that you can imagine. And I strive here not to be sentimental or maudlin. But it was a time when the nerves were ablaze, possibility was alive and the world resided in a smile and a wry conversation, and hope nestled like some early robin secure and happy as spring awakes. And the many casual weekend farewells resound: "Yes. See you on Monday. Don't forget that Math homework. Yes. Yes. I know, what can you do! Probably forever, you know. Don't hold your breath! Yes, take care. Have a weekend! Yes. Yes." And yes!

ADDENDUM:

ode of sorts to purdy
(on first hearing al purdy read)

'keep your ass out of my beer'
he leaned across the podium
running freight car fingers through straight grey hair
attacking the audience as if they were all americans
then he hesitated in his loping stance
retreating in memory to rummage out his solemn lines
'go ahead strike go ahead'

god damn it purdy move over
im from massassaga
thats only a couple miles from ameliasburg
and wild grapes grow there too
and more important i was born there
not in that damn dilapidated queens hotel
mired in the ghettoes of trenton
where you gained breath
and my ancestor didnt just inherit roblins mill   he built it
agreed my village doesnt have some sort of freudian store
with old women complaining about dirty poetry books
the ones you tried to sell there a few years back
theres no lake either
but theres a marsh that the sun tries to glimmer across
and where tall blue herons stand
so ive got my walden too
and experience with trains and hauling mattresses will come
but youve got books and canada council grants
and some pretty good poetry
more every time i turn around
so i guess for now you bastard
ill listen to you talk about
the gold hairs on your wifes belly
and your mice and your huskies and your pontiac
your burning buildings your rhododendrons
and the country of your defeat
but watch   out one of these days soon
im going to grow long straight grey hair
and drink beer all the time and
wear wrinkled white shirts with the sleeves rolled up
and believe me
i can smoke those cheap white owls too

ps: spring 2000

silent now
but your voice still resounds across the land it found
a respect deserved
as for me   well cigars have gone quite out of public fashion
                  and long since resigned at never achieving what you did
a defeat   perhaps   yes
but somehow in that defeat i find myself quite satisfied

> (One of my first published poems, originally written
> *circa* 1970; published in *Quarry, Canadian Forum, Pom
> Seed, white pelican, Waves* and elsewhere, and included in
> *redirection* Hidden Brook Press 2015)

26

the reader, the text, the meaning, o my!

It is a revelation to compare Menard's *Don Quixote* with Cervantes'. The latter, for example, wrote (part one, chapter nine):

...truth, whose mother is history, rival of time, depository of deeds, witness of the past, exemplar an adviser to the present, and the future's counsellor...

Written in the seventeenth century, written by the "lay genius" Cervantes, this enumeration is a mere rhetorical praise of history. Menard, on the other hand, writes:

... truth, whose mother is history, rival of time, depository of deeds, witness of the past, exemplar and adviser to the present, and the future's counsellor...

—Jorge Borges "Pierre Menard, Author of the Quixote" *Labyrinths* 1962

Ostensibly, that passage from Jorge Borges' "Pierre Menard, Author of the Quixote" represents one of the most remarkable moments of all contemporary literature. In Borges' story a critic examines the writing career of one, Pierre Menard, and encounters his rewriting of

Cervantes' *Don Quixote*, in appearance a duplication, a copying of the original, word by word. In effect what Borges is suggesting (among many things) is that as readers, and writers, all that we read is an intensely personal act, and all that we read becomes, in effect, a reflection of ourselves. So the reader and all that the reader has experienced becomes as integral a part of any text as the author or the text itself. Like that tree falling in the forest, perhaps, without the response of the reader, in fact, there is no text, no author. And thus, in reading, the text becomes as much ourselves as anything else—such is the essence of what has come to be known as reader response theory. And reader response is a postmodern theory which has proliferated among writers and artists of our time. And since the 1980s, reader response theory has gained a widespread acceptance and transmission into practice in elementary and secondary schools; David Bleich, Stanley Fish and Wolfgang Iser have been recent well-known scholarly proponents.

From da Vinci to Zang Heng to de Pizan to Verne, some people seem to live ahead of their time, and so it was with Louise Rosenblatt who, in 1938, published *Literature as Exploration,* the first extended discourse on the phenomenon of reading theory. She was mostly ignored at the time (Modernism and the New Critical approach were dominant and, of course she was a woman and a Jew). In particular, Rosenblatt talks of Transactional Reading, characterizing reading as a kind of business deal between the reader and the text and she speaks of two kinds of transactional reading, efferent and aesthetic: in efferent reading, we receive from the text (which she always labels *the poem*), we read to acquire information, as from a cookbook; in aesthetic reading, we provide a response to the text, emotions, feelings, thoughts:

> The poem must be thought of as an event in time. It is not an object or an ideal entity. It happens during a coming-together, a compenetration, of a reader and a text. The reader brings to the text his past experience and present personality. Under the magnetism of the ordered symbols of the text, he marshals his resources and crystallizes out of the stuff of memory, thought, and feeling a new order, a new experience, which he sees as the poem.

—Louise Rosenblatt *The Reader, the Text, the Poem* 12

For Rosenblatt, the reading of the text is akin to a musical performance and so the focus shifts from the text as "a thing in itself" to the reader's interpretation of the text:

> The reader's initial response to a literary text is an inextricable part of the reading experience itself and is simply not available for immediate articulation or crude external examination. We think-feel it. To articulate this response requires us to organize and "re-symbolize" it and this process renders us exposed and vulnerable. Yet, this exposure to the negotiating community of the classroom and the questioning of text and of self, attendant upon it, is essential for apprentice readers if they are to grow in their ability for literary experience. Hence the teacher's delicate task.

In this vein, a text does not have a meaning. Meanings occur only in the interaction between the reader and the text; based on personal experiences, each reader will bring a different, and genuine, interpretation to the text. Responding to the story of a barn being burned, the child of the farmer will naturally have a different understanding than the urban child. Your *Adventures of Huckleberry Finn* or your *Anne of Green Gables* will be different from mine in that we naturally bring different experiences to a reading. The musician plays the music; the music plays the musician. One thinks of the opening lines of Stevens' "Peter Quince at the Clavier," where not only is the music put into the instrument by the musician, but it is also extracted from it:

> Just as my fingers on these keys
> Make music, so the selfsame sounds
> On my spirit make a music, too.
> Music is feeling, then, not sound;…

—Wallace Stevens "Peter Quince at the Clavier" 1915

Individualistically, the *Don Quixote* you read is yours, not mine, nor Pierre Menard's (nor Borges', nor Cervantes'). This also means that, every five years or so as we, ourselves, grow and our understanding and experience change, texts will change, too. I recall reading *Catcher in the Rye* in high school and really admiring Holden Caulfield, then reading it during the year I was earning my teaching degree and thinking what an *a-hole* that kid was. I have read it again in the years since and changed my opinion again, and I have come to the conclusion that none of my interpretations was the right one but all were legitimate in the time in which they were made. Now, as one's experience and expertise increases, the refinement or nuance of one's understanding may be refined but the essential mutability remains. That is the judgement that a reader response approach demands. The teacher as sage on the stage has retired. The teacher's role is no longer to offer up, as such, *the correct meaning* (and really, no such thing exists anyway—this is, in a sense, the pedagogical fallacy); the teacher's role is now to foster an *interpretive community* in the classroom where the most logical and persuasive meanings can be shared. And in my experience, a kind of massaged and shared perspective usually occurs. If some student suggests that Romeo is an alien invading the earth, others will invariably suggest that he may be impetuous, or spontaneous, or irrational, or breaking the moral code of the social order of Verona, or just *a teenager in love*, and the alien idea usually fades away. And if it doesn't, perhaps the clever teacher will ask what an alien is, anyway, and a discussion will be generated on that rich topic (from ET, perhaps, to farm labourers or asylum seekers) and why violence and feuding and the like often accompany alienation (in old Verona as well as our modern-day world), topics apropos to themes of the play in general anyway. And so, often new life can be given to old works—reader response may be able to do what the school's budget can't; replacing old texts with new ones simply by altering how they are read.

Teachers have had some basic issues with reader response applications in the classroom. One, it tends to undermine the authority of the text and place more authority on individual interpretation—yes, probably true, but that may not be a bad thing. Students will need to be shown that their responses have merit and be encouraged to share them with others. The class needs to work together to solve or sort out literary issues and must always be willing, in the end, to accept differing interpretations and to allow for those—all of us do not need to think the same thing as long as we can support differing opinions that have fairly reasoned and evidentiary claims. (Therein might lie a better world anyway, one supposes.) Secondly, reader response pedagogy may undermine the authority of the teacher as critic and expert; as noted, the era of the sage on the stage is over. *Joltin' Joe has left and gone away.* The elementary or secondary classroom should have no podium—even in some colleges and universities, that mainstay of educational oligarchy is starting to waver, if not topple.

Ultimately, I suspect, the influence and practice of a reader response approach does not produce significantly different understanding in a classroom but—and this may be a significant *but*—it probably produces a student who feels that she or he has more ownership of the critical conclusions made in the classroom than ever before. And there are many positive tendencies for teachers:

> – telling less and listening more
> – clinging less to our initial agendas or, even, lesson plans
> – putting more faith in the genuine if sometimes naive
> responses of our students.

In my first few years of teaching, I remember generating worksheets with questions for students and, as part of my prep, carefully scripting "correct" answers for each question prior to taking them up. As a reader-response approach took over, those days evaporated and classes became much more fluid and spontaneous, and more effective, I think, more open-ended and interesting. I still prepared a supply of effective questions but worried less about the answers.

And my sense is that a reader-response sensibility is not simply an English/Language Arts or Humanities thing but a benefit to teaching any and all subjects. It is a method that empowers students to have a voice and an ownership of their learning, a genuine engagement with whatever the subject matter might be from an experiment in Science to a problem in Mathematics to a drill in Physical Education. Most often the intellectual integrity of the text or activity and of the classroom atmosphere and of a generally shared culture will play a positive role in leading students toward insightful and reasoned responses or actions. In effect, reader response leads toward a classroom with less (and delayed) teacher intervention, with more of a collaborative, truly educational ethos. And toward the understanding that many creative writers and artists have understood forever, that virtually nothing under our sun can ever (should ever) be pinned to a singular idea or interpretation. As Yeats so eloquently says:

> The best lack all conviction, while the worst
> Are full of passionate intensity.

> —William Butler Yeats "The Second Coming" 1920

27
Grade Thirteen

It's a strange, strange world we live in, Master Jack
You taught me all I know and I'll never look back
It's a very strange world and I thank you, Master Jack

—David Marks 1968 (recorded by *Four Jacks and a Jill*)

Grade Thirteen! Today, even the words seem arcane, anachronistic, the naming of some dimension that existed once in the far reaches of *The Twilight Zone*. But from 1921 until 1988 (really, 2003), it was the crown jewel in the school system across Ontario (and in many other jurisdictions in this country and elsewhere). Even today, *Cégep* exists in Quebec, typically, a two-year program taken after Grade Eleven to prepare students for entry into higher education in that province. And for years Grade Thirteen in Ontario was simply considered the natural endpoint of education, the most challenging achievement in the formal education of most individuals in the province, capped off by the often-brutal province-wide Departmental Examinations, which ran until 1967. Many students had to retake Grade Thirteen because of the difficulty of those exams. But in terms of the scope of education, the fifth year of high school was a landmark; remember, for the twenty-five years or so after World War II, Grade Thirteen, plus six weeks of summer training, qualified individuals to become full-fledged teachers in the province. So for a long time it was a tangibly significant educational summit.

But by the 1960s, with mass communications and the emergence of McLuhan's Global Village, with nationalism and Canada's growing presence on the world's stage, the pressure arose for Ontario to align with national and international communities and, in so doing, among other things, to eliminate the fifth year of high school. Opposition by parents to the Departmental Examinations may also have played a role. And so, provincial governments from the sixties on began the never-ending process (it seemed) of streamlining the curriculum to twelve years. It came to pass eventually that, to earn a high school diploma, students were required to earn thirty credits, usually with some caveats, such as the requirement of five English courses and "X" number of hours of unpaid community service and the successful completion (around Grade Ten) of something called a Literacy Test. The Excellence in Education movement was somewhat influential here. This meant students in Grades Nine through Eleven typically took eight credits per year, and then six credits in their fourth year—a fifth year was hardly needed. Then, on to university, college, or work! The graduation of students after Grade Ten was gradually phased out—these were the Occupational Classes, the oft-labelled "treads" and "retreads," the real-life sweat-hogs of high school. For earlier generations in the twentieth century, finishing their formal education after Grade Eight (as my mother did) or after Grade Ten (as my father did) was acceptable, even the norm—decent jobs were available and going to work was often necessary to support oneself and the family. The postmodern world seemed to be more technical, more complicated, however, so more formal education seemed necessary. And, in truth, as years have gone by, many of those occupations that required a minimal academic skill-set, parking cars and pumping gas and the like (which nonetheless sometimes opened the gateway to apprenticeships), have disappeared under the never-sated gaze of a technically-driven information age. Even life on the farm or in the mine or on the fishing boat or along the pipeline now benefits from some form of higher education be it in business, or computers, or in clever electronic ways of moving manure or finding ore or fish or the leak in the line.

By 1984 Grade Thirteen was formally phased out in the Ontario Ministry of Education's curriculum—sort of! Remember, curriculum is always a matter of politics, not education. And so, behold the beautiful tango of politicians. In 1984 Grade Thirteen was replaced with … *Grade Thirteen*! One thinks of Swift's courtly rope dancers in *Gulliver's Travels*.

> When a great office is vacant, either by death or disgrace (which often happens) five or six of those candidates petition the emperor to entertain his majesty, and the court, with a dance on the rope, and whoever jumps the highest, without falling, succeeds in the office.

Grade Thirteen became a set of courses called OACs—Ontario Academic Credits—and these became the *new* fifth year of secondary school (at least, until 2003, when the OACs, too, finally had their rope cut). Something lost; something gained, perhaps! The politicians, of course, were reacting to pressures to eliminate the fifth year but also demands from parents, businesses, universities and school boards who were concerned that reducing time spent in high school would impact one or more of what have always been the four pillars of the educational temple:

One—Standards:
The OACs gave the illusion of higher academic requirements. The lament over declining standards is a perpetual theme in education, a dirge continually bemoaned by the general public and particularly bellowed out of colleges and universities, and yet, one factor—those institutions keep expanding. At the university where I taught, fewer than 10,000 students attended in 1970; now the enrolment is nearly 50,000. And at the community college where I worked, attendance in 1970 was 430 students; now it is nearly 4,000. And all colleges and universities in the province, save one or two, have expanded in like manner. In addition, by the millennium, the number of official degree-granting universities in Ontario had nearly doubled, from twelve to twenty-three, and now with "virtual" universities added to the mix, enrolment consumption continues a voracious devouring. Places of higher education have become businesses where the bottom-line rules—more students equals more income from tuition and grants and, thus, more profit. But, one asks, how fertile is the field of talent? These days, students with high school averages lower than 65% are being admitted to institutions of higher learning, and to achieve a high school average like that all you really need to do is show up in class every now and then and sneeze! And certainly the province's population has not kept

pace—around 8 million in 1970, it is currently about 13. And so, really, educational abilities have not declined as much as admittance standards have been lowered—to the point where most colleges and universities are forced to require incoming students to take courses in writing or communications or complete literacy tests to demonstrate their language proficiency. Some institutions of higher learning, I understand, now administer exhalation tests to see if all new admissions can still draw breath. In the U.S., entrance examinations (generally, the SATs) have been redesigned and universally made easier (often altered under the criticism that they were too culturally biased). Another associated fly in this academic ointment involves the cultural expectation in society-at-large that everyone has the right to a higher education and there is pressure from all concerned for higher marks and grade averages; consequently, the issue of grade inflation has arisen. When I graduated from a high school of a thousand students, only four or five had averages above 75%—they were designated Ontario Scholars and given a small grant; now over sixty percent of graduating students have those averages, and the Ontario Scholarship program is an acknowledgment only. And all is fueled by the competition to get into preferred places of higher education, accompanied by the pressure on and from high school Administrators to get their teaching Faculty to comply. Such grade inflation has also become a significant concern at the university level and the land of winkin', blinkin' and finger pointing prevails. In point of fact, educational skills (numeracy, literacy and the rest) have increased significantly in the last one hundred-plus years—about fifteen per cent of the Canadian population could read in 1900; that number is close to ninety per cent today. In that regard, at least, teachers have done a fine job!

Two—Curriculum:
Curriculum is typically a reflection of the society at the time of its making, always reflected through a glassy political template, and often modulating accordingly. In Ontario by the late 1960s, under the Hall-Dennis report—an inventive curriculum introducing courses in drama and film studies and a lot of options for students—education seemed driven by hippie-dippy flower power, the spirit of the time; that quickly changed in the general and specific outcomes and expectations outlined in documents issued by the 1990s under Mike Harris' right-wing common sense revolution and then rewritten again in the early Liberal

2000s and again by Ford's conservatives thereafter. And so, Ontario's curriculum has always seemed a boat caught in the winds of political flatulence, tossed by the currents of social correctness, whatever they may be from front to front. That colleges and universities complain that the students they receive do not seem to know this or that, more than anything else, probably reminds us that those institutions by their very nature are always behind the times, always wrestling with the vagaries of the past, dreaming up a future for which they are not responsible, and always slightly out-of-step with the present. And wonderfully so, as many professors would exclaim. (This reminds one of the old chain of blame: the profs complain about the secondary teachers, the secondary teacher complains about the elementary, the elementary about the parents, the parent about God, and God creates Mondays.)

Three—Behaviour:
Even in Plato's time, adults have complained about the behaviour of youth and its lack of discipline; in *The Republic* (c. 375 BCE) Plato attributes Socrates as saying:

> The children now love luxury; they have bad manners, contempt for authority; they show disrespect for elders and love gossip in place of exercise. Children are now tyrants, not the servants of their households. They no longer rise when elders enter the room. They contradict their parents, chatter before company, gobble up dainties at the table, cross their legs, and tyrannize their teachers.

Not behaving as adults expect, in fact, may be part of what being young is. Students and their behaviours and attitudes, and what is or is not permitted in school, are also a reflection of the culture—times change, and children are influenced by the changes they see and feel and hear. Gone are the stocks and the strap. In my time in high school, students were sent home if they tried to wear blue jeans to school, chewing gum was not allowed and you were admonished if you forgot to stand when answering a question. Later wearing a baseball hat, raising a hoodie or lugging a backpack to class were forbidden. Now vaping in class or the use of a cell phone have replaced those sins. Who knows what the issues of tomorrow will be? But most of these things are just surface noise. Dance the Charleston or the Fox Trot; boogie to the Twist or the Futsai Shuffle. Such dance moves or hip clothes really do not determine who you are? Most likely these things are but the transitory mirrors that reflect the attitudes and values and habits of the time through which you pass; like Alice, you come back through the looking-glass and find the living-room again. Hopefully, I suppose, some of the darker ideas may change permanently over generations (racism, sexism, and the like) but, it is a slow process (humans have been at it for about 40,000 years now) and, in some way, certain concerns never seem to go away. Humans are human. The magic of our technology is a momentary cosmetic. Deeper down, where we think things really matter, where the true human heart beats, students feel and think and hear. They'll work and learn. They'll twist a microscope (or manipulate its keyboard) and march to the social justice issue of the day and try to read Kant and understand what they can of Keats and that alluring urn with which he engages:

> When old age shall this generation waste,
> Thou shalt remain, in midst of other woe
> Than ours, a friend to man, to whom thou say'st,
> "Beauty is truth, truth beauty,—that is all
> Ye know on earth, and all ye need to know."

—John Keats "Ode on a Grecian Urn" 1819

Today's students, by and large, are good people—not better or smarter or kinder than those who came before, but no worse either. Unless, of course, we envision some apocalyptic change to be at hand.

Four—Costs:

And the fourth pillar, the cost of education. Financial costs in education always soar. Education is a people business—a lot of money will always be absorbed in salaries and benefits and student means and milieu. Buildings age and teaching materials will always need renewal. As an extreme example, between 1962 and 1971, spending on education in Ontario inflated by 462%. Today, the lure of shiny technology is the apple in the garden; its sweet taste never hints of the plagues and hurricanoes to come. Software to drive the machine will cost a great deal more than the machine itself. Memory is replaced with slate is replaced with chalkboard is replaced with notebook is replaced with laptop and tablet and cortical implant and who knows what *AI* lies ahead? And what's true today of the soaring cost of education will be true in a hundred years, and a thousand! Wait 'til the taxpayer sees the bill for that first school on Mars!

A last word or two about Grade Thirteen. For many years (certainly when I was a student), it was more or less unfunded; that is, students had to buy their own textbooks. And while this seems like a curious thing today, even bad, it actually enabled Departments in schools to be very creative in designing their courses, especially, in Ontario, after the discontinuation of the province-wide exam in 1967. BCI had a new English Department Head, and under Mr. Richardson's guidance the English program was as creative and challenging as imagination allowed. It was this English program at BCI that propelled me into a world from which I have never escaped, nor ever wanted to.

To this day, I recall many of the texts we purchased for and read in Grade Thirteen English and, compared to what I have seen in schools since, I am still awed by the depth, breadth and exigent nature of those choices—we read authors like Kafka and Ellison and Ibsen which might challenge students in university graduate courses let alone high school. And so, I suppose, we read and understood what we could. In general, in that pre-semester world, we typically studied a novel and a play or two in each of the three terms—we covered a lot of territory. By comparison, in a modern-day semestered school, while the daily time in class has been doubled, the breadth in curriculum has been lost—a class that used to spend four weeks or so studying a play like *King Lear* (about 7 or 8% of the year), still requires that in *real* time to allow the play to *sink-in* (now, in semestering, that's about 20% of the year). And so quantity is lost, true in English as it has been across all grades and subjects. And continuity, where students might take a course in first semester one year but not until second semester a full year later, can be lost, too, especially in subjects like Music or French for which such close connectiveness seems most important.

For what it is worth, some of the books we read and studied (and purchased ourselves) in Grade Thirteen English included:

King Lear (Shakespeare)
The Wild Duck (Ibsen)
The Beaux' Stratagem (Farquhar)
Death of a Salesman (Miller)
The Glass Menagerie (Williams)
Invisible Man (Ellison)
The Sun Also Rises (Hemingway)
The Winter of Our Discontent (Steinbeck)
The Metamorphosis (Kafka)

What a reading list! Our poetry anthologies were also remarkable and included *20th Century Poetry and Poetics* (ed. Gary Geddes) and *The Blue Guitar* (eds. Rutledge/Bassett)—I still have the copy given to me by Al Revill, with his signature and phone number in it (962-3287—if you want to give him a call in 1969). So, we read a large variety of Modern poems and poets, often having to memorize pieces—I still recall bits and pieces of "Spring and Fall" and "The Average" and "A Subaltern's Love Song" and "Anthem for Doomed Youth" and "Futility" among others. And we read samplings of Frost, Stevens, Thomas, Purdy, Nowlan, Layton, Auden, Birney, Cohen, Klein, Sandburg, Souster, Yeats and more, with Canadian writers getting their due.

In particular, I remember Hemingway's *The Sun Also Rises*, initially thinking, what a stupid book, about a bunch of people who party in Paris all year except to take two weeks off to party in Spain and … and then it hit me like that proverbial *fifth glass of Manzanilla* might! Exactly…that's exactly what Hemingway was saying about these people, about this post-war life. Lost. Impotent. Wasted, partly because of themselves, partly because of the way of their world, because of the first Great War. The War! The bull fighting ring! Death as a spectator sport. The numbing of alcohol. The carnival. The physical disability. The lost generation … the only state in which the true hero can exist—a world that has no heroes, no meaning, no love. As emasculated Jake Barnes succinctly replies to Brett when she contemplates what a "damned good time" they could have had together: "'Yes,' I said, 'Isn't it pretty to think so'." Although he has currently drifted out of fashion, I read most of Hemingway in the years after that and came to admire the stark way he lived the world and saw it, his style and his stories. He was really the first writer I came to know and who had a significant influence on me. Right next to Al Purdy, of course—formidable writers, each of whom adopted a unique style both in the words they wrote and in the lives they lead.

And so, Grade Thirteen and high school ended. I was an Ontario Scholar and Valedictorian of my class (see Addendum) and moved on to Queen's University, the first ever in my family to do so, and where none of any of that really mattered. And Grade Thirteen, itself, like the fate of all things, I suppose, has now become but a faded memory. There is no doubt that the fifth year of high school produced a student who was a little better prepared to handle university or college both in terms of maturation and in academic acumen—in that era, by graduation many students had, not the minimum of thirty, but thirty-five or more high school credits. But, Grade Thirteen was also a year that held many back—few are the individuals that did not feel more than ready to get out of high school by the middle of that fifth year (when semestering arrived, many did leave after four-and-a-half years, often finding jobs to help supplement the cost of higher education). And, when Grade Thirteen finally disappeared as the millennium turned, the fear of a double cohort overwhelming institutions of higher learning in Ontario never materialized nor was there any great sense of distress or rates of failure among the students who moved on, one year younger (and yes, we had some sixteen-year-olds in first year university), but by and large, like those who came before, those students conquered their first year or, at least, weathered and endured the challenge. That old wisdom of *Ecclesiastes*, passed along by Hemingway, endures:

> One generation passeth away, and another generation cometh; but the earth abideth forever... The sun also ariseth, and the sun goeth down, and hasteth to the place where he arose... All the rivers run into the sea; yet the sea is not full; unto the place from whence the rivers come thither they return again.

ADDENDUM:

Valedictory Address

This is the Valedictory Address that I gave in late October, 1970—a time when issues of Canadian identity and nationalism and separatism were all in the air; when pollution and the gender gap and China entering the U.N. and the hippie lifestyle were often topics for discussion and debate. While I was tempted toward revision in retyping this, I resisted and present the text exactly as I gave it in my youth and naiveté all those years ago—it was also written during the new, hectic weeks of university. It was well received (perhaps all such speeches are—I recall Jim Bateman, another first year student from BCI, coming to my dorm room for a preview and giving it a big thumb's up) and, while I suppose it seemed insightful, even visionary, to me in its time, now it reads like the conventional blueprint that so many of these speeches must have adopted. So it goes, I guess, as Mr. Vonnegut would say. At the very least, many thanks to Mr. Buckley for somehow preserving the only copy and passing it back to me at BCI's fiftieth anniversary.

Mr. McKay, honoured guests, staff, fellow graduates, ladies and gentlemen:

This evening for the graduating students is a night of reflection. A night of remembrance. A night, perhaps, of sadness. A night which for many of us will be our last time in BCI. For five now seemingly short years, we got up early in the morning, some of us having to catch those motorized refrigerators they call school buses, others having to walk several blocks in the freezing snow, still others just crossing the street in order to make that nine o'clock bell. And then there were the assignments, the tests, the exams, and of course the marks and the report cards. But, as well—if those weren't—there were many good times and many accomplishments during our days. The Renaissance of the Assembly, the rehabilitation of the Honour System, Reformation of Student Government, a scoreboard for our good old gym, and perhaps even some deodorant for the football change rooms. No, we don't claim sole credit for all of these but we helped. Yes, to re-formulate a slogan which has often been used and which, I think, effectively qualifies itself in this case: "To us, BCI is not just a school, it's an institution," an institution in the technical sense of being an organised society dedicated to the promotion of a worthwhile goal. It has been for us in the last one-twentieth of a century a *way of life*, if you will, a torch of solicitude. And this torch we have grasped hard and held high with pride for, in most cases, five now seemingly short years. And we are gathered here tonight in the presence of emblematic diplomas and red, black and heliotrope streamers to let this torch, which in the last four months has been lowered, to let this torch slip from our grasp. From earth to earth, from dust to dust, from kindergarten and public school to life beyond graduation.

And so we are here, many of us in BCI for the last time. But look about you. Tonight the old walls of the Collegiate are seemingly brighter than they've been before. The gyms are gaily decorated. The costumes of the graduates are radiant. The staff is gaily decorated. And there seems to be an aura of happiness, of joy dominant, and perhaps some melancholy, too. But mostly, this seems a festive occasion and in thinking about it, well it should be. A poem might well illustrate the point. The style is trite, the title non-existent, but the theme apropos:

> the sun shining brightly in the april dawn
> awakening the dew on the sweet sweet lawn
> and youth slowly rises from its playful bed
> honey bees swarm the tulips red
> —o we laugh to see that youth is so
> think not of the advancing snow
> as knowledge with its green-gold wings
> replaces fancy with more concrete things
> and shining hair spins to silvery grey
> wisdom—what a costly price to pay
> cold grows the dew as youth is gone
> for others now the april dawn
> —laughter rises above the dead
> and none remember the tulip red

But, we'll never forget the tulip red, symbolic of our youth, of that which we learned in youth. And for the graduates, that pragmatic picture presents itself to us in the esteemed shape of a four-story institution on John Street. And so, we cannot be overly saddened tonight because, you see, we'll never really leave BCI. BCI has been the focal point of our youth, a stage of life, of growth toward maturity, so vital in so many ways. A great deal of what we do from now on as we age and adapt our knowledge toward understanding will reflect the imprint that this institution has made on our lives.

And what memories there have been in the last five years and what years they have been. The 1970 graduates, more perhaps than any who have come before, have lived in an age of change, an age of experiment, both in education and in experience. We leave this school at the threshold of a new decade with many still pondering and perhaps rethinking the last. When we first arrived on the scene in the peach fuzz days of Grade 9 and began to stack our first lockers, the educational system was based on the final provincial exams, girls' dresses were just an inch or so above the knee, and perhaps on a more serious side, Vietnam was still just an obscure confrontation somewhere in Asia, ideologies were something that only someone like Karl Marx had any time for and, of course, a trip was something that you took in your father's automobile. But in the short span of a demi-decade how things have changed. Final exams have all but succumbed to the seductive promises of progress. Inflation, pollution and female fashions have all skyrocketed. And perhaps here we should give a moment of remembrance for those casualties lost in the line of youth, cut down by the narcotics of mind and of body. But I am not sure if society really has time to mourn those lost souls, nor, in fact, if it really wants to. To those dropouts of society into illusion perhaps we recall only the stark words which Lucifer gave to the miscalculating Dr. Faustus: "What weepest thou? 'Tis too late. Despair farewell! Fools that will laugh on earth must weep in hell." Or should they be forgiven, for they knew not what they did? Be their colour black, red, white, or French, the choice may be ours to make and the consequences, well, surely they will impact only individuals and nations.

So, from this era of rapid change, of milk in plastic bags, of internal and external wars, of loss and separatism, we have graduated.

Or perhaps as the Hemingway character says, "Isn't it pretty to think so?"

Through these years, BCI has stood, not always winning all its games, not always passing all its flock, but always remaining as a guiding force to its youth. But don't take my metaphor incorrectly. I'm not really portraying the Collegiate as a beacon of solidarity or a staunch lighthouse, although in practise it has guided its souls, with success, around and through the oft-times "choppy" channels of education. The problems of mathematics, the intricacies of physics, the misdirections of society have all been confronted and, although not all solved, at least outmanoeuvred in our time. And as tradition or perhaps heritage demands, so they will be tackled in the future.

The future. That is what now remains to us, the graduates. Some will become doctors, others patients. Some will become lawyers, others lawbreakers. Some might build the world anew, others try to create anarchy. True, all of BCI's products will not reach that earthly material heaven which we call success. But whether we liked all of the process or not, we've been given an equal shot at it. An equal start, a lot more than many others in the world can claim.

In this future, many of the graduates here will forget each other, will forget teachers' names and faces. Some will forget how to find the asymptotes of a hyperbola, others won't be able to recall Romeo's last name. Many won't remember either of these. But *none* will forget the path that led them to their positions, be it one of satin and sapphire or of sand and solitude, and *none* should forget the true lessons learned. The Collegiate, its essence located somewhere in a democratic past, representative, I suppose, of our general educational processes, provided and enforced the primary lessons, supplied and applied its vitality into a universe of minds yearning for illimitable hopes and promises.

This product has been freed to think and to live as this night it steps forever forth from BCI.

And so tonight is really just a start. A germination. The bulb of that 'tulip red' has been planted and watered and has begun to sprout. BCI is saying farewell, but we cannot bear to repay the compliments. For BCI, its traditions, its spirit, its knowledge, its soul have been instilled in us and will forever remain with us whether we realize it or not. The future will reflect the past. One contains the other. There can be no end without a beginning. Whatever we do or accomplish, part of that success will belong right here. And so tonight we are not really saying goodbye to an old school, we are just saying hello, and welcome, to a new future. A continuation of the path. We are not losing an old institution; we are just gaining a new world.

My fellow Canadians. Thank you very much!

28
Writing Backward

The Imagination then I consider either as primary, or secondary. The primary Imagination I hold to be the living Power and prime Agent of all human Perception, and as a repetition in the finite mind of the eternal act of creation in the infinite I Am. The secondary I consider as an echo of the former, co-existing with the conscious will, yet still as identical with the primary in the kind of its agency, and differing only in degree, and in the mode of its operation. It dissolves, diffuses, dissipates, in order to re-create; or where this process is rendered impossible, yet still at all events it struggles to idealize and to unify. It is essentially vital, even as all objects (as objects) are essentially fixed and dead.

—Samuel Taylor Coleridge *Biographia Literaria* Ch. 13

I was once fortunate enough to hear James Britton speak at a conference; while he was a very old man by that point and had left his notes on the plane (the lecture he gave was a bit on the erratic side), Britton exists as one of the most influential scholars in contemporary educational history. Spending most of his career as Reader in Education and Goldsmiths Professor at the University of London's *Institute of Education*, he was a member of the Bullock Committee which produced the influential report "A Language for Life." Britton published his principal theories in *Language and Learning* (1970); *Prospect and Retrospect*, a selection of his essays, offers a cogent sampling and is still widely read.

Essentially, in these publications, Britton proposed the personal growth model of education, which to this day is probably the single most dominant paradigm in the contemporary classroom. Like writing rough drafts or stretching to warm-up for some sporting activity or using a Bunsen burner, or the presence of a TV screen in our home, it is so pervasive we are almost unaware of its presence. It was popularized, for the most part, from the famous Dartmouth Conference in 1966 which was a combined British and American language/teaching conference where James Britton's ideas were widely introduced and then disseminated through books such as John Dixon's *Growth Through English* (1967) and H. J. Muller's *The Uses of English* (1967). Until that time, the Modernist way of thinking had dominated, with its focus on canon, on content, and through a language instruction that focused on a grammatical discourse, teaching students about the mechanical form and the presumed correctness of language, essentially laying a Latinate structure over English, whether it fit or not (you know, the issue of 'split infinitives" and "dangling prepositions" and the like). Britton, on the other hand, emphasized student growth and imaged the classroom, predominantly, as a place where language is used as much as it is taught, and where students were more important than the subject being taught. Britton's theory of *language categories* lies at the heart of this paradigm. According to Britton, language has certain generic functions or roles:

> A – *The participant function*: "As participants in the events of the world we use language instrumentally to get things done..." Language enables us, it is participatory, experiential. We order a coffee and a doughnut or say "excuse me" if we bump into someone or we ask an employee at a gas station which direction to get to some destination.
>
> B – *The spectator function*: "On the other hand, in a contemplative mood, we reflect on the meaning and significance of these activities, thus assuming the role of spectator. We use language in this way to generate and refine our value systems and characteristically what we create are the stories of the events of our lives..." Language allows us to reflect on our experience, to sort out ourselves, to engage in moral imperatives. Britton

says: "… looking back, our representation is a storehouse of past experiences, selective of course, not total. But looking forward, that same storehouse is a body of expectations as to what may happen." In this manner we construct and reconstruct the process of our lives.

I included the quotation from Coleridge's *Biographia Literaria* above because, in so many ways, Britton's theory reminds one of Coleridge's distinction between the Primary and the Secondary Imagination, what we perceive in the Primary becomes dissolved, diffused and dissipated in the Secondary to recreate the world, to explain, to idealize, to unify the experiences of living, to make sense of what we sense. For Coleridge and the other Romantics, it was a stab at accounting for the wellspring of the poetic process, itself, those "caverns measureless to man" that Coleridge describes in "Kubla Khan" or that which Shelley tries to animate in his famous analogy of the "fading coal" in *A Defense of Poetry*:

> The mind in creation is as a fading coal, which some invisible influence, like an inconstant wind, awakens to transitory brightness; this power arises from within like the colour of a flower which fades and changes as it is developed and the conscious portions of our natures are unprophetic either of its approach or its departure. Could this influence be durable in its original purity and force, it is impossible to predict the greatness of the result; but when composition begins, inspiration is already on the decline; and the most glorious poetry that has been communicated to the world is probably a feeble shadow of the original conceptions of the Poet.

Britton seems quite Romantic in his theorizing, then, imagining a way in which the veil of the world can be torn open for our students, by our students. For such revelation begins and ends with the hearts and souls of our students themselves, not in learning about dangling participles or split infinitives or something else.

From his critical distinction in language between participant and spectator, Britton extrapolated three modes of written language:

1 – *Transactional language* correlates to the participant function. It is the form of language that enables us in daily life, that we use in essays, in instructions, in directions, in editorials, in arguments, in writing that gets graded.

2 – *Poetic language* correlates to the spectator function of language. This is the reflective form of language one finds in literary artforms, in litspeak and artspeak, in plays and poems and fiction.

3 – *Expressive language* is neither exactly transactional nor poetic, but can be a starting point for either. It is the casual, colloquial, personal, self-expressive form of language that constitutes most of our utterances from day to day. It is the formative, "gut" level of language, casual talk, conversation, "writing at the point of utterance." It is the kind of utterance that, today, generally fills X and Facebook and Instagram and all the other social media sites.

From his experience in teaching and in visiting classrooms, Britton argued that he found in the teaching of writing a great deal of transactional writing being taught, and used, and evaluated, with little poetic and almost no expressive. Schools in general, and colleges and universities, in particular, are dark satanic essay mills. Most of us understand and have experienced this—in academia, probably from Grade Six or Seven on to wherever our classroom days ended, writing the essay or the lab report or the argument or the analysis or the article dominated. And, of course, arguments in favour of being skilled in such transactional writing can be made. Very few professors of Law or Physics or Surgery will ask students to write a poem about their findings or experiments, and with reason! (And you probably do not want the Poet-Surgeon hovering over you (like some fluttering daffodil) in the operating room.) But Britton argued, in earlier education, especially, the lack of expressive writing meant that children could not develop the base of "fluency" they required for ease and achievement in learning how to write; and personal growth also stalled. In other words, Britton argued, schools were teaching language and writing skills *backward*. To achieve fluency in writing, and confidence in self, in social and emotional being, one needs to begin with natural expressive writing, and lots of it, before one moves on to poetic and/or transactional. And so, allowances were needed to make room for much more expressive language and personal growth in classrooms. And Britton's ideas caught on. From the 1970s forward, Britton's views changed the fundamental educational philosophy that underpinned the teaching of language and writing, and of education broadly. Out of his ideas, like foam on the high tide, came the birth of the "student centred classroom" and "writing as process" and "the journal." The real agenda of a classroom should be children's language; literature for Britton represents "just another voice" and needed to be de-emphasized; the key is to get kids "languaging." Britton, by the way, was the first to use such terms as "collaborative," "facilitator," and "student talk." And his philosophy always emphasized the importance of process, not product. In rather quick succession by the 1970s and 1980s, Britton's ideas on writing were picked up and extended by the Process Approach theorists (people such as Nancie Atwell and Donald Graves) and developed into the writing process model which, for better and worse, became quite institutionalized (see Chapter Thirty).

Beyond Britton's specific language theory, his broader philosophical stance had far-reaching influence. The Personal Growth Model placed the needs, experiences, and language of the individual child at the centre of the classroom, at the centre of education. Britton says: "In English class pupils meet to share their encounters with life" and such became true of almost all classrooms. At this writing, Teachers and Administrators and Boards of Education everywhere seem to express essentially these same sentiments, often in catchy slogan-form: *Every Child Matters*; *Success for Every Student*; *Student Centred/Learning Centred*; *Our Students, Our Future*; *No Child left Behind*; *Every Student, Every Day—A Success*; *Every Student Learns in His or Her Own Way*; and so on. The new school classroom is egalitarian, collaborative, user-friendly, intensely language producing, full of varied individual activities, authentic (whatever that can mean in an institutional setting), with the teacher often taking on the role of a "facilitator" of learning, a "mentor," a "coach." Especially in the elementary grades, the focus is on children's talk, children's activities, on journals, on process versus product, on group learning and on collaborative discussion within those groups. And all of this can be traced back to James Britton.

As an aside, coincidentally, the arrival and accession of Britton's philosophies aligned perfectly with the emergence of a post-war, postmodern western culture that canonized the existence of childhood, in daily practice and in legislation. In fact, Britton may have helped create a kind of childocracy in which children are held sacred in our society, morally and legally, worshipped and pampered without question from soccer field and hockey leagues to the *Conventions* of UNICEF and Canada's *Coalition on the Rights of the Child.* While one acknowledges the positively enlightened ethos this has created, one also understands the dark spirit of entitlement born of this shift.

Whatever one thinks about the sanctification of children, this *Britton invasion* certainly brought a beneficial breath of fresh air to the classroom, opening up subject matters and making children more active participants in their own educational journeys, giving them a greater ownership of and, presumably, interest in their learning than ever before. Are there some misgivings—of course, there always are! Some fear that the philosophy has been driven too far so that the passengers are now steering the bus, that there is an overemphasis on the child's own language at the expense of literature, discipline, and the requirement to learn some basic content deemed important. Children choose what they want to study, to read, and given such choices, the child may never choose literature, for example, or science, or math. And even then, for traditionalists, the idea that a canonized literary work has no more credibility in the classroom than a piece of student writing is difficult to accept. The idea of all students in a class studying a single core text has started to fade away. In general, the Britton approach often ignores questions of merit or value—the activity undertaken by the student is all that counts and, sometimes, it does not seem to matter what is being done. Senior high school students make posters of *King Lear* or read the romance fiction of Danielle Steel and Stephen King—is that demanding enough? And, along those lines, for teachers, many feel that a loss of identity has occurred—the exact role of the teacher is now one of ambivalence, at best. Facilitator, mentor, coach, guide, bystander—who knows? As psychologist A. Lloyd Brown says:

> There seems to be then a coming down on the side of response to the subject rather than knowledge of it, enjoyment and playfulness rather than discipline, the individual rather than the subject, the teacher as guide rather than authority. Must we choose these polarities.

Language theory may be oversimplified in Britton's approach along with an overemphasis on individual goals at the expense of a social or cultural context; the individual decides his/her directions and the rest be damned. At this writing, the phrase *Every Child Matters* seems to be everywhere as if a pandemonium of parrots had escaped their cages. But, conceptually, what does that phrase mean especially in a democratic educational context where (especially in Canada) individual rights are subsumed by the collective, where *other* children matter, too? And besides, for teachers, adopting such a philosophy is surely an impossible quest, a tilting at windmills that is destined to end in failure. Is that what any effective teacher wants? It reminds me of the fallacy inherent in the idea of *student-centred learning*. Should learning be *student-centred*? Is any education that is *student-* or *self-centred* much of an edification? I know, if my own learning were simply *Way-centred*, it would not be much of an education at all. Perhaps *student-active* would be a better phrase. And, perhaps, treading wisely around all such pop-phrases would be the best policy. And for the grammarians, if such rough beasts still exist in this postlapsarian Brittopia, the unending volume of writing done surely tends to enforce and re-enforce many irregularities—or as students might write, *it's volume alone tends to surely enforce alot of iregularities.*

But, in spite of the questions and concerns and the quibbles we express, as one gazes across the landscapes of education today, it is difficult not to see and be impressed with how deeply ingrained James Britton's thinking has become. His ideas have truly changed the idea of what school means. As he wrote: "We can no longer regard school learning as simply an interim phase, a period of instruction and apprenticeship that marks the change from immaturity to maturity, from play in the nursery to work in the world. School learning must both build upon the learning of infancy and foster something that will continue and evolve throughout adult life. School is not a place we go; it is the place we are." Now, learning is forever.

29

University One

Queen's College colours we are wearing once again,
Soiled as they are by the battle and the rain,
Yet another victory to wipe away the stain!
So, (~~boys~~) Gaels, go in and win!

> Oil thigh na Banrighinn a'Banrighinn gu brath!
> [*tiddley*] Oil thigh na Banrighinn a'Banrighinn gu brath!
> [*tiddley*] Oil thigh na Banrighinn a'Banrighinn gu brath!
> Cha-gheill! Cha-gheill! Cha-gheill!

—Alfred Lavell "Queen's College Colours" 1898

On the first weekend of fall, before my classes begin, I leave Brockington House Residence just after supper and meander across campus, an activity that I would do illimitable times in my years at Queen's University. Lower Campus is a recreation field, an expanse of rich green on the southeast border of the campus just across from Kingston General, the university's huge teaching hospital; to its far east across a driveway the field is an extension of the lawn of Somerset House, the President's gentile residence. This is before the time when a grey-cement parking garage would be burrowed beneath this emerald field. I stop to watch three older (upper-year, I presume) students tossing a football back and forth, casually enjoying their time away from their studies, whatever those may have been. The brown spheroid spirals through the early fall air and is softly snagged in one of the young men's outstretched hands. And perhaps I had stood watching for too long, or perhaps I appeared to be a lost and lonely fledgling (which I probably was), I don't know, but the fellow who had just caught the ball looked toward me: "Want to join us?" I nodded and he eased a pass my way. And I spent the next ten or fifteen minutes lightly tossing the ball back and forth among these strangers. Each of them could throw the ball well, and jog to catch a wayward toss, and so could I. We never exchanged names nor did I ever encounter these three spirits on the green again. They vanished like the weird sisters on the heath save from my memory where they have long resided. Somehow, more than anything else, the magic spiral of that football through the early September air prepared me for the world of books and ideas into which I was about to be submerged. And the kindness of strangers, too, on which old Blanche always relied, is a thing I recall and which I have always marveled at and treasured. Somehow, all of the orientation shenanigans aside, this was the most convivial invitation university could provide.

I chose to go to Queen's. Why … well, they accepted me! That's one. I suppose, so did the University of Toronto and York, but Queen's University was closer (about a hundred kilometres from home) and I had a brother (Robert) living in Kingston so, every now and then, a free ride back home to a decent meal. I also know that Mr. Mott, the Head Guidance counselor at BCI, was a Queen's grad and tried to get all of the good students to choose Queen's. I don't think he influenced me too much—everyone knew about his bias, anyway, and all of the good students knew enough just to nod and then make whatever independent choice they wanted.

Queen's was then and is still known for its stellar academics, also as a *beer and football* school; it is one of the oldest and most established universities in Canada, and one of the few recognized internationally. With most of its core buildings constructed in the Collegiate Gothic Revival style, a durable grey limestone that sang of authority and solidity (and often matched the foggy greyness of small-town Kingston), it was an institution very aware of its own high scholarly standards and was determined to maintain that reputation by giving most students very low marks, especially in the Arts. High school averages generally dropped fifteen to twenty percent in first year. I was fortunate in that I was the first person in my family ever to attend college or university and my family had no zealous expectations for me. My father's ancestors were Loyalists who had come north from revolution-bound America to settle in Prince Edward County in the 1790s, farmers and mill-builders, Quakers and Puritans. The great-grandparents of my mother (Kathleen Winnifred Gaffney) came direct to Canada from the blight-ravaged potato fields of Ireland during the famines of the nineteenth century— they were lured to Canada for some free dirt, property along the infamous Opeongo trail near Bancroft (the land was free, but it was also swampy, rocky and often quite useless, those details left out of the advertisements that enticed settlers to Canada's near north. As to my decision to study at Queen's, being the first soul in my family to venture beyond high school, my parents simply told me to do the best that I could, and I realize, in retrospect, that was the best thing any parent ever could do. I saw many students swelter under the pressure of university, much of it the result of the burden from home; either intrinsic or extrinsic, pressure was pressure. And Queen's always seemed ready to remind you it was Queen's. That's why the readings and work-load and assignments were difficult; that's why high marks were hard to achieve. I suppose it's also why the reputation was high. But there was a toll—in my couple of years in residence, alone, I saw at least two suicide attempts rushed off by ambulance, another restrained and taken away by mental health officials. And many students never returned for year two, and more simply drifted away in some self-induced purple haze. My parents, to my recollection, never said a word about my marks.

The first week at Queen's was Orientation; Frosh Week as it was more commonly called. The abusive practice of hazing had been eliminated in the Arts (and Queen's banned fraternities and sororities) so the first week was a fairly civilized, calm affair (although I did see several first-year Engineers forced to stand on cafeteria tables, turn in circles and say the word "lighthouse" over and over, and I saw some pushing jelly beans with their noses along sidewalks—and those were probably just the more visible of undertakings). The Arts and Science students were divided into "Gael groups" of fifteen to twenty students—I recall one of our two leaders was Peter Raymont who went on to have a noted film career in Canada (just recently I viewed a CBC/doc he produced/directed on Margaret Atwood); appropriately one of our activities that week was previewing a new Canadian release, Don Shebib's *Goin' Down the Road*, still a gritty, lyrical film that I admire (a 2011 sequel is equally poignant). I do remember, by the end of the week, Peter carrying around the prettiest female in our group on his shoulders—ahh, the perks of leadership, I guess. And I remember *The Rose*. At the start of the week, posters went up all over campus advertising *La Rose*, the first showing in Canada of a risqué, avant-garde French film, some rumored that it had been smuggled into the country past customs, and that, even in France, some cinemas that had dared to show it were closed by the gendarmes, and it was free to all first-year students—just show proof at the door. So, Wednesday evening, Dunning Hall is packed with about 400 Frosh, standing room only. There is a palpable sense of excitement in the crowd. And as the large red curtain on stage begins to open, the auditorium slowly darkens and a spotlight shines down directly on the stage revealing … a rose in a flower pot. And that's it. Lights come up; *The Rose* is over. As I recall, the audience is slightly miffed but mostly amused; we understand the joke and it is us. A well-managed set-up for an albeit flowery punch-line. And it's still early and the pubs are open. I also recall watching the Greased Pole climb by the first year Engineers (beyond description, that unctuous composition in the pit beneath the pole) and riding the ferry over to Wolfe's Island to a drunken party and going to the football game on Saturday at the original Richardson Stadium, surrounded by its beautiful oval wall of limestone. Beyond that, a few hamburgers and a few beers, not much else—I was far more interested in starting classes, to see what they were all about, than I was immured by the manufactured antics of this week. That said, I volunteered and was accepted as a Gael Group leader for the next year, and became one of the leaders of Gael Group Four, *Cha-gheill! Cha-gheill! Cha-gheill!*

Enrolled in Arts and Sciences, I took the courses that I was most interested in from my high school experience. I felt certain that one of those would be my major, or maybe I'd do a double major. Becoming a lawyer was always a possibility. Beyond that, I took courses that I was curious about: English, History, Philosophy, Geography and Political Science—all were full-year courses; half-year courses had yet to be instituted, at least not at Queen's. Political Science turned out to be more science than politics; I seemed to learn more about theoretical politics (Marxism and Fascism, and the like) in History. All I really remember about Poly-sci—a couple years later, I did meet the Australian man who was my first-year T. A. on the stairs in Weldon Library. He had been a pleasant teacher and, somehow, he remembered me, probably more than I did him, and happily shook my hand and told me that he had just passed his Ph.D. dissertation. Relief and joy were all over him, and it was only a moment I understood, years later, when I had the same experience—years of intense research and study suddenly rolling away like Sisyphus's stone. He was returning Down-Under with the highest academic accolade possible and I only hope that the career that followed was a fertile one. Parts of Geography were interesting; it was divided among Physical, Urban and Economic, each third taught by a different professor. I enjoyed the Physical studies, which even included lectures on dinosaurs, and the Urban was ok, with anthropological insights into human evolution but the Economic was very *Mathy*, dry calculations and computations, charts and graphs, and the like. As part of the Urban, we were paired up and sent out with surveys. The Prof was trying to collect information about the concept of community, the idea of social distance, a city's regional divisions and individuals' sense of private space. My partner was an attractive blonde woman and we had fun gathering information until a woman opened her door and, while we were explaining the questionnaire, her cat came at us like a rabid bowling ball, escaping into the streets of Kingston. We looked for a while but to no avail—that cat was lost. In all likelihood, it had its own sense of community and decided to prove it and, I reasoned, when it became hungry enough, it would probably seek out its own private space again (unless it didn't survive the perils of the streets, of course). We did not include it as some sort of *felis silvestrus catus* data-entry in the survey. Philosophy was a different cat. My professor was Peter White—he was on sabbatical from the University of Toronto and, for reasons all his own, had decided to teach for the year at Queen's. All year, he never wore an overcoat, even on the most wintery of days, a philosophical thing, I guessed. And we spent the first three months or so of the year dissecting the first two pages (yes, three months, two pages!) of A. D. Woozley's *Theory of Knowledge: An Introduction*. We seemed to cover the book word by word, comma by comma. And I am still not sure what the hell the professor was getting at, and that may be epistemology, I guess. I do remember that the Teaching Assistant sat in on all the classes; he was a young Grad student and about the only one to ask questions and he managed to get into several very long and complicated epistemo-logical (I think) arguments with Professor White. One day, I recall him challenging the professor and saying: "All right. I am a bear. Prove to me that I am not a bear." Next week, when we returned to class, we discovered that the Teaching Assistant had been fired and we never saw him again. To this day, I can only assume that somewhere, lumbering around Queen's campus and Kingston at large, a very philosophical bear remains continually perplexed at the answer he received. Perhaps that, too, is epistemology.

History 121—the intellectual history of the western world. The History course for those who might want to major in the subject (the alternative first year course was a study of revolutions). History 121 had to be one of the most notorious history courses in the history of History courses! We read everything from Plato and Augustine to Machiavelli and Marx, including the day's morning newspaper, I think, all original writings. It was not the History of High School! And while, in retrospect, it was a remarkable course that covered incredible materials highlighting the thinking beneath all the battles and beheadings and musings of the western world, it often required three to five hundred pages of readings per week, all dense original texts. It was as heavy a course as courses get, at least at that year and level. Most of us struggled just to get the reading completed let alone understand what we were reading—Kant and Hegel and Comte and Voltaire and Rousseau, and the rest! And in the class there was a long-haired dude who wore John Lennon glasses and smoked a pipe—yes, in this era people, including professors, still smoked pipes and cigarettes everywhere—we often sat under a smoky haze in classrooms, but that was normal, we knew no different. (Department socials were actually called 'Smokers'.) Anyway, whenever the History professor asked a question, this long-haired dude would lean back, take a puff on his pipe and slowly respond in an erudite scholarly manner, usually making reference not only to the reading we'd been assigned but to a half dozen other works that the author in question had written. Among other things, I came to realize that in the high noon streets of university, there is always a faster gun. So, this pipe smoking student in first-year History was always a wonder to behold; either that or, I figured, maybe he had flunked the course innumerable times and came to his knowledge through having to reread everything over and over. Any way you cut it, it was a helluva course.

The first-year English course was taught by Professor Susan Dick, a kind and capable educator, albeit formal in her approach, always addressing us with the prefix-titles Miss or Mr. As with History, the English course is something entirely different from anything High School ever offered, using a two-volume Norton Anthology, a linear historical survey of English literature from the Medieval to Modern, from the Gawain-poet and Chaucer to T. S. Eliot and Dylan Thomas. Some of the material is difficult but most of it is magical and my fate becomes sealed as an English Major-to-be, and whatever will follow that. *Cha-gheill! Cha-gheill! Cha-gheill!*, indeed.

At the end of first year, we receive the Queen's yearbook, *The Tricolor* (red for Arts and Science, gold for Engineering, Blue for Medicine—a purplish blend for Commerce has just arrived but the yearbook remains the *Tricolor*). Over fifty years later I still have my copy and glance through it as I write this. See all the long straight hair held with beaded or leather headbands, the exaggerated bell-bottoms and short skirts, decorated with stylistically flowered embroidery, the first-year tams and long tri-colour scarves, the shiny-new leather jackets, scruffy beards and young faces. O yes ... how fresh those photos are, how young all of us look, and how old we thought we were.

30
The Process of Process

Show up, show up, show up, and after a while the muse shows up, too.

—Isabel Allende *Why We Write*

Writing is hard for every last one of us... Coal mining is harder. Do you think miners stand around all day talking about how hard it is to mine for coal? They do not. They simply dig.

—Cheryl Strayed "Faith, Humility, and the Art of Motherfuckitude"

The idea and classroom practice of 'writing process' swept through education from the 1980s on. Affixed to a postmodern sensibility, this approach closely aligned with Britton's Personal Growth model, focussing heavily on the "expressive" mode of writing. Wherever it was effectively used, process writing generally provided a sense of freshness to classrooms. **In traditional teaching**, some stimulus would have been provided, often in the form of a composition topic or a lit-crit question (see the samples provided in Chapter Twenty-four); then the students would write for a timed period, perhaps edit their work if time and inclination allowed, and submit the writing for teacher evaluation. **In the process approach** (call it postmodern constructivism if you wish) some prewriting activities take place usually motivated by a teacher-suggestion or provocation, generally under the label of brainstorming (often the random jotting down of ideas and/or discussion with classmates); then organizing or clustering (connecting similar themes and ideas); then a rough draft is written; then revision (more conferencing with peers and/or teacher, more drafts, editing); and, finally, the final draft (*aka* publication); and then evaluation and feedback. The belief is that writing is a recursive activity and emphasis needs to be placed much more on the perceived process of that writing than on the mere product.

The writing process approach became very formalized, institutionalized. You may have seen models in chart form pinned to classroom walls (as dead insects in shadow boxes used to be in previous iterations of education):

- Brainstorming
- Organizing
- First Draft
- Editing and Revising
- Final Draft

While this approach made eminent sense, and really did pay off for most students, like so many things in our society, it probably became overused. I saw students, after they had put together some near-perfect piece of writing, actually creating a *rough draft* because that was a necessary component of the assignment. Were you one of those, writing the rough after completion of the final? If so, you were not alone!

Such was not the only fallout of the writing process approach. In ongoing classroom proceedings, instead of being the expert, the teacher became a facilitator using a bag of tricks to enable students to be progenitors of their own learning. Some teachers found this disconcerting. Their students no longer sit and take notes or complete the odd numbers of some series of textbook questions but are active partners, creating flowcharts, mind maps, graphs or pictorial diagrams, engaging in debate or think-pair-share activities, developing alternate scenarios, critiques and examples, interviewing one another, and so on—creating the 'lesson plan' as they go. (See process promotional texts such as Kirby/Kirby/Liner's *Inside Out* or Barry Bennett's *Beyond Monet*.)

As with all things, some reservations need to be voiced about the Process Approach: like some recipe for baking a cake, it has been regularized a bit too formulaically—does all writing need to be processed, or does all writing need the identical set of processes? As Raymond Rodrigues reminds us: "... there is no such thing as the writing process; there are only writing processes. Different writers write in different ways." Furthermore, how many diagrams or mind maps can students create before they become skeptical and bored with this repetitious and manufactured "creativity?" Genuine process work uses up a lot of classroom time—students in pairs or groups do not work with the same efficiencies as adults may (in point of fact, adults don't either). This form of classroom is sometimes described as the cafeteria-style of learning. In the end, a certain volume of curriculum may be lost; the teacher needs to be the arbiter in deciding whether what is gained is of greater value. And whenever students are teaching students, some ownership may be gained but a lot of expertise and knowledge is invariably lost.

Worth noting—another phrase that could be used for *writing process* is *word processing*; it is probably no coincidence that the dissemination of the process model paralleled the widespread distribution of computers and word processors in school classrooms in the 1980s and beyond. One fit the other like a bit fits a byte.

ADDENDUM:

Practice and Theory

Writing process has now become as universal as writing the in-class essay was in years gone by. And at times, it is done in classrooms in the same way the *Lord's Prayer* or the national anthem used to be performed, *sans* thought or feeling. The following are some of the skeletal ideas that underpin process practice and theory and may be useful to keep in mind:

1 – Learning to write is similar to learning to read—one learns to write by writing.

2 – The writing process is enhanced by massive doses of writing.

3 – Ideally, formal rules of grammar and spelling should never interfere with the flow of language in the creative writing process—revision should come later. (In effect, though, as computer writing programs have taken over, with ingrown spell-checks and style guides, writing has tended to become a recursive process of continual revision, one's words and phrases constantly being altered, redirected, as one composes. And newest versions of word-tech and AI using random Auto-Save features, Editors, Co-Pilot, Instant-Rewrites, the Cloud, and such, have only added complexity to this maze.)

4 – The very act of writing gives the writer the impetus to pursue writing.

5 – Writing is hard work—it requires time, energy and endurance.

6 – It is a trial-and-error exercise and requires many drafts and revisions before a polished product is ready. Then again, on rare, rare occasions, the Muse may speak clear in a first draft.

7 – It does not always flow on demand—students should not be asked to produce something instantly for display purposes. A genuine developmental process needs to be employed. And it may be idiosyncratic. Thirty students in a class may require, on some days, thirty processes.

8 – All writing needs to be supported by reading. Arguably, the best way to become a great writer—read everything great that has been written. Just that simple!

And for the teacher:

1 – Provide time for the student to write daily.

2 – When at all possible, the teacher should set the example (write and share writings with students).

3 – Peer or whole class discussion prior to the actual writing.

4 – Student / teacher and student / peer conferencing during and after the process.

5 – Provision of an audience. Reading and sharing days. Publish broadsheets and digital zines for school-wide consumption (carefully edited, of course).

6 – Show that you value students' writing.

7 – Always use a process approach.

8 – Respond quickly and consistently to students' writing.

32
University Two

Oh, and while the king was looking down
The jester stole his thorny crown
The courtroom was adjourned
No verdict was returned...

—Don McLean "American Pie"

I choose to live in residence for my first two years of university. It was a good decision, a resolve, I suppose, that put-on-pause many of the practical life-decisions that I would need to make later. Things like rent and cleaning and groceries! The Residence fees at that time were about $800.00 and paid for room, three meals and housekeeping services from September to May. In first year, I am placed in a shared room on second floor in the limestone-clad residence called Brockington House (named after an influential CBC executive), four floors, all male (co-ed residences were just on the horizon), with a TV room, hand-ball court, some study rooms and vending machines in the basement. Each floor is divided into three sections (north, middle, south), each with washroom and shower facilities, a floor senior in charge and a Don with family living in an apartment on first floor. The floor senior in my first year is Cowboy Mike, a second-year engineer from western Canada, and my room-mate is Bryan Kotila, from Sudbury, Ontario. Bryan is a Science student and an excellent chess player—we play after supper almost every night and he beats me every time all year long, once in five moves, until the very last time in April that year when I manage a stalemate (he may have let me, I don't know, but I considered it a victory then and I still do). Bryan was a joke virtuoso, one of those people who could retain and tell hundreds of humorous anecdotes; while I could never recall one, he could spin an endless stream for hours on end. But Bryan struggled a little bit with some of his courses—it is a common challenge for many at university, of course, especially for those from smaller or remote population centres. Andy Tilley, for instance, a jovial first-year engineering student on our floor, was best in his class in Cochrane (his father was a doctor there), but that class only consisted of eight or ten students; suddenly, in the larger university environment, performance was enacted before a much larger orchestra. Another student on our floor, a wild and hilarious trickster, a joy-seeker named Lloyd from Kapuskasing, soon all but abandons his studies for good times and beer. After first year, I only see Lloyd a couple times; he then resides at Elrond, Queens' high-rise downtown residence. He has gotten himself in trouble for dropping an empty bottle or two onto the street from high above and, eventually, he vanishes like so many into those infamous mists of time. The same with Bryan (and I to him, I suppose)—after first year, we more or less go our own separate ways and rarely encounter each other on campus again, and never thereafter. But, given that we were strangers dropped into a living space roughly six meters by eight, we got along just fine. He tolerated my eccentricities and was a good person; I can only hope that the fates of being have been kind to him since.

Residence can come with its challenges. Most of the rooms are shared and I did know several roommates who just did not get along, for all kinds of human reasons. On occasions, fists even flew … boys being boys, as they used to say. And, conflicts aside, distractions are always in the air. There is always someone who has nothing to do, which is to say, no assignment or reading due tomorrow, and always ready to suggest a trip to some local place of entertainment, or just to sit in your room talking. Several of us got into the habit of working until one or two in the morning—after eleven, things tended to quiet down in residence and I found that's when you could get some serious work done. I also learned to work with background music playing lowly in my room; somehow this inside music nullified the outside noise. What I am saying, I guess, one learned to cope. Meals were served in the old-fashioned cafeteria-style, not the foil-wrapped warmed-up fast food issue of today, and the fare, though a bit repetitious week to week (hamburgers on Tuesday, fish on Fridays, *etc.*), usually wasn't too bad. Breakfast was always palatable, but you could also always tell a night when the food was terrible because, about ten o'clock, pizza cars would arrive, delivery after delivery.

For second year, I am elected as one of the three Floor Seniors. Our residence Don was a Mathematics' Professor named Malcolm, a young Australian academic who lived with his wife in a decent-sized apartment on first floor. Malcolm had a small budget and invited we three Floor Seniors (Bob Alexander and Gord Silver and I) to a meeting early in second year where he served us sherry—I am not sure who in this world likes sherry but, I suppose, someone must; a beer would have been better. Malcolm and his wife Deanna were pleasant—they had just recently had a baby—and, in the course of conversation, they did discover that all three of us did come from working class backgrounds which, I thought, given the many students of economic privilege at Queen's was interesting. Later, I discovered that many of the wealthier families actually purchased houses for their children to live in while attending university … a fact I always found incredible! The Don also invited each section of residence students to the apartment to chat and, presumably, get to know a little bit about everyone—not a small task, four floors, three cohorts per floor. During this visit (and everyone was aware this would happen from the previous visits of other groups), Deanna would breast feed their infant in front of the boys. I understood the contemporary freedom of this gesture and Deanna's right to do as she chose but, to this day, I have always wondered at the reason she must have had for this exhibitionist urge—to bare herself in front of nearly two hundred young males. In this time and place, it was an act of liberation, true, but also a kind of ecdysial sensationalism, as curious then as it would be now. Everyone attended. Everyone waited. The babe must be suckled. Other floors had prophesied this. And given the antici-pation, one had to restrain oneself from laughter at this most natural and this most holy of moments.

Residence was the place where you met those who became your friends, sometimes life-long friends. The classes, especially in the first couple years, were a bit on the larger side and subject to a routine. You trekked across campus, arrived at class, sat there, took notes, and then left for your next class or back to residence, and often you did not really connect with anyone. (That said, I should point out that the populations of most of my first-year classes at Queen's were not too large in size, generally forty to fifty students, and if larger, usually had tutor-led seminars once a week. Larger institutions, like the University of Toronto and Western, were notorious for class sizes pushing into the hundreds. Today, of course, online aside, in house classes can be in the one thousand range). Nevertheless, one usually met those who were to be your friends in residence and living there really made university, university. Living off-campus, especially in first year, cast you as a stranger in a strange land. Residence life gave you a sense of place within the place; and friends with whom you did everything. All the activities from intra-mural residence sports to campus concerts and clubs and guest-speakers and the Library and the Art Gallery and Thursday night at the Manor and Faculty-sponsored Smokers and your classes and all the rest were but a footstep away. And I remember, in the company of this residence band of brothers, attending a seemingly never-ending series of pop concerts by the likes of Lighthouse, Leonard Cohen, Gordon Lightfoot, Stevie Wonder, Willie P. Bennett, John Hammond, The Grass Roots, The Guess Who, and Blood, Sweat & Tears (opening their act, an unknown folk singer named Don McLean, performing his catchy, as yet unrecorded tune: "American Pie"—the audience started by booing this warm-up but ended by singing along—the song would become a mega-hit, still played to this day). And another of the glories of university had to be all of the renowned speakers that various departments invited, most of their presentations free of charge. Over the years, at Queen's and elsewhere, I have had the opportunity to listen to the words of: Buckminster Fuller; Germaine Greer; Northrop Frye; Linus Pauling; R. D. Laing; Edward Said; Hugh Kenner; Balachandra Rajan; Marshall McLuhan; Irving Layton, Thom Gunn; Ted Hughes; Margaret Atwood; Michael Ondaatje; Alice Munro; Earle Birney; Milton Acorn; George Bowering; Fred Wah; Margaret Avison; Dennis Lee; bill bissett; b. p. nichol and, of course, the irrepressible Al Purdy.

I am also reminded here of the wealth of theatre that university often provided, offerings that usually skirted the boundaries that more commercially-minded companies could afford—*What the Butler Saw*, *The Tomorrow Box*, *The Caucasian Chalk Circle*, *The Balcony*, *No Exit*, *Our Town*, *Waiting for Godot*, *The Threepenny Opera*, Reaney's *The Donnelly Trilogy*, Ondaatje's *The Collected Works of Billy the Kid*, just some of the offerings that I remember. And comically I recall a production of *A Midsummer Night's Dream* that, word 'leaked' out, contained nudity. The theatre was packed for each show—there were Science and Math students and even Engineers in the audience (people who never went to live theatre), and true to its rumors, just as Act III closed, a topless woman (a wood nymph, I suppose) wandered across the stage. She had nothing to do with any of the show (except maybe the box office) but there she was. The magic of a midsummer's dream, I suppose.

As noted, many students at Queen's were from substantial families, the old guard of Canadian gentry. Buildings frequently held the names of corporate and industrial entrepreneurs of the past. And I met students with familial links to mining giants like Jamieson, and business moguls who owned and ran Eatons and Caterpillar industries and Howard Johnson franchises. Wealth was in the air. A couple friends and I used to sit on the Library steps and play a game we called "Count the Fur Coats." One fellow we knew traded his car one time, he jokingly said, because the light in the trunk went out. Queen's was old money.

But, cars were not really an issue for some of us. Financial issues were. In the summer months before university and in the years after first and second year, I worked at Wray's Home Furniture in Belleville; after third and fourth year I landed a job at DuPont in Kingston. The job at Wray's was the result of my friend, Randy Kerr, leaving it for something else and recommending me to the boss, Charlie Bristol. The job mostly involved driving truck and delivering furniture, some of it, heavy slugging, though I also learned how to install drapes and helped the carpet layers at times, Harry Neale and big Don Vance, a giant of a man and twice as strong (although he was the first adult individual I met who actually could not read or write). Wray's was very good to me. I made a dollar an hour, eight dollars a day, six days a week (except all Front Street stores closed at noon on Wednesday, a longstanding tradition in Ontario commerce, at least until malls took over the world). Forty-three dollars! Of that, I banked thirty-eight each week, keeping five bucks for my expenses. I stayed at home for free, got a ride to town each morning with my dad where I helped him sort mail for R.R. 7 before I walked over to Wray's, sometimes stopping at the *Cozy Grill* for a cup of coffee—10¢. (I was even bonded by the Post Office, swearing an oath to the Queen with my hand on a Bible, then having my finger prints taken at the Police Station in the old-fashioned inky style; so, to this day, as they say, enshrined somewhere in Ottawa, there sits a portrait in black and white of the ends of my hands and, ever since, I can tell you, I have been very careful to avoid robbing banks or smashing into jewelry stores—unless I was wearing gloves, of course!.) I walked and hitchhiked home every night—it was the great era of hitchhiking when the act seemed relatively safe for hiker and driver. You know, "all across the nation such a strange vibration / People in motion ... be sure to wear some flowers in your hair," *and so on.* In those years, *sans fleurs*, I started work at Wray's the day after my final university exam and worked through until the day before my first class began. Every dollar was vital; but beyond that, I actually liked the job; each day brought new experiences—and, of course, there was always the chance of visiting Mme David on Moira Street. She was a young and attractive French-Canadian woman who always ordered small items for delivery, throw rugs, tub chairs, lamps and such—she could have carried most of the items home but she preferred to have them delivered. She lived in a townhouse complex and would arrive at the apartment door wearing only a sheer negligee or, sometimes, what was then called a baby doll outfit. I could pronounce her name in the francophone way and she always seemed to appreciate that. She was married to a man in the air force, stationed in Trenton, but I think he was away a lot and I guess she was lonely.

Like so many students, I received a student loan and grant, in most years around $1500.00 (600 loan, and the rest grant) but, without the income from Wray's, I could not have made it. In fact, at the end of first year, I recall having eighteen dollars left in my account; at the end of second, I had about thirty-five. As I have often said, it was Charlie Bristol and Wray's furniture that put me through university. Charlie was a hard-core, profit-driven businessman but he kept hiring me back and, for that, I am forever grateful. At the end of it all, when I acquired my first teaching job, it took me nine years to repay that student loan; repaying Charlie and Wray's, I can never do that. (At this writing, Charlie is long since retired; the original Wray's store burned down in the mid-1990s.)

My other summer job, following third and fourth year, was at DuPont in Kingston. My brother worked there and they hired relatives as a first priority for summer relief to cover for employees on vacation. One bonus, the job did not start until about the end of May so I actually got some time off. One summer I ran the mail route for a week or so while Mom and Dad drove down to the east coast for one of the only actual vacations of their lives; Dad visited Sandy McSephney, his closest pal from WWII, and Mom got to visit the Green Gables' house on P.E.I. which she had read about all her life. At DuPont, I worked on fifth floor among senior employees, most of whom had joined the plant in its early days in the late 1950s. They treated me well but it was like entering a time warp, slicked comb-back hairstyles and rock 'n roll music with suburban homes and attitudes to match. The actual job was classic assembly line. I learned to operate a huge polymer machine that moved on railway tracks. You used a chain to open a wide nozzle that released a forty-centimetre-wide band of hot polymer which you grabbed and pulled down through a stream of water and around a revolving drum, then back up a set of metal stairs where you threaded the polymer band, now hardening, through a cleaving device, operated by stepping on a pedal; then you forced that trimmed-end through grinders which chopped it into small pieces that filled a huge tank hanging on a ceiling rail. Then you sat for twenty minutes or so and monitored the process, at the end, closing down the machine, pushing the tank to an appropriate grate in the floor, and dumping the minced polymer to the floor below where it would be re-melted as the process of making nylon continued, eventually spun out like a fairy's cobweb and wound onto large spools as thread for shipping. It was all like an absurd Rube Goldberg design come to life. And the large old machines with their chains and pulleys and gears seemed to echo the age of mid-Victorian industrialization. But once you got the hang of the enormous polymer machine, it was a very good job. The men on the floor rotated shifts and we did about four or five cast operations each per shift. We processed nylon for use in tires, and in women's stockings and for everything in between. There was a lot of free time between casts—one summer, I read all of Kurt Vonnegut's novels; the next, I ploughed through the Beats. And the pay was amazing—on the midnight shift, I made close to fourteen dollars an hour, and considerably more on weekends and holidays. (Remember, this was an era when a case of beer was $4.50 and a decent house could be purchased for ten or twelve grand.)

The great reward for me, through fourth year and heading into graduate school, money on a day-to-day basis was no longer as much of an issue. I was hardly rich but, on a student scale, neither was I impoverished. I was even able to afford a direct-drive Technics' stereo system and often sang along:

> So, bye-bye, Miss American Pie
> Drove my Chevy to the levee, but the levee was dry
> And them good ol' boys were drinkin' whiskey and rye
> Singin', "This'll be the day that I die
> This'll be the day that I die."

32
The Whole Hole

My ... advice [is] exemplified in what I call the Russian Novel Phenomenon. Every reader must have experienced that depressing moment about fifty pages into a Russian novel when we realize that we have lost track of all the characters, the variety of names by which they are known, their family relationships and relative ranks in the civil service. At this point we can give in to our anxiety, and start again to read more carefully, trying to memorize all the details on the off-chance that some may prove to be important. If such a course is followed, the second reading is almost certain to be more incomprehensible than the first. The probable result: one Russian novel lost forever. But there is another alternative: to read faster, to push ahead, to make sense of what we can and to enjoy whatever we make sense of. And suddenly the book becomes readable, the story makes sense, and we find that we can remember all the important characters and events simply because we *know* what is important. Any re-reading we then have to do is bound to make sense, because at least we comprehend what is going on and what we are looking for.

—Frank Smith *Reading Without Nonsense*

No issue in the last few decades of teaching has caused more controversy than the appearance and adaptation of a teaching strategy called Whole Language. The "Phonics vs. Whole Language" wars raged across the continents and continue to bubble and boil here and there to this day. Originating in the late 1950s, a new approach to the study of language came to the forefront—an approach that came to be known as new linguistics or psycho-linguistics. Linguistics studies and Linguistic Departments popped up across university frontiers. Part-science, part-anthropology, part-sociology, the study of linguistics took a comprehensive, holistic look at language as it was spoken and as it was actually used—it attempted to study real language, its origins and histories and the dialects and idiolects of its day-to-day usage and evolution. Long-held, traditional ideas about language were pressured. Primarily, the assumption that there was somewhere a perfect English, or even a preferred English, was held to a sceptical flame; this, of course, challenged the assumptions of behaviourists, of traditional grammar teachers, of those who used Phonics to teach reading, and of many others, as well.

By the late 1960s, these linguistically-based ideas (Lev Vygotsky, Noam Chomsky, Jean Piaget, and others) were adopted by theoretical educators such as Frank Smith and Ken and Yetta Goodman and disseminated into theories which, in general, came to be known as "Whole Language." The results were quite astonishing. Essentially, whole language teaching called for an entirely different approach to the teaching of language and reading, an approach that very easily meshed with the postmodern thinking that underscored the ideas of Britton and Process and Reader-Response Theorists. The value of behaviourist skills-based programs was decried and such programs, and their reams of support materials, discarded. As always, publishers were quick-to-the-draw, though, and rapidly spewed out tons of new "Whole Language" texts and supplies. The Whole Language system was embraced and implemented by many Boards of Education, some of whom bluntly forced elementary school teachers, in particular, to accept and adapt to the new pedagogy. And for many teachers, disenchanted with the ineffectiveness of past practises, this change in strategies was fully accepted. The time had come for nonsense to be replaced by genuine stories that children could read and find compelling in their own way; the time had come for Dick and Jane to retire, to dine on pureed entrées in a faraway rest home. And, as many teachers will tell you, they had endlessly taught the inane intricacies of grammar for years, all the while realizing that such instruction never seemed to improve students' writing or speaking. Grammar had simply become an independent subject in and of itself and, when formal grammar instruction began to go away, many were pleased. And for many, phonics instruction, with its myriad of arcane rules and exceptions, played in that same ball-park. Let the wrecking ball have its day.

A great deal has been written about the arrival of this whole language philosophy, and a lot more discussion has ensued. Suffice it to say, here, that it did create a new orthodoxy—textbooks and workbooks and online programs and Ministry guidelines and all the rest. And, just in itself, such a universal reification may be cause enough to make one sceptical. Teachers, being the inherently independent beings that they are, of course, often did their own thing. Some resisted the change, some accepted it whole-heartedly (pun intended, I suppose), and many developed a blended approach using both whole language and phonics, and other tricks of the trade, all tailored to the individual child's needs, in their efforts to help children, all children, learn to read. In its essence, whole language encouraged children to learn how to read by reading. Do not be hindered by a few minor mistakes in pronunciation or meaning—just keep reading. As with Frank Smith's Russian novel one supposes. And so children learned, correcting their interpretation of a text when needed, and they found stories they liked and they read and learned to read. And that, of course, was always the goal, anyway. As Ken Goodman claims: "No one will teach your child how to read. Reading isn't taught. Reading is developed. ... They have learned how to speak—a much more difficult process—and they will learn how to read! All you have to do is set the right conditions."

In the main, the shift to Whole Language learning did constitute a revolutionary overthrow of the behaviourist sensibility which had ruled for a long time. Combined with the other postmodern trends that evolved in the closing decades of the twentieth century, whole language symbolized a kind of egalitarian sensibility, aligning with the natural and idiosyncratic processes of learning and absolutely fitting the multicultural nature of the world in which we now live and teach. Like it or not, it was a pedagogy that was here to stay ... at least for a while!

ADDENDUM:

A Disease for All Seasons

If one reads much nineteenth-century literature, from novels to diaries to medical reports, even death certificates, one will discover that many succumbed to the fatal disease of 'brain fever,' and yet, in our own time, that disease essentially seems to have disappeared. Where has it gone? Has it been cured? Well, probably not. In fact, it has not really gone anywhere; the disease has simply been renamed, re-categorized in name as several different afflictions. We live in the great age of inventive diagnosis—our culture seems to thrive on the isolation, parsing and naming of different maladies. For example, if you suffer from the misfortune of stubbing your toe too frequently, sooner or later someone will diagnose you with Stubbed Toe Disease, probably STD, for short! And in all likelihood, the pharmaceutical industry will invent a new pill to be taken regularly (at a 'healthy' profit, of course). So whenever some new disorder or alteration is discerned, like Adam branding the Garden, a new name is devised, a new learning disability is categorized and discussion erupts on all the talk shows, for a day, at least. And whether the disorder is ADD, ADHD, dyslexia, dysphemia, ASD, ID, LD, RND, DDD, or any one of many others (even STD, perhaps), debate and disagreement always seem to flourish. Most critical to our understanding, all of these recently defined disorders have had their impact on the classroom, most (I think) helping those students most who most need that help. So the phenomenon is not necessarily a bad thing, it is just a thing! The communication disorder, dyslexia, provides a good example.

In a conference on issues surrounding world illiteracy in 1968, the Federation of Neurology Research Group defined dyslexia as "a disorder manifested by the difficulty in learning to read despite conventional instruction, adequate intelligence and socio-cultural opportunity. It is dependent upon fundamental cognitive disabilities which are frequently of constitutional origin." This issue—*i.e.,* certain individuals being unable to read, unable to decode language with accuracy—has been an educational concern, at least, since the seventeenth century, the word itself meaning "word blindness," generally attributed to German neurologist, Adolf Kussmaul, in 1877. Although research in the twentieth century intensified, little concrete aid or action was done in the classroom, really, until the 1960s. Some felt that the use of phonics would help although many argued that the disorder was a social construct, changes in society and social structures allowing it to emerge. As such, dyslexia came to be known as the "middle class disease" (as anorexia or bulimia were once categorized, or in the way that AIDS was initially cast as "the Haitian" or "the Gay disease"). Frank Smith (*Reading Without Nonsense*), even suggested that there was no such thing as dyslexia—it simply meant that a child couldn't read, but when the child learned to read, dyslexia went away. In time, however, theories of cerebral dominance gave way to studies associating dyslexia with psychological cognitive development, and attitudes toward dyslexia became more clinical and receptive; Macdonald Crichley's *The Dyslexic Child* (1970) is generally seen as a clarion call. By the 1970s and on, government policies came to define the disorder and initiate learning programs aimed at assisting dyslexic individuals (those who exhibited difficulties in verbal processing speed, phonological awareness, verbal memory, and the like) in the same manner that blind or deaf or autistic, or other individuals with various disorders, would be helped. The research continues; dyslexia tends now to be seen as a learning disorder or reading disability and continuing psychological diagnosis and help is made available. While there is little doubt that many individuals through the years suffered a good deal of unfair assessment, embarrassment and alienation, hopefully in the contemporary classroom identification and assistance is readily at hand. Individualized instructional programs including phonological awareness, multisensory approaches to reading and anxiety-reducing exercises and open discussion have all helped. And recent research in subjects such as eye differences, inner ear function and on processing in the brain's auditory cortex hint at causation and maybe even a cure. Perhaps the most important note to make in the educational and human context is that no link exists between dyslexia and individual intelligence. None!

33
University Three

Yeah, we're drinking and we're dancing
But there's nothing really happening
And the place is dead as Heaven on a Saturday night
And my very close companion
Gets me fumbling, gets me laughing
She's a hundred but she's wearing something tight

—Leonard Cohen *Closing Time*

While I always tried to place sobriety and classes first, there were plenty of distractions to be had as an undergraduate, some good, some not so much! As noted by second year, I was elected to the position of Floor Senior, responsible in general for the conduct and well-being of fifteen residents in the North section of second floor, Brockington House. I met some of my best university friends there, Frank, who became a successful lawyer in Toronto, Rob, who was elected and became a long-serving Conservative Member of Parliament, serving as Attorney General, Minister of Justice, National Defence and Foreign Affairs among other high-ranking posts. And Peter, with the eternal soul of a hippie and artist, and with whom I continued to meet in the continuing university years to discuss poetry and art and time. I think that I learned more in my interactions with Peter than I did in most of my classes. His partner and later wife, Jean, had roots deep in mother earth and was always the possessor of a kind goddess's soul. Many a time I dined at their wonderful third-floor loft in downtown Kingston above the Whig Standard offices, and many a time did Peter and I sit with a loaf of crusty bread and a bottle of wine and sort out our poems and projects and visions. Peter and Jean did take a year off and, with another couple, did a passage to India in the fashionable hippie way. They flew to Europe, purchased a VW Microbus and drove across Europe and Asia to what was once known as the Jewell in the Crown, a journey of a lifetime inspired, of course, not so much by E. M. Forster as, I think, by the Beatles. I still have some of the incense that they brought back to me from halfway around the world.

A weekend for the ages!. The classic football rivalry—Queen's vs. U. of T. The Victory Burlesque. Rochdale Co-op. The Toronto Maple Leafs. Partying in the lap of the rich. It was a Toronto weekend for Queen's students and a group of us, the usual cabal, joined the feast. With rye and wine in hand, we took a chartered bus on Friday afternoon to downtown Toronto—in retrospect, I pity the poor bus-driver although I think he got a good tip. After *oil-thighing* the Toronto Bus Station, our first destination was the notorious Victory Burlesque. I am not too sure why; I suppose someone suggested it and it seemed like a good idea at the time. It was an infamous strip-joint in T.O., at a time when prohibitive laws and moral codes had just started to ease across Ontario-the-good and such establishments were starting to spread beyond the Big Smoke, but their presence in smaller towns was still rare. Perhaps that was part of the attraction; this was forbidden fruit? Once the location of a church, the Victory was a converted movie theatre, now shabby, old, worn. Three bucks each to get in. The five or six of us in our group sat near the front. And the production was what I imagine vaudeville must have been like. A saxophonist played the national anthem. There were some short bad films—one on Sudbury of all things—the saxophonist again and an old man stepped to a mic—I still remember how threadbare and shiny his grey suit looked in the glare— he sang a song and told a couple jokes and introduced the first act. Music began anew and a woman did her thing, pasties and g-string kept in place as the law then required; the man returned, had a couple somewhat less-than-snappy one-liners (one, "you ain't seen nothing yet" to which Frank quipped, "you're right"), told a couple more jokes and the second stripper came onstage. No alcohol was served at the Victory and, as we began to sober up, any charm the place might have had began to sober down; like most bars when the lights come on at closing, it became seedier and seedier. Nevertheless, at one point, the second stripper managed to borrow a pipe that I was carrying and, while she did return it to me, take my word, I never smoked it again. More M.C., then the grand finale, called *double vision*, or something like that, two strippers, one already undressed, one fully clothed. Music played and they reversed the process; unfortunately, for the desired effect, the person dressing was far more attractive than the woman undressing so our attention focused on her. And that was it—we tumbled back into the street and went searching for a bar to refuel the illusion of the weekend. I will add that the Victory was one of the few establishments of that sort that I have ever entered. While I have known some men, in particular, who found great delight in strip clubs, I have always been overwhelmed by the palpable sadness that permeates those spaces—you know, the cloying redolence of excess talcum and cloned perfumes, cheap rye and the stain of stripper tears, subjugation and sorrow, heightened all by the imitative paraphernalia of the erotic.

We spent that night at Rochdale, sleeping on pillows and couches in a common room somewhere high up in its eighteen floors. Rochdale was a co-ed co-operative residence of one of U. of T.'s satellite colleges, an experiment well ahead of its time, or any other as it turned out. The place was situated near Yorkville, then a hippie enclave resembling a kind of Haight-Ashbury North. In my memory, all the people we met at Rochdale seemed very friendly, one young woman, like the Lady of Shalott on her shallop, floated down from floors above carrying a huge bowl filled with pills of various colours, offering a choice to any who wished to partake. Next day, I remember drinking beer from ping pong and pool tables in the basement of one of U. of T.'s female residences, then on to the football game, where Queen's lost, of course (I don't think Queen's ever won a game while I was there), but that didn't seem to matter, we still invaded the field at game's end and, though some cheerleader kicked at us, we knocked down the Toronto goal posts. That was a weird fan ritual at football games in those days, to defend the posts while at home, and destroy them when on the road. As proof, I still have a blue piece of the Toronto goal post that several of us snapped off that day (strangely, one student we did not know took a six-foot piece and, actually, cut it up and, as he had promised, made sure we got our trophies—honour among rampaging fools, I guess.) Of course, these days, with metal goal posts anchored in concrete or in metal sleeves beneath the artificial turf, I suppose that goal post tradition has become anchored itself as a part of lore-gone-by.

That night we dined in elegance at the home of Mary and George, Frank's sister and her husband, then a CEO of Caterpillar industries. The dinner was served by an African-Canadian actually wearing one of those French-maid outfits—the only time I've ever seen that. I can't imagine what a sight (and smell) we must have been but such things did not seem to matter to us then—we drank expensive beer and wine and dined on shrimp and steak. And later we were chauffeured down to Maple Leaf Gardens for the hockey game, taking our million-dollar corporate seats in a row just behind the Leafs' bench, the likes of Keon and Henderson and Ullman and Ellis and Baun on the ice. (I do remember later, as a thank you, we sent Mary and George an antique doorknocker; it had come up in conversation, I think, that it was probably the only thing that they did not have.) After that, a car picked us up and delivered us to a modern-day mansion in the Don Valley, the house of Frank's uncle who owned the hotel chain in Canada known as *Howard Johnson*. I remember seeing a Jensen Interceptor and a Rolls parked in the four-car garage. We were entertained by two teen daughters in an area that had a huge indoor pool with a bar across the entire end. The next day, the uncle joined us at a *Howard Johnson* for a breakfast that included everything on the menu and tried to send each of us home with a tub of ice cream, an item *Howard Johnson* had just developed for sale. All in all, it was an interesting weekend although I do remember that the two-and-a-half-hour drive back to Kingston felt like forty hours.

It was an era when the practice of *jogging* began. Presumably for reasons of health, students could be seen loping across campus and along the lake at almost any time of the day and night. I never partook—exercise was not my thing (never has been, I am sad to say). This was also an era when a short-lived fad called *streaking* became popular; often, it and jogging would join hands and do their thing. For no reason, really, other than releasing a spirit of the rebellious, both personal and societal, individuals and sometimes groups, would disrobe and, usually wearing only a mask of some sort, race off on a visible jaunt here or there. Streakers were generally not really joggers so their gallivants were typically brief, albeit spirited. I never partook—as jogging was not my thing, so, too, jogging nude—but one evening Rob and I were out walking near the residence and, around the corner, a sizeable group of fifteen to twenty masked joggers approached. As they passed, we saw one of the joggers perform a small hop in his running stride and, instantly, each of us said aloud: "Frank!" While he had a mask on, true enough, it was Frank. Whenever Frank ran, like a gambler with a tell, every so often he made a little hop and that gave him away and gave us fuel for ribbing well into the future.

Residence life, with evenings often full of noise, water fights that shrunk the carpets, envelopes filled with shaving cream exploding beneath unsuspecting doors, rooms filled with balloons or stripped of all their furniture—residence life ended and, in third year, I moved on to a calmer life in a house, together with four friends from the floor: Doug McLean (Halifax), Bruce McClaws (Ottawa), Bruce Raddatz (Arnprior), Gord Silver (Guelph), then (Gord and Sheila were married after third year) Iain Scott (Kingston). We rented a house on Collingwood Street, about a seven-minute walk to campus. The house, which was one third of an ancient triplex, probably built fifty years before, had been fixed-up by our landlord (sort of—new plumbing, a veneer of panelling and a tiled floor). But rent was manageable and we got along; there were no major issues or disagreements that I recall. Each of us had a bedroom and there was a kitchen and a living room and we decided that we would share a supper-meal week-days. Two offered to cook all the time, three of us did the dishes. I think sharing that meal was a brilliant decision; it kept us in touch communicably, and offered a casual time to deal with any house matters, finances, annoyances, *etc*. Beyond that, we went our separate ways, had separate friends and different areas of study. For all of us, those studies intensified in third and fourth year and, for the most part, the house on Collingwood became a quiet refuge. Scotty brought Burin with him; she was a Saint Bernard puppy, spoiled rotten by all of us. Her name was the outcome of Scotty's throwing a dart at a map of Canada, landing on Newfoundland between Conception Bay and Burin Peninsula, the latter seeming to be a much-safer name for the female pup. She would sleep with her feet on the doors to Scotty's room and mine, each door moving as she breathed and stretched. Our kitchen table was an old aluminum table-top set on a broken portable washer-dryer, quite low, and as she grew Burin began to hover over our shoulders during meals, watching intently for her turn, I suppose, drool spiraling down as it does from all Saint Bernard's. It was quite a sight and quite a life for her, surrounded by continuous attention and a lot of treats.

One of our best friends, Sharad Tembe, boarded in a house a couple blocks away; his landlady was an elderly Scottish woman, Mrs. Tea (pronounced *Tay*). We got to know her and often did small jobs around her house, just because—raking leaves, fixing up a trellis, shovelling snow, and so on. And she would ask us in for tea and biscuits every now and then, and she gave us an entire set of dishes, J. & G. Meakin, English ironstone china, gold leafed with a rose design. We used these for all of the time we lived in the house and divided them at the end—I still make use of some and, whenever I do, I cannot help but think of Mrs. Tea and the kindness that strangers can share. As to Sharad, he showed up in the B.Ed. program when I returned to do that at Queen's and we enjoyed many cups of coffee in the cafeteria there. The last I heard he had landed a teaching job in the Pickering area and life was unfolding as it should.

Toward the end of third year, many of the classes I took were filled not only with third but also with fourth-year students. Three-year degrees were still common and viable at that point and so, along with the 'four-year' students, thoughts of life-after-Queen's were in the air. The grim reaping of graduation was nigh. For English students, the three most obvious exit options were teaching, graduate school, or law. Other options were available, of course, but were less obvious and more intangible (jobs in publishing or journalism or advertising or the like). And so, discussions often ranged away from our literary studies—the quest for Mistah Kurtz or the ungraspable white whale were replaced with thoughts of finding a job or, at the very least, thinking about what you would really like to do for the rest of your life. Vividly, I remember walking back across campus from a class in old Carruthers Hall and thinking "what would I really like to do" and the answer appeared as clear as the North Star on a cloudless night. Having never really considered this before, I thought, the ideal job for me would be … a university professor.

34
Daisy, Daisy ... I'm half crazy!

Daisy, Daisy, give me your answer, do
I'm half crazy, all for the love of you.

—"Daisy Bell" Harry Dacre 1892

(first song sung by a computer, the IBM 704, Bell Labs 1961; also performed by **HAL 9000** in *2001: A Space Odyssey* (Kubrick 1968)—the name HAL derived from each letter preceding IBM)

Adults ignorant of computers will soon be as restricted as those who today are unable to read.

—*Apple* advertisement 1994

In days gone by, every now and then posters would go up around a town and, a week or so later, wagons or a train would arrive, a parade would ensue with elephants and a tiger in a cage and acrobats and clowns. A tent would be set up on the edge of town and the circus would begin—trapeze acts and fire eaters and scantily-dressed women riding upright atop huge stallions. And there would be sideshows, a boy with the tail of a monkey and an enormous fat lady, two-headed rattlesnakes and magicians making the impossible, possible. The circus was always balanced on the razor's edge, manufacturing illusion and danger, conjuring exotica to life in an oh-so ordinary world. P. T. Barnum, the

Ringling Brothers, James Bailey, the Garden Brothers, although these names have faded into the fog of time, in essence the circus remains, reincarnated in the lure and in the magic of consumer technology. Barnum and Ringling Brothers have morphed into Microsoft and Apple, ASUS and Sony, the process and the desire to manufacture illusion, to create tangible magic, to conjure the exotic and the erotic—all remains the same. And so the circus has never left town, it is only the click of a mouse away.

Technology has probably always captivated us as a species. How marvelled the earliest cave-community must have been when that first cave-woman or cave-man used reeds to tie an angular stone to a sturdy stick to make a lethal club. It must have seemed magical. Whether that artefact was used to improve the hunt or grind the seeds or keep the spouse in line, I'm not sure, but how quickly must others have formed and fashioned their own, redesigning and reshaping and improving these weapons of local destruction until the tool was perfected and it was time to move on to slings and arrows and nuclear missiles. In so many ways, the instinct of human curiosity and competition drives the development of technology. While the lion cub mimes its parent and follows its natural urges in prowling and ripping at the throat of the wildebeest, and the cub's offspring will do the same, generation after generation, the human impulse is to alter the process, ostensibly to make the act more streamlined and efficient and, always, faster. But, at the end, the wildebeest is still dead and the feast begins. And so humans learned to make magic, inventing gods and myths and invention, itself, and, invariably, the sleight of deception was always in the air. And the true point of magic, the crucible in which the impossible manifests itself, is that moment when the magician can make the senses of the audience disappear, make its sight unable to see what it should be able to see. We snap the selfie and behold the wildebeest still.

SOME SLOGANS of TECHNOLOGY:

Can you hear me now?
A magical and revolutionary device at an unbelievable price
Pushing limits
Nothing like anything
Software for the Open Enterprise

Empowered by Innovation
Strength on your side
We make IT happen
You've got questions, we've got answers
Your potential. Our passion.
A Virtual World of Live Pictures
We make sure
Reach out and touch someone
Think outside the box
Think different
Your vision. Our future.
Where do you want to go today?
Connecting people
Sound. Vision. Soul.
A better way
Choose freedom
Committed to people. Committed to the future.
Computers help people help people
The Future of memory
The Future of people
Ideas for Now
Leap ahead
Be direct
Get more out of now
Changes for the better
Has it changed your life yet?
Evolve wisely
Get in the game

So, every now and then, from Ditto Machines to Handheld Calculators to Overhead Projectors to Interactive Smart-Boards, technology will emerge that is suited to the classroom and, like the circus days of old, the hype will be hyperbolic, irresistible. Call it 5G or 12G or 77G. Salvation by Machine. The Deficit Model reincarnate. The list of Technology Slogans above is an illustration. It could be a long imagistic poem or, perhaps, a Hip-Hop rap, a rhythmic vocalization chanted to the deconstructive scratch of a couple old LPs, or, for that matter, to the mystic rising of the moon seen from the entrance of the cave. It is, of course, a somewhat random list of Technology Slogans that successfully fronted international advertising campaigns over several years. Poetry and marketing are never far apart, it seems, nor are marketing and religion. (We must always recall the old idea that poets are liars, carnival hucksters—the Romantics sometimes thought of themselves as just that, liars, or lyres, Aeolian harps, forces of Nature flowing through them like modern-day wind chimes, a source of inspiration for the music they made, the illusions they poetically conjured into being with words. So, beware says the poet Coleridge, "*weave a circle round him thrice and close your eyes with holy dread.*" And as such, warns Plato in *The Republic*, these fanciful makers (*poiein*—Greek for maker, poet) were too dangerous and unpredictable to be allowed to reside in Utopia. The poets were banned from Paradise.) By which we conclude, there are probably no billboards lining the streets of Heaven, no circuses encamped beyond the Pearly Gates on high with alluring Tattooed Ladies or Monkey-tailed Boys. No international corporations allowed. As to the slogans (and note all the poetic and rhetorical devices used), on first glance, don't all of these offer diabolic possibilities we'd like to embrace, propositions that would make us wealthy or cool or happy, or all of these. And doesn't everyone want to be so! Just taste the apple (Apple? Mac?)! But, of course, beware the magic they sell, the snake oil that cures all our ills and fears. Weave a circle, indeed!

Of course, one can take any one of these slogans and challenge its logic or deconstruct its semantics. Question what it actually means! For example, "Get in the game"—a rhetorical command that makes anyone who doesn't respond in the positive seem like an outsider, a loser. But who is asking this of us? Why should I join some game? And what game? Whose game? What are the rules? How does one win? Lose? And when all is said and done, a game is but a game. It is a construct, with artificial rules and pointless results. It is a reality play that does not really matter. Even the Super Bowl or Stanley Cup are illusions, two-headed snakes, a side-show curiosity. Or consider another slogan, "Evolve wisely." What does that mean? Both ideas, evolution and wisdom, are processes that occur naturally, not facets over which humans (or technologies) have any real control—we cannot suddenly decide to become wiser or grow another digit. And in the aftermath of the "woke" world, *Reach out and touch someone* would probably get you arrested.

So, as many media scholars have noted, few of these advertising slogans stand up under scrutiny, but they have been very successful. They speak, not to rational logic, of course, but to those infinitesimal dimensions of the human psyche where, in Leonard Cohen's phrasing, "magic is alive and God is afoot." Who does not want to behold *The Greatest Show on Earth*! Who does not want to own the newest smart phone or dance to the hottest music! Who does not want to get in the game! To be cool and wealthy and happy! Still, while to a great extent, most of these slogans sound fascinating, gnarly or chill, we must remember they really mean nothing. Their promises are empty. Just an infamous swig of Dr. Thomas' Eclectric Oil. But we are continually under the influence of their 'mental bombast' (Coleridge's phrase for those overblown moments in the poetry of his friend, Wordsworth); and, to be honest, there may exist a kind of joy in the encounter and in knowing that we need to resist their allure, like playing a game of chess on the beach against Death, I suppose. It may be the only way most of us as common citizens can be heroes. To see through the hype. To avoid being trapped. To enter and emerge from the labyrinth. Not to buy into the latest trend. And boast about our achievement (while showing off the T-shirt we just bought!). Many slogans still catch on in the popular imagination—how many times have you heard someone speak of "thinking outside the box" and not recognize its origin in the "nine dots puzzle game" and that it was a phrase most popularized by *Jysk*, the Danish furniture corporation. Bottom line, if you can, I suppose, be the lion, not the wildebeest. Now—wouldn't that make a fine marketing slogan! For what, I'm not sure! But who knows ... hey, perhaps there's an *App* I can download? Or a Siri I can ask? And even deeper...while we may know that a piece of chocolate cake is not good for us, we also know the pleasure to be had in each bite, and such pleasure is probably enhanced by our knowing. And we do not want to live in a barren world without cakes and ale, anyway! And even deeper, perhaps, the psychological drive to be a victim, to be part of that community, to know that we are being hunted and understand the power of identity we gain from that. To know that monsters live among us and massage our shadows. To understand our lives as wildebeests.

Consider the following:

Education of Our Youth is Doomed If...
... the hammer and chisel are replaced by chalk and slate (953 CE)
... chalk and slate are replaced by quills (1215 CE)
... quills are replaced by pencils (1795 CE)
... pencils are replaced by fountain pens (1845 CE)
... fountain pens are replaced by ballpoint pens (1888 CE)
... ballpoint pens are replaced by typewriters (1930 CE)
... typewriters are replaced by keyboards (1988 CE)
... keyboards are replaced by speech-to-text programs (2030 CE)
... speech-to-text programs are replaced by AI implants (?)

Reductive as this comical chart seems, as I have mentioned, I was a student in a time when ballpoint pens were forbidden in the classroom; we had to use fountain pens to perfect our cursory writing skills and it was thought that ballpoint pens were detrimental to such a skill. As often seemed the case in my schooling, I used a fountain pen in school but ball points everywhere else. In the early days of calculators, similar fears were expressed; use of such a gadget would destroy students' abilities to manage basic Arithmetical operations, adding and subtracting and calculating averages. To some degree the critics were not wrong. I have seen contemporary students, given 7 out of 10 on an assignment, use the calculator function of their iPhone to determine the percentage they received. And cursory writing has all but disappeared, discontinued as a curricular practice in most educational jurisdictions at this point (although, recently, some Boards are reconsidering this).

Technology is often the harbinger of change, and resistance is natural. As humans, we settle into comfort zones and are not often fond of displacement. But, often, like confronting Star Trek's *Borg*, resistance is futile. And in education, in particular, we need to be open to change, and learn how best to use technologies as they come along, how to qualify the hyperbole of the salespeople and, when we can, use new technologies in appropriate ways to help our students, and to enable them to help themselves. Showing some film on Friday afternoon just because one can does not cut it—that is the sign of an ineffective teacher. But adapting and improving our classrooms with appropriate technological change only makes sense. To use one past example, as various studies have indicated (see Kidwell, Gardner, Reiser, Knowlton), the acceptance and use of the overhead projector involved a gradual process; when the viable technology emerged in the 1970s, PD sessions were given and its praises were sung *but*, until the projectors were made readily available to teachers and placed in most classrooms, it was not made a part of most lessons. Then, its use became ubiquitous. Now, of course, the wheel has come full circle and, in most places, these projectors can be found in storage closets covered in dust and made fun of in films like *The Suicide Squad* (2021). (A few years ago, I was even given one as Loyalist College culled its dregs—the projectors, not me). I recall the same progression with regard to digital projectors and programs such as *Powerpoint*. I never made much use of them at Western where I had to pre-order a projector and whiteboard, go get them in a Tech-centre before class, roll them to the classroom through crowded hallways, set them up, return them after, and so on. By and large, the nuisance outweighed the benefit. Only when I began to teach at Loyalist College which had digital projectors and smart-boards and computers in every lecture room did I start to use this technology, and then I used it all the time. It was an amazing tool, allowing for creative presentations that supported the lesson, complete with access to websites for information, examples, searches, and all the rest. I do not think it made me a better teacher, as such, but it may have added some light and colour to my lessons. So, when Technology is practical, readily and easily available, teachers will use it and students will benefit. Appropriate, wise and effective use are the keys. In this regard, technology should always augment the education at hand, not replace it. Like a sword in some Medieval battle, having it is important, but knowing how to use it is even more vital. Technology requires thought, and a skilled hand—it remains an aid to education, not the thing-in-itself.

Caveat emptor: flipping on a digital slide and then reading it is almost never an effective instructional method. Never! *Hic sunt dracones*. I recently sat through most of an hour-long webinar where that was the *modus operandi*—showing a wordy slide, reading it to us, moving on to the next. It was dreadful. Thank the fates, the webinar was free (although it did cost an hour of my life).

And sometimes technology takes a wrong turn. I remember electric readers that eased a ruler down the page of a book, supposedly improving reading skills by prompting focus and speed. Heralded at the time and used everywhere by reading specialists, in retrospect, it was a terrible, counter-productive technology, debilitating the reading process. So, all that educators can really do is be vigilant and do our research. Mostly the test of time will be the arbiter—some inventions will falter quickly and disappear, others will run a short course, and others will become a part of the evolving fabric itself. And so, verily, in accord with the old design, counting on one's fingers begat abaci begat adding machines begat slide rules begat calculators begat smart tablets begat AI implants, and the universe continues to unfold.

Of course, in recent time, the technology that has led the parade of all technology is the personal computer. The days of the so-called super-computers, UNIVAC and Colossus and IBM 702 and the like, had little direct impact on elementary and secondary schools, but the arrival of the PC changed the educational world. (Anecdotally, once, after they had removed much of the roof, I recall watching a crane lower a computer into a building at Western—it seemed like the future had arrived but, I suspect, that old super-computer mainframe had little more computing power than the laptop you might carry into that building today.) While some personal computers such as *Tandy*, *Apple II* and the *IBM PCjr*, appeared in schools, by the 1980s far and away the product that became the greatest mover and shaker of all was the *Commodore 64*. It really instigated the era of the personal computer, and so-called computer literacy, in schools. In fact, when Boards of Education purchased two *Commodores*, they were given a third. The *Commodore* arrived in 1982, initially priced around $600.00 and on sale everywhere from Walmart to Canadian Tire; it had 64k of RAM, a 1MHz processor, a decent audio chip and BASIC programming built into the ROM. It was a relatively indestructible machine and fostered the burgeoning needs of schools everywhere, with prices dropping to as low as $200.00. And when trouble occurred with the *Commodore*, you simply reached around the side, flipped the OFF switch and started over. It also competed well in the Gaming market, actually signalling the death knell for Atari. It was discontinued in 1994; by then, other forms and formats took over, in particular, the arrival of Apple and the mouse. But the *Commodore* had a huge impact, the rocket booster that got a couple generations, teachers and students, into the digitalized ether. In the beginning, we were cautious—I recall, in those early days, being absolutely distrustful of the electronic storage system that captured one's work invisibly, somehow magically imprinting it on a flimsy 5¼ inch floppy diskette. Remember with a typewriter you always saw the fruits of your labour and, at the end of the day, could hold the proof in your hand. So no, I confess in those first days, I was compelled to print out everything I did. In my mind's ear, I can still hear the ratchetting of that nine-pin printer, its paper stack with perforated margins unfolding and lurching through the machine. And paper proof of my words in hand. Now, in this era of text messaging and electronic submissions, I know people who do not even own a printer. And from the software—early word processing programs such as Easy Script and Paperclip to contemporary versions of Word and Visio and WordPerfect—to the storage devices—3½ floppies, RW CDs, thumb drives and the Cloud—to the computing power of the machines, themselves, doing all the lesson building and the behind-the-scenes stuff (prepping and printing of handouts and tracking and managing marks), the PC world rolls on. While I suspect that the use of PowerPoint or GoogleDocs or the like to prepare classroom lessons may actually take longer than earlier methods, surely the world of the Gestetner and the Ditto Machine are but historical memories.

The age of information technology has not answered all of the questions, of course, in education or elsewhere; in fact some would say that it has simply added a lot more contentious mystery to the mix. From the Frankenstein monster to HAL, Tyrell's Synths to Skynet, Mustard Gas to the Atom bomb, we all know what dangers lurk in science untended—one thinks, perhaps, of Yeats' chilling imagery in "The Second Coming": "…what rough beast, its hour come round at last, / Slouches towards Bethlehem to be born?" Issues such as the misinformation (and worse) embedded in the web; the plagiaristic lure of *MyEssayWriter*, *ChatGPT* and the like, the cost of software (very expensive; it is an issue that haunts school budgets—what is spent on licensing rights drains what might be spent elsewhere); instant obsolescence (whatever one purchases will be "virtually" obsolete by the time you download or unpack it); and economic inequality among students (some students will not have easy access to contemporary technology; for others, as several early studies have shown, students able to submit printed, coloured, pretty assignments received higher grades).

And in the future, one can only imagine what 'AI' will bring to the classroom—students will not study a text as much as become a text: they will see through Juliet's eyes as she peers from her balcony or become Romeo calling out from below; not studying but mired in the trench-mud of World War One; riding the first rocket-ship to Mars. Imagine the possibilities and imagine the issues that will arise. Or, in the extreme, as the Marxist critic Richard Ohman says: "I see every reason to expect that the computer revolution, like every revolution from the top down, will indeed expand the minds and freedoms of an elite, meanwhile facilitating the degradation of labour and the stratification of the work-force that have been hallmarks of monopoly capitalism from its onset." Theodore Roszak writes:

> People who think education equals information have no idea what either information or education is. … Kids don't need much information anyway. Not first of all. Teaching them that they do is bad teaching. They need ideas, values, taste and judgement without which information is useless. Ideas, values, taste and judgement are found in other human minds. And most cheaply in the minds of the authors of books and teachers in classrooms. Kids need to learn about those other minds. Let them.

In the wake of such strident views, the need for something called computer literacy has been widely touted but the courses that have arisen seemed to become mostly a pursuit to improve mechanical skills and not to delve into an intellectual or psychological understanding of the potential impact this technology would impart. The propagation of the cell phone has only amplified this need; if vaping and soft drug use is an issue among youth, cell phone addiction is far worse. Rules regulating the use of computers and cell phones have trumped exploration. Skewing the issue of computer literacy, the word, itself, devolved to become a noun for all seasons, attached to almost every concept, especially in education: media literacy, math literacy, digital literacy, financial literacy, cultural literacy, health literacy, legal literacy, scientific literacy, information literacy, critical literacy, social literacy, game literacy, news literacy, and so on. I have even seen the phrase *literature literacy*. I wonder, did we ever discuss pencil literacy or fountain-pen literacy? No, at this point, perhaps what we really need is a course in literacy literacy. Yikes!

But we must resist the urge to throw the baby out with the bath water (parents will know what I mean). While technology in education may not be the new messiah on the block, it is a tool with which teachers can enhance the message they are trying to convey. And, especially today, with wide-screen televisions and noses pressed to the shimmer of smart-phones (those dark mirrors), at the very least, the tech that teachers appropriate and use effectively can vitally redirect and capture the attention of students (and, in itself, that is significant!). Most certainly the *Covid-19* pandemic underscored the educational value of technology where for a year or more online education was often all that was possible. And while that situation also clarified the limitations of online learning for all concerned—we came to understand how important the human presence is in education, teachers and classmates and the physical ambience of the school—the available technology proved itself to be better than nothing at all. It reminded us once again of the resiliency of students and of teachers, too. And reminded us, too, that like the Horn Book or blackboard, digital technologies are but a tool to focus interest and enhance learning opportunities, to enhance the educational moment for the teacher and for the student. And with no need for posters or parades, we are reminded again that the greatest show on earth is right here in the classroom.

35

University Four—my Honours B.A.

It was agreed, that my endeavours should be directed to persons and characters supernatural, or at least romantic, yet so as to transfer from our inward nature a human interest and a semblance of truth sufficient to procure for these shadows of imagination that willing suspension of disbelief for the moment, which constitutes poetic faith.

—Samuel Taylor Coleridge *Biographia Literaria* IV

Courses at Queen's, generally and logically, follow an ordered pattern: 100-level courses are for first-year students, 200 for second, 300 for third and 400, fourth. To earn a degree in the Arts, nineteen courses are required, ten in your major, in my case English: the first year Honours course (*Introduction to Language and Literature*) plus three each in the other levels. In second year, I take courses in Shakespeare, Chaucer and American Literature (plus a History and a Film Studies), in third, I take Renaissance Non-Dramatic, Romantics, Victorian, Linguistics, and Canadian literature. And in fourth, I study Eighteenth Century literature, American literature, Modern British, and another Film Studies. Right or wrong, I came to feel that focusing on English courses gave me everything I needed in academia: philosophy, history, psychology, sociology, art, music and all the rest seemed embedded in the scope of my English studies.

I was fortunate at Queen's, I think, to have a series of excellent professors. Antony Alpers, a New Zealander, was a dramatic lecturer, emphatically and theatrically leaning across the podium often as he quoted from poems and stories. He taught American literature and I remember to this day the metaphor he gave for the course—reading American literature is like the pioneers crossing the continent, he said, eventually they will have to climb the Rocky Mountains as, eventually, you will have to read *Moby-Dick*. And so I read that great novel for the first time—I had seen the movie and read the comic, but the book was different. In particular, a lot of cetology. Professor Alpers was also the only university professor I ever had who gave us the option to do a creative assignment and not just the standard literary analysis. For this, we could choose a character from the course and, in that voice, write about another. So, I became Huck Finn and, using all the unintentional wit and wisdom I could muster, I wrote about Benjamin Franklin. I recall writing "God help them that helps themselves," Huck mimicking something Franklin might have said as Poor Richard. Alpers actually phoned me up in residence and had me come to his office; he was very amused and impressed by my effort and I was impressed by his. Professor Alpers was a scholar of Katherine Mansfield, having exclusive academic access to all of her papers (he had known her family); his impressive book on her life and art sits by me as I write this (*The Life of Katherine Mansfield* Viking 1980).

It was an honour to be in the Renaissance course taught by A. C. Hamilton. He was a kind and delightful man who made our entrance to an understanding of some truly distant, dense writers (the likes of Sidney, Spenser, Milton, Donne, Marvel) comprehensible by using a low-toned, relaxed approach. He was the first person to suggest that the best way to understand poetry (all writing really) was to read it aloud and I have been doing that ever since—I still read poems that way almost every day and, at whatever level I taught, I tried to do that in class as well. Reading aloud, and listening, somehow transports all of us to a quieter, simpler moment even in complex worlds, a childlike moment that opens the sensibilities to clarity and insight—enabling that famed suspension of disbelief, I suppose. It is probably a skill that all teachers should perfect—reading aloud. Professor Hamilton was an internationally recognized scholar (I recall his having to cancel a class once because he'd been asked last-minute to do a lecture at Johns Hopkins);

he produced a variorum edition of *The Faerie Queene* as well as the monumental three-volume *Spenser Encyclopedia*. And yet, busy as he must have been, he always returned assignments personally by having students visit his office—he would type his comments on the title page. And if A.C. saw you while walking across campus, he would stop and chat.

George Whalley, whom I had for Romantics, always seemed to carry the same small blue book and smoked endlessly, twisting his cigarette in an ashtray as he lectured through its smoke. (In those days, by the time a class was half over, seminar rooms would be filled with a desultory, low-hanging cloud of greyness.) In his lectures, Professor Whalley shifted flawlessly from commentary to quotation and back again, never consulting a source; his discussion on any day could range from Coleridge's *Biographia* to "Lycidas" to the Hebrides to weather fronts in the Western Hemisphere to Dorothy Wordsworth's power of observation as she beheld the last leaf of autumn still clinging high in a tree. Although the course was supposed to cover the Romantics (Blake, Keats, Shelley, Byron, Burns, and so on), we spent the entire year engaged in the *Biographia* with allusions to Wordsworth dropped here and there. But Professor Whalley was an engaging figure and, as long as you did not try to take notes, his classes were wonderful. And I always remember his advice on becoming an effective writer; "use help not aid" he would say, meaning that we should always say what we wanted to say in the simplest, most direct way possible (echoing the theme advanced by the "Preface" to *Lyrical Ballads*, perhaps)—although by their very nature his lectures always seemed far apace from that counsel—simple words, perhaps, but an abstract and challenging stream of ideas, not unlike the Romantic literature we read.

Professor Douglas Spettigue was a significant midwife in the nascent study of Canadian literature, a Frederick Philip Grove scholar who emphasized the need at the time for more critical and biographical background material to help the subject mature. We approached Canadian literature in a broad historical manner, reading *Wacousta* by Richardson, the Confederation poets, *Roughing it in the Bush* by Susanna Moodie and *Settlers of the Marsh* by Grove before we got to twentieth century writers like Callaghan, Hood, MacLennan, Roy. Two things I recall in particular: doing a seminar on the obscure Canadian imagist poet, W. W. E. Ross, and coming out of a class one afternoon in September to see people shouting and cheering all the way across campus, students slapping strangers on the back and floating on air (it seemed). Canada had won the final game of the later-labelled *Summit Series*, Cournoyer passing to Henderson for a goal in the last seconds, Canada defeating the evil empire known as the U.S.S.R. Instead of watching the game, I had attended class although I was sorely tempted to skip as so many others must have. But the entire game was replayed that evening and our house watched as the ultimate drama unfolded again—in the nationally immortal words of Foster Hewitt: "Henderson made a wild stab for it and fell. Here's another shot. Right in front. They scored! Henderson has scored for Canada!" For me, fittingly enough, that course in Canadian literature is forever linked to that famous goal which now stands as such an iconic cultural moment for Canada.

Modern British was a course taught by the Professor Tom Marshall, a poet then working on his series of books on the Elements. Tom's lectures often seemed diffused and slightly indifferent but he was responsible at that time for literary readings offered by the Department, usually introducing the writers. Being known by him, I regularly got invited to the after-reading receptions where some food and a lot of alcohol were generally served. I sat on the floor with Margaret Laurence drinking beer, talked with John Newlove about hitchhiking across Canada and with Stephen Mayne about living in Montreal and hockey, watched Milton Acorn dance an East-coast reel (or try to) and heard Thom Gunn and Ted Hughes playfully speak in British accents so dense no-one could understand. Tom was a very good friend of Al Purdy—I still have a letter from Al asking me to come down with Tom to visit him at the A-Frame sometime. Sadly, Tom died far too young.

Having spent my entire life in the profession, one of the things that I have learned about teaching is that personality matters. And that is especially true, I think, with certain subject matters. Eighteenth-century literature is filled with verse bound in the confines of topical issues and the complexities of the heroic couplet (the verse of Pope and Dryden) and with long dense prose fiction (*Clarissa*, *Tom Jones*, *Moll Flanders*, *Robinson Crusoe*, *Evelina*, *Roderick Random*, *Tristram Shandy*, *Life of Johnson*). Professor Charles Pullen, with a background in Law, was a wonderful, funny story-teller and taught us how to understand the condescending voice of the eighteenth-century gentleman, words spoken with an attitude that often turned in on itself in the finest satiric pings, to use Professor Pullen's word for the effect. While the works, themselves, were sometimes a struggle to get through, the classes were a joy to attend.

Kerry McSweeney taught two courses I took, Victorian literature in third year and American studies the next. Professor McSweeney always arrived at class with an armful of books that tumbled onto the table as he sat down and which he used throughout class to add extra literary and critical insights to the materials at hand. Under his tutelage I read Dostoevsky's *Notes from the Underground* and John Fowles's *The French Lieutenant's Woman* to set the Victorian Age in perspective and then we plunged into the layered worlds of the Brontës and Dickens, Tennyson and Browning (although I never came to appreciate Browning as an undergraduate, I was finally impressed with his works when I ended up teaching that master of the dramatic monologue—teaching something often has that impact). I spent most of one Christmas holiday reading *Little Dorrit* and, next year, the same, only this time reading *Moby-Dick*, again. There is no doubt that Professor McSweeney's course influenced the future scholarly voyages I undertook—I certainly followed Ishmael to sea in my M.A. year. As editor of the *Queen's Quarterly* at that point, Professor McSweeney also hired me once to distribute copies of the magazine around campus to other departments. Having some extra money was always a welcome thing. He was a kind and generous individual to me and also delivered classes that followed the prescribed course outline (there were some profs who did not seem to do that very well); I liked Professor McSweeney's orderly approach and his sense of humour, and he challenged and enlightened my learning. I was actually saddened somehow, several years after, to learn that he had transferred to McGill. Most certainly, Queen's loss.

In reflecting on this time, and others have certainly made this observation in many other ways—what a remarkable passage it was, to be immersed in this sea of literature, an intense and luxurious experience where the only pressure, really, was managing the arbitrary due dates for all the assignments. To be young and explore the world with Keats and Melville and Eliot and Yeats and Dickens. To be young and in their arms. O what a time it was!

Most of that time at Queen's, I was a poet. Professor Bill Barnes, who edited *Quarry* magazine, was kind enough to like some of my writing and publish several poems. The same with *sweven*, the campus creative writing magazine; the editor, Steven Winnett, saw promise in my writing and printed numerous pieces. I was also published in *Canadian Forum* and *waves* and *white pelican* and elsewhere across the country. And so, by third and fourth year, whenever any campus Arts' event occurred that involved readings, I was invariably part of it. And I enjoyed it … the attention stroked my ego and, whether I read to an empty room or to a coffee house crowd, I did the best I could … I had several funny poems and crowds always enjoy those. But there was probably a price paid. Whatever the art form, there is a personal isolation inherent for the artist, and it does not matter if you are successful or a failure, good or terrible. But, as I have noted earlier, it was not really a choice for me— I have been compelled to write and draw since I was a kid. For me, writing is breathing. And part of my writing process has always been momentary withdrawal and that has shaped my personality. I recall my parents going for Sunday drives and asking me if I would come along and I would refuse, even though I really wanted to go. Other times I went, and enjoyed myself. But some force inside—call it a self-imposed suspension of disbelief, perhaps—that force often arose and made me not do what I would have liked to do, and that has always separated me from others, caused me to step aside like Wakefield or Bartleby from the flow of the world in which I was living. I remember once going out on a date with a bright and attractive woman named Sean—we had dinner, attended a concert and then landed in one of the hottest bars in Toronto, a post-disco palace that had a unique all-metal dance floor. We were having a great time and then, suddenly, I went away, just sat with my beer, my brain elsewhere, and even Sean noticed. It killed the evening. That process, my "Walter Mitty syndrome," has happened throughout my life and continues with me to this day. I suspect that, after my dust is scattered over the Way Pioneer cemetery, my soul will probably be somewhere else ruminating on some arcane idea. For yes, I have come to know Ishmael, isolato to the core, orphan of the sea and shore—for better or for worse, we are soulmates. As to what friends and confidantes through the years might conclude about me and my behavior, well, I will leave that up to them and their memory, if such exists at all. I suspect that most would be less than kind.

In June, I graduate. My parents and my Aunt Irene and Uncle Francis attend the ceremony (My Aunt and Uncle, without children of their own, have always been like second parents to my brothers and me.) They are all impressed by the colourful pomp and ceremony of the affair. And for the granting of my degree itself, a pretty cool moment in my life—I kneel in front of His Excellency the Right Honourable Roland Michener, former Governor General of Canada and current Chancellor of Queen's; he touches my hands, smoothly and amiably asks me what plans I have and, after four long years of study, I have been conferred with the piece of paper that proclaims my Honours Bachelor of Arts. As to Chancellor Michener's question, I have set myself on the paths most obvious for those with an English degree. I have been accepted into two Law schools (Queen's and Windsor), I have gained entrance to a teaching degree (the B. Ed. program at Duncan McArthur College) and to English Graduate Studies at the University of Western Ontario (where, I later found out, they added seven per cent to my average because I come from Queen's). Grad Studies has the advantage over the other choices—they are offering me a paying job as a Teaching Assistant and giving me a scholarship to boot. Being paid to be a student. That sounds like a no-brainer. And so the choice is made. Although, to be honest, money is not the only factor. For me, the lure of literature and literary studies still fills the sails. My B.A. has given me the taste but there is more to be learned and Ishmael hovers high in the mast-head, ever-searching the rolling horizons of the vast deep. I will follow where that lost soul leads.

36

Ishmael and Ahab and Al—my M.A.

What is it, what nameless, inscrutable, unearthly thing is it; what cozening, hidden lord and master, and cruel, remorseless emperor commands me; that against all natural lovings and longings, I so keep pushing, and crowding, and jamming myself on all the time; recklessly making me ready to do what in my own proper, natural heart, I durst not so much as dare? Is Ahab, Ahab? Is it I, God, or who, that lifts this arm? But if the great sun move not of himself; but is as an errand-boy in heaven; nor one single star can revolve, but by some invisible power; how then can this one small heart beat; this one small brain think thoughts; unless God does that beating, does that thinking, does that living, and not I. By heaven, man, we are turned round and round in this world, like yonder windlass, and Fate is the handspike. And all the time, lo! that smiling sky, and this unsounded sea! Look! see yon Albicore! who put it into him to chase and fang that flying-fish? Where do murderers go, man! Who's to doom, when the judge himself is dragged to the bar? But it is a mild, mild wind, and a mild looking sky; and the air smells now, as if it blew from a far-away meadow; they have been making hay somewhere under the slopes of the Andes, Starbuck, and the mowers are sleeping among the new-mown hay. Sleeping? Aye, toil we how we may, we all sleep at last on the field.

—Herman Melville *Moby-Dick* Ch. 132

I am the final student to arrive at Geoffrey Ran's class on *Romance in America*, a couple minutes late because I had difficulty finding the room in old University College, one of the two original buildings at Western, now a sprawling university campus ranging over the original grounds of the London Hunt and Country Club—"the country club" is still a nickname borne by the university, in part, in recognition of its *nouveau riche* reputation (as Queen's was old money, so Western is new, located in London, Ontario, one of the financial hubs of Canada at this time). As the last student seated, Professor Rans immediately assigns me the very first seminar to deliver in the course, on the two volume *Arthur Mervyn* (1799), an early American novel, which no-one has ever heard tell of, written by Charles Brockden Brown, an author whom no-one has heard tell of either. This early American novel is marginally a Romance, its clunky events sliding between the real and the supernatural; much of it involves the real, albeit surreal, plague of yellow fever that struck Philadelphia and area in 1793; in particular, it was a book that had some influence on Edgar Allan Poe and "The Masque of Red Death." But I'm happy to receive the assignment and present first—the novel is both eighteenth-century in feel and American to boot, both literary areas in which I have some confidence, and it will mean one more thing out of the way early on. (As it turns out, the Book Store does not get the class books in soon enough and my presentation gets shoved back until nearly the end of the course.) The course, in general, focusses on the great era of Romance in American literature—we read Washington Irving and all five of Cooper's *Leatherstocking* novels, Poe and Hawthorne and Melville and James. Professor Rans is an uneven, eccentric academic but I like him and, in general, enjoy the course. And my understanding of America and its literature continues to be expanded exponentially.

The Masters of Arts degree has two options. You can take four graduate-level courses, or do two courses and a thesis (approximately, a one-hundred-page research paper), plus, for each option, students are required to take one course in a foreign language and a short course in *Bibliographic Methods*. Most students take the four-course option; it is probably easiest with a line-of-study clearly laid out according to the courses available and the professor's deadlines. But I choose the thesis option because, to me, that makes the M.A. different from undergraduate and will prepare me, I think, in case I ever wish to go on. (It did!) Class sizes in courses are twelve to fifteen students with a mix of those working on M.A.s and on Ph.D.s.

The second course I am admitted to is Stan Dragland's *Long-Form in Canadian Poetry*, offered in the evening. Professor Dragland is a young and engaging professor and everyone seems to enjoy the remarkable course he has put together where we read poets almost all of whom are living, poem-length books such as Jay Macpherson's *The Boatman*, Margaret Atwood's *The Journals of Susannah Moodie*, George Bowering's *Geneve*, Michael Ondaatje's *The Collected Works of Billy the Kid*, Wilfrid Watson's *the sorrowful canadians*, Gwendolyn MacEwen's *The Armies of the Moon*, Stuart MacKinnon's *The Intervals*, and several more. While long narrative poems had an established tradition in Canada (one thinks of Goldsmith's "The Rising Village," Richardson's "Tecumseh," Isabela Valency Crawford's "Malcolm's Katie" and several by Pratt including "Brébeuf and his Brethren" and "Towards the Last Spike"), the latest trend at this time was for poets to create long, book-length poems, often twisted, obscure, arcane. In retrospect, it was a movement that probably signalled the end of poetry in Canada which had been a country that, relatively speaking, devoured poetry and poetry books at least until the end of the 1960s. But, whether moving away from the memorable individual poem to these long esoteric selections was the straw that broke that old moose's back, or an attempt to re-ignite that straw, either way, sadly I think, it was the era that marked the end of poetry in the popular mindset. Prose fiction seemed to take over. Accordingly, it was a time of great scholarly debate on hyperbolic topics such as the death of literature or the death of the author; George Steiner famously predicted the end of civilization where all that would remain was "math, music and silence." Technological innovation was on the rise in the machine and in the human psyche and that seemed to mean the annihilation of all previous forms of communication.

Initially, at least, I am very impressed by some of the grad students in the courses I take. One woman makes some brilliant connections between Canadian poetry and the works of Joseph Conrad and a male makes perceptive associations between the symbols of Egyptian hieroglyphs and Canadian petroglyphs referred to by several poets. And then, as time progresses, I spy the one-trick that these ponies are repeatedly performing; the woman has just taken a summer course in Conrad, the male a course in Egyptology—they are just using materials fresh to their studies and playing the old lit-crit game that I learned so long ago. And understandably so! After that realization, the courses and fellow classmates become easier to understand and competition becomes less daunting. I also met a man named Nino Basacco in that evening Canadian class (Western's Department of English always offered at least one grad class in the evening so individuals with day-time jobs could pursue their studies); Nino was a remarkable high school teacher from Woodstock, Ontario, working on his M.A. part-time and we often talked about what life as an English teacher was like. Nino also gave one of the most interesting seminars of the year breaking down Wilfred Watson's bizarre *the sorrowful canadians*.

Al Purdy had just published his book-length poem, *In Search of Owen Roblin*, so that fit the theme of Professor Dragland's course perfectly and became the topic of my major seminar and paper. Purdy's voice, grounded in the soil of home, once again provided me with direction and substance, with a place to stand on, as Al so eloquently says in "Roblin's Mills."

For my second-language course, I study German mostly because it fits my schedule (a couple hours every Friday morning) and all of us take the *Bibliography* course taught by Professor Jim Devereaux, one of wittiest men I have ever met. Professor Devereaux also operates the *Belial Press* in the basement of University College, a Stanhope-style manual press that is used to design and print posters and flyers for events on campus. I volunteer to help out and learn how to set the type and ink it (a messy job reserved in the day for *the printer's devil*) and press out the posters. It is fun and a welcome physical distraction from the regular academic order of the day. I also serve as a Teaching Assistant, working with Professors Bieman and Atkinson covering two tutorials for the Introductory English course. While Atkinson is an enjoyable fellow, he has had some health issues and Bieman is partnering to help him keep the course on course, as it were. And, for the most part, save for one moment in a lecture on *Othello* where the discussion seems diverted to goats in Spain, the year runs smoothly. As to sitting at the head of the seminar table as a T.A., I enjoy pretending to be a professor but do not let myself fall into the trap that some Graduate students do, that is, spending far too much time and effort at the expense of one's own studies and workload. I do an honest job and help my students whenever and wherever I can but, like the past T.A.s I have had myself, including one notably unemployed bear, I realize that I am but a very small pebble on the road these students are travelling. I am fortunate, though, to meet another dear and brilliant friend, Michael Hurley, my partner as a T.A. Michael is a poet and peacenik at heart and will reverse the path I have chosen, travelling east to earn his Ph.D. at Queen's and landing a teaching job at the Royal Military College in Kingston on whose Board of Governors I later serve. Michael will teach poetry to soldiers, surely the noblest act of all.

This is the post-pill, pre-AIDs world. Relationships slide freely and fluidly—evening classes are frequently followed with trips to the campus pub and all kinds of impulsive and twisted things occur. I am sure that you are not interested in reading about that kind of thing, about my various adventures and misadventures of the amorous kind. Suffice it to say, that professors and grad students and undergraduates, too, move in and out of various kinds of trysts and, however we may judge the human folly of that time and place in retrospect, tears and heartaches, and even inappropriateness, aside, the world spun on and the sun continued to rise every day. And the last time I checked, they still do.

Having chosen to do a thesis, my interests direct me toward Herman Melville's *Moby-Dick*. Who knows why, really? I mean the work intrigues me … it still does. It is such a rich and deep and, in many ways, to use its own metaphoric sensibility, such an ungraspable phantom. I remember having a copy of it as a kid in the form of a *Classics Illustrated* comic and, careful as I was with all of my things (we were poor; I did not have many things), somehow that comic book became lost. So maybe that's one of the deep reasons I returned to the text—like I say, who knows why we choose to travel the paths we do. Like Frost's persona, we are always choosing one diverging path or another. Professor Rans agreed to be a supervisor and Professor Ernest Redekop, another American specialist, agreed to be second advisor. As had happened in History in high school, Professor Rans has me do an impromptu presentation on Melville for the class. By the time May rolled around, I had narrowed my topic to a consideration of the narrative structure of the book. For the first couple months of summer, I found and read all that I could pertaining to my study. I read all that

Melville had written, including *Mardi*, a novel I figure only four or five other people on this planet have read. (I also read his book-length poem, *Clarel*.) This was that old-kind of library-based research, pre-Google, where you would read the critical books or their chapters on *Moby-Dick*, note what sources the scholars had used, then ascend or descend into the marvellous stacks, combing through the mountainous volumes and periodicals and micro-fiche tracking down what you could. It always felt like a small satisfying miracle when you finally found *827.2 Vol VII Section III* of some thick brown-bound periodical, opened it and actually saw the article, cited elsewhere, for which you had been searching. Occasionally, library-loan had to be used to retrieve some material that seemed as if it might be pertinent (sometimes it was; sometimes not); and so, the research got done piece by piece—there was a physicality involved that was satisfying—it felt like a quest conquered. For better and for worse, this kind of hands-on research seems to be a fading artifice—in fact, in recent years, I have encountered senior university students who have never even visited the stacks. The psyche is now devoted to electronics and the ease and perceived efficiency they provide—while something is lost (at the very least, not all materials are yet in digital form), much is gained as well, accessibility and downloading and the rest. In any case, this is the present and future form of research; like blacksmith's liveries or cobblers' shops, libraries with shelves of books and echelons of librarians are fading away, transforming into different manifestations, efficient and aloof.

In my research, I quickly discovered that a lot had been written about Melville. Although he was an author almost unknown at the time of his death—his name was misspelled in the *New York Times'* obituary—he came to be revered as a great author, as the man who wrote one of the most significant American novels ever. Melville was discovered, as it were, in the 1920s, and then again in the 1950s where attention often turned to the narrative complexities of the novel, and Gregory Peck became Ahab in Hollywood. The whale, shamefully, was uncredited! And scholarship on Melville has never ceased since. I worked away on my thesis, essentially on my own, and finished a draft by early in August: *Because I Could Not Stop for Death: The Quest of Ishmael in Moby-Dick*. Geoffrey Rans read it and had me over to his home one afternoon; he was excellent, a great help in smoothing out some of the mechanics and telling me that he thought I had arrived at the right conclusion, that Ishmael survives at the end of the book because he comes to an understanding that Ahab and the crew who follows him do not, the understanding that multiple beliefs can be held at the same time (as a whale has monocular vision). And even beyond that, Ishmael comes to accept the truth that there some things in our universe simply beyond human understanding. The great white whale swims away while monomaniacal Ahab and the *Pequod* sinks, with Ishmael the lone orphan surviving. And Professor Rans told me that I had done the thesis in the "good old fashioned English way," namely, by myself.

I tidied up the thesis, delivered a copy to Professor Redekop, then, summer over, I turned to the next stage of my pursuits, a return to Queen's to get a B.Ed. degree. A couple Profs, including the Head of Grad Studies in English, asked me to continue on into the Doctoral program but that would take at least four more years (probably longer) and I just felt that I needed a break from the academic grind and from the meagre living, just above the poverty line. Professor Rans kept in touch but I never heard from Redekop. Embarrassed by his colleague, Geoffrey finally said he would prod him to read the thesis and, finally, near the beginning of March of the next year, I received the thesis in the mail. To be honest, it looked the same as it had when I sent it to him— to this day, I do not think that Professor Redekop ever read the thing. A defense date was set in September, and, by then employed in a teaching job, I got the day off work and drove to Western (about four hours away) to make my defense, which went very smoothly. Professor Rans was ill that day and did not attend and, at the end, Dr. Redekop's only comment was that he disagreed with everything I had to say in the thesis. So it goes. I made final corrections, including using a manual page stamping device to add numeration, mailed three copies to the university and, in time, received a copy back from them, bound in black. And now it sits in a bookcase in my living room and has not been opened in fifty years.

ADDENDUM:

My Pods of Whales

My pods of whales. One curious offshoot of my work that I should note. Having learned of my academic interests, over the years friends and family have given me hundreds of whale replicas. If you were to visit my home, you would find scads of these trivial knick-knacks, representations of various cetological creatures in wood and plastic and porcelain and metal and glass and marble and even the tiny tail of a whale carved from actual whalebone like the scrimshaw ancient mariners toiled at to fill the empty hours of their day. Kitschy as they tend to be, these pods of whales are not always a trivial thing. Wherever I turn in my world, these whales swim about me and always remind me of those who for some reason cared enough to give these gifts and they remind me of that great writer, too, unheralded and solitary but magnificent in mind, and of that pure mythic beast that breached his fingertips so long ago. So, no, my pods of whales, they are not always a trivial thing at all.

Arrowhead, Melville's residence in the Berkshires where he wrote *Moby-Dick*; I snuck under the cords and sat at the desk where he wrote that great book and gazed upon the humped-back mountain through his window on the world. Below; one of my pods of whales.

37

Teachers' College—my B.Ed.

Let Sporus tremble –"What? that thing of silk,
Sporus, that mere white curd of ass's milk?
Satire or sense, alas! can Sporus feel?
Who breaks a butterfly upon a wheel? …"

—Alexander Pope "Epistle to Dr. Arbuthnot" 1735

Duncan McArthur Hall, named after a History professor who had once been the provincial Minister of Education, houses the Teachers' College at Queen's University and is located far to the west, well away from main campus, the building, itself, sandwiched between the Federal Women's Prison and the new football stadium. The land was once a quarry where inmates pounded away at limestone rocks. I must remind myself not to be too unkind to McArthur's—that's why I include the quotation from Pope above: "Who breaks a butterfly upon a wheel?" But coming out of the tough academic grind of a Master's degree, Teachers' College was really like a vacation. It was the early days when these teacher training institutions were just being conceived in Ontario and almost all of the instructors were former teachers or secondments and all of our assignments were short, simple, practical exercises devoid of much academic weight. University academics did not think much of these Teachers' Colleges with their Faculties mostly a random assortment of people without high academic qualifications. (I was once asked with some disdain by a friend who was an English professor at Western, in reference to my working at UWO's Althouse College, why would you want to teach there? I replied by asking him the same question—why do you want to teach here? Our conversation then moved on to other things.) Nevertheless, whatever their reputation, Education Departments were often situated physically in marginalized locations on campi (at both Queen's and Western, the Education buildings were far off main campus, and the same was true of OISE, north of Bloor and well away from mainstream academic life of U. of T.)

I never applied to McArthur's College; I simply phoned them up, indicated that I had been accepted the previous year and, like a contestant in some game show, they said *come on down*. That was generous of them but recent B.Ed. students will understand the irony, given that, currently, acceptance to such programs is so incredibly competitive (Since 1990, on average, Western had nearly five thousand applicants per year for some seven hundred spots, or so—the worse the economy, it seems, the greater the number of applicants.) Now, to complete a B.A. in English, I took nineteen courses over four years; to earn my B.Ed., I needed to cover some seventeen in one year. This included two major options: for me, I take English and History—I started in Theatre Arts with a desire to learn about the technical aspects of theatre but the instructor there seemed only interested in turning us into actors, so I walked across the hall and joined the History class (I let the Registrar's Office know several weeks later what I had done—they were kind). As it turns out, later in the year, the College mounts a production of *Macbeth* with that Theatre instructor playing the lead. He is quite old, short and plump and not instantly my idea of the gallant battlefield warrior and doomed Scottish thane. Mostly what I remember is the bloody facsimile of his head on a short stick being dipped under a cardboard drawbridge and waved at the audience at the end. It was in many ways a memorable production of the Scottish play… "full of sound and fury"… you know the rest!

I take a required variety of short courses—Group Dynamics, Soviet Education, Film Making, Educational Materials, Discipline, Assessment, and so on—in the dismissive vernacular of the day, much of it seemed *Mickey Mouse*. But, I must confess this—as much as I thought that so much of what we were taught was trivial, in the early years of my teaching career, I was surprised at how much I used from those classes. I think of the comment frequently attributed to Mark Twain: "When I was a boy of fourteen, my father was so ignorant I could hardly stand to have the old man around. But when I got to be twenty-one, I was astonished at how much the old man had learned." While there are some extrinsic requirements to the program (like a volunteer assignment where I help out a local theatre group and a trip to the Women's Prison, just across the street, to teach some inmates how to write poetry—in retrospect, a skill they surely needed), the key component of the B.Ed. is the practicum where we are slotted as student teachers into four different schools for two-week sessions. For the first time in my life, really, I have to learn how to tie a tie and I have to purchase some sports coats and dress slacks. In those days, to be a teacher, you have to look like a teacher, I guess! I am placed into English classes at Quinte Secondary (Belleville) and Port Hope and for History in Cobourg and at Centennial (Belleville). My previous experience as a Teaching Assistant at Western is greatly beneficial to my teaching, to my comfort and confidence in front of a class, and, mostly, I breeze through these placements.

The teacher with whom I am placed first is a former Headmaster from a Bermuda school and he is Hindu. With my reading in Melville and Emerson and such, and their interest in Transcendentalism and Eastern religions, I have great fun chatting with him and learning all that I can—he is the first actual Hindu believer I have met. As an Associate, he has his own approach: he watches me teach one day and then does not return to the classroom until my final day the next week. He simply scrawls across my final report: *Brian will be a fine teacher*!

In Port Hope, I teach History with a man who is a teacher god. He is the football coach and a teacher liked and revered through the entire school. A walk through the halls with him is like a stroll on the red carpet at some awards ceremony. I learn a lot—his feedback is precise and helpful and the school, at large, emotes a constructive ethos, the staff room full of positive energy and humour. I learn to adapt what I know to what I am teaching; in one instance, teaching a unit in Medieval British History, I speak to the class in Middle English, quoting Chaucer's great poem:

> Whan that Aprille with his shoures soote
> The droghte of March hath perced to the roote,
> And bathed every veyne in switch licóur
> Of which vertú engendred is the flour; …

This captivates the interest of the students, and my Associate Teacher, too, and generates a healthy discussion on language, on how language can change, how culture has changed, and why, and so on. (It is also at this school that I meet an English teacher and, in conversation, he recommends that I read an author by the name of Richard Brautigan who, he says, is writing in a way like no other. I write the name down and, the next time I am in Toronto, I find and purchase a book by Brautigan called *The Hawkline Monster: A Gothic Western*. That book will change my life; more about that later.) The only drawback of teaching in Port Hope, because it is so far away, I need to find local accommodation and rent a room at a small motel for five dollars per day. It is late fall, off-season, no heat and only a Gideon's *Bible* for protection against creepy-crawly creatures of the night. The College provides twenty-five dollars per week to cover accommodation. In the placements in Belleville, when I stay at home, I give the money to my mother.

For English in Cobourg, I stay at home and drive. Dad has helped me purchase my first real car, a sporty 1972 Toyota Celica—it's an hour-long drive but it's only for a couple weeks. I am placed with the Department Head of English and she is very helpful. The school is on a winter festival schedule which means that, some days, I do not teach at all but help out monitoring events. And that's 'ok' with me; while it is the best part of the B.Ed., I have found that being a student teacher is still an artificial exercise—not the real thing. Students always know who their actual teacher is, who really doles out the real marks. Notwithstanding, I teach one of her Grade 12 classes (mostly chip-on-the-shoulder females—you know, that age) and they respond well to what I try to do, which impresses her. At the end, she tells me that she would hire me if a job ever materializes. But, from what I can tell, it never does. And I realize this may be a comment that she makes to every student teacher.

My final placement is with a History teacher named Chuck Bovey at Centennial in Belleville. That is a new school, built so all the classrooms are in the inner realms of the structure with no windows. You can enter the building and never see the light of day again until you exit. In teaching History, I also confirm to myself that, no matter how hard one tries, the lessons you offer outside your subject area are never quite as fulfilling as those within—your comfort level and ease with the subject, the background materials you have at your fingertips, are absent. And I have heard from others about a tactic Mr. Bovey has of not completing the final report and making student teachers wait. I simply tell him to forward it to the College and leave on that Friday when my session is done.

I meet several people who become friends for the year at McArthur: Lenora, from the Niagara area—we shared a lot of cigarettes and good humour—and Jim, whose dad was a doctor and a member at Kingston's only private golf course, Cataraqui. We golfed there free on several occasions; all Jim ever did was sign in at the Tee-house, usually empty. And I often sit in class with Moe, a refugee from a Ph.D. program at USC who looks like Allen Ginsberg and has a wickedly sardonic sense of humour. And Sharad shows up as only Sharad can—on the second or third day, I am sitting having a coffee in the cafeteria and there he is. Like a ghost. We share a lot of time and good conversation through the year.

The last assignment at Teachers' College occurs during the final week of the year when students are supposed to find their own placement and observe classes for a week. It's a chance for us to try different settings, secondary teachers in elementary classes, and *vice versa*. But no one from McArthur is checking on this so many students simply go home; I manage to land in an Elementary School for a couple days. It is an open-concept school, with a large circular library in the centre, the class areas spread out around it like the spokes of a wheel. Teachers wear a relaxed wardrobe, T-shirts and jeans; I see one instructor wander through the place smoking a pipe. Another class of students sits in a darkened area, each with ear-phones on watching a film as other students on either side wander around and chatter away, sometimes pointing across at the screen and whispering to their friends. I am not sure that I entirely understand this form of education—I think somehow that it is supposed to be an environment that resembles everyday life—such "open classrooms" is a philosophy that comes and goes over the years. Similarly, the idea of having students in permanent groups (even in high school) was a practice that I encountered several times, the theory being that students could learn from each other as much as they learned from the teacher. The classroom became a kind of cafeteria without the food, at least most of the time.

And the year ends. All in all, the B.Ed. year was not too bad. It was quite fragmented and went by quickly; I lived in a dingy basement apartment behind a furnace in a house across the street from Bellevue House, Sir John A. Macdonald's residence in Kingston. My English instructor, Ron Turner, was a genuine, well-meaning man with lots of practical ideas, and the pub in Portsmouth and the Manor (Queen's go-to bar) were never too far away. McArthur's grading format is a progressive system using H/P/F—Honours/Pass/Fail. This system seems appropriate to the tasks at hand, offering an incentive to those who need that and indicating a qualified success to the rest. I do not go to graduation for the B.Ed, nor do I attend the M.A. ceremony. Mostly, save for those brief crossings of the stage for high school and for my B.A., I think of graduations as pretty tedious things, listening to mispronounced names and watching strangers parade back and forth in (mostly) borrowed robes. And I am reminded again of Mark Twain and Huck Finn and their attitude toward the rituals and rules of society: "… Aunt Sally she's going to adopt me and sivilize me, and I can't stand it. I been there before." That said, later as a professor, I end up participating in numerous ceremonial roles at such Graduation occasions; for the most part, they are still pretty tedious although I come to understand their place in university goodwill and marketing.

38

To BCI Once More
(and my first years of teaching)

> You can't go back home to your family, back home to
> your childhood ... back home to a young man's dreams
> of glory and of fame ... back home to places in the
> country, back home to the old forms and systems of
> things which once seemed everlasting but which are
> changing all the time—back home to the escapes of
> Time and Memory.
>
> —Thomas Wolfe *You Can't Go Home Again*

There are no teaching jobs. There are never any teaching jobs. Ever!
Every new teacher graduate knows that (particularly in the last forty
years). Gone are the baby boom days when entire sections of the *Globe
and Mail* would be filled with ads for employment in teaching. Gone are
the days when Boards of Education would fill the Park Plaza Hotel in
Toronto and sign candidates on the spot, sweeping them away like
joyous waves at some drunken football stadium. Gone are the days when
qualified teacher trainees could pick and choose what area of the
province in which they might prefer to live and work and grow old.

Like most of the graduates of the B.Ed. program, by the end of
April I have completed a resume and filled out numerous application
forms for the various Boards I think I might like to work for—
Kingston, Ottawa, Peterborough, Hastings. And I continue to scour the
newspapers, the Tuesday *Globe and Mail* and the local *Ontario Intelligencer*.
I am staying at home, doing some work on the farm and helping my

father with the mail route, optimistically figuring that some prospect will appear sooner or later. And they do at scattered times—I apply for a job and am offered a part-time position in a school in Northumberland County, north of Cobourg. As I am thinking about that, an ad for an English teacher appears in the local paper at, of all places, my old high school, BCI&VS. I do not really want to teach there; after all, it is only six years since I graduated and many of my former teachers would still be in the building. Working around them, with them, well, it would be strange, uncomfortable, even creepy in some way. But … what can I do? I apply … and get an interview.

Part of that interview team is Mr. Hildebrandt, my old Math teacher but now Vice Principal. Another member is Ruth Boyce, another rookie V.P. but former member of the English Department, and the Principal Jim Walker. As I recall, the questions are broad and soft: would I have any objection to the requirement of wearing a coat and tie? Would I be willing to coach? What is my opinion of teaching in a semester system? To this last question, BCI had just decided to switch to semestering, which among other things meant that the school day would begin at eight AM, not at the traditional nine o'clock, and the issue had apparently raised a huge and divisive debate among the staff, only being accepted by a narrow margin. I had no problems with any of the questions and returned home. About two days later the phone rang and it was Harold Hildebrandt; he indicated that the English job had gone to another applicant (a teacher with several years' experience from Stratford, I later learned) but that BCI was prepared to offer me a job made up of two English, two History, and two Geography. And O, the bravado of youth, or maybe the stupidity! I thanked him for the offer and declined, saying that such a teaching load just seemed too fragmented for me. I hung up and went out to cut my parents' lawn and then, after fifteen minutes or so, call it one of those fateful moments of serendipity, if you will, the lawn mower sputtered and died, running out of gas. It was at that very moment that I heard the telephone ring. I went inside and answered it to hear Mr. Hildebrandt again, this time offering me a teaching schedule of four English and two of my choice, History or Geography. What could I do? Obviously BCI was bending over backward to accommodate me … I accepted and, thinking a moment, told him that I would prefer to teach Geography. I am not entirely certain why I chose the subject in which I had no teaching experience, or much academic background, except that I figured there might be lots of maps to be created, film strips and other visual aids to use and so on. And maybe, having taught History in practice teaching sessions, I thought that I would prefer something else. Also, I think, one of the teachers I most respected in all the world, Mr. Bruce Retallick, was still in the History Department at BCI and I think I was intimidated at the thought of teaching in his shadow.

As it turned out, BCI was an excellent place to learn how to teach or, at least, to start to learn the craft. Over time, one thing that I came to understand is that, as in many things, one is always in the process of learning, but especially, it seems, in education where students change, subjects change, pedagogies change, technologies change, cultures change, political powers change, expectations and goals change. And, most of all, you change. Understanding and recognizing that human change is probably the key in becoming an effective teacher (maybe the key in being human)—that essential understanding that we never arrive, that we are always evolving, we are always in a state of becoming. To be rooted, cemented, in a specific psychic place is probably the greatest act of failure any teacher can ever execute. And, sadly, I think, teacher or no, such a petrification happens to so many people, even by their teens, and they are mere zombies for the rest of their lives. The walking dead. In some way, the purpose of education may be to keep the living alive, and sometiomes to re-animate the dead. This does not mean that old ideas or tested virtues are not valuable nor does it mean that they are not useful to offer for consideration in contemporary classes but … the ink for the Ditto Machine, my friends, has long since evaporated—we must not be ossified by its Circean scent. We must avoid being Gryll.

As to BCI, itself, it was an old school whose facilities were often deliciously out-of-step with the times. Some classrooms still had varnished rows of folding desks bolted to the floor with art-deco iron legs; the first working door key given to me was an actual skeleton key. The Physical Education facilities were quite archaic; there was no full-size playing field and space in the basement gyms was hampered with a huge overhead beam. (The Men's Head of Physical Education, Brian McKenzie, had kindly invited me in to cover his classes one day in June so I got a refresher day, as it were, in reminding me what the school was like—as a mark of change, I recall that one of his classes was a Grade Twelve Girls' class learning the rules of football. When it came time to scrimmage, they wanted me to let them play tackle. I did and no-one got killed so the day ended well.) The Shops, too, were filled with museum-quality planers and jointers and automobile engines from the 1940s. This meant that most Technology and Occupational students went to newer schools, better equipped for the skills they needed. But BCI, it had its charms, too. Rooms had fifteen-foot high ceilings, huge metal windows that cranked open, a classic 800-seat auditorium with its faux-marbled proscenium stage and large domed lights hanging from above on chains. The corridors of BCI were wide, wainscoted with glossy red brick and lined with plaques and trophy cases that housed over fifty years of past glories. BCI's students now generally came from the affluent homes of the city and from the north end of the County, doctors' and lawyers' kids, the children of successful business-people and traditional farm families. Discipline was not often a real or unmanageable problem. There were a few rebels and miscreants, of course—there always are—but, generally, it was a very ordered place to learn to teach. I could focus on improving my teaching skills not my classroom management.

All of the newest teachers to Hastings County are invited to the Education Centre one afternoon in early September for an orientation. Among many speakers who talk to us is Mr. Eric Runacres, the Director of Education for the newly amalgamated Hastings County Board, and one thing that I recall him saying remains with me as clear today as when he said it. He advised us to immerse ourselves in our teaching and to "take risks." That is the only time in my teaching career that I ever heard any Administrator anywhere say anything close to that; usually the suggestion pulsed more along the "keep in line" or "don't rock the boat" tone. But not Mr. Runacres; for him, it was "take risks" and, to this day, I recall that advice and remain impressed that such was his message. And to me, for teachers starting out in their teaching career, it remains an excellent a piece of advice now as it was then.

On that first day in September, I remember stopping on the sidewalk before I entered school, groups of students noisily chattering away and brushing past me, and me, wondering—what have I got myself into? But, in the end, I pushed on and my first teaching job turned out just fine. I taught a couple Grade Nine Geography courses for two years before I moved to all English all the time for the rest of my career. The members of the Geography Department treated me well; the Head, Bob Ross, a geologic rock hound, made every resource he had readily available. He was an hilarious man; I always remember in particular one of his funniest stories. Bob used to preview educational films for some film distribution company and would typically show them to his students, having them respond critically. One time he received a film on Sweden and, not thinking too much about it, proceeded to show it (without preview) when, suddenly, its focus shifted from the industries of Sweden to the culture of the Swedish bath house, the screen filled with images of nude Swedes cavorting about. Bob said his first impulse was to rush to the screen and try to cover the images with his hands which, of course, really served no purpose except perhaps to refocus those students who weren't paying much attention. Bob always seemed to have such humorous stories to tell. And while I would never claim that I was a great Geography teacher, I worked at it and did come up with some good ideas. Once I had students create their own imaginary island kingdom, like Earthsea or Never Land or Laputa, inventing a series of maps showing contour lines, political divisions, meteorological systems, and so on. It was an exercise that really drove home the concepts at hand. What do contour lines do when they depict a mountain? How do isobars change from land to sea? And under the category of "serendipity," I suppose, I think that the experience of working with film strips, films, and projectors in teaching Geography nudged me into an understanding of how powerful, how motivating, visual media can be for students and certainly encouraged me into learning how to transfer the use of such technology into my English classroom.

At the end of first semester, I recall calculating the final marks for one of my Geography classes and struggling over whether or not to pass Eddie. He had done little all term except disrupt the class and had completed a horrendous final exam. He hardly tried, leaving most of it blank. In the end, in spite of my arduous re-evaluations and anxieties, I felt that I could not pass him. And next fall, who is one of the very first students I meet in the hall, but Eddie, who comes straight up to me—I was expecting the worst, but he says in a somewhat cheerful tone: "Hello, sir. Guess whose class I'm in? I can't wait." And he was genuinely happy. In spite of all my concerns, he was as pleased as a muddy pig to be in my class again. Failing did not matter as much as the comfort zone which he knew he would inhabit, and he worked harder and achieved a well-earned C+ that semester and never failed to say 'hello' with a smile whenever our paths crossed again. There were lots of things to be learned here but one … I came to understand that, as teachers, most of us come with an academically-oriented initiative, driven to success especially in matters related to learning and school. But not all of our students are like that. Learning how to recognize and understand those differing spheres of existence is vital to so many aspects of being an effective teacher. Not all students will pass, but all students can learn. So can teachers! And marks are always a momentary and superficial thing—they are not a selfie of anyone's soul.

As to English, well, not to wax nostalgic, but one's first class is always one's first class. The first class you can really call your own is forever your best class, your most memorable. For me that was the Grade Eleven academic class that I taught in my first semester, about thirty students in total, their names memorialized in a poem I wrote many years later, "A Prayer for My Students" (see *Addendum* following). First of all, unlike any teaching experience before, although I followed the prescribed curriculum, I was responsible for, in control of, what went on in that classroom, in the first days starting with a series of open-ended warm-up exercises (some playful short pieces of literature from John Lennon and Richard Brautigan and James Thurber, some word games and Mad-libs and creative writing) and moving on to short stories ("A Cask of Amontillado" and "By the Waters of Babylon" and "The Lottery" and "The Machine Stops") then a "Poetry and Film" unit (see next chapter) and a unit using contemporary songs with interesting lyrics (Dylan's "Subterranean Homesick Blues," John's "Daniel," Reddy's "I Am Woman," and Springsteen's "Thunder Road" were a few) then on to *Lord of the Flies* and *Romeo and Juliet*, finishing the year with a fun reading of *West Side Story*. The only literary hiccough during the year was Dickens' *A Tale of Two Cities* which students found very difficult to read or comprehend; it was a literary left-over from the long-standing tradition of reading a Victorian novel in high school each year. This was a class filled with strong students and even they struggled. I think that was the last Victorian novel I taught at high school—later, teaching *Great Expectations* in a first-year university course, I saw the same reading issues arise and could understand why. Once, students had had a dose of this kind of writing throughout Elementary and Secondary school but in the modern curricula, particularly under the influence of personal choice and whole language, lengthy descriptive prose and long convoluted plots, as one finds in Victorian lit., made them strangers in a strange land. Beyond that, this Grade Eleven class involved itself in almost everything we did—even to this day I remember explosive debates (arguments?) within the class over issues such as the fate of the elderly in our society and whether or not inheritance should be allowed. I have taught lots of other engaged and engaging classes since but this was my first and to this day there is a magic in my memory of these young people. At the end of the semester, every one of them passed and, in itself, that speaks volumes.

Margaret Werkhoven, Head of the English Department, is one of the most earnest and hard-working teachers I have ever encountered, the first I knew to institute a journal-writing program among her classes. She also has a political bent and, after a couple years, moves to a job at the Education Centre—eventually she will work at the Ministry level. She is replaced by Kevin Manion, a gregarious, likeable person who becomes a good friend. I attended several English conferences with Kevin; touring around Toronto in his freezing-cold VW-Bug and, one time in Ottawa, at his in-laws' house we watched that famous play-off game in which the Bruins took a "too-many-men-on-the-ice" penalty and Guy Lafleur scored to send the game to overtime where the Canadiens won. (I had the opportunity to travel to Montreal a couple times in the late 1970s to see those spectacular Canadiens' teams play— Lafleur winding up behind his net and soaring down the right wing, blonde hair flying and the noise of the crowd rising to a crescendo; that Hardyesque madding of the crowd was breathtaking.) By my fifth year, Kevin has me create a special Grade Thirteen English course which I nickname *Visions*; it dabbles in cultural and literary works from the time of Plato and Sophocles through Swift and Brontë and Yeats and Munro and other contemporary writers, even living ones—I have writers like Ralph Gustafson, Robert Allen and bill bissett visit the classroom. The course is packed with some of the most gifted students in the school, oversubscribed really because I can never say no. For a high school English teacher, this is as good as it gets. The class is eager and witty and never a day goes by that it is not a pleasure to teach. And for me I realize then, if not before, that teaching never feels like a job to me. That I get paid to talk about poems and stories to interested students is merely a curious bonus. And I feel that way throughout my career.

As to working alongside teachers who were my teachers, the likes of Mr. Buckley, Mr. Retallick, Mr. Green and the rest, the environment is always cordial, respectful, but my friends tend to be found among the younger folk, nearer to my age and interests. I often have lunch with Art Tait and John Smith and Bill Miller, the wittiest Physical Education teacher I have ever known. What Thomas Wolfe said holds true—although I have returned to my home turf, I move into my own apartment away from home (to my mother's dismay, I might add) and carve out a space that is certainly not the space in which I grew up. The "home" I return to is not the "home" from which I graduated.

I teach at BCI for five years; I learn how to be a teacher there. Part of that is getting involved in other things at the school. I have always done that, trying to be engaged in various aspects of school life, trying to be in the bloodstream of the school. It is a part, I think, of becoming the school and knowing yourself as a teacher and, in particular, getting to know students in different settings, students in an environment where each wants to be. So, I coach; in first term, I help with Junior Boys' football, then coach the Junior Girls' Volleyball squad. In second year, I co-coach a Junior Boys' Volleyball team, and so on—I don't think I ever teach in any high school where I do not coach at least one team. Volleyball becomes my specialty, I attend training-theory sessions and take courses, do a lot of reading and, over the years, a couple of my teams actually manage to compete at the highest championship level. Although one year at BCI, while coaching a Midget Girls' Volleyball team (the label used in that time), an amusing issue arose—after our early morning practice, the female Physical Education Head catches one of the girls smoking-up in the changeroom, a place to which, obviously, I have no access. This creates a mini-crisis; although I think it is somewhat hilarious, I play it serious and the entire team, *sans* the guilty person, comes to my room after school to beg me not to quit being their coach. Through much soul-searching, we push on. As to the guilty person, the most talented player, by the way, and a really likeable young woman, her parents withdraw her from the school; her name (yes, of course, she is the child of that old nemesis from the County)—Sherry Salisbury. What were the odds! At BCI, I also get involved in school and union duties, being PD rep. and serving on PAC and CBC and being Staff President. And I present several PD sessions (The Use of Film in English, Linguistics and English). And for most of my time at BCI, with Dave Handley, I help produce the annual school variety extravaganza, *Kampus Kapers*—a tradition at the old school for as long as the school has existed, preparation begins in late fall and extends to late Spring when the show will finally unfold in all its glitzy glory.

After the end of my first year of teaching, I take on a summer school course, a combined Grade 11 and 12 offering which runs at Quinte Secondary each afternoon from 1:00 to 4:00. I do this for several reasons—one, I figure it will give me more teaching experience; two, Quinte is only a two-minute walk from the apartment building in which I live, so it's convenient; three, a bit of extra cash will be handy (teacher salaries and benefits in those days were not that great); and four, I did not have any plans for the summer anyway. The school is not air-conditioned and the afternoon classrooms are like saunas—Math courses outnumber all courses and get all the morning slots (failure in regular-school Math is the force that drives Summer School in those days)—but discipline is well-maintained by the Administration and the students are no trouble in that regard, so I can focus on the teaching. Although I am repeatedly asked to return for the following year and after, I do not teach Summer School again. It was a good experience but, for some such experiences, once is enough.

There were also lots of other distractions in my teaching life at BCI. The Toronto Blue Jays were a new thing and I organized a couple year-end trips for staff to see games, the first using a van we rented, the second with teachers from Trenton High School in a Greyhound. To use the vernacular of the day, these were pretty wild and crazy affairs. We played cribbage in the Staff Room and a silly little curling game that was wonderfully competitive for quarters and, on Fridays, a group of us regularly walked down to the *Cozy Grill* for lunch—their mincemeat pie was an addiction. And there was the *Batchelor Club & Friends*, invented by Art Tait and I where, on occasions, we would have staff sign up and we would come to their house for food and drinks; ridiculous as it was, people actually did sign and we did tours. Art was from L'Amable, near Bancroft, where my mother was born and grew up—one of my earliest childhood memories was the savage sound of a fiddle being played by one of Art's relatives, the sound mingling with the ever-present scent of wood and tobacco smoke and drifting up to my grandmother's house from the valley below. So Art and I had a natural bond, coached a lot of teams together, ate a lot of meals and closed down a lot of bars together, both around Belleville and in Lake Placid during March Break. Ours was a beautiful friendship for many years and we still touch base from time to time.

Paul Temple was a classics' scholar who taught Latin until the subject disappeared and he shifted to English. Paul used to do those cryptic Crosswords which I could never understand; I loaned him my copy of Joyce's *Finnegans Wake* one time and he actually understood it, reading certain sections to me, explaining the jokes and laughing and laughing. And Paul had lots of wonderful stories; he always claimed that once, as a college student, he had completed a translation of *The Aeneid* and later found out that his professor had it published as his own work. Once, Paul claimed, he was telling this story to a stranger in a bar, as personally poignant and treacherous a tale as it seemed to him, when the fellow turned and said, "Who gives a fuck!" Paul loved to play golf and we walked many a fairway together blathering away about this or that witty or quasi-intellectual thing. He had that academic bent of mind which I have always enjoyed, the ability to see the ordinary world in a surprising, extraordinary way.

I quit teaching after five years at BCI through a combination of circumstances. Probably key to that was my mother's death. Early in my third year, she came home one Saturday from working at Barber's Flowers, where she did most everything including the design of floral arrangements, and her right arm would not stop twitching. Hospitalizations and tests and surgeries later, it was determined to be incurable brain cancer. Her health slowly declined over the next couple years until she was placed in the chronic care wing of the Belleville General Hospital unable to discern the present, ultimately losing her ability to speak. I used to go to the hospital after school most every day to help feed her. She died in July; I taught one more year at BCI. My solution to her ongoing illness, I think, was to bury myself in work. One year I coached four teams, two in the winter term (early morning and after school) and I took on the job of Night School Principal—four nights per week, I hired and supervised over fifty instructors and courses including an arrangement with newly founded Loyalist College providing some Business courses. We also offered Board of Education credit courses in subjects like English and Mathematics and Typing, and interest courses for the general public in specialized areas like Cooking and Baking and Auto Shop and Ikebana and Jazzercise and Violin Making (I still remember the craftsman Broder Johannsen holding a piece of wood he had chosen, knocking on it with his fingers and telling me that he could hear the music in the wood), and more. The job wasn't all management; at break, I used to set up and sell coffee and donuts for twenty-five cents apiece—aside from making some pocket change I passed on to day-school charities, this also gave me some good time to kibitz with our "night-school" students and get to know them a bit and, actually, it was simply a lot of fun and got me out of the office where, I must add, my secretary Gerry did phenomenal work. As a result of this kind of successful management, I think, part-way through my fifth year, the Administration at BCI offered me a unique opportunity to take on a newly-created position—I would teach half-time and travel throughout the community the remainder, meeting with and talking to community groups about special programs offered by the school and the Board.

But at that point, the die in my head had been cast. Things in my life seemed changed utterly. There were even days in that year after my mother died, when I left school and automatically turned the car toward the hospital—surely it was feeding time in chronic care. And then I'd realize my error. I felt worn down, used up, and needed a redirection. Adding to that, as a result of declining student enrolment and as a legal precaution, each year I worked at BCI, I had received a letter from Hasting County laying me off—while we were always told to ignore these letters (they were just a legal formality), somehow they always reminded me, as Pink Floyd said about those students, I, too, was just another brick in the wall. One's value was no more than that proverbial bean being counted somewhere by some indifferent accountant or lawyer. As it happens, my birthday falls late in May and, in my fifth year at BCI, the termination letter from Hastings County was imprinted with that date. I framed that letter and still have it to this day. Being fired on your birthday—how cool is that! And surely it was a sign, I thought.

In retrospect, my departure was not perfect—as Keats wrote, "I always made an awkward bow." I decided to return to graduate studies and made that decision, in practice, quickly, even rashly. Finishing my M.A. always made me feel as if I had climbed only halfway up a mountain. I knew that I still had some academic chops inside me and the job was not finished. So, I reapplied to Western and they seemed pleased to accept me. There were practical aspects, like finding accommodation in London before the summer crush of students, and so I finished my responsibilities (mark entry and other paperwork) by the third week of June and left Belleville to find an apartment. This necessary abruptness meant I could not attend a special send-off that had been arranged for me (renting a hall and all) but I never wanted, nor felt that I deserved, that kind of special treatment. Rare is the retirement or send-off that I have ever attended for anyone, including myself. I have never enjoyed a funeral.

And so, as much as I had learned at BCI both as a student and as an emerging teacher, and as many friends as I had made there and as many students as I may have influenced and who had an impact on me, I handed in my resignation and would never enter that building again—it was closed as a school in 1992 and demolished twelve years later. Nothing sits in that empty space now. But there are ghosts, of course. Some evening, park your car in the empty parking lot and watch carefully, especially on those nights when the moon is full—you will see them shuffle along, shadowy figures with a hopeful stride, carrying their armful of books through that space, and climbing invisible stairs into the deep night sky, the faint summons of distant class bells singing like lost choirs. The past and future ever just a step away.

Belleville Collegiate Institute & Vocational School, cornerstone 1927

ADDENDUM:

a prayer for my students

i

as things wind down for me like some old fat clock
and time begins to tell me more than i tell time
schools and clubs   teams and faces
rise like gaunt spirits from hungry yearbooks
teaching in five long decades   nearly forty years   forty years
and ten thousand students
ten thousand bodies full of energy and doubt and cockiness and wonder
and the conceit that they know it all or nothing or dont care or do
and they are always fifteen
year by year this talking body came to know the crease and ache of age
but they are always fifteen
keeping me young and making me grow old at the same time i suppose

ii

after the banality of teachers college
the artifice of imprinting on anothers classes
and the passing rite of beer and beach of ex and telethon
sudden september is upon us
yellow beasts with red eyes slip through the morning fog
prowling a young and disquiet jungle
i remember pausing on the sidewalk before the doors on that first morning
'what have i gotten myself into'
and then i push on because i have to

i remember my first class   most teachers do
mine a group of grade elevens emerging as all grade elevens do
from childhoods placentic cartoon
        to the awe of a new and brave world
a world of idea and insight and responsibility and freedom of body and mind
where car keys rattle like rapture in the palm and tobacco is in the air
where skipping a class is tempting as the illusion that free will affords
where academic grind truly begins and a new light-just-met kindles—

tom and tricia and dawn and terry-lynn and andrew and
darlene and judy and debbie and ginny and mary and richard
and bruce and dorothy and mark and barbara and chris and
angela and paul and eric and nancy and rick and alan and
kathy and rob and jill and tammy and dianne and catherine
and john (because theres always a john and this one passed
though barely because he despised the illogic of poetry and
the banter of mercutio but he liked the logic of grammar and
that seemed enough at the time and i have felt no regret since)

iii

a curious mixture of joy and sorrow sweeps over me
one goes with the other in such matters i guess
over the years
some flirted some raged some shared music and laughter
        and opinions about movies
some carried that dark chip on their soul as teenagers do best
        in building their moats and walls
some dropped by to say hi as i sat after school to mark or plan
some were probably wronged by me in some institutional way
        but they managed to escape alive
some shared pizza at seasons end or coaxed this worlds worst dancer
        to their proms sway
some later brought their children to view the old relic
        who once taught them something years before
        exactly what—well such is memory's blur
some slipped away when no monitor was in sight—
one shot in a calgary bar one taken in an alcoholic car crash on highway 19
one with cancer in the brain another whose double lung transplant didnt take
yet another with sorrow on her wrists and nyquil in her belly
and some went on to deal darkness and consume shadows
our world demands that too
for the race that allows only one runner is no race at all
success for every student is the pledge
whatever that may be is the prize
most i believe found the benchmark that our culture demands of its systems
websites are filled with images of their families and friends
        and the revel of their lives

nurses and doctors and lawyers and police officers and computer wizards
and family makers and factory workers and sales people and stratford stars
and so many as teachers of course from my years at althouse
and all the rest

iv

and so in the end what prayer do i have for these students passed
beyond the cliché of health and joy
what fear do i have if i have any fear
especially today when the world seems so stark
        bombs flying and towers dying and covid constant
the rush of technology worshipped in every silicon of sand
and a carnival of misery aired as amusement across the land
dark mirrors in hand
but of course time is no orphan as all of us know—
drag that horse inside nail the heretic to a tree
        smokes always rising where it shouldnt be—
the dark dogs of havoc have growled down the ages
        in different shapes   different dreams
like the ghost lines that faintly remained on all the blackboards i ever erased
slight scars embracing each new day begun
        so we take back the night and meet ourselves in the pitch
        a prayer imprecise just whets the fangs of the bitch
so think again think again
what is the purpose of the bell rung the hand raised
the poem the equation the experiment and the lap run
field trip and science fair debate fought and musical done
what the end in this hearts haunt of all these chalky rooms
but that these students received the power for their own prayer
placed true at their fingers touch whatever that touch can be
as near as minds echo or faiths will

v

and so my prayer then lies in its own souls way
after all the care you have been given
after all the paths made bare
beyond the busy web find a pure space in the air

a space both genuine and fair
and be aware
with opened eye each day
just be aware

and see it new   see you   and come to knowing
and the wonders of the gods will dance
like some magic firework that explodes again
just as you think its done   and again
and you and your prayer will be one and true
but always new
and so better the world too

that is my prayer

and then you must get on with the living of things
the swaddling of the babe
the working of the sod
the cheering of the wide tv
and this old teacher for one   illusion or no
will be satisfied to imagine his journey not entirely spent
or accord denied beyond the endless sere

(previously published in *redirection* Hidden Brook Press 2015)

39

It's Full of Stars

The thing's hollow—it goes on forever—and—oh my
God!—*it's full of stars!*

—Arthur C. Clarke *2001: A Space Odyssey*

I can see the grass is growing on the streets I knew
And through the trees I can see the sun is shining on the sea
And the ruins of the city are in flower now
For the great electric experiment is over...over now

—Noel Harrison "The Great Electric Experiment"

During my first semester of teaching, I created a unit entitled "Poetry
and Film"—my Department Head, Margaret Werkhoven, was intrigued
with it, followed my lead in her section of the course and, ultimately, we
delivered a P.D. Day presentation based on the use of film in English
(my first of many such "media" offerings through the years). I was
always a big fan of film and television and had taken a couple film
courses at Queen's, one of the first universities in Canada to create a
Film Studies Department. Getting into those courses was the first
challenge (they were very popular); there, I studied *An Introduction to Film
Studies* (we learned the terminology of film, dating back to the days of
Cecil B. DeMille, and studied several genres: the western, film noir, the
thriller, among others). And in another course, *Film as Auteur Art*, we
viewed the works of great directors such as Ford, Kurosawa, Hitchcock,
Fellini, Bergman, Ozu, Peckinpah. To one who had watched John Wayne
and Jimmy Stewart in countless westerns all my life, it was astonishing

to see such popular icons and their movies being talked about by university professors, to see the symbols and motifs of these films identified and analyzed as a matter of serious study and fine art. (Here, among other things, we are reminded that there is always a fine line between what is considered, by some, to be high or fine art and that which is thought of as low or popular art—Shakespeare and Mozart, we recall, played for the people of the streets as well as the aristocratic elite.)

Teaching with film in these early days was not always an easy thing. The 16mm film projectors were large and sometimes cantankerous things, chewing on and frying celluloid at a whim's notice. And the films, themselves, had to be located and requisitioned early on, sources included the Education Centre, the local city library, NFB, CBC—often the first thing I did in late August was order the films I wanted and when I wanted them. As films became known and noted, competition increased. In those days, Education Centres had libraries and a full-time Librarian to manage such things; by way of example in London, the School Library at the Education Centre was renowned, containing all sorts of print materials for research and a huge selection of films and film-strips—university professors regularly used its resources. For my "Poetry and Film" unit at BCI, I searched out and found a large variety of short, creative films from various locations (mostly Education and Public Libraries, and the NFB), including:

> *Rainshower*—without dialogue, a sumptuous film tracks the arrival and dissipation of a rain shower and its impact on life in the country and the city.

> *Neighbours*—Norman McLaren's NFB film creatively uses pixilation animation to show two neighbours coming to a pointless war over ownership of a flower; as the concluding card reminds us, in several languages, "Love Your Neighbour."

> *Omega*—an open-ended, experimental film about humans and the ending, or beginning, of a new universe. Mercurial, enigmatic, mesmerizing to this day.

> *Da Duva*—clever parody of Bergman's *The Seventh Seal* using "pig-Swedish," or as the *Mooska* says, "Moo."

The Rise and Fall of the Great Lakes—Bill Mason's comic adventure depicting a canoeist paddling around the Great Lakes in geologic time and dealing with all of the changes encountered; as its soundtrack folk song says, "…changes keep the world goin' round…"

Flat Flip Flies Straight—a true film-maker's film, a fluid work showing a boy tossing a frisbee to his dog on a beach with Wagner's potent "The Ride of the Valkyries" as soundtrack. A joyful, colourful and mesmerizing short film.

Cosmic Zoom—a lyrical animated short that begins with a boy and his dog in a canoe on the Ottawa River, then zooms out to the farthest reaches of the universe, reverses and plunges back to a mosquito on the boy's arm and then continues a dive to the core of the most minute atom.

Evolution—the NFB animated classic humorously tracing the development of life on this planet and beyond—warning: there always seems to be a bigger fish.

Nahanni—a Canadian odyssey set amid the rugged and beautiful land of the northwest, the aging Albert Faille struggles to find a mythic gold mine near the head of the turbulent Nahanni River.

Joseph Schultz—a 1975 film that promotes values clarification and a lot more; a German soldier refuses to take part in a firing squad and is, himself, executed.

The Shopping Bag Lady—a teen learns a life lesson when she comes to see through the eyes of a homeless person whom she and some friends had earlier harassed.

Two Men and a Wardrobe—Polanski's student film, an allegorical account of two figures who emerge from the sea and of the prejudice they encounter as they journey inland carrying their wardrobe. (As an aside, I still have a 16mm copy of this film; in later years when videotape took over and the Oxford County Board dismantled its Media Library, they sent me the film to keep—I guess I was the teacher who had used it most, maybe the only one who had used it?)

The Red Balloon—a helium-filled balloon exhibits sentient qualities and magically comes to the aid of the small boy, Pascal.

The Log-Driver's Waltz—Animation takes over from live-action in this joyful musical account of love, logs and rapids: "The log driver's waltz pleases girls completely"—an NFB gem.

I presented these films along with a study of poetry, in particular emphasizing the power of precise imagery, motif, structure and symbolism, techniques essential to both arts. In the classroom, the balance between the two forms seemed to enhance the power and magic of each. I will add that, one time, some forty years later, I had the occasion of meeting a student from one of those classes, Peter Luscombe, and Peter actually still remembered those long-ago classes, in large part because of the film unit, recalling them as a huge influence on the career he pursued: Peter was then head of the Department of English at Lucas Secondary School in London, Ontario. (Of note, I might add that all of the film examples mentioned above are still readily available from online resources, a testament to their enduring quality, I think.)

I also did a unit I nicknamed "combos" where I used film versions of several short stories that I taught, always reading the story first, having students analyze it in one way or another, then viewing and analyzing the film, comparing the two, and so on. It seemed to work well in engaging students especially in regard to inevitable gaps between genres. Why were some things omitted in the film versions, why were certain things added? Which was better, story or film? In what ways did each affect the "reader"? How were the genres irrevocably different? What did they share in common, in methods? I think the process helped students read both stories and films more effectively and gaps often became the subject of observation and heated discussion. (Understanding gaps, what is absent, is often a key in understanding literary fiction or scientific experimentation—what is not stated or present being as important as what is.) Among others, I used story and film combinations of "The Lottery" (the 1969 Encyclopedia Britannica version, not later TV adaptations); "Dr. Heidegger's Experiment"; "Occurrence at Owl Creek Bridge"; "The Red Kite"; "Boys and Girls"; "The Lady or the Tiger"; "The Gift of the Magi"; "The Fall of the House of Usher" (the fine *Short Story Showcase* version, not the *Netflix* series).

Full length film had to be ordered at significant cost from the distributers and generally had to be returned in twenty-four hours. One time, I remember travelling to the Belleville bus station early in the morning to pick up a copy of Zeffirelli's *Romeo and Juliet,* four reels in a huge much-travelled canvas-strapped carton, so we could gather classes together that day and then get the film returned by the next (all in the hope that the projector would not exhibit some hunger-tantrum that day). As the 1980s unfolded, some schoolrooms had televisions installed, hanging from the ceiling and capable of being hooked into an intra-board network of "Educational Programming." Usually, the teacher would book a time and, at that moment, some selected television program would flicker to life. But Educational Television was an awkward, clunky system, often with limited or second-rate programming with cheap production values; generally, its use disrupted the flow of the day and surrendered the control of that flow to external forces. It never really caught on; for a lot of teachers, the trouble outweighed the value. And then, beginning in the mid-seventies, personal recording technology began to blossom. Betamax and VHS battled in the format wars, and very slowly, Boards of Education bought into one or the other; the practice of teachers using materials taped at home exploded and, in step, the video rental business was born— remember the time when *Blockbuster* or *Jumbo* or *Videoflicks* lurked on every block, and every corner store had racks and racks of tape— sometimes video player and tape rented together? And other technologies quickly followed: Laserdisc, Video8, DV Video, DVD, DIVX, MPeg 4, Blu-Ray, HD-DVD, Video-On-Demand, and the current technological immediacy of cell phones and computers and tablets which enable access to various forms of video download and streaming, YouTube, Spotify, and all the rest. The accessibility of programming for use in lessons now seems illimitable.

There is a double-edged caveat, I suppose. The display of the magic lantern, the tantalizing light on the wall, comes with so much ease today and the process of education, especially in our post-*Covid-19* world, seems swallowed in such a technological maelstrom—*ReadWriteThink* and *Socrative* and *Moodle* and *Grammarly*, Zoom, Google, X and the rest. One issue, the nature of contemporary technology—by the time you read this, these sites and programs just mentioned may be ancient history. Obsolescence is immediate—babies are born with walkers and catheters inserted. The portentous conclusion of Orwell's *Animal Farm* comes to mind:

> The creatures outside looked from pig to man, and from man to pig, and from pig to man again: but already it was impossible to say which was which.

As you gaze into the contemporary classroom, sometimes it is difficult to tell the students from the screen and *vice versa*. Indeed, as Marshall McLuhan predicted so long ago, not only is the medium now the message but, in fact, the day has come when we wear ourselves. Dark mirrors are held up everywhere. A monumental change has occurred. Students have become their screens; like Alice, they have passed into these mirrors of their lives. Many teachers have, too. One might conclude, of course, that this technological immediacy has made teaching easier—if students do not know what a *one-horse open sleigh* is or a *dodecahedron* or a *rotogravure* well, *voilà*, push a Google button and there one is. Just that easy! But, for contemporary educators, to teach a thing to the thing-in-itself is a challenging and intricate task. Like teaching dance while dancing to a dancer. We are Chaplin's Tramp rolled inside the great machine, Sisyphus seeking liberation by embracing the very act of his enslavement. An evolutionary layer has been added to the pedagogical mix. And there is no going back, no coaxing the genie back to its lamp, nor would we want to. As concepts like gender and race, ethnicity and class have changed irrevocably (we think, for the better) so, too, the idea of what a student is, of what a child is. Students not only reside in Plato's Cave; they have evolved to become the Cave, itself. Behold the apotheosis of the "Data-Child." Besieged by a tsunami of information and adept in the tech of the moment, for humans, especially the young, this has become the age of the selfie, a world of narcissistic social web-sites where people do not interact as much as they endlessly express their own interests and opinions, casting images of themselves for the world to see like a life-buoy adrift trying to stay afloat. As if Viktor Frankenstein's creature had self-replicated, the spawn of some mad 3D printer—something horrible, or something wonderful—remember, though monstrous, filled with rage and capable of extreme violence, Frankenstein's creation is also erudite, reading Milton and Plato and the Bible? Black holes or the birth of stars?

Recently, a friend visited with her nine-year old. They have no televisions in their home (never have); my friend, an avid reader, and her decision, TV is unnecessary, its viewing habits negated, never initiated. And yet, over their weekend visit, my guess is that, instead of being outside exploring or playing or swimming, or inside colouring, drawing or reading, the child spent at least ninety percent of his time viewing a cell screen, a tablet or my TV.

We know that technology always evolves in discernible but sometimes subtle ways, elusive, too, as Roy Amara's 'Law' states: "We tend to overestimate the effect of a technology in the short run and underestimate the effect in the long run." Our human relationship to the phone is an excellent example: once tied by cord to the home or office or phone booth, by the 1980s compact flip phones became common, gradually replacing the house phone; while mobility was their gift, generally they were still used for talking with people, setting up meetings, coffee with friends, and so on, but when the cell phone replaced the flip phone in the early 1990s, technology changed from a device for *communication* to a device for *information*, from a device that projected out to one that burrowed in. Cell phones affixed the user to a world of information (albeit sometimes quasi- or even mis-), to a galaxy of web-sites and social platforms, most with the intent to sell something—merchandise, ideas, values, attitudes. For children, play-time was replaced with screen-time. AI, cell-screen addiction, omnipotent corporations, secretive Big Brother governments, deep-fake fear— ubiquitous forces able to control us with a string of numbers, a beep or a blip on the screen—little wonder that many people are currently obsessed by a sense of having no control over their lives, that the walking dead and other forms of the aimless zombie seem so prevalent in popular culture. The recitative selfie, the social web-site (far more idiocentric than social) was the understandable defense. Zombiest or not, there is no point in trying to ban or cancel or ignore these media—without cells, humans now suffer from psycho-nomophobia; it is an age of idiosyncratic synesthesia. Cell phones are here and here to stay—at least until they morph into something else. Indeed, the best path to avoid having our brains consumed, to avoid becoming real zombies, the best path is understanding our contemporary media. So, don't put your cell phone down or cast it into some drawer or ban it—but look at it—hold it close and really look at it! Whose face do you see? Who must we educate?

(Incidentally, as I write this, the Government of Ontario has just issued regulations to ban cell phones in classrooms (vaping, too)—phones must now be silent and out-of-sight at all times. Here, as is so often the case, the politicos are treading in uninformed spaces— they do not understand the issue at hand, or the students and, rightfully, intuitively, teacher unions have immediately voiced their opposition. Of such government intervention, as Hamlet might say, "the time is out of joint." As teachers, as humans, we must not ban the cell phone from our classrooms, we must learn what it is, how to teach it, how to teach using it, and enlighten our students accordingly.)

When I came home from elementary school as a student circa 1960, I would sometimes listen to short programs on our old console radio, shows like *The Lone Ranger* and *Superman*, about fifteen minutes in length but filled with dynamic action and despicable villains—Butch Cavendish or Lex Luthor—"Hi Yo, Silver", "Up, up and away," all empowered by such telltale radio cues, and all the rest. The radio was taller than I was, a large piece of varnished art deco furniture fuelled by an array of vacuum tubes and two large A/B batteries. Then for Christmas one year, my two older brothers each received a transistor radio—each radio was about the size of a brick and weighed as much. Times were a-changing. What transistor radios did was personalize entertainment and information media and emphasize its portability; instead of sitting at home, usually sharing the experience with family and friends, now the media was mobilized and individuated. My brothers' radios had earphones. Very quickly, as technology evolved and transistors morphed toward integrated circuits and micro-processors, products like the Sony Walkman and Discman, the personal computer, the flip phone and the cellular phone followed. The primary purpose of that cell phone was no longer to send or receive personal calls but to join the vortex of the world, a funhouse mirror both clear and distorted, angelic and demonic. And so a distinct process of individualization and isolation took place; in that dark looking-glass, human youth has become the Data-Child incarnate, the obelisk full of stars. And the monumental challenge for the post-modern teacher now becomes how to ask questions of the question, how to educate the cave itself, how to bring light to the stars.

40
Second star to the right

Five years have past; five summers, with the length
Of five long winters! and again I hear
These waters, rolling from their mountain-springs
With a soft inland murmur—

—William Wordsworth "Lines Composed a few miles
above Tintern Abbey"

I have quit teaching to begin my Ph.D. studies. The doctoral program in English at the University of Western Ontario is possibly as complicated and difficult as any in the world. In some universities, Ph.D. students are assigned an advisor, create a reading list and show up every now and then to discuss their progress. But, in my time, Western's program is delineated and extensive, designed at the very least to turn out competent generalists and, in practice, generating a huge number of incomplete candidacies. In some sense, the Department of English at Western seemed to be trying to prove itself as an academic institution; and one way was to ramp up its requisites:

> 1. a full consecutive year-long residency, during which one is to meet with one's Advisory Committee (by the way, in all my time in the program, I never saw such a group and here, over forty years later, I still await that first meeting);

> 2. an extra foreign language course beyond what you did in your M.A. (I take a correspondence course in

Latin from Waterloo University; pre-online, keeping up with and mailing in the basic monthly assignments is the primary challenge but I manage and earn what is probably my highest mark in any course ever, 95—there are times when I wonder what the doctoral program at Waterloo might be like!);

3. Four to six full graduate courses (or eight to twelve half courses; these became more common in time; and a *caveat emptor*, most half courses really turn out to be three-quarter courses in content) and you must earn a minimum grade of 80% in each of these courses to continue on in the program;

4. Bibliography course;

5. Three extensive general examinations (written; three to five hours in length), at least one must be pre-nineteenth century literature and at least one must be post-nineteenth, and you need to earn at least 70% in each to pass; all three must be written in a one-week period (I opt for Restoration and Eighteenth Century; Romantic and Victorian Literature; and Modern (including British, American and Canadian Literatures) a period from 1670 to contemporary time covering all of the major writers, period and contemporary criticism);

6. Two additional examinations, one written, one oral, in your area of concentration (these are pass or fail);

7. Dissertation (around 300 pages in length, with proper margins—the registrar's office will use a ruler and measure these when you finally submit your work);

8. Final examination focusing on the depth, thoroughness and quality of the dissertation; examiners—one Department; one external to the Department; one external to the university.

It is a long road and many are the graduate students who get lost along the way. Strangely, many succeed quite well in the course-work but disappear when the matter of study is in their own hands, in prepping for the examinations and in conquering the dissertation. I was mostly the reverse; once I got to the specialized exam and the dissertation, I felt confident that the battle was won. Ideally, the doctoral degree should take four years to complete, one year for the courses, one for the general examinations, and two for the rest. But most take longer. In the gentler days of the 1970s, there were numerous students who were well beyond those temporal boundaries; I recall my M.A. office-mate as a man in his tenth year of Ph.D. studies. Eventually, he drifted away. And by the 1980s, a new Department Head of English began to expedite things and this new sheriff-in-town pressured candidates to get on with things. Being an eternal Grad student, apparently, was not a career.

I take two courses in that first year of studies, Professor Woodman's *Shelley and Keats* and Professor Gedalof's *Eighteenth Century Literature*. Dr. Woodman is a well-respected scholar, especially in the works of Shelley—he once wrote *The Apocalyptic Vision in the Poetry of Percy Bysshe Shelley* and was still quoting from it twenty years later. His class is filled with several of his acolytes, students who worship him and have taken other courses with him and/or are working with him on certain academic projects. And Woodman is quite caught up in new approaches to literary interpretation. The so-called New New Criticism has just hit its stride, especially it seems among the world of the Romantics; critics that I have read for enjoyment in undergraduate years, writings superfluous to all things scholarly (Barthes and Bloom and Foucault and such) now seem to be taken as the new divinities of literary study. Derrida has arisen like a third-day god called *deconstruction* and something called the Yale school, Fish and deMan and Hartman, is conjuring volcanoes. To my mind, their works in general are written in obfuscated styles and tend to play a lot of linguistic games that complicate as much as clarify—I think of an essay by Hartman where he latches on to the word "parasite" in Shelley and presumes to write an essay that burrows into the poet's work without ever mentioning the writer or his work. In my experience, these critics rarely speak clearly about any literature and seem to give permission for other lesser academics to do the same. It is cleverness in the place of substance and I never find the genuine there. But that's possibly just me. For a short while, in the bewilderment of this new talk, I wonder if I have made a mistake in taking five years off from graduate studies, but then I come to the realization that no-one else understands this stuff any more than I. It's the same old shit, just a slightly different animal. And the gravitas which it is given seems a sham to me. It's where literary scholars go when they get bored with trying to understand what the poets have to say. And no matter the clever intricacy of the labyrinth established, at some point the onus must fall on the critic to provide some clarity to the reader, otherwise, those critical writings are not worth reading.

The worst case of this kind of academic sleight-of-hand came during a seminar on Shelley's "The Witch of Atlas," given by one of Professor Woodman's disciples. The woman was ploughing through all kinds of arcane insights into the androgyne and the hermaphrodite and the Platonic splitting of the soul when Professor Woodman asked her a question pertaining to the poem, at which point the student admitted that she had never read the poem, the poem on which her seminar was based. Woodman said something like, "well, we should read the poems" and the world spun on. Now there was a time when the ceiling of the seminar room would have been blown off, but that was a time when Graduate seminars were like Julius Caesar's welcome party at the Capitol. I had heard the tales of times when some professors would choose a different grad student each week and proceed to crucify her or him—that was part of the crucible of advancing through this most advanced of degrees. But mostly those days were gone, and this case involved a devoted follower so no discernible punishment was given. To note: I did my seminar on Shelley's *The Cenci* and I did read the work.

This is not to say that literary scholarship and pedagogical method-ologies have not benefitted a great deal from this new new critical wave, this new way of thinking about poems and stories. Feminist perspectives have certainly provided many new handles; surely any reading of *Romeo and Juliet* is bolstered by a consideration of the cultural role of the females within that manipulative chauvinistic society. And most certainly the struggles of Tom Wingfield in *The Glass Menagerie*, trapped in a world of blue roses and gentlemen callers, is enlightened under the eye of Queer Theory. And a Marxist consideration of the role of Willy Loman crushed under the bourgeois juggernaut symbolized by tape machines and silk stockings can offer insight. But as I have said before, the theory that has no traction in practice is of little use. It is simply a form of intellectual masturbation, a moment's pleasure perhaps but no progeny to live on.

Dr. Gedalof's *Eighteenth Century Literature* course is almost the direct opposite of Dr. Woodman's. This course is relaxed and enjoyable and things said are mostly comprehensible. The literature, from *Moll Flanders* and *Robinson Crusoe* to *Clarissa* and *Tom Jones*, from Dryden and Pope to Smart and Swift is often mammothite in size and challenging in scope. But the class feels right; there is plenty of humour and I recognize the place that I would someday like to be. With interests in *Detective Fiction* and *Film Studies*, Professor Gedalof is a kind of modern-day Renaissance scholar and the recipient of numerous teaching awards on-campus and nationally. He later becomes a very important part of my academic journey.

My assignment as a Teaching Assistant for the year is to Professor Constance Hieatt and her course in Children's Literature. This opens up another whole new world for me, working with a subject about which I know nothing. Connie Hieatt is a formidable figure, she and her husband have been stolen by Western from Columbia University, reportedly, for obscene salaries; she is a Chaucer and Middle English scholar, a specialist in Tolkien and Old Norse and Anglo-Saxon languages and literatures, a writer of Medieval cookbooks and of children's literature and one of the founders of the serious study of that sub-genre. Professor Hieatt is a well-organized lecturer although the students find difficulty with her New England accent and a slight speech impediment. I usually manage to ease their concerns in our seminars. I often "man" the slide projector and surprise her, I think, with the ease with which I manage jams, upside down slides, focusing, and so on—my five years of experience as a classroom teacher pays dividends. The same with the teaching where I usually take only five to ten minutes to prepare each seminar. The reading requires a bit more but it is enjoyable. I generally read the course materials in the hour or so before bedtime, usually around midnight; it seems to be a perfect time to be reading Nursery Rhymes or the tales of Grimm and Andersen, the likes of *Peter Pan* and *Alice in Wonderland* and *The Secret Garden*—the load for *Children's Literature* is somewhat heavy, about twenty-five novels, but most are entertaining and straightforward. And Hieatt's lectures reinforce the underlying formulae and themes of this literature; while labelled Children's Literature, it is never entirely just for children. Professor Hieatt is like the Billy Goat from one of the tales she has translated, gruff and distant, but I break through by casually talking with her about everyday matters and, the following year, she asks for me back as a T.A., apparently something she almost never does. I truly consider that as important a conquest as the grades I achieve in the courses I have taken. My return to Graduate Studies after a five-year break ultimately feels like the right thing, the thing I needed to do to clear my life, the meaning lost is found once again in the wonders of the world of literary things. While the workload is heavy, the demands themselves seem to be a liberation of mind and soul, and the path true as that eternal child Peter says: "… second star to the right and straight on 'til morning."

41

Sex, Lies, Videotape and Teaching

You're traveling through another dimension, a dimension not only of sight and sound but of mind. A journey into a wondrous land whose boundaries are that of imagination. That's the signpost up ahead— your next stop, the Twilight Zone!

—Rod Serling *The Twilight Zone* 1959-1964

Space: the final frontier. These are the voyages of the starship *Enterprise*. Its five-year mission: to explore strange new worlds. To seek out new life and new civilizations. To boldly go where no man has gone before!

—James T. Kirk *Star Trek* 1966-1968 (*aka* Gene Roddenberry)

I am not a Luddite when it comes to the Information Age; far from it. I have, in theory and in practise, tried to promote the effective use of technology in teaching, really, since the first day I stepped into a classroom. Even before—I remember during my B.Ed. year using Dylan's poetic "Three Angels" as soundtrack and, with a partner, shooting an 8mm film to align with its words (a music video ahead of its time, I suppose). And in that year, I used Bunuel's film *Un Chien*

Andalou along with Dickinson's "Because I Could Not Stop for Death," slides of Brueghel's "Triumph of Death" and part of "Desolation Row" as a media collage/presentation. I have always been fascinated with the collision and collusion of media, like Keats use of synesthesia, I suppose; how contrapuntal disharmonies can be enlightening, revelatory. As noted previously, "Poetry and Film" in my first year of teaching was a memorable success for many students, and later when the "fifth" credit required for high school graduation became a course in Media English, I was tagged in three successive high schools as the person to design and teach that course. At Clarke Road in London, within three years the enrolment had grown from two sections to eight—almost every student in that Tech-oriented school wanted into that English course. It was such an unusual phenomenon, Administration actually had me give a presentation to the Teaching Staff about the course—I used some snippets of student films and kept that very upbeat, aware of the politics of such an occasion. Later, in my professorial years, I taught *Media Studies* in the Faculty of Education and *Reading Popular Culture* for the Department of English (it was one of those large super-courses with about 1000 students) and I designed and wrote an online version of a media course in the early days when that university cash cow was just calving. And since the 1980s, I have offered numerous Professional Development and information workshops for teachers and for the public at large, some in province-wide conferences, dealing with the topic of media and its impact on education and culture at large. Topics varied—the image of women in media, the image of men, high school in film, television and the family—the title of this chapter was the moniker I gave one presentation in St. Thomas—from the title alone, I think, the seminar was so much in demand that the venue had to be moved to a larger auditorium. The power of a provocative title is never to be underestimated, I guess. As Calvin Klein proclaimed so long ago, "Sex sells!"

This is the twenty-first century. All of us, from womb to tomb (as the gangs in *West Side Story* might say), will be exposed to a great deal of media no matter what kind of hermit- or bookworm-style of life one strives to adopt. We live on the yellow brick road, the film or the song more than the book. And so it has always seemed logical to me that the better our skills in "reading" media, the better off we will be in understanding that beast and in understanding ourselves. Such literacy is critical both for our students' and for our own good health. Whether society creates the media or media creates society is one of those chicken and egg conundrums but an understanding of that dynamic, one way or the other, can reveal a great deal about both. As an example, in the early television anthology series, *The Twilight Zone*, which ran on CBS from 1959 to 1964, show after show was built around the obsessive idea that some force, some thing, was out there ready to attack us, to get us, "to serve man"—literally—monsters or aliens or next-door neighbours who lived on Maple Street. Rod Serling's ominous voice drilled that message home week after week. And of course, such themes reflected the paranoia of the late 1950s, the ever-present cold war with its fear of Communist infiltration and nuclear annihilation. Similarly, by the 2020s, *Black Mirror*, a contemporary anthology series streaming on *Netflix* and often compared to *The Twilight Zone*, offers show after show that spin around themes in which individuals are taken over, or fear being taken over, trapped, manipulated by some intrinsic force beyond their control. And surely such themes provide us with a valuable insight into our own contemporary culture, the world of immersive video entertainment, of existence in a post-*Covid-19* tech-world on which we rely but which few of us really understand or over which we have any real control. Siri…are you listening?

So, if you are a parent, most certainly you should let your child have access to the media, to films and TV and the web—screen time as it is called these days. If you do not, then you are simply making your child into an info-leper, an outcast in body and soul from the world in which she or he is living, undermining an understanding of the world in which we live and condemning your child to techno-death. Like living next to a lake but forbidden from touching the water or swimming. BUT as a parent, you should also engage in the media that your child is consuming so it does not consume your child. Do not protect your children from the evils of the world in forbidding them to go out at night or play unsupervised in the park, and then send them alone to their room where cell and computer and TV screens offer shortcuts to that same world. Work with your child to understand the nuances of the technological age and its messages, and that may be as simple as helping your child understand when the show stops and the commercials begin. And, as a parent, of course, you need to be educated yourself—perhaps some of the material in this chapter will help at least as a place to start.

If you are a teacher, use media. And as a teacher who uses media, teach media. Understand media. This will speak to the identity of your students. They are Star-Children. The Data-Child. They have stopped being those who sit in Plato's cave and view the shadows cast by fire; they have evolved to become the cave itself. As I suggest in Chapter Thirty-nine, in our current age technology and the student have merged and the effective teacher will understand that and work with it accordingly. In the following, let me offer some fragments from my own teaching which you might use to enhance yours. (And I should add, in my experience, many contemporary teachers have a solid grasp of most of this already.)

Obviously how one teaches media is up to the individual. Presenting media courses, I have known teachers who do something different every class, pop music one day, TV the next, Ads the next, and so on. I have seen courses based on themes (sexism, racism, violence or escapism); on history (decade by decade, perhaps, or 1968-1972 (the era of American film's great Renaissance), or even just one year, 1939); on genre (film, TV, Pop Music, detective novels); on sub-genre (Film Noir, Silent Film, the Blockbuster, Sit-coms, the Western, Soap Operas); on *auteur* (Hitchcock, Spielberg, Lucas, Zhao, Norman Lear). Textbooks are also available which divide and subdivide the study in a variety of ways. And now, there are numerous online sites each with its own spin. (In teaching, the key to all of it, as always, exists in the teacher's own awareness of the subject itself, preparation, and enthusiasm.) In the next couple pages, let me lay out my own approach to the subject, the approach which I thought was most effective for the students I taught. I tried to keep things organized and always found that most students benefitted from such a logical, ordered approach. At the very least, what follows will provide a real snapshot of the pedagogy I employed, an approach which seemed to work.

The basis to my approach for students, and this was boiled down from the work of Barthes, McLuhan, Chomsky, Baudrillard, Postman, Duncan and others, was to establish a theoretical framework in the first couple weeks of the course that high school-age students could understand and use throughout. Here are what I call "the Four Cs":

One: Construction: all media are created, from print or TV news to blockbuster films, whatever the medium, someone begins with a blank slate (a new page or an empty sound stage or an unprocessed piece of film) and fills in the desired information. Philosophically, I suppose, the *tabula rasa*.

Two: Convention: all media develop and use common images or motifs or methods, sometimes overusing them to the point where they become bathos, ludicrous. Some common conventions: good cowboys wear white hats; car chases will involve crashing through flower or vegetable stands no matter the time of day; perps chased by police will run into streets and get hit by traffic; news programs will have young, attractive women as anchors, and, maybe, allow older men; pop songs will typically be built with verse, chorus / verse, chorus / musical bridge / verse, chorus; TV sitcoms traditionally use a three-camera shoot, perfected long ago on the set of *I Love Lucy*. At times, actors will get typecast to play the same role forever and, on a darker trajectory, conventions can become stereotypes that have sinister connotations along the lines of racism, sexism, agism.

Three: Creed: this is the double-edged sword of media; one, all media are driven by certain sets of belief—Fox News and BBC, for example, will report the same news story with a radically different perspective—and two, viewers will bring their own codes of belief to their consumption of media—this is often the arena where issues of protest and censorship go to war.

Four: Commercial: all media are driven by sales and profit margins. The books on the *New York Times'* "Best Seller List" are not necessarily any good, they are just best sellers. Excellent television shows get cancelled when ratings, not quality, decline. Product placements in television and film are a distracting nuisance but seem to work. Look at the niforms worn and cars driven in professional racing, the boards surrounding any NHL game, the shoes of basketball stars, the patches on the shoulders of baseball uniforms. Apocryphally, the origins of television are said to have occurred when a furniture store owner in Philadelphia purchased some televisions in the early 1940s, placed them in empty store windows around town, running ads for his stores with a few entertainers (jugglers and clowns) in between. Sales shot up and, to this day, that's what television is—advertisements with a little bit of entertainment in between.

I would work through these "Cs" using examples from various media as illustration and then watch a contemporary television show with the class, often of the students' choosing, and have them apply the theories. Students would generally demonstrate remarkable insights, seeing what they had not seen before, and the hook was in. And, from advertisements to blockbuster films to television shows, the Four Cs would always provide some critical opening for the students; it would always unlock some perspective even in something old. Consider the opening of a film like *Casablanca*—the construction, conventions, creeds—a montage tracking from the spinning earth to Europe to North Africa to Morocco to Casablanca, itself, Nazis in pursuit, and through its streets to Rick's Café Americain, then through the bar to the centre of all, a back room and Rick Blaine, himself, playing chess, smoking his cigarette and wearing a white-jacketed tuxedo, black pants. To wait… and wait… and wait. The master of the game. The possessor of the trump cards, a pair of exit visas. A world all black…all white. A world in which a beautiful friendship is about to be born.

In the secondary school media courses I taught, I focussed units on the genres which I felt had the most direct impact on teenagers, namely, television, film and popular music. And mostly American in origin because, as wonderful as the CBC or TVO may be from time to time, American media is the force that drives the world, especially the world of our students here in Canada. So, about a month on each genre with a nod here and there to print media and giving students a chance to make a short film, take a trip to some media hot spot (like a local news channel or Sheridan College or the NFB studios or CityTV) and the course was complete. I used an historical approach in my units for a couple reasons: by its nature media is ephemeral—a pop culture icon one day is yesterday's news the next, so an historical approach meant that I did not have to reinvent the wheel each time I taught the course. Current material would always be fed in, but the entire course did not have to be re-done each semester. In addition, students generally found it easier to examine older materials for which they did not have as much ownership. Distance makes critical perspective clearer, easier, for students and for adults. Today, from afar, it is much easier to see the sexism of *The Honeymooners* or the racism of Mayberry than it is to see the same in more contemporary shows whatever they may be. Of course, it can be complicated—sometimes culture shapes the media (the routines of *The Smothers Brothers* or *Saturday Night Live* responded topically to everyday events, some long forgotten and/or irrelevant); sometimes media shapes the culture (a show like *X-Files* gave rise to all kinds of UFO sightings and conspiracy theories).

TELEVISION:

On television, I would start with some contemporary sitcom and have students apply the Four Cs. Sitcoms are twenty-two minutes in length and, like short stories or poems, are perfect for use in classrooms. I always showed these in class (one must never assume students can watch such things at home; in many cases, for many students, that kind of home does not exist). So, we watched these together—in the same manner that I would always read stories and poems aloud in a regular English class. What better thing to do in an English classroom than listen to the sound of literature! I broke the history of television into segments and, in each, we often focussed on different thematic concerns—innovations and technical production, images of women, images of men, images of family, themes such as nostalgia, violence, satire, women's liberation, Black Lives Matter, and other concerns of interest.

1 – 1940-1955   Innovation and Experimentation

We viewed clips from shows like *Your Show of Shows*, *You Bet Your Life* (Groucho Marx not Jay Leno), *Ernie Kovacs*, *The Honeymooners*, *The Milton Berle Show*, *The Jack Benny Show*, *I Love Lucy* and, often, anything else from that early period that I could find. In effect, these shows were often just visual radio and sometimes felt as if they were being made up on the spot, sometimes with shaky minimalist sets and flubbed dialogue and advertisements maintained or inserted as part of the programs. Without allegiance to any of these shows, students generally found it easier to spot faults and foibles, identify roles and outline formulae. Often they were surprised to find brilliance in many of these early samplings although, most certainly, they almost always noted, television in the 1950s was not black and white—it was white. In terms of technical things, we would research such terms as kinescope and electronicam and DuMont; I would get students to shout out "one, two, or three" each time a camera cut was made in *I Love Lucy*—significantly, it was really the first show that filmed its episodes and cemented the format of the situation comedy in content and in method, also in marketing strategy, establishing *Desilu* as a force for years; I encouraged students to count out at home that evening to see if the "three camera set" was still in use (it was; it still is … although the portability afforded by the Steadicam and lightweight cameras with balance-effects has changed production somewhat). I envy contemporary teachers; in the earlier days, finding content meant trolling *TV Guides* and late-late nights on obscure channels; now, virtually all the material I searched so hard to locate can be found in abundance on the web (sites such as *YouTube*) and clipped directly to the classroom. And most of it is in Public Domain, and short clips of anything can be used at any time in line with Fair-Play regulations.

2 – 1955-1965   Violence and Ratings

This is the great era of the television western; by the late 1950s, there are over twenty-five of these dusters on TV every week averaging three or four killings on each show, bloodless but violent nonetheless. (As a kid, I loved westerns, watching everything I could, including shows most people have probably never heard tell of, like *Tate*, *Yancy Derringer*, *Black Saddle* and *Wichita Town*. I carried a *Lone Ranger* lunch box to school for eight years.) A strange and foreign genre to most contemporary students, I would show a few clips from shows like *Bonanza*, *Rawhide*, *Have Gun Will Travel*, *Wagon Train* and *Gunsmoke* where Matt Dillon, standing in Boot Hill cemetery, provided the following *Introduction*:

> Out here I remind myself how violence ends. Buried in
> the rim of a nation, the edge of a wild frontier. Some

of these Boot Hill men are the victims of aimless slaughter. The rest, I killed myself. I'm a lawman, United States Marshall. The law comes hard to the frontier. Men like these didn't want it. And more men, still alive, there in Dodge City, they don't want it. They're the drifters, the killers, and the spoilers. And they have to be met. It's a chancy job; makes a man watchful and a little lonely. But somebody has to do it.

And Matt Dillon did it, week after week, killing a stranger in the opening credits and more in almost every show. But Matt was a likeable character, a hero, and a man's man—so this became a natural place to get the class considering such ideas. What is it to be a man, a male, at least as the media presents this? What is a hero? Why has this western genre all but disappeared from our screens? What killed the western? (Later in the course I might get to show clips from some of those late 1960's western films which begin to interrogate their own codes—the spaghetti westerns of Sergio Leone, late John Ford films and Sam Peckinpah's—and when it erased its codes, the western erased itself.) Beyond the western, this was also the television era which perfected the sitcom … in a show like *The Dick Van Dyke Show*, the genre never got any slicker. But images of family and the male are issues certainly fired up in sitcoms like *Father Knows Best, Leave It To Beaver, Ozzie and Harriet* and *The Andy Griffith Show*. Students had the perspective that distance-in-time provides with these shows (they did not usually mind the viewing) and the stereotypes could be defined readily. Among other factors, I suppose, I generally accessed only the better shows and most interesting moments—shows like *Car 54, Where Are You* and *My Mother the Car* were not easy to find in those days although I did use clips from *Gilligan's Island* and *Mr. Ed* on occasion.

3 – 1965-1975   Realism and Social Conscience

In the time after the assassination of President John Kennedy and protest movements to end the war in Viet Nam and achieve equal rights for Blacks and women, show after show emerged on American television trending toward issues of dramatic realism and social injustice. *Naked City*, *Mr. Novak*, *The Untouchables*, *The Avengers*, *The Man from U.N.C.L.E.*, *Julia*, *I Spy*, *Mission Impossible*, *Dragnet*, *Marcus Welby M.D.*, *Ben Casey*, *Dr. Kildare*, *60 Minutes*, even *Star Trek* and sitcoms like *M*A*S*H* and *All in the Family*—while these shows could not always be taken too seriously, many times their plots did stab at serious social issues. (Norman Lear's productions all dealt with social matters and *Star Trek's* five-year mission to spread American values across the universe included socially conscious episodes like "Let That Be Your Last Battlefield" or "The Omega Glory"; Prime Directive aside, of course, *Star Trek* of the 1960s was also inundated with mini-skirts and sexist attitudes, the Star-ship Enterprise often driven by Captain Kirk's unrestrained libido.)

4 – 1975-1985   Nostalgia and Escape

With the loss of the war in Viet Nam, American television did a recognizable about face, ignoring the present (in the same way American society initially ignored the vets returning from that war) and embracing a time when life appeared to be less complicated, simpler, easier. TV returned to the time of its imagined cultural roots or invented escapist worlds, places where one might like to live: *Happy Days*, *Laverne & Shirley*, *The Waltons*, *Little House on the Prairie*, *Fantasy Island*, *Charlie's Angels*, *Love Boat*, *Police Woman*, *Three's Company*, *The Six Million Dollar Man*, *Wonder Woman*, *The Bionic Woman*, *Mork & Mindy*, *Wheel of Fortune*, *Cheers*. Wouldn't it be wonderful to find someplace where everybody knows your name or spin a wheel and win a fortune (presented to you by the eternally-lovely Vanna). The shows of this era always generated some interesting discussion about topics such as nostalgia, collectibles, sentimentality, memory and what a culture values and how it represents such values, or not! Why does Grandma collect those old tea cups; why does your friend keep those unpackaged hockey cards or Barbie dolls? In the exhausted post-*Covid-19* world, similar trends have appeared—a slew of game shows returned to broadcast TV as did the revamping of past shows like *Fantasy Island*, *Will & Grace*, *Frasier*, *Saved By the Bell*, *Hawaii Five-0*, *Lost in Space*, *Punky Brewster*, *Miami Vice*, *You Bet Your Life*, and a host of others. Nostalgia seems to thrive in times of stress and defeat.

5 – 1985-2000   Cable and Conservatism

Perhaps one of the most significant inventions of the twentieth century was coaxial cable. I even remember when early cable companies tried to maintain ownership of small lengths of coaxial cable; if you cancelled your subscription or moved to a different apartment, that piece of coaxial had to be returned. As I have noted earlier, I grew up in a house without television (without electricity) but when we finally hooked up that 17" Admiral, only four different broadcast (analog) stations were available, CBC channels from Kingston and, faintly, Peterborough (identical programs except for local news), and NBC, CBS and ABC (the new kid on the block), all from Rochester across the lake. PBS existed but only in *TV Guide*—Mr. Rogers never entered my neighbourhood. With the arrival of coaxial cable in cities across the world by the 1980s, and later, into the countryside, the potential to broadcast nearly 500 channels arose. Demand and supply worked their magic. Channels came into being that, surely, no-one would ever watch, entire channels devoted to news, weather, shopping, sports, music, religion, food, and on and on. There seemed no end to it, and, these days, in the wake of digital video compression which allowed satellites with twenty-five transponders to increase their output almost incalculably, and fiber-optic cables which expand that even more, streaming a galaxy of channels for which we pay but never watch. And so not only do we have a dozen Sports channels, several showing the same event, but we also have stations dedicated to fishing, golf, poker, motoring, Nascar, Indy Racing, NHL, NFL, MLB, NBA, Bundesliga, video gaming, *etc.* One assignment—I would have students in groups choose an obscure cable channel from a hat and prepare a presentation in which they explained the mission of the channel, ratings figures, programming, ownership, probable success or failure. And then, create a channel that did not yet exist and make a pitch for its development. Another exercise—a clip of Jim Anderson (*Father Knows Best*) next to Al Bundy (*Married ,,, with Children*), each father giving advice to *his* Bud (sometimes I would add the conservatism of Cliff Huxtable (*The Bill Cosby Show*) or Roseanne to the mix). And long-running shows like *The Simpsons* or *South Park* almost always provide teachable moments. So-called *Reality TV* can also be interesting to study, unpeeling the onion that is *Survivor*, *Big Brother*, *The Bachelorette*, *America's Got Talent*, and such. Game shows, cheap to produce and having especially risen in popularity during recent *Covid-19* years, can also reveal a great deal about TV production and cultural values.

6 – 2000-+   Beyond Cable and Chaos

We have entered a television world of delightful chaos … "57 channels and nothing on" sings Bruce Springsteen. Long gone are the days when students would show up at school, almost all of them having watched the Beatles or The Doors perform the night before on CBS's *The Ed Sullivan Show*—such pop culture continuity no longer exists, diametrically constructed today by the diversity of social- and info-media sites. (Although, one supposes, if you wish, your students can still see the Beatles on that *Sullivan* show, the performance readily repeated on *YouTube* or other such platforms—their electronic ghosts will probably rock there forever.) Although it has been much criticized over the years from that time in 1961 when Newton Minow infamously declared it a "vast wasteland," television is essentially not unlike most of the Arts— yes, about 90% of it is terrible but 90% of the novels written are terrible, too, as are 90% of the poems and songs and plays and films. We need to do with television and all electronic media what we do with every artistic product and expression—we need to apply a critical perspective. And we need to provide our students with the capability to wield a similar critical perspective. Choose what is best based on select criteria and then watch what you choose. Some of the most enriching moments of my lifetime have been spent watching television, in movie theatres, or listening to music. Shows like *M*A*S*H* or *The Singing Detective*, films like *Field of Dreams* or *Old Yeller*, singer/songwriters like Leonard Cohen and Bob Dylan—all have made this planet 'a better place to be' (to quote Harry Chapin). For fun, I have added a page listing the best of these media at the end of this chapter; you should make your own lists. It will help your ancestors know who you were. It may help you, too.

Network TV, itself, has almost faded into memory for many. Traditional television has been replicated (for some, replaced) by other screens, other devices of amusement and illimitable broadcast or streaming sources. Cable is succumbing to Fiber-Optic and Wireless transmission. What began with those transistor radios my brothers received for Christmas long ago has now been amplified into portable machines we carry around, continually plugged into and stared at and attached to our bodies, awkward devices like Andorian antennae protruding from our heads. Surely, artificial implants are just around the corner when the latest episode of *Jeopardy* or *The Late Show* or that most recent *Facebook* update will be streamed directly into our cerebral cortex, the blink of an eye or the twitch of a nose away. I can hardly wait!

FILM:

For teaching film, I would use selected clips and show examples of what, since the days of DeMille, has become the standard language of film (shot, cut, track, tilt, zoom, pan, close-up). Then I would use some clips from silent film (usually comedies—the work of Buster Keaton or Charlie Chaplin)—the idea here is to try to give students some appreciation for the magic and creativity of film long before sound and colour came to be. I always made a deal with classes that I would show one "old" classic film of my choosing (usually I picked *Casablanca* or *Horse Feathers*) and they would be able to choose one film of their choice (with acceptable school/course viewing standards in mind). In between, often I presented a sub-genre unit I nicknamed "high school films," and all classes seemed to enjoy this. Here, students were viewing themselves or, at the very least, Hollywood's version of them and their lives. Essentially, we would view one complete film and a series of film clips depicting life in and around high school. And from *Blackboard Jungle* and *To Sir With Love* to *Mean Girls* and *Clueless*, from *Fast Times at Ridgemont High* and *Carrie* to *Rebel Without A Cause* and *Dead Poet's Society*, from Prep Schools to East L.A., Ferris Bueller, Tracy Flick, Jeff Spicoli and Cher Horowitz, there were hundreds of film possibilities. Usually, the complete film we watched in the time that I taught was a John Hughes film entitled *The Breakfast Club*—while it is a somewhat static film where, mostly, stereotypical versions of students sit around and talk as they serve out a detention on a Saturday (the supervisor, V.P. Dick Vernon, really should talk with his union), the film always seemed to generate a magnetic attraction for my students. And even to this day (as I write in 2024, it has just been added new to *Netflix*), its phrases are a part of pop culture—"when you grow up, your heart dies" or "My God, are we gonna be like our parents?" or "Screws fall out all the time. The world's an imperfect place" or "Don't you, forget about me."

MUSIC:

As to popular music, more than any other form of media, it always seemed, students had degrees of ownership and intransigence—they tend to like what they like. So I would always remind classes that, of course, each had her or his favourite and that we would get there but the idea was to have a look at (or listen to) the history, to see where their favourite came from—and besides, if you did not like something one moment, just wait and it would change quickly. Fortunately, I was able to gather several documentary films on various eras in Popular Music following World War II covering the Rock and Roll-likes of Bill Haley and Chuck Berry and Little Richard and Buddy Holly; I used a film called *Elvis '56* to account for the King in his most important time and, after the day the music died, I filled in the Folk Revival with music and information from my own resources—Woody Guthrie, Leadbelly, The Weavers, Pete Seeger, Peter, Paul and Mary, Gordon Lightfoot, Joan Baez and the rise of Bob Dylan. The appearance of Motown and Funk and then, with the arrival of The Beatles and Rolling Stones and Dylan and The Band switching to electric (inventing Rock), the eras came quickly—Glitter-Glam, Disco, Punk, Metal, New Wave, MTV and Muchmusic and video, Michael Jackson and Madonna and the emergence of many female performers, then Garage and Grunge and Rap and Hip-Hop and Electro-pop and the rebirth of Country. Music videos, in particular, were often rich topics of study, alluring advertisements that sold a style of music and a lifestyle, too, complete with values, attitudes, wardrobes and a whole lot more. Clips from Ken Burns' *Country Music* offer useful insights into that genre, and provide an interesting view of another, the *Documentary Film* (Michael Moore's works can be helpful here, as well).

All in all, I think that I got more writing out of students in my Media classes than in any English class. Beyond required assignments, anytime they viewed a new film or TV show or listened to a new album, they could write a review for bonus. And I had them do a short film in an assignment I called a "One-Period Shoot." We had no video editing suites at the time so I bought a VHS camera and tripod and, once they had completed their storyboards and rehearsals, a group of students would be given the camera, a tape and one period (75 minutes) to do their film, to be shot in sequence at a length of three to five minutes (which is a significant film as any know who may have shot one). And most did just fine, demonstrating an understanding and even some skill and innovation as they completed their works. We would have an "academy awards" period when all efforts would be shown and best picture, best actors, *etc.*, would be voted upon.

So, in conclusion, teachers need to embrace technology like never before—it's where the students are. It's who our students are. Use the media and teach the media as you are using it. To abandon or reject media would be like sailing across the ocean and, part way into the voyage, deciding that you'll no longer use the boat. Or, like Yeats' Cuchulain wading into the sea with his sword to fight the "invulnerable tide"—an heroic gesture, maybe, but also one of folly and certain defeat. I am a literary person—reading, writing and teaching literature have always been situated at the centre of my life. I've written two or three books on grammar and had several literary works published, novels, poems, plays (all available through *amazon*, by the way!). But, I have also always understood that, at least in the last seventy years, no matter how much we read, we will always experience more via screen, through TV or film or computer or phone or tablet, Siri or Alexa or Cortana. And that dimension exists to an even greater degree for our contemporary students. And so, when I began to teach, and ever since, I tried to incorporate the use of such Tech for my classes and, as a natural progression, I think, the study of such Tech—how they work, how they change us and what we see and know, how we think and perceive the world, how we interact with that new world, how to deal with that technology. And for students today, that means how to deal with oneself. Technology is now the currency of education, of living, and must be situated as the substance and soul of education. That signpost up ahead … it has a binary base and the frontier is seated in our classroom, a reflection in the screen of a cell phone, maybe iconized as a Zoom chatroom. And in a revelatory moment we realize … the wizard and the curtain are one and the same.

ADDENDUM:

The G.O.A.T.

It is always fun to make lists along the lines of those which follow and to make your argument for one inclusion or another. I have not included anything from the last decade or so; the dust of some time needs to settle before the true contenders emerge and shallow prospects materialize as the hollow shams they are. I will not try to explain all of my selections, that would take too long but, suffice to say, there are good reasons for each. And, of course, many excellent and influential items have been omitted—*Twin Peaks, Lost, Boardwalk Empire, Game of Thrones, Your Show of Shows, Ernie Kovacs, 60 Minutes, The X-Files, Survivor, I, Claudius,* among others, come to mind in just thinking about the abundant wealth of television let alone film or pop music or fiction. But these lists have been made with thought and purpose; these are all shows, films, songs or books that have had a distinct and long-lasting impact on Western culture, low and high; these are the best of their genre.

The Best TV Shows

M*A*S*H, with a combination of humour, satire, poignancy, drama and purpose, and a creative consistency over a long time, is hands-down television's best show ever. Many other TV shows have had a significant influence but none more than that medical band of brothers (and nurses) surviving the madness in 1950's war-besieged Korea (really, of course, Viet Nam in the 1960s and '70s, and really all times of war and conflict, which seems to be all times).

> 1 – M*A*S*H
> 2 – The Twilight Zone
> 3 – The Singing Detective (Dennis Potter)
> 4 – The Tonight Show with Johnny Carson
> 5 – The Ed Sullivan Show
> 6 – Gunsmoke

7 – Sesame Street

8 – Star Trek

9 – Roots

10 – The Sopranos

11 – Saturday Night Live

12 – Hockey Night in Canada

13 – The Honeymooners

14 – I Love Lucy

15 – The Dick Van Dyke Show

The Best Films

"I love the smell of napalm in the morning." I first saw *Apocalypse Now* on a 70mm screen in the University Theatre on Bloor Street in Toronto; direct from Cannes, it was a minimally-edited version with no credits. The opening image of helicopters slipping across the screen and napalm erupting, devouring that green palm forest accompanied by The Doors' guttural lyrics: "this is the end, my friend, of all our elaborate plans..."—it was not a film but an experience, a picaresque journey exposing the pointlessness of war and the frivolity of our culture, an acid trip into the human heart of darkness where "all the children are insane." Strikingly powerful episodes follow one after another after another...from Colonel Kilgore ("Charlie don't surf") to Chef and his encounter with the tiger to the Playboy Playmates with their scant cowboy outfits and toy guns to the brilliant photojournalist ("I'm a little man") to Kurtz, himself...Viet Nam, War, America, contemporary culture, humanity were never unveiled more artfully, more absurdly, more savagely—"the horror, the horror," indeed.

1 – Apocalypse Now

2 – The Godfather

3 – Casablanca

4 – Cabaret

5 – O Lucky Man

6 – The Man Who Shot Liberty Valance

7 – Blade Runner

8 – Deliverance

9 – Psycho

10 – The Wizard of Oz

11 – Jaws

12 – Battleship Potemkin

13 – The Shawshank Redemption

14 – Little Big Man

15 – Chinatown

16 – Nashville

17 – Jurassic Park

18 – The Seven Samurai

19 – Ben Hur

20 – Citizen Kane

21 – Batman

22 – Horse Feathers

23 – Modern Times

24 – Vertigo

25 – King of Hearts

The Greatest TV Characters

Like Shakespeare or Tolstoy or some other force of genius, television has produced a remarkable gallery of memorable characters covering the vast and intricate dimensions of human possibility. And none is better than Barney Fife, that woefully smug and delusionally sympathetic ever-deputy of Mayberry, forever fumbling in his shirt pocket to find the single bullet for his gun or whispering awkward love poems into the phone to his girl Thelma-Lou, always the butt of the joke, always at our heart's core. Don Knotts' was brilliant in shaping the character and bringing Barney to life and making us realize that there is, at the very least, a little bit of Barney in all of us. (Knotts also made Ralph Furley on *Three's Company* memorable.) Because of the comedic nature of his work, Knotts was probably an underrated talent. We should always remember that comedy is just as difficult to enact as tragedy, some would say more so.

1 – Barney Fife
2 – The Fonz (*aka* Arthur Herbert Fonzarelli)
3 – Matt Dillon
4 – Ralph Kramden
5 – Tony Soprano
6 – Mr. Spock (*aka* S'chn T'gai Spock)
7 – Andy Sipowicz
8 – Archie Bunker
9 – Murphy Brown
10 – Mary Richards
11 – Lucy Ricardo
12 – Les Nessman
13 – Frank Columbo
14 – Walter White
15 – Homer Simpson

The Best Pop Songs

Indisputably, the greatest musical entity in popular music in recent time is *The Beatles*, and, after their teeny-bopper beginnings ("I want to hold your hand," "Love me, do," and such—slick but imitative, superficial), the group evolved to a remarkably sophisticated ethos-phere, and at the apex of that is "Hey Jude," a technically brilliant and lyrically enchanting song that means everything and nothing, a love song, a canticle for a psychedelic age, a portent of things to come, a universal testimony for hope and renewal, an existential awakening. Pop music gets no better than this (although not far behind, Dylan's apocalyptic howl for a culture lost, "Like a Rolling Stone"—"When you ain't got nothing, you got nothing to lose").

1 – Hey Jude
2 – Like a Rolling Stone
3 – Maybellene
4 – American Pie
5 – Hotel California
6 – Highway to Heaven

7 – All Along the Watchtower

8 – Me and Bobbie McGee

9 – Hallelujah (Cohen)

10 – Layla

11 – Born to Run

12 – Long Tall Sally

13 – American Woman

14 – Imagine

15 – Thunder Road

16 – Seventeen

17 – Mr. Bojangles

18 – Bohemian Rhapsody

19 – Bridge Over Troubled Water

20 – Smells Like Teen Spirit

The Best Musical Films

The Musical Film, not unlike the Western genre on television, used to be a huge attraction, often attracting blockbuster crowds and capturing numerous Academy Awards. For the most part, those days seem to be gone—in part, generally, contemporary musicals seem to have become more complicated, with darker premises than the joys of *Easter Parade* or *White Christmas*—still very popular in theatrical presentations, shows like *Les Miserables* and *Hamilton* do not seem to translate effectively to the silver screen. Also gone are the influential days when such musicals would have received widespread exposure on TV shows like *The Ed Sullivan Show*. That said, the greatest Musical on film is probably *Cabaret*, its music and dance logically fitting into its action, the story of the divinely decadent Sally Bowles performing at the Kit Kat Club in Berlin. Fascism is on the rise as the Nazis steadily overtake the Weimar Republic but no-one is looking: "Fatherland, O Fatherland … tomorrow belongs to me" chills the heart. Directed by the legendary Bob Fosse, and based on Isherwood's novel about a licentious life in Berlin, the film's message is compelling and the characters, from the wonderfully creepy MC of the Kit Kat to the irrepressible Sally, herself, are mesmerizing. Given the time and place, the heavily ironic advice of the main theme seems inarguably appropriate, then and still:

The day she died the neighbors
Came to snicker:
"Well, that's what comes
From too much pills and liquor."
But when I saw her laid out like a Queen,
She was the happiest... corpse...
I'd ever seen.
I think of Elsie to this very day.
I remember how she'd turn to me and say:
"What good is sitting all alone in your room?
Come hear the music play.
Life is a Cabaret, old chum,
Come to the Cabaret."

1 – Cabaret
2 – Jesus Christ Superstar
3 – Fiddler on the Roof
4 – West Side Story
5 – The Umbrellas of Cherbourg
6 – Singin' in the Rain
7 – At the Circus
8 – The Sound of Music
9 – Moulin Rouge
10 – The Wizard of Oz

Best Novels (or Literary Romance) **in English**

All of the fictions listed below are sophisticated literary classics but, for me, Richardson's *Clarissa*, an epistolary fiction at over two thousand pages in which stubborn virtue triumphs through death, has to be the greatest novel of all. Even its full title, *Clarissa; or, The History of a Young Lady: Comprehending the Most Important Concerns of Private Life. And Particularly Shewing, the Distresses that May Attend the Misconduct Both of Parents and Children, In Relation to Marriage*, is a masterpiece and the title character, heroic, virtuous, determined, stubborn, but caught in a tragic social spiral from which there is no escape, is surely one of the most remarkable ever created.

1 – Clarissa
2 – Ulysses
3 – Moby-Dick
4 – Wuthering Heights
5 – Fifth Business
6 – Tristram Shandy
7 – Adventures of Huckleberry Finn
8 – The Portrait of a Lady
9 – The Great Gatsby
10 – The Prince of Leroy
11 – The Sound and the Fury
12 – A Passage to India
13 – Alice in Wonderland
14 – Invisible Man (Ellison)
15 – The Scarlet Letter
16 – A Canticle for Leibowitz
17 – Trout Fishing in America
18 – Great Expectations
19 – Tom Jones
20 – 1984
21 – Beloved
22 – The Grapes of Wrath
23 – Heart of Darkness
24 – To the Lighthouse
25 – Under the Volcano
26 – Cat's Cradle
27 – The Catcher in the Rye
28 – The Horse's Mouth
29 – For Whom the Bell Tolls
30 – One Flew Over the Cuckoo's Nest

Best Pop Lyrics You Have (Probably) Never Heard
(Song/Performer)

1 – Brownsville Girl (Bob Dylan)
2 – The Doll House (Phil Ochs)
3 – Cellophane City (Steve Forbert)
4 – Geronimo's Cadillac (Michael Murphey)
5 – Beirut (Peter Sarstedt)
6 – Master Jack (Four Jacks and a Jill)
7 – Bruised Orange: Chain of Sorrow (John Prine)
8 – The Great Electric Experiment Is Over (Noel Harrison)
9 – Kansas City (Melissa Etheridge)
10 – Closing Time (Leonard Cohen)
11 – Black Diamond Bay (Bob Dylan)
12 – Changes (Alan Price)
13 – Jesus, The Missing Years (John Prine)
14 – Beans in My Ears (Pete Seeger)
15 – The Road Goes On Forever (Robert Earl Keen)

16 – Peter Kagan and the Wind (Makem and Clancy)

17 – Sweetheart Like You (Judy Collins)

18 – Hurt (Johnny Cash)

19 – The Guitar (Guy Clark)

20 – Eve of Destruction (BarryMcGuire)

21 – Desolation Row (Bob Dylan)

22 – Where do you go to, my lovely? (Peter Sarstedt)

23 – Black Day in July (Gordon Lightfoot)

Some Poems to be Read Aloud

1 – Spring and Fall (Hopkins)

2 – The Country North of Belleville (Purdy)

3 – Daddy (Plath)

4 – To His Coy Mistress (Marvell)

5 – The Lady's Dressing Room (Swift)

6 – A Subaltern's Love Song (Betjeman)

7 – Tarantella (Belloc)

8 – The Man with the Blue Guitar (Stevens)

8 – Incident (Cullen)

10 – Sonnet 116 (Shakespeare)

11 – Ode on a Grecian Urn (Keats)

12 – Skunk Hour (Lowell)

13 – Because I could not stop for death (Dickinson)

14 – The Love Song of J. Alfred Prufrock (Eliot)

15 – Sailing to Byzantium (Yeats)

16 – After Apple Picking (Frost)

17 – The Snowman (Stevens)

18 – The Lady of Shallot (Tennyson)

19 – The Waste Land (Eliot)

20 – Kubla Khan (Coleridge)

Now, in the charts which follow, enjoy making your own lists:

Best Films	
1	
2	
3	
4	
5	
6	
7	
8	
9	
10	

Best Television	
1	
2	
3	
4	
5	
6	
7	
8	
9	
10	

Best Characters in Television or Film	
1	
2	
3	
4	
5	
6	
7	
8	
9	
10	

Best Pop Music	
1	
2	
3	
4	
5	
6	
7	
8	
9	
10	

42
Finding in the Souwesto
My Teacher-self

Finding is losing something else.
I think about, perhaps even mourn,
what I lost to find this

—Richard Brautigan

And the lady from the lake
Helped me to escape
And led me to myself at last, at last
Though I danced with the dolls in the doll house

—Phil Ochs "The Doll House"

In August after my first year of doctoral studies at Western, I am leafing though *The London Free Press* and see a single advertisement, a temporary teaching position, one month, perhaps two, in a school in Tillsonburg, Oxford County. For no reason that I can recall (I often apply for jobs that I don't even want), I send in an application package and I am invited to an interview. I do not get the job—a laid-off teacher from London gets it—then a day later, when this teacher is rehired in London, I am offered the Tillsonburg position, somewhat sheepishly, by the principal of Glendale High School, Joe Sweeney. An English teacher, Frank Kuhl, has had a leg amputated and is not ready to return to his teaching duties. So, out of the browning, near-to-harvest tobacco fields, a job materializes; I say 'yes', drive to Woodstock (I have never been there and do not really even know where it is) and sign a contract. It is one of the most foreboding things I have ever done—I really do not know where this will lead me, if anywhere. I will have to take a leave of absence from Grad Studies at Western and if this job ends after one month, I will be stranded. But, from redirection, direction comes. Such has become a kind of mantra for me. And, I have come to understand, we never really control the winds of change, anyway, even when we think we do.

Glendale High School—Tillsonburg:

Glendale turns out to be the most pleasant school in which I ever teach. Although located in a small town, it is a rural school, almost all of its 600 or so students coming from local area farms, many of whom grow tobacco (it is said, a hundred acres in tobacco makes you a millionaire). The students here dress very well and their parking lot is filled with very nice cars. Tillsonburg is a community of affluence with a school to match. Shops downtown sell designer clothes and accessories, and a new mall has been constructed to the west of town. It is not exactly rural Canada as you might picture it. Designed by founder George Tillson, a turn-of-the-century entrepreneur, the main street is a wide boulevard designed so that horses and their carriages or wagons could make an easy U-turn. The town has its own radio station and newspaper and two high schools. Before my time at Glendale, a feud of sorts raged between these two schools, Glendale and Annandale. Glendale was the newer school and had modern shops; Annandale considered itself to be the 'academic' school with advanced Art and Music programs—commonly, Annanadale's "death sentence" to troublesome students was the threat of banishing them across town to Glendale, the school for dummies (in the Fred Sanford-vernacular of the day). This feud had apparently become so entrenched and detrimental, in the year or so before my arrival, some programs had been shifted between the schools and several Department Heads forced to switch, to calm the distrust and emphasize the idea that both schools were equal; nevertheless, a degree of cynicism and enmity remained among many staff members. Like most feuds, Capulets and Montagues, Hatfields and McCoys, Lilliput and Blefuscu, it made no sense, at least to me. Adding to the general malaise, the teaching staff went out on strike for the first couple days of the year in which I was hired, a dispute about all of the usual suspects, salary and benefits and the like.

In spite of the union's bad relations with the Board (which was noted for its conservative, even backward leanings, educationally speaking), as a part-timer, the staff at Glendale treated me very well and assured me that they understood my situation, that I had no choice but to cross the picket line, and the strike only lasted a day or two anyway. One of the first things I did as the year got rolling was volunteer to coach; the senior boys' volleyball team had a need. One, I liked coaching and, two, it was probably a good political move, showing the Principal that I was willing to get involved in the school even though my sojourn might be brief. As a bonus, the volleyball team had an excellent setter (Chris Coyle) and one of the most talented offensive players (John Telford) I have ever coached; he was a magnificent athlete and loved the game. He was one of those players who could hang in the air like a hovering gull, then hammer the ball wherever he wanted into the opponents' court. And one month of teaching became two, then three and, after four, the County offered me a permanent contract and gave me the full year in terms of seniority. Oxford County, whatever one may say about it, was always very good to me; the local Kinsmen even offered to fund me for international research if I wished and, at one point, the Board offered to pay for the courses I would need to become a Principal, but by that point I was bound to a different direction.

Still unsure of my job security with Oxford, I often apply for other jobs—a University promotional job with the Registrar's Office at Western (nine individuals ask questions at the screening interview; only two at the next); a position to sell insurance at *London Life* (my old housemate, Scotty, works there); a teaching position at a private school, St. Andrews' College in Newmarket. I am offered a position there based on my first job ever, taking care of Revill's English-style jumping horses—St. Andrew's has a stable of horses and needs someone to coach its equestrian team. The job is appealing but requires my in-house residency as a Don in an apartment at the end of a hallway no bigger than my current garage. They wine and dine me (sans wine) in a huge auditorium with a horde of well-dressed, uniformed children—a lot of prayers are said, though as Huck Finn says, "…there warn't nothing the matter with the victuals." I respectfully decline the job but this process continues to enable my competence and confidence in the skill of being interviewed, and, as I found out through the years, that is not a bad skill to have. As an aside, regarding uniforms such as the St. Andrews' children wore, while a dress code is supposed to bring about conformity and eliminate the competition of clothes, students in such schools seem to find a zillion ways to wear shirts and sweaters and skirts to make difference seem viable. And the nicely uniformed children of Golding's *Lord of the Flies* often come to mind.

Don Wharram, a poet at heart, was a fine Department Head at Glendale, even giving up his senior OAC courses for newcomers to teach—Don, Kathy Robinson (also new to the school) and I were the only three in the Department (occasionally, the Librarian Christine Burns taught a course; Chris and I carpooled from London in my first year at Glendale and she became a good friend). Murray Adams, a Commerce teacher about my age, played on an evening Mens' basketball team together and we regularly toured the local hot spots; Phil King, a Special Education teacher who organized a Glendale rock band, had a quick-witted sense of humour and became friends as well (more than once trying to set me up with girlfriends). And on several occasions, fellow teachers I barely knew kindly invited me to their homes for meals; the staff room at Glendale was always a place of lively and friendly banter.

Ralph Cook, a Math teacher, became a dear friend, a true eccentric who drove a twenty-year old Land Rover and played the bagpipes; Ralph had the world's largest collection (I think) of bagpipe albums and, in British tradition, always kept some warm Guinness beneath the sink of his apartment. Ralph had a deep interest in local history and was thrilled when I did a scholarly research project on the history of Dereham Township (by then, subsumed into Southwest Oxford); he arranged for me to speak to numerous local groups (my *Tweedsmuir* Tours) and fly over the area in a friend's plane to take photographs. It was my first experience flying; the plane was a small two-seater (one of those 'Buddy Holly planes' as comedian Billy Connelly would say) and we flew on a day when convection currents would lift the plane and then let it drop twenty feet. Quite a ride; and add to that, the pilot was a man who had been forced out of teaching because of mental illness; I recall to this day his dipping of the nose of the plane as we flew over the high school and saying: "That's where they did it to me." And yet, here I am, still! Ralph also introduced me to a gentleman who was an amateur archeologist and had a wonderful collection of Indigenous arrowheads and pottery shards—he loaned several cases to me for presentations. I also helped

Dr. John Cooper finish a book on the history of Tillsonburg, completing *Contents'* and *Indices'* pages for him; especially of interest to me, Dr. Cooper had taught at McGill University in the same Department as Stephen Leacock—he had several wonderful personal reminiscences, especially of Leacock's last years when his lecture hall would be filled with random people just there to listen to rambling lectures and often hilarious stories about Leacock's experiences and the famous persons he knew.

My sixth year of teaching high school passed at Glendale and I think I was just hitting my stride. I remember, when learning to drive, after one year I thought I knew it all; then after two years, I realized how much better I was than I had been, and the same after three and four. I would look back and marvel that I had ever been allowed on the roads at all (wisely now, I think, restricted 'graduated licensing' is in place in Ontario.) The same is true of teaching—no matter what we think, it probably takes five years or more before we really have enough experience to be in control of our teaching abilities and our classroom management. I taught in a wonderful room at Glendale, a former Art room; it was about a third larger than a regular classroom. I got rid of rows, placing the student desks in a large semi-circular curve, backs to the window, only about three rows deep, the centre area open. I kept the teacher's desk to the side and put a small table and chair at the front. This was the set-up I used for the rest of my secondary school teaching days. This amphitheatre-style seating allowed an open middle space for presentations and performances, kept all student eyes toward the front for paying attention, for viewing film or TV or the overhead and eliminated any back row—at most, any student was only three desks deep. (There is a theory of classroom arrangement called the "Big T"—when desks are in rows, students seated across the front and down the middle (*i.e.*: a "T") get the best marks; students to both sides often disappear in those rooms. Eliminate the "T" and everyone does better.)

At Glendale, I connect well with the students. With the bent of a literary soul and an academic, to boot, from outside their world, and making use of a wide variety of text and media, I am probably a bit different than the other teachers they have known in this relatively conservative enclave. I have the natural ability to natter away with students on all kinds of silly things and, when I meet them in the hall outside of class, never rag on them about classroom stuff or matters of assignments. At students' bequests, I routinely get invited as a supervisor on school trips in History and Music, the Shop students service my car and do welding for me and the Home Economics classes invite me to their after-school fêtes every Wednesday. At noon-hour or when I have a spare to do marking and preparation—the door always open, always—students regularly drop by my classroom just to chat about this or that, sometimes in groups, sometimes alone; mostly we talk about everyday things, about the rock and roll of living. I never give unrequested advice or preach at them or tell them what to do, ever! We just talk about stuff!

As an aside, first rule of being a teacher: never believe anything a student tells you; simply, they do not see the entire picture. And never listen to any student who begins to talk about another teacher; simply tell them that is inappropriate. (There are some students who, for whatever psychological need, will simply travel from teacher to teacher telling the same story, but switching-out one teacher's name to another's like some fill-in-the-blank exercise.) And if an issue of suspected abuse should arise, legally, of course, one must report that to an appropriate Administrator—in the five decades in which I taught, no such issue ever arose. Friendly but never friends is the role the teacher plays.

Probably the strangest incident at Glendale, in fact, probably in all my teaching days, occurs one sunny fall day around noon. Suddenly an Amish horse and buggy shows up in the school parking lot, then glides out to the football field and around the track. Physical Education classes stop and stare; students and staff peer from windows and congregate outside. The buggy, with a person yelling "giddy-up," moves back off the field, across the parking lot and on down the street. By this time, two police cars appear and slide in behind and the entourage disappears into the maze of the nearby subdivision. The driver of the buggy is a Glendale student, an uneven character named Brad Aerd, given to explosive incidents. A staff member tells me about one time he saw him jump out of his car and begin screaming at an older couple who had stayed too long at a stop sign. Apparently, a peculiar rage runs in the family, a younger sister having attacked a VP in her office a year ago, biting her so she had to get shots (rabies' shots, I assume). Brad, on a whim only his brain could manufacture, had decided to steal an Amish buggy from downtown. He removed a sleeping child from the back and drove to the school, finally to be arrested by the police. The noontime ride of Bradley Aerd—not something that one sees every day and an incident that will show up in my novel, *The Prince of Leroy*.

So, absurd buggy rides aside, teaching at Glendale in Tillsonburg was generally very pleasant and, to be honest, it was more than nice to have an income again after a lean year as a Grad student. After commuting for a year (it was about an hour's drive from London, across the sometimes treacherous and snow-blown flat lands of southwestern Ontario), for two years I rent a bungalow in Brownsville, a smaller-than-small community just west of Tillsonburg. During one summer of those years, I toured the east coast of Canada and, another year, I did a humungous tour west accompanied by the best friend of my life (staying in the old quarter of New Orleans, then west across Texas to visit sites such as Carlsbad Caverns, the Grand Canyon, Billy the Kid's grave, LA and Disney-Land, Alcatraz and City Lights, camping among the Sequoias, and north to Vancouver Island, the Columbia Ice Fields, the HooDoos and where Louis Riel fought and was executed—it was a spectacular trip, all the while enhanced by my ride, a 1983 black *TransAm* glass top with *Recaro* detailing, just like the *Knight Rider* on TV but *sans* KITT).

But time marches on, as the cliché reminds us. A position arose at Glendale for someone to establish a Gifted Program; I applied, nailed the interview in speaking to issues of theory, budget, curriculum, and so on (one of the interviewers later privately told me that I was far and away the best) but the job went to another, for political reasons, I think. Just days before that, Nino Basacco and I had crossed paths at an English Conference—Nino was transferring from Woodstock to Ingersoll to be Department Head there and asked me if I would be interested in being an Assistant Head. I had resumed my Graduate Studies again and, for practical purposes, thought that living in London (IDCI was only a twenty-minute drive away) would be more efficacious. And so, a couple days after Mr. Sweeney told me that I did not get the Gifted position, I informed him that I would be transferring to IDCI. If I didn't like Joe and think that he was one of the best Principals I had ever known (and a golfing friend, as well), there would have been some smug satisfaction.

Ingersoll District Collegiate Institute:

As Glendale was small, IDCI is a huge school, having been expanded upon three times with plans forever in the works for a community swimming pool to be added. It has over 1500 students, three separate gyms, two sports' fields and takes fifteen minutes to walk from one side to the other. And as Joe Sweeney was one of the most effective Administrators I have known, Al Ward of IDCI is not. He is a curiosity, a smart man but a micro-manager and an overt control monger. Once, after members of the English Department had mutually agreed upon teaching assignments for the next year, for no reason, he intervened and shuffled everything around. And such was a common occurrence. The morale of the school, especially in the English Department, was as close to depression as anything that I could imagine. As many laughs as we used to have, there always seemed to be a palpable tension in the air— it was like Donald Trump's erratic reign as president, one always wondered what would come next. Nino Basacco, on the other hand, is an excellent Department Head, and has a brilliant strategy for the Department. He tries to shape the school's courses of study into an intelligible progression using a set of anthologies based on literary tropes and developed by Northrop Frye and W. T. Jewkes. Grade Nine will study Romance, Grade Ten, Tragedy, Grade Eleven, Comedy, and Grade Twelve, Satire and Irony, and OAC I will review all. Nino becomes a good friend, one of the most well-meaning and sincere men I have ever known. And he loves rock music and has a huge collection of vinyl; one of our most memorable excursions happens one July 4th when we travel to Buffalo (with a stash of mushrooms—hot dogs never tasted as magical) for an all-day concert by the likes of *The Grateful Dead*, *Tom Petty and the Heartbreakers* and Bob Dylan. I learn how to coach soccer, helping Nino with the senior girls' team, and I have a junior girl's volleyball squad at IDCI, skilled enough to medal in the championship tourney for southwestern Ontario.

I teach a range of English classes in my four years at IDCI from Basic Level to Gifted students (often finding similarities between these two academic extremes; among other things, their insecurity and their competitiveness). I enjoy working with the students there. One year I have a creative writing class (OAC II) of about fifteen students; the next year there are more than double that number because, as the students later tell me, they have told others how much they have enjoyed the course. Memorable: together we produce a newspaper, actually being given access after hours to the local newspaper office to prepare, cut and set the columns in the old-fashioned ways of wax and ink, and the class completes a book, a poetry compilation à la *Spoon River Anthology*. And, one experience in particular, I enter the mental ward of the local hospital to visit a student who has tried to commit suicide, her arms pale, her wrists still bandaged as I am locked into and, later, out of the ward. Sadly, it will not be the last time for that kind of experience.

I also complete my final Ph.D. courses and write my comprehensive exams while at IDCI. I take two courses from Professor James Reaney, the wonderful poet and playwright, a gentle and visionary man who essentially changes my way of seeing the world. I take Reaney's *Southwestern Ontario Culture and Literature*, his revolutionary course that aimed to prove (and did) that one, Canada had a literature and a culture, and that two, it was regional in nature. And that, in 'southwesto' Ontario, literature was often driven by those same Gothic elements found in southeastern American culture, the writings of Poe and O'Connor and Faulkner. I recall Reaney once saying that Alice Munro was the first writer to take us underneath the verandahs of Ontario, his point being that the source of our literature is in our own back yards. Like Munro, Reaney's own stories and poems often focus on local events and characters, including his monumental trilogy of plays symbolically retelling the saga of the Donnellys, the victims of one of Canada's most grisly mass murders. The other course I take from Professor Reaney is a half-course on the Brontës where, in addition to reading the seven chunky Brontë books, I work on their connection to Sir Walter Scott, no writer of short novels himself. But I learn a lot from Professor Reaney and his often whimsical, childlike view of the world, from charming chats with him and with his wife, the poet Colleen Thibideau—the first time I ever ate pear pie was at the Reaney house on Huron Street. Most important of all, through Reaney's vision, I come to understand a new way to see the world, that all that truly matters can be found just off the back porch, in one's own back yard.

The other Grad course I take is Professor Joe Zezulka's Canadian literature where, once more, I turn to a consideration of Al Purdy applying Martin Heidegger's existential ideas to the Purdy oeuvre. Joe is brilliant, an expert in the emerging field of literary magic realism, but also an earth-bound academic with whom I can relate—I recall once sitting on his back porch drinking a beer and talking about fishing in eastern Ontario's Salmon River.

I spend much of a year preparing for the set of qualifying examinations I have to write. I am prepping for exams in Restoration and Eighteenth Century, the Romantics and Nineteenth Century, and the Modern Period (including British, American and Canadian literatures). One is responsible for the principle writers and their works, as well as criticism of the period, and major critical responses since. I get in the habit of using as much time as I have available while at school (spares, chunks of my lunch hour, before and after class) to work on school work, prepping and marking, and by five o'clock I turn to the Grad work. It means that I am busy most of the time but I remind myself, and any others who ask, that no-one is making me do this. I am being buried, true, but I am being buried in a world with which I am one. I teach through the entire process—the examinations all have to be written in the span of a week. I get permission to use a Friday P.D. day to write the Moderns, I write the Romantic/Victorian on a Monday evening after a day of teaching, and I take a personal day on Thursday to write Restoration/Eighteenth Century. I recall getting out of my car before that first exam with a feeling much like soldiers must have felt before they went over the top for the first time, hesitancy, fear, the notion somehow that identity and reputation, everything, is on the line. I hesitate, then take a big breath, and push on. A week and a half later, Pat Dibsdale, the Grad secretary and all-around matriarch of Western's English Department, phones me to tell me, almost unbelievable to this day, that I have passed. All the first round of exams. Passed! For the first time, as I hang up the phone, I feel burned out and just sit at my desk for several minutes. In the exams, I really only used about twenty per cent of what I prepped but I still had to prepare in that way. Everyone does, I suspect. Now, it is just a matter of creating a reading list for American literature, writing an exam, completing an oral, and then on to the dissertation. And straight on 'til morning, Mr. Pan. I suddenly feel relaxed, confidant. I know that I have it made.

I leave IDCI after four years. I have written a letter to the Administration outlining my concern over the low morale I see in the school; the Principal is unimpressed. I meet with Mr. Ward and the two VP's to discuss this and, I recall, in talking about the ethos of effective schools, at one point the Principal said to me, "What, did you write a book on the subject?" to which one of the VPs responded, "Yes, he did." It was a charming moment—by that point, I had co-authored a book on excellence in education for an OSSTF summer workshop. Coincidently, a hiring bubble popped open at this time and I apply to teach in the London Board; there is a screening interview, and I bring along samples of the newspaper and the publications that my writing class has done; essentially, at that point, my interviewing skills prevail and I take over the session. Later I discover that I get ranked as first on their list of teachers with experience. And so, I move on. Living in London and working there simply makes sense. I am placed at an east end composite school, Clarke Road Secondary, only about five minutes from the apartment in which I live. The commuting days that I have endured for most of the last seven years are over. In my years in London, I will grow to become the best teacher that I can be.

43
The Road

Sherry buys a paper and a cold 6-pack of beer
The headlines read that Sonny is goin' to the chair
She pulls back onto Main Street in her new Mercedes Benz
The road goes on forever and the party never ends

—Robert Earl Keen "The Road Goes On Forever"

While Oxford County treated me well, London Board of Education is a breath of fresh air. Oxford was a small, rural board with deep Conservative/conservative roots. It had no semestered schools well into the 1990s and much of its territory can be considered the Bible belt of Ontario. At Glendale, a representative of the local church organization actually stalked the halls during lunch hour, talking with any students he perceived to be alone or lonely. Margaret Freur, the Vice Principal of Glendale, once blocked members of an LGBTQ+ group from entering the school building; its representatives had been invited to speak to a Social Studies class—the teacher, to her credit, I think, promptly held her class on a lawn across the road (it was her final year at the school, though). The London Board seems much more liberal in thought and deed. Clarke Road sends me William Glasser's *Control Theory* to read (outlining an umbrella theory for pedagogy at the school) and the Board holds a full-day orientation at its Board Office handing out canvas bags full of information, and a free pencil to boot. The only sad thing that I see—a gymnasium full of brand-new TVs hooked to Beta-max recorders—someone has made the short-sighted decision to buy into that tech instead of VHS; it means that I will have to find some way to use or adapt all the VHS material I have.

Clarke Road, *the Road* as it is known, reminds one of those schools you see in films like *Stand and Deliver* or *Blackboard Jungle*, beaten, graffiti-scarred lockers and smashed toilets in the boys' washrooms. It is an east-end school, students from working-class homes often consisting of one parent, or none, with grandparents or older siblings taking on the role of caregiver. I learn to adapt quickly. I recall once, with a Grade Ten class, having students in groups doing a review assignment. We had read *Romeo and Juliet* and *To Kill A Mockingbird* and the assignment was to compare the relationship of father and daughter. I circulated around the groups, coming to one, it so happened, with five young women who complained that they were having difficulty with the assignment. I chatted with them about the works, at one point, asking them to think of their relationship with their own father and it was at that point when each student, one after the other, noted to me that she had never known her father. Clarke Road was always full of unsuspected surprises like that. One day, Tracy Laponder came to me at lunch hour and asked if I could help her write a letter. I agreed, of course, and found out that, since Tracy could not make it all the way to Kingston, the letter in question was to the Parole Board at Kingston Penitentiary asking that they not grant freedom to the man who had killed her mother—Tracy had come home from elementary school one afternoon to find her Mom bleeding out on the kitchen floor. On another occasion, I pull a young man into a room just before a mob chasing him comes crashing through the outer doors. He has mistakenly talked to somebody's girlfriend and a Vietnamese gang from the north end is after him. They have baseball bats and chains and, probably, other weapons concealed from view. Fortunately, police arrive at about the same time as the gang and they disperse. Another day, there is a knock on the door during a class, the VP is standing outside and asks to see a student named RonJon. I can also see a fully armoured police squad huddled along the hall. When RonJon, who is a friendly and likeable student, exits, he is tackled by the officers. From his gym bag, they extract a chrome-plated .44 Magnum—he has brought this to school and has shown it to several students, trying to impress them and asking if anyone knows where he can get some ammunition. I offer a character reference for him but the Board policy is zero tolerance for such an offence and he is given a permanent suspension from all London schools.

While these anecdotes are indicative of the environment in which the Road was located, the vast majority of the students with whom I work are down-to-earth, decent individuals, kids toughened by their world but proud of it. I have never taught in any place where I felt more a part of the school than the Road. And by request, I develop a Media Studies English course whose enrollment expands from three sections to eight in a couple years. At different times, professors from Faculties of Education at Western and the University of Toronto visit to see 'what's going on' (to echo Marvin Gaye). And, while I do have a text for the course, mostly I use the media, itself, as text (TV and film and Pop Music) and get as much writing and discussion from those classes as from any I have ever taught. (See *Chapter Forty-One* for a full discussion.) I also take the Media classes regularly to the NFB, CityTV and *Muchmusic* studios in Toronto and to New York City where we tour the city and visit the Paley Centre, the *Saturday Night Live* studio, Yankee Stadium, Madison Square Garden, the United Nations, Trump towers and other sites of interest. I coach volleyball and golf at the Road and am involved in several school activities including tutoring the *Reach for the Top* club.

Incidentally, I finish my doctorate while teaching at the Road to become, as they say, that kind of doctor who does nobody any good. I pass the specialized examinations for American Lit. (written and oral) without any real difficulty, although I am sick as a dog with flu during the written portion—my recollection is that it was like writing in sludge, each idea being squeezed onto the page one sluggish word at a time. And I remember little about the oral, offering my view of the ending of *The Great Gatsby* as a summation of American literature as a whole and an interpretation of Wallace Stevens' "The Snow Man" to the nodding approval of the examiners. And Ernie Redekof, the prof who never read my M.A. thesis, asking a trick question about the bower scene in *The Red Badge of Courage* trying to see if I would confuse that realistic novel with the tenets of romance. And Geoffrey Rans offering up what he must have thought to be a softball question on *The Color Purple* because I had sat through one of his lectures on it, except it was not actually a novel on my reading list. But I managed, passed my oral and pushed on to my dissertation.

In the July following my completion of the doctorate, Ian Underhill contacts me. Ian is a teacher at South Secondary School in London and, for years, has been teaching the four-week summer course that allows teachers to get their Honours' Specialist designation. Once, beginning teachers were hired on a two-year Temporary Contract and then, assuming the teacher was relatively competent (usually a Superintendent would visit your class), you would sign a Permanent Contract. In the 1980s as Faculties of Education emerged, Honours' Specialist Qualifications courses were developed to replace the Temporary/Permanent contract model. Ian wonders if I would be willing to take over the teaching of this summer course and I am pleased to do so. For me, while it meant giving up most of July (the course was offered four hours per day, five days a week for four weeks), it is an irresistible opportunity to put some of my academic training to work, and there will still be five or six weeks of vacation remaining. It is a money course (with the Specialist Qualification, teachers' salaries jump a category on the pay-grid and it is also a requirement for any who wish to pursue a career in Administration); beyond that, once they got involved in the course, the students are keen and delightful. I found that old academic interests were refuelled and, as we focused on theory most of the summer, the desire to understand and sort though their practice was often palpable. Again and again teachers showed me that latent need to get involved in intellectual matters, an occasion that Staff Rooms rarely allow. And having had at least two years of teaching, the timing for them was perfect to examine some of the theories, trends and beliefs floating around in education and infiltrating their classroom. (Some of the content of this book has its origins in those course lectures.) And I, too, became a better teacher through this exercise, exploring the intellectual dimension of thinking about what I was doing as well as doing it. And, for later practical purposes, the experience made me a somewhat recognizable presence around the Faculty of Education building.

The English Department at Clarke Road is a star attraction—the previous Department Head has insisted on permanent group-learning in all classes at all times and the program has worked so well groups of educators from across the southwest regularly arrive for visits. Dennis Johns, the Assistant Head, calls the place a fish tank. Funding has poured in and closets full of arcane supplies are available—there is even a class set of instamatic cameras (although, ironically, we run out of funds to afford the required film). Keith Watson, sincere and cerebral, is the new Department Head who arrives when I do along with a couple new teachers (Anne and Patricia) and one old vet who will become one of my best friends and most admired colleagues. This is Brian Charlton—we get nicknamed, *the two Brians* and find a bond without words. Brian has moved to Secondary School from teaching Elementary for complicated reasons connected to a divorce (his 'ex' becoming an Elementary Principal). Brian has done his M.A. at Western in the same era I did and knows all the Profs I do—he still plays on the

Department slow-pitch softball team, in fact—and he has also written a wonderful book, *Angel & the Bear*. It is a long poem drenched in Beat-felt themes and the magic rhythms of Jazz. We talk about writing and academic matters and share an endless sense of marvel at the folly of the world, Brian always able to see, ironically, at least, the positive nature of silly and passing things. We golf together and have many a drink together, one memorable night sitting down after school and closing the bar, the time disappearing, it seemed, in a sip of ale. It was the last great drunk of my life. Not too long after, Brian retires and he dies of cancer little more than a year later, aged 58. As Joe Zezulka said to me one day outside his office, "there is no fairness to that." I wrote "&", a meditative elegy for Brian, included in my collection *magic birds*. And I will forever mourn his passing, reflections from his writing and his spirit never far away:

> mother city shuffles you around
> her town like cards on a table
> pinball players fall down
> go home drunk
> if you're able

—"dedication" from *Angel and the Bear* Brick/Nairn 1979

44
Dear Richard—my Ph.D.

But I can't change the world
It was changed before I got here.

—Richard Brautigan *The Tokyo-Montana Express*

On January 14, 1967, the first Human Be-in and Gathering of the Tribes was held in San Francisco's Golden Gate Park and attended by some twenty thousand people including Allen Ginsberg, Ken Kesey, Timothy Leary and Jerry Rubin. Music was provided by the Grateful Dead and the Jefferson Airplane who offered their panacean advice, "feed your head." Later in 1967, the Beatles released their radical concept album, *Sgt. Pepper's Lonely Hearts Club Band*, and *Hair* opened. "Che" Guevara was captured and executed in Bolivia and revolutionary posters went up in university dorms everywhere. Woody Guthrie died, Elvis Presley got married and *Rolling Stone* magazine published its first issue. It was the summer of love, the time of the hippie. The Monterey Pop Festival, from June 16 to 18, became the first great rock festival, foreshadowing Woodstock, *Revival 69* in Toronto and Altamont in California. Over one billion dollars were spent in the year on record albums. In Mexico, the *Partido Revolucionario Institucional* recognized Carlos Fuentes with a major literary award and arranged for the construction of nine tourist hotels in Cancun; within a year, the Tlatelolco Massacre, *la noche triste*, forged alliances among students, workers and the poor and marked the beginning of the end for the *PRI*, heralding a political shift toward a more balanced democracy. And in Canada, change was also in the air with Confederation celebrations, Expo '67, and the resignation of Prime Minister Lester Pearson to make room for Pierre Eliot Trudeau, a Just

Society and Trudeaumania. In Viet Nam, although U.S. involvement escalated to include more than 485,000 troops by December, the Tet Offensive of January 1968 would forever change public opinion and American commitment to the war. In 1967, the times, indeed, seemed to be changing.

In 1967, as well, Donald Allen, editor of a small non-profit press called Four Seasons Foundation, re-acquired a small book that Grove Press had decided not to publish. Its author's only other prose work, *A Confederate General from Big Sur*, had sold fewer than eight hundred copies and had been remaindered. The author was a relatively unknown San Francisco writer named Richard Brautigan and the book, which he had originally completed in 1961, was *Trout Fishing in America*. It sold extremely well for Allen, rapidly going through four printings, and was purchased and reissued nationally by Delacourt Press. *Trout Fishing in America* achieved a remarkable popularity—in Brautigan's lifetime selling over two million copies worldwide—in part because, as a friend Keith Abbott suggests, it seemed to speak so precisely to the public sentiment and popular culture of the time:

> When *Trout Fishing in America* was published in 1967, its patchwork construction, its pastoral lost-paradise themes, and its funky, wacky and innocent voices appeared to mirror events in the Haight. Brautigan's active engagement with the Diggers gave him recognition and a *de facto* status as Poet Laureate for the street. At last the media had something written and so the novel became an emblem, an explanation, and a target.

Richard Brautigan quickly became very well-known and relatively wealthy, a pop culture icon. His image adorned posters and t-shirts (see below); and while many fellow writers eked out their living in part-time jobs, publishing only broadsides and chapbooks, as Joseph Mills notes, Brautigan was "photographed by *Life* and giving readings at places like Harvard." This economic liberty gave Brautigan the freedom to pursue whatever literary interests he wished and in the 1970s he did so, churning out a series of experimental (and brilliant) novels that blended different literary genres—gothic and western, crime and erotic, detective and fantasy.

In some sense, Richard Brautigan became a victim of his own success, his own unique style. Brautigan's writings so often appeared light and effortless on the page and expressed insights that frequently seemed so whimsical or quirky or temporal, they appeared to be the simple, artless and airy observations that anyone—hippie, flower child, whoever— could have made. And his work seemed so wedded to the popular *Zeitgeist*, like so many facets of such a feckless culture, it was here one day and gone the next; the critical establishment generally resisted, doubted, ignored or panned his work and, when the 1960s rocked to a close, what positive critical interest there had been for Brautigan's work ended as well—many of the reviews of his post-1960s' writings are savage, vitriolic. As Tom McGuane says: "When the 60s ended, he [Brautigan] was the baby thrown out with the bath water." As a west coast writer, Brautigan, himself, simply felt that he was disliked by the east coast publishers and their critical establishment which he labelled the "New York Mafia." Even among contemporary writers, he was often the subject of parody (as in pieces by Keiller, Burges and Percy)

and Ginsberg, one of the leaders of the Beat movement with whom Brautigan was first linked, nicknamed him Bunthorne, a reference to the inadequate poet in the Gilbert and Sullivan operetta, *Patience*. The irony, of course, is that Brautigan's so-called hippie novels were all written well before people put flowers in their hair and headed for Haight-Ashbury. As he once commented: "I never thought of myself as a hippie novelist. ... My writing is just one man's response to life in the 20th Century."

Conversely, one can argue that Richard Brautigan was no victim at all. In his lifetime Brautigan achieved the kind of financial success and international notoriety about which most writers can only dream, and he enjoyed it—who wouldn't! Emerging from a childhood of abject poverty and parental abuse in the northwest, unknown and without connections, Brautigan established himself in San Francisco by the late 1950s and, within a decade, had published four successful novels, two collections of poetry and an edition of short stories. As noted, he was photographed by and written about in international publications such as *Life* and *Time*, was in demand for interviews and readings around the United States and abroad, made a substantial enough income to buy properties in Bolinas, California and Livingston, Montana and travelled widely, including lengthy and costly stays in Japan. Brautigan mixed with the elite of Hollywood, achieved celebrity status, even mobbed on occasion by fans, and generally lived an independent life in which he did what he wanted, partied a lot and undoubtedly had many satisfying escapades. His was a remarkable achievement, and in spite of the understandably melancholy recollections of him after his self-inflicted death, sadness at his loss and at what might have been, all and all, his was a pretty good life for a writer (maybe for anybody else save the final gunshot).

In the years leading up to his death and in the years following it, Brautigan's works were often hard to find—most were out of print. Critical attention was minimal. Since the turn of the millennium, however, change seems to be in the air. Canongate's Rebel Inc. has reissued several titles including *Revenge of the Lawn, Sombrero Fallout, So the Wind Won't Blow It All Away, A Confederate General from Big Sur* and *An Unfortunate Woman,* a deluxe, limited edition of *Trout Fishing in America* has been printed, a collection of juvenilia and a posthumous novel have been published, at least two memoirs have been issued, one by Brautigan's daughter Ianthe and another by a friend and colleague, Greg Keeler, a recording of Brautigan reading his work has been reissued,

William Hjortsberg has completed a comprehensive and monumental biography for Knopf (*Jubilee Hitchhiker*), John Barber has created an online magazine dedicated to Brautigan entitled *Change* and has published a selection of new and old articles, *Richard Brautigan: Essays on the Writings and Life*. And in 2010, alone, at least three full-length books were published in homage to Brautigan's life and work (novels by Mesler and Sherman and a collection of critical articles and reviews by Surhone, Tennoe and Henssonow) and film versions of three of Brautigan's novels, *The Abortion*, *The Hawkline Monster*, and *A Confederate General from Big Sur*, as well as a feature length biography, are all in various stages of negotiation or production. And I, too, as this chapter probably indicates, spent a lot of time tangled in the magic words of Richard Brautigan and completed my dissertation on Richard and his works by 1990. And I think in some way at least I honoured the dead writer with some of the dues he deserves.

Richard Brautigan's works often made me laugh out loud and weep in the heart; his adroit observations and imaginative constructions seemed to lift a veil, comic and poignant and satiric and sad, on life as it was being lived in my time. During my early doctoral years, when I raised the possibility of working on Brautigan to Geoffrey Rans, he told me not to, suggested that I research someone like Toni Morrison, that a thesis on Brautigan would never get me hired in any university. But that was never my goal; I wanted to do the research because I liked Brautigan's writings, because I felt that he merited some serious study. And having done my M.A. thesis on Melville, I wanted to work on a contemporary author and avoid some of the immense critical baggage that comes with attending to a more established writer from an earlier time. The contrast intrigued as well. Melville wrote heavy; Brautigan light, but each achieved remarkable insights into the human condition. The sea was in their souls. Alan Gedalof graciously offered to help, being a kind of Renaissance academic in the department; Brautigan's interest in detective fiction and *film noir* also aligned with Gedalof's interests. And for some reason I will never understand, Professor Michael Groden, an eminent, internationally recognized Joyce scholar, kindly agreed to be second advisor. As it turned out, for the perusal of each advisor, I wrote and submitted my first chapter within the year, and then completed the rest of the dissertation on my own. In not pestering my advisors as some grad students are wont, Professor Groden, in particular, told me it felt like one of the quickest completions ever, like I wrote it overnight. The only challenge in the defence was getting to the defence. I defended in January (that date apparently saved me a term's tuition) but a winter storm had roared through that morning and, on my way to defend, I got stuck twice (once in my driveway, once in the university parking lot)—a true Canadian Ph.D., I suppose! Each of the four examiners commented on how well the dissertation was written— nothing makes you a better writer than teaching writing, I think, which by that time I had done for many years—and, at the end, the external examiner asked me what I was planning to do with the thesis, to which I replied, "Nothing!" Dr. Gedalof laughed with me about that after. But the answer was true. I did the doctorate for personal reasons, for purposes of finishing a doctorate, I suppose, to finish climbing the mountain that I had begun with my B.A. I avoided any kind of celebratory fete afterward (although the Department at Clarke Road hijacked me with a gift) and only attended the convocation ceremony because my father had asked me to do so in my mother's memory. My father died before that ceremony occurred. Dad was very sick in the last year or so (bone cancer)—in fact, there was a six-month period in which I could not write at all; then after he passed, the words came back and I finished quickly. And so I crossed the stage for him, too. It seemed a long way from the dark ploughed furrows of those fields of home where I grew up and yet, in memory, it was not far distant in many ways at all.

Richard Brautigan's ranch, south of Livingston, Montana.

45

Consulting...about what, I never figured out

the trouble is there is no
sorcerer but only apprentices
man is the political animal
who knows paranoia is power
demons rise up, atoms split
there is so much incomplete magic
inchoate worlds and spells
in the wind of power

—Tom Marshall "Second Legend"

I like teaching at Clarke Road; it has a remarkably genuine feel about it but, as is my nature, I feel the need to move on. I apply for a position as Consultant in the London Board and am offered an interview. As with most interviews by this point, I more or less control it—I know that they will give me the questions in advance, tell me I have fifteen minutes to review them, then ask me if I am ready after five. It is a trick they play to test your ability to think on your feet, I suppose, and I am ready. I have also readied myself for their questions in regard to current educational trends and theories and Board policies and procedures. And so I am appointed as Language Consultant for the Board (in theory, responsible for all the languages taught—French, English, Spanish, German, Japanese, others?—heavens, I think, does this Board know what trouble it's in!); Clarke Road, I might add, has already prepared me for the language of the street but, of course, no school alone teaches that. I am not assigned, as the other Consultants are, to a particular family of schools but, rather, to all schools. I do all my work from an office space in the Board Offices with no need to travel anywhere; my immediate Supervisor is an affable man named David Ennis who always wears a white shirt and black suit, everyday, always. Always ready for that snapshot in the local newspaper. He is a 'pit' as I come to nickname all such individuals—a Principal-in-Training. Until they get their appointments, these ingenues serve the Superintendents who serve the Director who serves the Minister of Education who serves the Premier who serves, well, only God knows and it is not for me to ask. Either the Premier or God?

The Superintendent I report to is Don Scanlon, a pleasant former elementary school Principal edging toward retirement (like most of the Superintendents I meet, he has reached the apogee of his existence on this diurnal plane); Don takes on the role of father-figure in each of the weekly meetings he oversees, telling all of the Consultants some cozy family-style anecdote about camping or Christmas and then spinning through the expectations of the week. The paternal role is one common to elementary school Principals from the time, I suppose, when males were arbitrarily cast as Principals in such places to guide the vestals of public schools—it took a long time for elementary teachers to rise up, overcome the stereotyped image of the elementary teacher as glorified second-mother and earn equal rights in pay and benefits (and respect) in comparison to their secondary colleagues and the public-at-large. In many jurisdictions, that same struggle is still being waged among the ranks of Kindergarten, Day Care specialists and other Early Childcare Educators in general.

On my first day at the so-named Education Centre (it isn't, by the way; the classroom is always the true Centre of Education), I need some tape and find a roll in a storage closet, but this is a kind of tape I have never seen before. It looks like a regular dispenser of Scotch tape but, when I go to use it, it is tape that does not stick. It peels off like a tired sticky note, which, apparently, is what it is supposed to do. I quickly come to see it as a metaphor for the world I have just entered. This is a political world. Nothing sticks! Everyone here is treading water, trying to get somewhere else while not drowning, but not moving either so no waves are created. No boats are rocked. The Board Office seems filled with an anxious sea of bobbing heads. Even the tape doesn't stick. As shy, wise Tom Marshall once wrote, "paranoia is power." The assumption is that even a Consultant such as I must be trying to get somewhere, but I'm not. I never learned nor have any desire to know how to swim. For me, this experience is just another trip to a sideshow in the carnival of the world. Besides, T. S. Eliot's phrase always lurks in the back of my head: "Fear death by water."

As a Consultant, I never do any consulting. I don't really do much of anything, no reading or research or analysis; instead of using its own intelligent resources, the Board seems to buy its pedagogy in pre-packaged installments, disseminating a different set of ideas every two or three years before switching to some other. (This strategy will lead to the emasculation of the Boards. The Mike Harris Tories will usurp Board power, the government-at-large taking charge and buying a chosen curriculum instead of designing one.) Whoever does the shopping, the source is almost always America which teems with high profile, sleekly marketed programs and testing methodologies— education is a decidedly lucrative endeavour south of the border. While I am a Consultant, Outcomes-Based Education by Bill Spady is the rage. Wildly promoted in the fashion of carnival hucksters by his High Success Network, with glossy handouts, progressive booklets, telemarketing videos, ready-made overheads, fill-in-the-blank classroom materials and other slick and simple propaganda, it is the newest dance craze and Consultants are sent forth to promote the method school by school. For the most part, thankfully, I am kept apart from that sales pitch; I meet after school with several teacher-writing groups and assemble endless and mundane documents to be passed on to others and destined for dusty shelves—in the main, I seem to be a well-paid secretary. I get along with the people with whom I work, have nice lunches with them, tidy up a storage closet that is near my desk, sign a bunch of stipend-notices for something or other and, I suppose, get a break from marking (although I never really minded marking). But quickly I know that I do not fit here; lots of good people do and good for them. So, although the appointment can last five or six years, to the surprise of my supervisors, I think, I resign after six weeks. I thank everyone for the opportunity but indicate my desire to return to the classroom as soon as the next semester begins. As later Director of Education and wise friend, John Thorpe, commented, I probably served the shortest term of any Consultant ever. And I take pride in that accomplishment.

46
The Theory of Cutting Corners

About a hundred and fifty horsemen were at once scattered over the downs, riding at the top of their speed, in almost all directions; some following the hounds, but a greater number, not liking the undulating nature of the ground, cutting corners, and hustling each other by cross riding.

—Knightley William Horlock "On the Management of Hounds" 1852

I do not believe, either, in what we used to call cutting corners or going short roads to places. The short road I have always found is in the end the longest.

—"Going Straight On" *Oxford Magazine and Church Advocate* (V. III October 1863)

'Cutting corners' was once a topic of moral discussion in society; in education, it has been a persistent trend particularly since the end of World War II. And cutting corners, as the quotations above suggest (where the phrase first appeared in English), is never by accident or without purpose, nor does it typically end with the positive consequences for which it is intended. Usually, it has been done under the name of efficiency or modernization or, just, re-organization, to cut bureaucracy and reduce administration. In Ontario, with the recommendations based on government policy reports such as the *Robarts Plan*

(1962) and the *Hall-Dennis Report* (1968), school boards in the province were reduced from over 4,000 to just over one hundred; Harris's *Ontario Curriculum* and *The Fewer School Boards Act* (1997) reduced them even further, from 129 to about seventy (31 English Public, 29 English Catholic, 4 French Public, 8 French Catholic). Ostensibly, this was to solidify and streamline the educational standards of schooling across the province, but the merging of Boards is expensive as is the operation of larger Boards. And, in general, this took away a lot of local control as well as sensitivity to and understanding of local needs. And the old question always arises in regard to common standards, does a student in smaller communities like Pickle Lake or Moosonee need to know the same as the student who lives along the metropolitan Jane/Finch corridor in Toronto, and there is no easy answer. Even as I write this, the number of boards in Ontario is once again under threat of reduction by the Doug Ford Conservatives. So, the beat goes on.

Another blow to the significance and autonomy of local school boards and their elected Trustees, Harris's government removed education from the residential property tax base so that the central government, not the School Boards, collected and controlled distribution of all property taxes. Trustees, who were once the most powerful group in education, controlling matters of finance, have now become an anachronism, little more than decorative wind chimes around Board Offices, or to use an old country phrase, useless as teats on a boar hog.

Corners have also been cut in curriculum development. Once, when curriculum guidelines by the Ministry were created, drafts would be forwarded to schools for perusal, and Departments, led by their Heads, or Area Leaders, would review them. Often this resulted in significant modifications and even wholesale changes—curriculum was often massaged to fit local needs. The Heads, experienced teachers and the chief arbiters in these matters, came to be seen as blockers of policy. Thus, in recent years, the Department Head system has come under direct attack ranging all the way from the elimination of Heads to the amalgamation or clustering of subjects under clever new arrangements colloquially calling those in charge Super Heads, but essentially reducing the number of Department Heads in positions of influence. Sometimes, now, with no input at the local level, fully printed Curriculum Guidelines will arrive at the school level (often in late June, or through the summer) with no voice to respond. The cutting of corners, indeed.

Frequently in our society, and in education in particular, complaints arise when things become "too theoretical" or "too technical," when things are not practical enough. Medical doctors are asked to explain diagnoses in lay terms, car mechanics use a language that is fifty years out-dated to describe automobile maladies. In educational realms, one often hears that everything done in ivory towers is of relative merit and little use and is generally out of touch—it is all "too theoretical" to be of any use in a real classroom. While some of this may be true, in this, a common tendency of our society is evident, the desire for "common sense" solutions, the tendency to split theory and practice—theory may be ok (maybe) to study somewhere but it sure as hell has nothing to do with my classroom on a Friday afternoon. Recently, perhaps the most egregious instance of this kind of flawed thinking came about in Donald Trump's dealing with the *Covid-19* crisis, rejecting science and, at one point, even suggesting that the injection of disinfectant might provide a cure.

The tendency of our society to scorn theory and to separate theory from practice is widespread and deep. It echoes an essential anti-intellectualism, evident by way of example in many literary works and throughout popular culture—one of the most common occupations of villains or buffoons in American Literature, for instance, is the scholar-teacher—from Ichabod Crane ("The Legend of Sleepy Hollow") to Dr. Spivey (*One Flew Over the Cuckoo's Nest*) to Barker Flett (*The Stone Diaries*); the hero of North American popular culture is almost never the debonair Sherlock Holmes or erudite James Bond but rather the non-thinking man of true grit and action, Davy Crockett or John Wayne or Rambo or John McClane (Yippee-ki-yay, you ***; Ferris Bueller always outsmarts Mr. Rooney). The intellectual person of theory simply lacks the chops to get the job done, lacks the common sense to fix the car or put out the fire. And even teachers, although they are among the best educated individuals in our society, often seem to buy into this sceptical stance at least in staff room banter.

In many ways, however, theory is power; our society differentiates professionals from technicians in a variety of ways, not the least of which is monetary. In some sense, with the pressure in many jurisdictions to eliminate professional activity days and/or take absolute control over what is presented, with the attempt to make teachers more "accountable" for the time they spend at school, with the effort to increase instructional time, with the regular surfacing of plans to test and re-certify teachers, with the notion to increase the time needed to earn a B.Ed. from one to two years (or four or five), with the tendency to reduce the study of English to a set of language skills, with the effort to program exactly what teachers teach (I have seen daily automaton-like print-outs from a Chicago Board outlining (ordaining?) precisely what teachers say and do during the day), with the amalgamation and neutering of local Boards of Education (spaying, if you prefer), with the attempt to eliminate non-academic teaching positions, and so much more, there is, without a doubt, steady and certain, an attempt afoot to cut corners by de-professionalizing teachers.

When I began to teach, it was mandatory that I belong to the OSSTF, the Ontario Secondary School Teachers' Federation. Part of my salary was arbitrarily directed to the coffers of this umbrella organization, providing legal protection for various things and a superannuation plan. When it came to contract negotiations, though, salaries and benefits and the like were negotiated Board by Board, District by District. And for years it was always made clear to us in OSSTF that we were not a union, we were a Federation. While the difference wasn't always made clear, somehow, I think the status of being a Federation made us Professionals and not Labour. And in some curious way, that always made sense and seemed acceptable, classist as the consideration tended to be. What it meant province-wide, in practice, of course, was an oft-time dizzying matrix of negotiations, Public and Catholic and Private, Elementary and Secondary, English and French, and all Board by Board so often there seemed to be a never-ending spate of educational disruptions or threats of disruption, all made exponentially worse with the onslaught of electronic and social media.

Labour issues aside—days of protest and weeks of strike and hours of frustrated angst—perhaps the most productive way for teachers to combat this attempt to delimit their status is through the power of owning and implementing theory, through understanding the interlocking principles which exist behind daily classroom activities. In the truest sense possible, I have never met a teacher who did not, in some way or another, teach from theory. Every teacher acts from a set of hypotheses, but often only partly thought out—quite frankly, teachers can't always research or formulate complete theories while performing their everyday tasks. They've got hall or yard supervision, a Video-chat session to set up, a data projector to locate, a team to coach, or mark entry to do. But theories do play vital roles—in fact, our most powerful theories become our myths, our religions. So fundamental here is my belief that theory does have a place in the classroom and, in fact, the more teachers know about the theories that influence them, the better off classes will be, and the better teachers they will be. There is no cutting this corner. And I know from my work with teachers through the years, that they have the intellectual curiosity and the inherent desire to garner and articulate this knowledge. Theory provides power and the more empowered teachers are, the better education will be, the better off our children will be. In so many ways, I suppose, that is the reason why I write this book, to quantify some of the various theories and trends that surround the contemporary classroom and tempt further interrogation.

A brief word about Professional Development Days; briefly, in the immortal words of the Daleks … "Exterminate." PD Days should be exterminated! Long ago, when there seemed to be more money and teaching was viewed as a learned profession, grand Conferences were held, often with national and international presenters, and Professional Development Days were often like mini-versions of those conferences. As the concept currently exists, most jurisdictions have between four and eight PD Days—students stay home and teachers attend some scattered workshops or presentations often arranged locally by either the Principal of the school or the Director and Superintendents. Over the years, I have actually witnessed many conflicts (sometimes quite comical) over who controls these days, but mostly the themes offered are mundane, simply the indoctrinating transmission of some Ministry dogma or trendy methodology. I found many of them so inept and boring and incomplete, I started offering to give them myself on various topics (usually related to media and technology or language and linguistics). Not that the presentations I gave were not, in themselves, inept or boring, but at least I was not the person forced to attend— thankfully, it is hard to fall asleep during your own presentation. The grand PD conferences that used to be held (where I saw the likes of Britton, Rosenblatt, Postman and Frye) have essentially costed themselves out of existence, and *Covid-19* was a final nail. And the narrow, scattered, postage stamp days that currently exist are generally a waste of time—for teachers, these days might better be spent to catch-up on marking or prep for next week's classes, or to read a good book. Many teachers slip away to do this anyway.

That said, I firmly believe that the teaching profession is a profession and, as such, vitally needs time and space to research and mull over the ever-evolving ideas of educational change. As you would not want a medical doctor who has not updated her- or him-self in the last twenty years, so you do not want a teacher instructing your child who, at least, has not been exposed to currently unfolding ideas and theories by professionals in those fields. And this needs to be done in some formal, in-depth manner. Instead of dropping in a PD Day here or there, it might be far more useful to set aside a solid week, or two, each year, and provide teachers with a set of readings, a group of articles or a pertinent book or two (print or web), and offer meaningful Professional Development, a kind of mini-course or extended workshop in which teachers are actively engaged in the give and take of learning, provided with a real opportunity to sort through the academic underpinnings of the profession in a serious manner. A paper or a project could be the end requirement, some kind of tangible research or action that might even be connected to a specific area of need or interest in their local school system. The students would not lose any time in class—these PD weeks could easily be amassed in the week before Spring Break or at the beginning or end of the school year. (Suggestion: offered in real space and time, these courses would NOT be on-line or virtual. They would be immersed in human experience, human connections.) As to the source for instructors, with government prompting, some combination of Consultants, Administrators and University Professors could be made available, and certain lead-teachers, too. In this way, at least, substantial Professional Development could be made a lot more meaningful and useful, and interesting, too. And, having taught teachers in summer courses for years and seen how starved so many were for some renewed academic challenge—teachers are, after all, in the main, *university graduates*—I know that the response would be positive and, in the end, it would be the students who benefit most. And the educational ethos at large.

ADDENDUM:

The College of Teachers

And speaking of the Daleks and extermination …. since teaching began in this province, among the supervision of Principals, Board-level Superintendents and complementary governance by the rules and mandates of their own Federations, teachers had been duly regulated and suitably disciplined. Censure, when and if required, was properly meted out. In 1994, the *Royal Commission on Learning* recommended that teachers continue to be so regulated. Two years later, out of thin air, in July of 1996—summertime when schools were out of session—the Ontario College of Teachers was born like some toxic sea-scum arbitrarily washed ashore by the tide and its mandate included such broad powers as the licencing and disciplining of teachers and the accreditation of teacher qualification programs. It is in charge of all things educational in the province. Who this College is and where it came from is a mystery but, like so many entities of this type, Iago worming his designs into Othello's conscious, the longer they exist, the more they become entrenched, the more convinced they and others become about their need to exist as if they have always been. And the more legitimacy they gain in the eyes of all who behold them. Let it be said: the College of Teachers in Ontario is an unnecessary organization, simply another bureaucratic cesspool into which tax-payers' dollars are flushed. This College does nothing that was not done before and is simply another attempt to control teachers and minimize their identities as professionals. July 5, 1996, the day the College came into being, remains one of the darkest days ever for education in the province of Ontario.

Initially, this College decreed that, before they could receive their B.Ed., teacher candidates were required to write a test, something akin to the American SATs. As you can imagine, this did not go over well after students had paid for and completed the work assigned them at Faculties of Education; the Faculties were less than impressed either. And the tests were 'very American' in content and slant, created by a test-publishing company in New Jersey (NJASK), and not only in content, but in how they were administered—I knew a couple students who lived just north of Toronto and were assigned to sit their exam in Sudbury. On a map in New Jersey, I suppose, that looks close enough. The College of Teachers decreed (initially, at least) that all practicing teachers were going to have to sit for regular exams and re-certification, criminal record checks were demanded of all teachers, language fluency checks were imposed, discipline hearings and punishments were published in their quarterly magazine, *Professionally Speaking,* and its insidious *Blue Pages* seem to have become the obsession of the College, their true *raison d'être*—recently they even went all the way to the Supreme Court of Canada to appeal one of their judicially overturned discipline decisions. For years, teachers tore the address labels off and tossed this magazine in the mail to be returned to the College at its expense. But the entrenchment continues; recently, the College changed from an elected member set-up to a *selected process for membership,* under the presumed goal of fine-tuning the ranks of their membership. Cutting corners, I suppose! That same manoeuvre was carried out quietly in the early days of the Third Reich, a regime that pushed the cutting of corners to a brutal perfection. Exterminate, indeed! One is compelled to think of the dark words of Martin Niemőller:

> First they came for the socialists, and I did not speak out—
> Because I was not a socialist.
> Then they came for the trade unionists, and I did not speak out—
> Because I was not a trade unionist.
> Then they came for the Jews, and I did not speak out—
> Because I was not a Jew.
> Then they came for me—
> And there was no one left to speak for me.

—Martin Niemőller 1946

47

Up in the sky, it's a bird...

"Well, as I always say, Johnny, there are three sides to every story. Did you ever think, maybe the fool's quest is staying here, boarding up this room, burying yourself in this place like some kind of old fashioned ... well, clown? Refusing to change, refusing to take charge of change. 'Cause, if you don't take charge of change, Johnny, it'll take charge of you! That's what hell is! And growing old in the same place. You wake up one morning and suddenly your joints ache just thinkin' about getting' up. Maybe you need to do for yourself before that happens? Maybe that would make what you do for others matter a bit more? Maybe this room's been boarded up long enough,..."

"You can't escape the past, Oz, any more than you can catch the future."

"...maybe the last circus has already left town, Johnny. Maybe nobody can change the world, but we can all change ourselves, or try to. Maybe it's what we're born for... "

"By God, old man, aren't you the poetic one this morning. You must be hangin' around the Professor too much. But you know, I think you're right, Oz. There is a storm comin'. I better check some of the windows around back. Maybe do some fresh caulking."

"Hell, Prince. I can do that."

'No, you keep helping Emily with the Gardens. I'll do it. Getting' ready for the storm before it gets here is something I need to do. And there are some things that have to be done you know, that you need to do by yourself.'

"Yeah, I know Johnny. What's the old sayin'—live as long as you can, close your own eyes when you die!"

"Yeah! Something like that. Sometimes it's easy and sometimes it isn't. But maybe it's really the only way to live your life, to save your world. It's how you know who you are when you get up in the morning, aches or pains, like it or not, have a cup of coffee, talk to strangers checkin' in at a cheap motel. You gotta be who you gotta be, Oz. It's just that, sometimes, it takes a while to find that, sometimes a lifetime. That's life at the Leroy, isn't it? Sometimes a blessing; sometimes a curse. But that's life at our Leroy! It's the life we know. See you later, old man."

Johnny squeezes Oz's shoulder with his hand and moves away toward the Office. "Errands to do."

—Oz and Johnny in conversation *The Prince of Leroy*

My exit from the Education Centre and my short life as a Consultant begins with a chance encounter with Ted McTavish. Ted was one of the V.P.s at Clarke Road Secondary School and he is visiting the Board Offices this day and I tell him of my decision to return to the classroom. He is now a V.P. at South Secondary School, an older academic school (structurally, it resembles BCI) situated in an established community in south-central London. Ted is an earnest fellow—he made a grand announcement on the P.A. at the Road following my completion of the doctorate—and a golfing buddy; along with Gerry Denomme (with whom I coached the Road's golf team) and Brian Charlton, we spent a couple summers golfing various courses around the south-west. Gerry was a scratch golfer and Ted, tall and athletic, could pound the ball a mile. Brian and I, mostly, went along for the ride (although I did shoot in the mid-eighties most of my golfing life). Anyway, long story short, political magic happens and, after my meeting with Ted, I am assigned a position teaching in the English Department at South.

South Secondary School:

In spite of the behind-the-scenes machinations to bring me to South, my stay there is only for one semester. I do all my teaching in a portable next to the school which establishes a kind of disconnect, anyway; I never feel much a part of things, so leaving is easy. Two highlights, I suppose: teaching an OAC Writer's Craft class in which the students are top-flight academics and we do all sorts of creative endeavours, including publishing a book of poems and stories; and two, a junior boys' volleyball team which, although their true love is basketball, is exceptionally athletic and willing to learn. They only narrowly miss winning the city championships (held in Western's main gymnasium), falling to Oakridge after a referee's egregious missed call (you know the story) but still go on to compete in what is called SWOSSA.

During my stay at South, interviews are held for the next round of Headship appointments for London schools; it is a position that I think will give me some control and freedom so I apply. Nothing ventured; nothing gained, you know. Although he worked to bring me to South, Ted kindly gives me some advice about dealing with budgetary questions and I nail the interview, placing first on the list of candidates for promotion. Very shortly, I receive notice that I should prepare for an appointment. Initially, it appears to be a return to Clarke Road, but I am not certain that I want to take on a position of authority over colleagues who were my friends. I contact John Thorpe, the Principal of Clarke Road, indicate my hesitancies to him and suggest that I will be happy to withdraw my application. But John tells me to wait; again, political gears inside the walls twist and grind and, when my appointment is offered, it is to Oakridge Secondary School. The current Head there, Wendy Thorpe (John's wife), is tracking to become a V.P. and needs some experience in a different kind of school other than Oakridge; so several personnel change schools and I am dropped into the role of Department Head at Oakridge Secondary Schools, which is the final high school in which I will ever teach.

Oakridge Secondary School:

Oakridge's school colours are red, gold and blue, the same as Queen's, so somehow naturally I feel at home there. And, while I live in the county north of London, the school is less than five minutes away so that is a good thing too. Oakridge is situated in an affluent suburb and has just been renovated to help it compete, I think, with a new Catholic school that has recently been built down the block. Both are new and shiny. About 92 percent of Oakridge's students go on to university or college and, in one of my years there, seventeen individuals or athletic teams compete in all-Ontario competitions. Those statistics are rare, unheard of; in fact, many schools never have one team or individual reach Provincials. At Clarke Road, by comparison, fewer than ten percent of the students go on to higher education (not always because of ability as much as peer influence—parents, siblings and friends didn't go, so neither do they)—this potential lost is an indelible sadness of teaching at the Road. At Oakridge, the reverse is true. Expectations from many directions provide a constant pressure on students, often, to reach beyond their capabilities. And sometimes, among students, expectations exceed effort. With an eye to international business, Japanese is even taught at Oakridge with a teacher from Japan on loan. French, German and Spanish, too. Huge musical productions are mounted each year, using professional choreographers, and set designers, and costing thousands of dollars. It is truly an elite academic school; and most of its students are interesting and engaging young people who will take their place in the positive echelons of society, whatever those are construed to be. Some sense of entitlement is evident, of course, but to me, that is not just Oakridge—by the end of the twentieth century, that is a universal trend slouching like some beast from the desert into the heart of contemporary society, children seem to be given so much (whether they want it or not), their lives become at once an astringent existence of privilege and prerogative. In addition, as the year 2000 nears, we have come to live in a world that perceives danger in all places. The age gives birth to the helicopter parent. Children are never safe; they are ferried everywhere with someone they can trust holding their hand. And so, as the young lion learns to crouch in the tall grass and slash at the throat of its prey, entitlement is a carnal instinct inherited as a right of survival. It is the new Golden Calf and a thing that teachers must now learn to expect. In that way, *Covid-19* was the perfect disease for the time in which it occurred—the ubiquitous threat, everywhere, anyone, at any moment. The breath of a stranger, lethal, invisible. An instant cure needed/expected; aged ones die alone behind plexi-glass barricades; indistinguishable refrigerated tractor-trailers serve as morgues. Who deserves to get the vaccine first! Well … those without entitlement finish last, you know, and may not finish at all! As a Department Head in the London Board, I teach four classes, not the usual six. That extra time is truly the best part of the position, time to take care of all the paperwork and bureaucratic demands of the role. Luckily, the Department at Oakridge is very good, diverse and talented and committed. The only problem is that, at times, they do not realize how good they are. When I arrive, there are minor squabbles well-brewed among factions of the Department, but I refuse to take sides. In the big picture, the students are doing well and the universe continues to spin. I recall a line from Leonard Cohen: "First you take Manhattan, then you take Berlin." Michael Nobes, an excellent teacher, becomes a friend, and we set up a Film Study Club and I help some students establish an Oakridge literary magazine we call *The Ridge*. I coach the Intermediate boys' volleyball team and manage to produce a compre-hensive Department Guidelines which clearly lays out the courses, texts taught, and general policies of the Department (previously, little of that information exists outside of the individual teacher's minds). I begin to create assessment rubrics for the courses, so trendy that a couple Superintendents actually visit to talk with me (one actually suggests that I should consider applying to be a Consultant—I smile and think of wise Huck Finn: "I been there before"). At Department meetings, I invite various members to present unique teaching ideas they are trying in their classes, and slowly try to break down any rancour that exists. I do not invite the Librarian to the meetings—she was a close friend of the previous Head, attended meetings and seems to have been a divisive force, which is something the Department does not need. My sense is that things are working, so I do not try to impress some overt philosophy—a quieting peace and calm is mostly what is needed. Trivial as this may sound, I always have some food and drink at these meetings which, somehow, makes the time communal—feed the body, you know, and the soul will take care of itself. That's an idea that has worked for a long time. Not quite bread and wine, but close!

And then one afternoon in spring, I receive a call from the University of Western Ontario. Ian Underhill, through unfortunate personal circumstances, is resigning his position as a full-time undergraduate instructor. The question—would I be willing to apply for the job? While only guaranteed as a one-year appointment, it is not every day that a university phones up and (more or less) offers you a job. And so I apply and, as is my wont, I do well in the interview—I actually know several of the people asking the questions, having taught the Honours Specialist course for several years, and I have a pretty good handle on what the job might require. Of those interviewed, I am also the only one with a doctorate. I am offered the job. But leaving Oakridge is not an easy decision. At the same time as this offer is being made, I am promoted to the role of *Superhead*. As a streamlining and cost-saving measure, cutting corners under the direction of the Provincial government, the Thames Valley Board of Education—London, Middlesex and Oxford have just been amalgamated—is reducing departments in all secondary schools to four. I will now be responsible for English, Theatre Arts, History, French and all of the other Modern Languages. It means five-grand more in salary but I also understand the overall political machinations at work. Oakridge is an excellent place to teach and, if I leave for a year, I will not get placed back there, and several members of the Department ask me to stay ... but, but, but. My friend, Michael Nobes, gives me a bottle of Glenfiddich long before I make my decision—he knows. All that time and effort spent to finish a doctorate and, suddenly, an opportunity to put it to use. And so, I accept the one-year secondment. While I keep the extra salary of the promotion, I let the *Superhead* position fly up, up and away.

48

Some New Clothes

For neither in tailoring nor in legislating does man proceed by mere Accident, but the hand is ever guided on by mysterious operations of the mind. In all his Modes, and habilatory endeavors, an Architectural Idea will be found lurking; his Body and the Cloth are the site and materials whereon and whereby his beautified edifice, of a Person, is to be built.

—Thomas Carlyle, *Sartor Resartus*

… No costume the Emperor had worn before was ever such a complete success.

"But he hasn't got anything on," a little child said.

"Did you ever hear such innocent prattle?" said its father. And one person whispered to another what the child had said, "He hasn't anything on. A child says he hasn't anything on."

"But he hasn't got anything on!" the whole town cried out at last.

The Emperor shivered, for he suspected they were right. But he thought, "This procession has got to go on." So he walked more proudly than ever, as his noblemen held high the train that wasn't there at all.

—Hans Christian Andersen, *The Emperor's New Clothes*

The clothes we wear are important to us, not only sustaining us through the deviations of the seasons but also providing some comment in certain times and places on what we think of as our identity, on who we are and what we value in those moments. And like the seasons, our fashions change. In Arts and Science Faculties, there was a time when, upon the retirement of a specialist in a subject area, Victorian Literature or perhaps The Tactics of Gallic Warfare, a specialist in the same field would be hired, or in some other similar historical designation or thematic need as perceived by the Department. By the 1990s, however, as Postmodernist values tightened their grip, that pragmatic practice went out of style. For the most part in the twenty years before, universities had been busy churning out graduates who had burrowed deeper and deeper into theory of various kinds at various levels and, accordingly, hiring practices shifted. A brave new paradigm strutted down the street. And its wardrobe was of many different hues and fabrics altering the very textures of the Departments themselves. While not all aspects of any change are entirely good—we may cringe as we think back to leisure suits and hot pants—for the most part, this makeover brought new perspectives, even new subjects, and overall, a fresh and changed power to envision the intellectual world in these very oldest of institutions. Feminism, structuralism, post-structuralism, deconstruction, semiotics, cultural and media studies, queer and gender studies, and a host of other theoretical frameworks, re-visioning old and contemporary texts and events and concerns and apotheosizing new ones, all re-animating the corpse of academia in one way or another with a new suit of clothes. In thumbnail versions and lay-person language, here are some of the mainstream theories that had the greatest influence both in the university sphere and, as the ideas spread out, in elementary and secondary pedagogies as well:

Archetypal Theory generally examines the significance of common images, motifs, narratives, and/or types of characters that recur among different works with a focus on myths, dreams and ritual. Influential scholars such as Northrop Frye and Joseph Campbell were central to this way of thinking; I saw teachers develop entire units and courses based on Campbell's thinking about the power and cycles of myth (themes centred around the journey, a search for the lost parent, the Romantic rebel-hero, the earth goddess) and Frye's contributions were illimitable—not only was he president of OCTE for years but, in Ontario, anyway, his work helped to anchor education in a broad cultural and moral context (his series of mythology texts alone (edited with W. T. Jewkes) were standards for many years across the province) and Frye's educational commitment to the literary world and the word were powerfully influential: "... nothing but literature, in a culture as verbal as ours, can train the imagination to fight for the sanity and dignity of mankind." (Northrop Frye *The Educated Imagination*).

Feminist Criticism, although it has now formally been around long enough to have many diverse branches, is still generally the school of thought which looks at the cultural and economic experiences of women living in a patriarchal society. It examines the "history" ("herstory"?) of gender roles, patriarchy, subordination, bias, and so on. From altering the way we may look at teaching and texts to changing the texts themselves and even to hiring and promotional practises, feminism has brought a lot to the pedagogical table and has fundamentally transformed the sensibility of teaching, revolutionizing schools, and society, in general.

Marxist thinking has dominated certain university departments, always considering class, conflict, culture and economics—who controls the material means of production has the money, and who has the money has the power. In school situations, political texts such as *Animal Farm* and *1984* are still commonly taught and the class conflict in works by the likes of Dickens and Shakespeare are read in a different light, and often Marxism links with other theoretical approaches to form powerful new ways of seeing and teaching. The 'social justice movement' owes a great deal both to Marxist and Feminist ways of thinking.

New Criticism, which I have covered earlier (Chapter Eleven) had dominated pedagogical thinking and practice for the last hundred years and was never entirely eradicated by the 'new' new critical approaches.. It advocated the close reading of text (and nothing but the text) with a focus on words and structure, on intense explication and extensive terminology. Its progenitors were heavyweights like T. S. Eliot, Ezra Pound, E. M. Forster, I. A. Richards, John Crowe Ransom and Cleanth Brooks and they insisted that there was only one no-nonsense way to read literature, one no-nonsense way to teach—understandably, New Criticism was the principal target for the onslaught of many of the newer critical approaches but, at heart, its procedures still infiltrate much of what happens, especially in the English classroom. Ask precise questions, get the 'right' answer, and move on.

Psychological and Psychoanalytic Criticism considers literature, in particular, as an expression of the personality, feelings, and desires of the author. The considerations and patterns of human motivation as described by Freud and Jung and others (there are numerous schools of applicable psychology) are often used to illuminate literary works from *Hamlet* to *Fifth Business* and everything in between. In education, this is often the territory of Dewey and the Laboratory Schools, and his advocates. And most schools have Student Services Departments where various dimensions of psychology are never far away.

Reader Response Criticism is the school of thought which considers the process and nature of reading and the experiences of the reader. As we read, the meaning is considered to materialize in the space between the reader and the text, so that, in a classroom of thirty readers, ostensibly, there will be thirty different texts. Rosenblatt, Iser, Bleich, Fish and a host of others present variations on this theory which, in the English classroom, has led to much greater onus on situating the interpretation of any text in the hands and minds of the students—their thoughts, experiences and assumptions come into play and shape the course of the study at hand. It is now the teacher who has stepped down from the dais to listen and learn. This theory sits at the heart of the notion of student-centred learning.

Deconstruction essentially focuses on the internal functions of language and conceptual systems, on the idea that language means nothing beyond relational meanings and assumptions internalized in expressions. The process of reading a text is based on understanding and breaking down its structures so one might read Shrek, for example, as a deconstruction of the Western European fairy tale, or as a Marxist allegory (Shrek as proletariat, Farquaad as bourgeoisie).

Historical Criticism is the school of thought that looks at the significance of historical time in a piece of work. Social, political, economic, cultural, and/or intellectual aspects of the era are considered. Examining the legal rights of females in the sixteenth century might be very useful in a reading of Juliet's plight in *Romeo and Juliet*, or the historical concept of the Canadian Residential School in reading *Fatty Legs* or *I Am Not a Number* or the trauma of differential racialization and diaspora in a consideration of Joy Kogawa's *Obasan*.

Structuralism considers the underlying universal patterns or ideas that recur in various individual and collective behaviours; essential is the idea that all human activity and production, even consciousness and perception, are not natural but constructed through cultural, social and psychological structures. To understand a work of literature, for example, or a particular historical event such as a war or a revolution, one must not consider it in isolation but look at the context in which it evolves. According to its proponents, the principles of structuralism could be applied to all human endeavours, to literature (Barthes/Derrida), psychology (Lacan), history and science (Foucault), sociology (Althusser), and so on.

And so on, indeed; there are many other theories and variations. And while the direct analysis and debate over these heady theoretical concepts may mostly seem a matter for the ivory towers, these theories now underpin so much of the everyday classroom in how teachers think, in what teachers teach and in how they teach it, in what they believe. When I began my career, teachers wore formal attire, skirts and blouses, jackets and ties—we asked questions and expected the correct answers. But now, well, how the questions and answers have changed. Now, truly, as that old show tune says: "In olden days a glimpse of stocking / Was looked on as something shocking, / But now, God knows, / Anything goes." And for the most part, it seems to me, such redirection is not a bad thing.

49
Professing

Send to us power and light, a sovereign touch
Curing the intolerable neural itch,
The exhaustion of weaning, the liar's quinsy,
And the distortions of ingrown virginity.
Prohibit sharply the rehearsed response
And gradually correct the coward's stance...

—W. H. Auden "Petition"

Leaving an assured situation in an excellent academic high school was not an easy decision, especially when I was setting out for a job only guaranteed for one year. Add to that, the somewhat dubious reputation that Faculties of Education possessed, an inconsistent vibe they seem to emit to this day like slightly dysfunctional nuclear plants—great potential and energy nestled inside disastrous reputations. But for better or worse, like Conrad's Jim, I suppose, I made the jump. And I became a professor, that role which I had once thought I might like to assume. (And one year renewal to another, the secondment to university eventually becomes a tenured job—the Faculty's Dean, Alan Pearson, was very kind to me—and I spent the rest of my teaching days in that role, over twenty years.)

Perhaps more than any other university entity, the Faculty of Education is constructed with an "ingrown virginity," an intrinsic insecurity about its own identity. All my while there, its Administrators squawked repeatedly about the fact that it was *not* a Teachers' College but a *Faculty* of Education. And therein lies the rub. In part, the composition of the professoriate itself means it is a community without a centre. The common thread that one might find in Departments of Biology or Earth Sciences or English seemed lacking. The Faculty of Education is an academic smorgasbord; various professors have expertise in Psychology, Law, Sociology, Philosophy, Kinesiology, Commerce, Languages and Literacies and a variety of Curricula and Pedagogies, and, from Gender Studies to Special Needs' Education, they parade an assortment of other interlocutory proficiencies in theoretical and practical discourses. Unity of thought or purpose is often a *rara avis*, which can make for a positive diversity but, too often, a discord is palpable. For example, as a high school English teacher, I once attended a P.D. presentation on writing by a prof from OISE who concluded by acknowledging that his copious *journaling* approach to writing meant that teachers would have *"to mark 'til you drop"* (a direct quotation); as you might imagine, that idea did not go over very well. And for good reason—it was a stupid idea, made all the more so given its presumably intelligent source. Accordingly, students in B.Ed. programs and teachers upgrading through Education courses frequently note how out-of-touch Education profs and their courses can be. And, by and large, aside from driving past a couple local schools on the way to their university office, a vast majority of Education Professors have no contact or experience with schools or young students and, as I witnessed on many occasions, actually felt uncomfortable, intimidated, at the very thought of being in an actual school.

But all feel that their own, particular academic subject matter serves as a critical foundation in informing how education should be shaped and in how the path to becoming a qualified teacher should be laid out. And they are not wrong—as I hope this book has illustrated in part, Education is a complex tapestry. Teachers benefit from a sweeping understanding of a wide theoretical and cultural spectrum. But teaching is teaching: in that conundrum alone, Faculties of Education need to be Teachers' Colleges, and Teachers' Colleges need to be Faculties of Education. To pretend that one is not the other is inane (and certainly not the "intense inane" of Shelley's visionary altitude). And to argue that the Practicum alone, where student teachers work in schools with Associate Teachers, is the place where theory and practice merge, where students get all the practice they need, is a lame argument. To be effective institutions, Faculties of Education must connect the dots—

courses that espouse theory must show its relevance to practice, and practical applications must always be grounded in theory. Only then do the wheels stay on the bus.

That aside, for me teaching at university is a phenomenal experience. While, as I often noted, the best part of being a professor may have been that it had no hall or cafeteria supervision, professors are also afforded the opportunity to push a pursuit of knowledge and understanding as far as possible. Being a professor is also one of the most egotistical professions on the planet—you enter a room, begin to talk and people start taking notes. Many professors actually fall under its spell and become what they think they are perceived to be. It is, often, a selfish and isolating sort of job. You work alone a lot and many professors horde their insights and discoveries for fear someone else will steal their intellectual property and outrace them into print. Get to grab that Nobel medallion first. Most professors teach about six to eight hours per week for about seven months of the year, and the remuneration is substantial. And every sixth or seventh year, a sabbatical, no teaching at all! And at Faculties of Education, generally, ten to twelve weeks of those "teaching" months have no lectures or classes when students are assigned to schools for their practicum. My teaching year in Education often ended in February, resuming in September. The unscheduled free time was wonderful—my spouse always said that I didn't have a job so much as a hobby, and often asked me how it felt to be retired. In general, professors are held to a responsibility ratio of 4:4:2, which is to say, forty per cent teaching, forty per cent writing and researching, and twenty per cent community service (meetings, committee work, union duties, and so on). 'Free time' aside, many profs struck me as workaholics—you will find them in their offices late at night and on weekends toiling away on one project or another. Some of that probably comes from the regressive work-regimen necessary to earn a doctorate. But for most professors, what one enjoys doing and what one does become the same thing. Consequently, divorce rates are often high, social skills minimal, and therapy sessions frequent. (On a personal note, I always tried to work weekdays in my office following regular 9-5 hours, and reserve evenings and weekends for leisure and pleasure and other tasks—there is always grass to mow or snow to shovel and my dogs loved their walks—don't all dogs! And, for me, as my mother trained me to do as a kid, there is a kind of sane normalcy in changing wardrobes at the end of day.)

Like Law or Engineering or Medicine, Education is an applied discipline; scholarly flights of fancy always need to touch base with the earth at some point. While in English lectures, one could ride deconstructive theory as high as Melville's Catskill eagle or dive deep into Freud's oceanic *id* along with that ubiquitous white whale; but in Education, some firm grounding seemed necessary—that rambunctious class of Grade Tens always waited on some Friday afternoon somewhere and Education lectures needed to acknowledge that. In some way, that was the greatest challenge in being a professor in the Faculty of Education, connecting theory with practice and practice with theory. And many professors failed—it is one of the reasons that Education Faculties are so often belittled by their graduates. 'Mickey Mouse' Institutes as once they were called. Obviously, Gender theory and Disability sensitivities are all important. But understand—as a school teacher, having students in my classroom who were Gay or Catholic or Deaf or inflicted with ADHD or from impoverished backgrounds made no difference—I taught the lesson I intended to teach to all students equally. I made necessary modifications or accommodations, usually quietly or casually behind the scenes— sometimes simply in curricular choices, changing a text or including some different issue or theme or angle. I recall once replacing a traditional single-piece desk with a table and chair for a student who was eight months pregnant and I recall printing out all assignments in a larger font for a student who was legally blind and I remember locating a hearing-disabled student at the front of the room and for several years I picked up day-old breakfast items for the school from a local Starbucks—whatever was needed (I think/hope all contemporary teachers do that kind of thing)—and then moved on.

To be clear, I do not think that any teacher should ever devise or deliver any lesson that is not supported by theory—like any competent professional, teachers need to read and research what they are about to do before they proceed. The capable surgeon does not operate on a brain tumor by first cutting open the stomach. Conversely, however, the theory that can not be demonstrated in practice is not much of a theory. Rocket theory is fine but not if every rocket explodes on take-off. If some theory spouted from the podium about education cannot be applied in an educational context, it is simply bad theorizing. 'Marking 'til you drop' is not feasible. And in some sense, anyway, the distinction between theory and practice is essentially a fallacy—one must not, cannot, exist without the other, except perhaps in a madhouse. Identify them as you wish, it seems incumbent to me that Faculties of Education are obligated in every way possible to prepare candidates to be effective teachers. Professors must not defend their absence of applicability by claiming that such is the domain of the practicum experience, offering the excuse that they lecture in their area of expertise and Associate Teachers in the field prepare student teachers to teach. No! Everyone in education is in the field. Professors and Associates are busy—all have many duties and responsibilities—but theory and practice (call it *praxis* as some have) must be connected.

As an aside, once I worked in English Education at Western with a colleague whose primary interest was gender—the plight of Gay boys in Middle School, in particular—and that's all he would ever teach. Research and articles and essays, all on that subject matter, all year long. While gender as an issue is obviously important in and of itself, that information alone was not enough to prepare students to become English or Language Arts teachers. And his students suffered when they got to practice teaching and beyond. I tried to help by offering him the hand-outs and lecture ideas that I used but he was set in his approach— he had not read much in literary realms, had no experience teaching in a school and, I suppose, clung to his area of comfort as all of us are wont to do. Once, I even saw him put out some marked assignments, then run down the hall (literally) to avoid his students. Among other things, it was an example of the old square peg not fitting the round hole. Universities seem filled with Bistro Marxists and Cashmere Feminists, profs at the podium who decry the capitalist ills of a bourgeois culture and the misogynistic oppression of females and then drive their BMWs home to a massive house kept clean by a maid service that pays its workers a minimum wage. "So it goes," as Mr. Vonnegut once said. (As an aside, a couple years after I retired, I did hear that the "gender prof" with whom I taught was charged with illegal possession of child pornography and forced into early retirement. As in the life of Hemingway's Jake Barnes, I guess, irony endures.)

I probably spent most of my teaching time at the Faculty of Education delivering courses to qualify students in becoming teachers of English and Language Arts from Grades Four to Twelve. We studied everything from the content of and politics underpinning the Ministry's Curriculum Guidelines to the preparation of basic lesson plans to teaching short stories and poems, grammar and Shakespeare. We covered the traditional Socratic approaches, open-ended Reader-Response methods, Independent Studies, Media Education and Cultural Studies and a lot more in-between. The Education students were superb, all of them mature in the sense that each had completed at least one degree (one year, I had three PhDs in a class) and all motivated by the tangible destination ahead—a job! At various times, I also taught courses in Media Studies, Children's Literature, Language and Linguistics, Graduate English, and a couple Graduate-level Independent Studies, one in Neil Postman and another, Michel Foucault; and I wrote and taught several online courses. Online Education was just beginning and, for universities, bluntly, educational quality aside, this was a hugely profitable enterprise. Within a decade, the robust tradition of offering on-site summer courses vanished into the digital ether; summer courses at the Faculty had filled every room morning and afternoon, spilling out to occupy space in several surrounding schools—all of that went away. Quickly! And it made sense. The *Honours Specialist Course* I had taught for years ran from 8:00 am to noon, students sometimes driving in from a couple hours away or even coming down from Northern Ontario to board for a month in spartan residences. Simply going online and completing whatever requirements were asked was much more convenient for the student and, for the university, no heating or cooling a room, no custodial services, 'summer courses' could now be offered all year round, and on and on. By the arrival of the Millennium, online Education was the wave of the present and the future. Quick. Efficient. Convenient. Easy access. User friendly. No class size was too large. Fast food for the Brain. I wrote at least four of these courses for the Faculty, and taught several. And I created the main introductory online English course for the Department of English and taught it for several years as well. Some students said they liked online learning; most admitted that they liked the convenience. And so, the universe of online education evolved and expanded. Basic platforms changed and online courses became even easier, easy to teach and easy to take, easy to develop in the cookie cutter world of digital technology, but as we all know, when things are easy, sometimes we get nervous, and sometimes for good reason. Teaching online courses was not really teaching; it was more like reading, and marking, eternal marking. And there was always an uneasy feeling about the students and just what they were learning, absorbing. In a classroom, the learning is often in the air among the teacher and the learners, in the eyes and in the movement of the body. You can look at a text lying on a desk and know whether or not it has been read. One sharp, rephrased question can sometime bring a flurry of hands and a moment of humour can bond a classroom and lift it up. But there is no humour in online teaching; keyboarded comments are all flat, tone deaf, unable to manage the timbre that wit can allow. So even in its pre-Zoom origins, there was an uneasiness about online teaching that some of us who were deeply involved in its development had felt. As the reliance on online education during the *Covid-19* pandemic of 2020 to 2022 revealed, education in a real classroom offered a great deal more than merely staring at a computer screen could generate. But, *Covid-19* aside, online education was a profit-maker for the university by a landslide and once the avalanche had started, of course, no one could stand in its way and survive. The ivory bean counters keep their ivory heads down and count their ivory coins, and none hear Socrates weeping.

As some consolation, in the online courses that I wrote, beyond assignments and tests generated each session by the instructor (now, in many such courses, these tests are all repetitively produced by some institutional bank), I always included a chat-room requirement, a space which students had to enter during each unit and respond to readings or activities or react to the comments of classmates. This was a personal component that, in part, helped the instructor get to know her/his students; of course, it also added some labour to the delivery of the course, but I always felt this was useful and worth while. For some students, at least, it worked and made the course a better learning experience.

I also worked in the Department of English at Western. There I taught *American Literature, English Literature and Language* (the Honours Introductory course) and *Reading Popular Culture* (one of those 'super' classes of 1000 students or so, held in a huge lecture theatre and I, microphoned-up on-stage, like some stand-up comic). I was always pleasantly surprised at the freedom given in teaching these courses. The *Pop Culture* course had no guidelines whatsoever and the other two provided cursory directions—in *American Literature*, for example, at least three weeks were to be spent on pre-1800 materials (and at least three on post-1900)—that was all. For one such as I for whom literature was the air I breathed, this was heaven on earth. I got to read and think and talk about poems and stories and novels and got paid to do that. I really looked forward to the classes—I even included Melville's *Moby-Dick* and Richard Brautigan's *Trout Fishing in America* on the reading list for the course. Twain's *Adventures of Huckleberry Finn*, Fitzgerald's *The Great Gatsby*, Faulkner's *The Sound and the Fury* and Toni Morrison's *Beloved*, too. Incidentally, in the first year I taught English, my very first lecture in the *American Literature* course was at 10 o'clock, a Tuesday in September, a warm sunny day that happened to be the 11th. I mentioned the news we knew to the students at the start of class and proceeded with the lecture—who knew the world was about to change. When I got back to my office, an e-mail from Marcia, one of my English Education students, had arrived—I include it at the end of this chapter. Sadly, the day did not end well for Marcia's family or for so many others. Understandably, it took Marcia a long time to decide whether or not she would return to complete her B.Ed. But she did, and to see her step through that classroom door was like seeing a survivor emerge from the rubble and grey dust of that dire day. To say the least, it was a gratifying thing that lifted the spirit.

Whenever I wasn't teaching, I kept my office door open. I kept specific office hours but made a point of letting students know that I was accessible whenever needed—I always felt that there was plenty of time to do the work that required solitude when no students were in the building. And as time went by, students would regularly drop by my office for important reasons and for no reasons at all. One young man talked about his brother's suicide, how he stabbed himself seven times, and Tom about his experiences teaching in Japan; he was a Mohawk from the Brantford area and found the behaviour of his students most peculiar (it was a time, apparently, when some daring young Asian girls chose not to wear underwear). Fred from Sault Ste Marie regularly brought me a coffee and we talked about a universe of things and, as a parting gift, Arlinda gave me a replica of Dumbledore's wand with the inscription: "Your magic changed my world. Thank you." As in all teaching, some students in class memorably stand out for all kinds of reasons—Ram reacted vehemently, and often negatively, to most that we did, Ram who, more than a decade later, still phones me every year on my birthday to ask how I am; and Andrew who went to New Orleans to help out after Hurricane Katrina; and Fraser, the musician with the wild hair and wry smile, whose CD I still play; and Ona with her ever-quizzical nature, ever-emerging from a fundamentalist upbringing; and Kylene who was so disappointed at not getting into the B.Ed. program first time around but succeeded the next year; and Lori who orchestrated an award to be given for effective undergraduate teaching and found and gave me a copy of the *Classics Illustrated Moby-Dick*, that comic book I lost so long ago. (In general, in teaching, I have always found that, for no reasons really, two or three students in a class will like you, two or three will dislike you and, for the most part, the rest won't remember you a month into summer holidays. So it goes, you know!) But I enjoyed my years as a prof, published several articles, including one I was especially pleased with on Richard Brautigan in the revived *Change* magazine, created *Passages to Literature,* a series of over sixty teaching guides through Althouse Press, and the textbook, *Print Preview,* a guide for undergraduate research and writing (Pearson Press). But my focus and my main interest was always on my teaching and my students. In that regard I was nominated for several teaching awards and won thirty during my tenure at Western, including one for online teaching and, also, curiously, in the mail one day, a commendation from the Minister of Education for effective instruction (still a mystery).

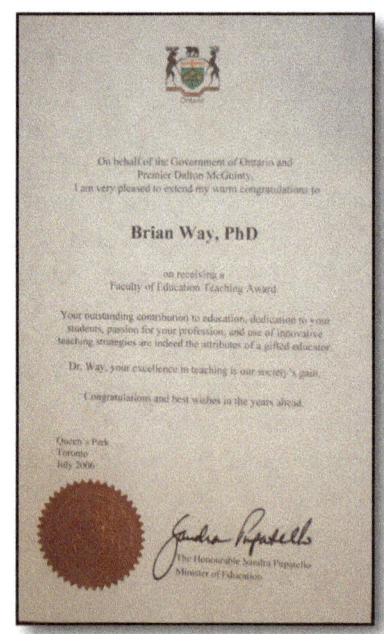

Subject: Re: English 30
  Date: Tue, 11 Sep 2001 11:55:11 -0400
  From: "Marcia ███████ and ██████ ███████ <████████████@███████████>
    To: <bway@uwo.ca>

Hello Prof. Way,
I can only write a quick note but I wanted to let you know that I will not be able to make it to english 30 on wednesday. My sister and brother in law are in New york city right now and while we know my sister is okay we have yet to hear from my brother in law (he was in the world trade center). My parents are driving to New york to pick them up so I have to go to Toronto to look after my nephew.
I hope that I will be able to make it to monday's class, but as you can guess I'm not sure yet.
Thank you,
Marcia ███████

Email from Marcia

Classics Illustrated *Moby-Dick* (thanks, Lori!)

ADDENDUM

Prince Edward County, My Home:

Stuck like a bent thumb into Lake Ontario, the County—that is, "the" as in 'bee' or 'see'—is a littoral peninsula of sandy shores and limestone ridges, rolling farmlands and roads with vague names that lead to other roads with vague names. I grew up in the County along Upper Massassaga Road on what was in those days a "typical" farm, one hundred acres in size. About twenty milking cows, a couple work horses (Jake and Min, by name), pigs and chickens and geese, occasionally a bull. Fields of alfalfa and timothy, oats and wheat and sweet corn, once or twice sorghum or tomatoes. An unpainted hipped-roof barn with upper mows for the hay and straw, a granary below and room for storing farm equipment including a binder and threshing machine, seed drill, mower, a stone boat made from the hood of an old Chevy, plows, roller and drags and tucked farther underneath old unused equipment, a corn-binder and hand-cranked windmill, cradle scythe, wooden fork and flail leaning against the wall. And high along the peak of the roof a dark trolley on a track with huge tongs that could be lowered to grasp loads of loose hay or hoist a canvas stretcher high from the bed of a wagon. (There was no electricity or plumbing—my grandfather Wesley, once a leading-edge steam-entrepreneur in the early century, had been maimed by the Depression, and subsequently adopted a fairly closed mindset about all-things 'modern.' Ours was the last property on Massassaga Road to get hydro nearly into the 1960s.) The farm stretched between a marsh on the north end sustained by waters from the Bay of Quinte and its tributaries flowing south from the highlands of Hastings and a southern marsh whose wetlands were indirectly fed by Lake Ontario. A lower field near that marsh was separated from the rest of the farm by a low stand of Poplar, Ash, Elm, Red and Silver Maple which we just called 'the woods'—white and red cedar and prickly ash and lilac flourished along the margins and several wild apple, plum and hickory trees were harvested regularly. There were wild strawberries, too, and asparagus to be found in the marshes in spring. And a seasonal stream flowed across the farmland and its lane, waters cool and quenching, taste as pure as Pishon.

When I was young, the County was mostly known for its farms (there were ten along Upper Massassaga Road—now there are none). Occasionally, visitors would come to seek the promise of apple stands or cheese factories, and on the western shores the Sandbanks with its white beaches and fresh surf always beckoned those who enjoyed swimming and tanning and a picnic. Beyond that, a plethora of homogenous hamlets, some with deceptively alluring names like Mountain View or Cherry Valley or Rosehall, but all a moment's blur, insubstantial as a quick summer shower. In truth, beyond a casual Sunday drive, not many visited the County and the County seemed ok with that. As I return in retirement, a new attraction, wineries, has sprouted up like burdock from the ditch. And there is summer theatre and a plethora of artsy festivals and shows. The County has been found, it seems, and an invasion is underway by those from away, outsiders from Trawna and beyond with outside ideas and a promotional plague-of-mind that, to me, never quite seems to be of the County—the tours and fests and studio shows all come and go, culturally insincere, inconsequential as motes of dust in the late afternoon sun. Although, I admit, I must be careful not to let my ancestral prejudices intercede, that old County way-of-knowing that if your generations do not stretch back twenty decades here, you do not really belong and you will never understand—for here, just now, see, see that lad across the street, that's young Sir John A. fumbling with some legal papers in the wind, and over there, why that's Sam Champlain resting on a fallen tree on the shore of the Bay, weary feet dipped in the waters after another endless portage, puffing on a clay pipe at close of day and scribbling in his journal: *"Toute cette belle région était inhabitée—car sa population indienne l'avait abandonnée par peur des pillards Iroquois."*

While I have travelled widely and lived in many places in my lifetime, spent more time out of the County than in it, for some irrepressible reason, this will always be the place I call home. The place that calls me home. Long ago, in passing, I met an old man-of-the-cloth on the steps of Shire Hall and he said something simple to me that has resonated since: "you can take the boy out of the County, but you can never take the County out of the boy." Now I suppose (gender-bias aside) that can be said for many people and places. There are few of us who do not identify some particular locale or another as home—all the cultural parades and celebrations of the diaspora regularly remind us of that. There are some pure nomads separate from space and time, I suppose, but not many. For me: my mother's ancestors came from the blight-ravaged fields of western Ireland to settle on the rock-strewn farms of North Hastings; my father's stock were Loyalists. They originated in Southampton, stayed in Holland for awhile, then settled first around Boston, then New York (Long Island, Fishkill Plains, Albany) before migrating to Canada West by the 1790s. Daniel Way settled in the County locating to Seventh Town by 1800, settling on farmland near the precambrian inlier, that stubborn igneous nub that solidified in the burning lake and floated north as the planet was being born four and a half billion years ago. Daniel married three times, rearing some seventeen offspring. One, John B. Way, built the first gristmill in Ameliasburgh (then Way's Mills), later trading it to Owen Roblin (that mill, now reconstructed at Black Creek Village in Toronto).

So the County is home. What that means, why that is—those are complex issues both physical and psychological, and probably spiritual, too. Certainly there is biological substance in the idea that the food and drink we consume, potatoes and carrots and milk and the like, generated from the soil and grasses of the place we inhabit, literally shape us and establish an indelible bond to the place of our growing years. Essentially, we are made by place. At least, that was true in my time before international corporations bought out everything and homogenized the world so that the radishes everyone eats are now from Escondido and the milk from Hortonville. Recent initiatives like the "100-Mile Diet" speak to that issue. Beyond that, intrinsically, of course, I have seen the sun rise across misty marshes filled with muskrat houses, sudden springs and precarious sinkholes, cattails, red-winged blackbirds and schools of smelt. I have crawled in the dirt under verandahs and through culverts to see the skeletons of small animals who snuck away to die alone—in memory, I always left the bones in their sacred resting place (my mother set limits on what 'collectibles' I could bring into the house, anyway). I have watched baby foxes cavort about their den at the edge of the woods and climbed high in the end of the barn to see a nest of newborn doves, squawking out as I neared, thinking I was a parent bringing food, I suppose. I was attacked as a child by a large and ornery gander as I ventured too close to his brood and, in the rickety attic above the old garage, I sat in an ancient one-horse open-sleigh and imagined swerving through huge drifts with voracious wolves in pursuit like a story my grandfather had told to me. I think I explored every unlit and private nook of that hundred-acre country that seemed mine. And I have slept with my head against the wall of our old house while midnight mice clamoured only inches away going about their nocturnal business and I have placed my feet against the warm wrapped irons that my mother set at the foot of my bed in the winter, any warmth from the main-floor space-heater a rare commodity in the upstairs of our house. And I have eaten thousands of meals around the old kitchen table and sat uncomfortably with tie and jacket for formal Christmas meals—turkey and stuffing and gravy and turnip and potatoes, and mince-pie and steamed-pudding and crackers that snapped with a hat and a prize. And I laughed and talked and shared the stories of our lives with family, with parents and brothers and aunts and uncles and all the rest, many of whom have now vanished into the shadows of time. And the snows that fell in November stayed, drifting around house and trees and always making the hill next-door behind Roseberry's perfect for sleighs and friends and my old toboggan soaring down, down and far out into the cold crunchiness of the marsh. And I think of the Christmas tree in the bay window of the living room, decked with round glass ornaments, some half, some whole, and incandescent icicles, small elves made from pipe-cleaners and silver tinsel that cast a magic spell through day and night, all illuminated by the illimitable belief and imagination of that purest of spirits, the spirit at the heart of being a child. The days, the hours leading up to Christmas were endless, a bright promise full of hope, sure as that new star about to be born in the ancient night-sky.

"There's no place like home" is the mantra that returns Dorothy from Oz to Kansas, to her home and into the arms of those who love her. Nostalgia, regret, love, loss, relief, recollection, and a host of other emotions surround the idea of home, always a place you know only after you leave it, a place always past and just beyond the present, never quite re-creatable in your own time and space. Many writers have written about the idealization we think of when we think of home. Thomas

Woolfe cautioned that we cannot go home again, and in the sense that our experiences as we age inevitably make us different, and changed, he is right. But that does not alter the ideal that always exists. Robert Frost simply suggests that "home is the place where, when you have to go there, they have to take you in." Toni Morrison reminds us in *Beloved*: "If a house burns down, it's gone, but the place—the picture of it—stays, and not just in rememory, but out there, in the world." There is a permanence in home no matter how old you are, or how far you've travelled, what you have or haven't become, no matter what you accept or deny, how long you wander or how close you stay. And the County— "the" as in "bee" or "see"—however I remember it or imagine it, however near or far away, for me, the County will always be my home. Its soil is my blood. Its soul, my own.

50

College and Comm and a Roof
for my Garage

"Are you that travelin' salesman that I have heard about?"
I said, "No, no, no, I'm a doctor and it's true
I'm a clean-cut kid and I been to college, too"

—Bob Dylan *Motorpsycho Nitemare*

I retired as soon as I was able to reach full pension status. I always said that I would do that; I had no desire to become one of those bleary-eyed Struldbruggians you see ambling about campus, noctambulant Methuselahs lost in time. And so I left Western and moved back to Prince Edward County where those Loyalist ancestors had settled over two hundred years before. I had several personal writing projects that were calling to me and the soil of home as well. So I kept myself busy with those projects and several volunteer activities—I served on the Boards of Governance for the Royal Military Colleges of Canada, the Al Purdy A-Frame Trust, and the Prince Edward County Library System, as "Captain of Trenton" for the Heart and Stroke Association, on the Ameliasburgh Recreation Committee and Fair Board Association and I took several local interest courses—Stained Glass, Caning and Cord Weaving, Genealogy, Watercolours, Acrylics. I kept myself as active and involved as I needed to be.

Then, one August afternoon in the second year of my retirement, the telephone rang. And for the third time in my life, an institute of Higher Learning invited me to come teach for them. A Dean at Loyalist

Community College in Belleville had retrieved my name from a list that the Registrar had—in a survey for one of the interest courses I had taken, I had casually ticked a box about employment-availability for Loyalist. The Dean (an affable man named Dan Holland) asks me if I would be interested in teaching a Communications course in their Biosciences Department. Humorously, I think of the line from *Godfather III:* "Just when I thought I was out, they pull me back in!" I go in the next day for a meeting and a tour—I was to teach two sections and,

PEARSON CUSTOM LIBRARY

COMMUNICATIONS
Dr. B. T. W. Way
Loyalist College
Applied Sciences, Skills and Technology

strategically, they had scheduled one in the morning, one in the afternoon on the same day (even in the same room). While I only had a couple weeks to prepare, what I was to teach was essentially my decision to make—I was the only one teaching Comm in the Department and could structure the course any way I wanted. I thought of the six Language Arts (Reading, Writing, Speaking, Listening, Viewing, Representing) and shaped the course around those, in future years actually crafting a textbook through Pearson using those concepts as guideposts.

The Community College system in Ontario sprang into being in the late 1960s with the passage of Bill 153—almost all of the twenty-four Colleges opened in either 1967 or 1968. Often located in smaller centres that did not have a university, and intended for students interested in practical rather than scholarly pursuits, colleges were focussed on developing skill sets generally necessary in a variety of trades and technologies, to provide "career-oriented post-secondary education," to quote the party line. From their inception, individual Community Colleges continued to expand (as noted in Chapter 27), far exceeding the intellectual evolution of the human gene pool. Simply put, the academic quality of the student population, especially in reading and writing competencies, reflects this tendency—as the College enrolment increases, the range of learning abilities and skills remains fixed and Comm courses, such as the one I am hired to teach, are born. (The same is true of universities, most now requiring a literacy test and/or a writing course in first year.)

I enjoy my years at Loyalist and quickly go from teaching part-time in Biosciences to delivering courses across the spectrum—I teach Communication to students in Esthetics, Justice, Construction, Computer, Electronics, Engineering, Manufacturing; I even teach an online Music course. In terms of technological tools for teaching, the facilities are superb. The building has wireless throughout, and every classroom has a computer, a digital projector and a Smart-Board so programs like *Power-point* and *Excel* become integral parts of every lecture and use of video and access to Internet resources like *You-Tube* and *Wikipedia* are universal, and commonplace. Whereas many of the lecture theatres at Western still have a nineteenth-century charm to them (many have not changed in the last hundred years or so), the classrooms of Loyalist seem borrowed from the holo-deck of the Star-ship Enterprise.

On the whole, for its students, Loyalist College offers a user-friendly and accommodating environment, in part, because of the wide range of students in its various programs more or less eager to get on with their lives and embrace new occupations. And most of the instructors I meet, from Auto-mechanics to Bio-scientists to Chefs to Lawyers, know their subject matter well and are dedicated to what they do. If there is any flaw, and this is probably true of Universities as well, it is in the understanding and application of instructional skills and theories and contemporary approaches. Most instructors seem to teach in the way that they were taught themselves, and this is not always a good thing and certainly does not account for pedagogical changes and innovations that may have occurred in recent years. Some of the instruction simply seemed inappropriate, at times almost comical. For example, one lawyer I met a Loyalist College, teaching part-time in Justice, seemed to be convinced that her Community College students were going to become lawyers, always complaining about their language skills and how no judge would put up with them in court. I only ever met one student in all my Justice classes who might have had the academic chops to do a Law degree; at best, these students were destined to be assistants and clerks and researchers, and that's what they wanted. No Judge would likely ever hear a peep from them! Another example—I worked with a Department Head who insisted on the use of weekly Spelling Tests, a practice generally discontinued in public school classrooms some forty years ago, and for very good reasons—such rote exercises in spelling do nothing to improve spelling or anything else. Ever! Spelling skill is akin to singing or dancing—some people are just naturally good at it, some are not. Spelling has to do with a certain a neural acumen, an adept visual memory, that certain humans have; that said, there are certain tricks and methods that can be taught, programs that can be implemented, to make individuals better. But Spelling Tests, which this Department Head insisted everyone use, do nothing, and never did except show a teacher who the best spellers were from Day One to the end of the school year. Another Department leader in Communications exclaimed at a general meeting that students at the College hadn't read anything since they were ten. When I asked her what she had done to help students improve their reading, she replied: "That's not my job." That kind of unresearched, prejudicial attitude always saddened me, especially among educators and, especially in that context when we know that literacy rates are greater now than they have ever been. This is, after all, the generation of students that flocked to read Rowling's *Harry Potter* series, the *Twilight* and *Hunger Games* books and work by Stephen King, J. R. R. Tolkien, George R. R. Martin and a host of others, not to mention all of the reading that takes place in social media and video entertainment, too. (In our western world, at the turn of the twentieth century, less than 20% of the population could read and write; now, literacy rates are close to 90%. However one views education, educators have done a very good job in improving literacy in the last hundred years.) I also chatted with one Administrator at Loyalist who seemed to envision all of the College's students as innocent Catholic school-girls and thought classes should be taught as if the students were in Grade 6; contrariwise, one Esthetics class I taught had a dozen students, none married but with fifteen children among them. A pleasant group of students indeed, but not exactly Catholic school girls (whatever that may mean)! So things at Loyalist were good but not perfect; but I saw my place as a small pebble here and, mostly, tried to keep my head down. I was tangential to this world and thought of Richard Brautigan's wonderful phrase: "I can't change the world; it was changed before I got here." And, of course, I was a part-time instructor; this is a cost-saving measure for Colleges and Universities but it always diminishes a bit from the continuity and integrity of programs at an institution. Part-timers have no job security and little loyalty and are generally cast as second-class citizens anyway. Ironically, humorously, one day, sitting in the storageroom office-space provided to part-timers, chatting to a colleague (he will get a full-time position as an Environmental Biologist at a University in Wisconsin), we realize that there are six part-timers using this space, all of whom have doctorates, probably a greater number than all full-time instructors across the entirety of Loyalist College.

Beyond providing a bit of extra coin to pave my driveway and put a roof on my garage, Loyalist College was a good experience for me; I spent five years there and enjoyed teaching in the Community College environment. It was a learning experience. The motivations of students were significantly different from those of university students; as a rule, these were pragmatic students. Trimming and decorating fingernails or cakes, hammering a nail or examining a blood cell, they embraced a world of practice that generally lacked the artistic spark of knowing for knowing's sake; the goal here was earth-bound and utilitarian. For the most part, these students were out to try to improve their lot in life in specific ways and, for that alone, I always felt honoured to help them in whatever small manner I could. While I was there, the College, especially Biosciences, attracted large numbers of students from India, trying to get that North American piece of paper so valued around the world. In Communications' classes that added another new challenge, working with many students for whom English was a curious and distant language skill, a language they rarely spoke except in Comm class, but, mostly, they tried and, as students, that's the best one can do.

With a lengthy illness, including about four months in hospital, my teaching at Loyalist, and my teaching career entire, came to an end. I had taught in five decades, over forty years, in a dozen different institutions, probably 10,000 students—and those students probably shaped me far more than I ever shaped them. And if I had to do it all over again, there is no doubt in my soul that I would happily do so. What a grand ride it was!

Sept. 8, 2015. Retirement for me, not for the buses; a "yellow beast with red eyes" slides by my house marking the first September in over fifty years that I do not return to school as a student or a teacher. It was finished. But, ahh, what a time! What a time well spent!

Epilogue
sex with students ... and other
teacher stuff

Suzanne takes you down to her place near the river
You can hear the boats go by, you can spend the night beside her
And you know that she's half-crazy but that's why you want to be there
And she feeds you tea and oranges that come all the way from China
And just when you mean to tell her that you have no love to give her
Then she gets you on her wavelength
And she lets the river answer that you've always been her lover
And you want to travel with her, and you want to travel blind
And then you know that she will trust you
For you've touched her perfect body with your mind

—"Suzanne takes you down"
Leonard Cohen *Parasites of Heaven* 1966

And so, much of my life has been spent in schools. Rural schools and urban schools, small schools and large schools, academic schools and vocational tech schools, elementary schools and secondary schools, college and university. I have been a teacher of Language Arts and English and History and Geography and Media and Music and Comm, a Principal of Night School, a Consultant, a Department Head, a Professor of Education, a Professor of English, and a Professor of Communications. And so, what have I learned from these years, from friends and colleagues and students, from my reading and research and experience? What have I learned:

▷ I have learned that teaching is the best job on the planet.

▷ I have learned that the ultimate goal of education can be stated in one word, AWARENESS—awareness of body or mind or skills or ideas or values or community or environment, an awareness that transforms a closed mind into an open one.

▷ I have learned that learning should never stop.

▷ I have learned that, as teachers, we cannot save them all.

▷ I have learned that the classroom is a sacred place—it is the centre of education and should never be profaned by trivial pursuits.

▷ I have learned that, for a teacher, Labour Day is never a holiday.

▷ I have learned that teaching is very hard work. This is one of the first lessons that teacher candidates are often surprised to learn as they train to become teachers—as a student, from Day School to Graduate School, one arrives in some space, sits for an hour or more, then leaves; as a teacher, every moment of that time has to be constructed, created, embroidered in some way or another. Preparation and assessment come with the territory. And while imagination, sincerity, passion and the rest have a role, for the classroom experience to be rewarding for students, nothing can replace hard work and academic acumen on the part of the teacher. Nothing.

▷ I have learned that all teachers teach a subject first, not the child, but always the subject.

▷ I have learned that a teacher should meet with a student only in a room with an open door.

▷ I have learned that a teacher should avoid physically touching a student whenever possible—from kindergarten to graduation, no hugs or handshakes or fist bumps or shoulder pats are needed. These are simply unnecessary cultural conventions particularly invented and embedded in our society in the last few decades, and we would be healthier in a variety of ways to shed them. At the very least, *Covid-19* taught us that. In the context of school, they are rarely genuine anyway; at home, perhaps, but students need to learn that school is not home. Sometimes, home is not home.

▷ I have learned that the effective teacher never condescends to students or speaks to them in any noxious manner; treat students as if they were adults and most likely they will respond in kind. Treating adults in that same way can also lead to positive things (sometimes!).

▷ I have learned, if an individual or a class does not know a thing which I think they should, never blame someone or something else for that lack of knowledge, but … take the opportunity to teach it myself. Mr. Buckley taught me that.

▷ I have learned that the best teachers see themselves as teachers, not heroes, or leaders, or saviours, or crusaders or some other such thing—those labels are generally applied to teachers by those who do not understand the profession; teachers are at their best when they are teaching, not crusading. As Vergil's *Aeneid* reminds us: "*Fascilis descensus Averno*—the descent to hell is easy." Teaching is not preaching. From critical race theory to environmental economics, as important as issues of social justice are, and worthy of being introduced, they are also one-eyed creatures that neither allow students, nor the classroom ethos at large, any fair space for debate or growth. They create rooms made of corners. They tend to be trendy and sanctimoniously politicized, and they are easy to venerate, apting to send students off into the world on ignorant blind missions; such pedagogy fosters what might best be labeled *the Miss Jean Brodie syndrome*. The child of the social justice classroom is often more an indoctrinated follower than a liberated benefactor; and classmates who hesitate, or deny, risk being outcasts, lepers. And most of the time, being a teacher of social justice is a path too narrow, too blind, easy and strident and inculcated— someone else, usually with a vested interest (perhaps justifiable, possibly monetary), has already given you the answers, and the buttons and the posters and the emojis, with no thought required. Again one thinks of Yeats: "The best lack all conviction / While the worst are full of passionate intensity."

▷ I have learned in suit that those clever ideological phrases that infiltrate the classroom from time to time, like "black lives matter" or "prawo odebrane" or "no child left behind" or "take back the night" or "every child matters," come and go like flakes of snow—while seeming admirable at a surface level (one understands the idealism), educationally, they are windmills of illusion, with the potential of doing far more harm to teachers and their students than good (or anything else). For teachers, they are simply unattainable projections that lead ineluctably to failure and disenchantment as, at the end of the day, those teachers discover they have fallen short of whatever herculean or messianic chimera they might have imagined themselves to be chasing. In effect, how can any teacher, anyone, be responsible for "every child"—defeat, failure, are inherent in these very concepts which, in themselves, are inane generalities, naïve and flawed; these are pretty flowers, but flowers of the hemlock. Baudelaire's *Les Fleurs du mal*. True social justice, if that is one's goal, is best achieved through the effective teaching of Math or Music or Science or Poetry—teach the subject beautifully and justice will prevail. As an aside, I recall working one summer at Mobile Drive in Toronto (Federation Headquarters) and discovering several bags full of buttons—this was 'the age of buttons' before emojis and GIFs took over—button after button discarded as one campaign of protest succumbed to another. Those discarded bags of buttons have always seemed poignantly symbolic to me. (Incidentally, to eliminate racism, current thinking among movements like Afrofuturism suggests that the best approach might be to adopt a less negative, more expansive view, to stop talking about racism and using phrases like "African-American", "white supremacist", or "Latinx", idioms which tend to codify and validate racial perceptions.)

▷ I have learned that there is neither glory nor satisfaction in being part of a league of victims, especially in teaching.

▷ I have learned that those who are so eager to change the world, especially through education, almost invariably want to change the world to align with their own values, to buff their own crown, cement their own comfort.

▷ I have learned that good teachers will understand and transmit the ideas and theories of others but that great teachers will take those concepts and transform them to fit the needs of the children they teach. Be not good but great. (I think of the phrase "good poets borrow; great poets steal" attributed to everyone from Horace to Yeats to Eliot to Picasso to Colonel Sanders, I think.)

▷ I have learned that, from one day to the next, keeping an even, balanced keel as a teacher always produces the best results and earns any teacher the surest trust. And trust is always vital between teacher and student—the best teachers are not roller coasters.

▷ I have learned that, according to research in Applied Psychology and Human Development, the growth of all children is best served with three ingredients: **authority** (set guidelines; occasionally someone needs to say "no"), **independence** (the child needs leeway to breathe and explore), and **a loving community** (a positive, supportive, safe environment). If this research is right, from Day School to Post-doctoral studies, the classroom is a natural place for all of these.

▷ I have learned as a teacher (as I write this 400+-page book) that I tended to talk too much; many teachers do. Our classrooms need to be filled more with the voices of our students than with the voice of their teacher. And ALL of our students—the females, the shy kids, the minorities, and the others who are different—the voices of ALL of our students, not just the confident, the males, the academically gifted and the aggressive (although their voices are important, too).

▷ I have learned that the least useful part of any teacher's day is time spent on tracking, assessment and marking. Grades reveal little and mean less about any of us, students or teachers (or schools or school boards).

▷ I have learned that the next least useful part of any teacher's time is spent on hall, yard or cafeteria supervision—the most effective schools find ways to get around such duties (with the staff's support, one high school in which I worked used monies allocated for Assistant Heads to pay community groups to cover such assignments—this became an excellent fund-raising activity for those groups and good PR for the school. In another school, the Administrators did this supervision; positively, it got them out of their offices and known among the students.)

▷ I have learned that the best teacher is the best prepared teacher, day by day, lesson by lesson. Time on task and task on time.

▷ I have learned never to believe anything (entirely) that a student tells me (like the children they are, students never see the whole picture).

▷ I have learned that a classroom functions best when it has a set of simple rules in place for students and for teacher; the "Three Ps" always worked for me—**Preparation, Participation, Politeness**. When everyone paid heed to those, no other rules were necessary.

▷ I have learned that Curriculum and Policy and all the rest, whatever the source, are always political, never educational. (Even as I write this, the Ontario government has just added a new "practical hands-on Tech requirement" to the provincial curriculum—there is a perceived housing shortage in the province and the government is being pressured to find a solution so, one assumes, come election time they will have guaranteed that every child knows how to use a hammer and pound a nail. After all, it's part of Curriculum!)

▷ I have learned that to be a good teacher you need to read—anything, everything, and poetry, too.

▷ I have learned that the greatest challenge for any teacher is the dual nature of the profession, the necessity to treat all students the same, equally, and, at the same time, to treat all students differently, as individuals. This is the great high wire act of teaching. *L'équilibre inconcevable*! (And it's the reason why teachers never blame or discipline an entire class for a misdemeanor one child has committed.)

▷ I have learned that teachers should be friendly with students, but never friends.

▷ I have learned that teachers should probably not have sex with their students. This is a practice generally frowned upon by most jurisdictions and, whenever such incidents are reported, the self-righteous saintliness of the culture arises. The world becomes 'holier-than-thou' or anyone else. The "Blue Pages" bluer! Even as I write this chapter, four American television shows, *A Teacher, Cruel Summer, Miller's Girl* and *Captivated: The Trials of Pamela Smart,* have spun around this issue—in three, the teachers are incarcerated; in the other, the teacher is shot. And TV in Great Britain, too, is involved, with the mini-series *The Teacher* and even the venerable *Coronation Street,* developing an ongoing sub-plot about a salacious teacher/student relationship. So, when such incidents get reported in the press or show up in government reports or in pop culture, at large, our society stops bombing some brown nation for a moment (or loaning them money at exorbitant interest rates) and casts all aspersions toward the evil teacher and the victimized student. But an easy hypocrisy exists here. Middle and Secondary Schools rage with rambunctious growth and hormonal complexities. Students at that age are growing into their physical selves and in conjunction with that, for better or worse, the very nature of teaching requires a certain degree of intimacy, of close contact both in intellectual pursuits and in physical proximities, in enlightened discussions and in simple manual tasks, pointing out the solution to a problem or overseeing an experiment or guiding some athletic pursuit or conducting the band. Add to the mix, many students use flirtation as a means of relating to adults and, naturally, as humans, teachers can find this flattering. This is not something that is new. From Johnny kissing Heather on the playground of my Public School or that time long ago when my father opened the Grade Eight classroom door to find his Principal fucking the Grade Four teacher, schools have been places filled with a certain degree of sexual dalliance. My own Grade Twelve Chemistry teacher was married to a former student and, in the years since, I have known many teachers of all genders and faiths in the same situation. In most communities, it is not unusual for teachers to encounter students by happenstance beyond the borders of classrooms where the students work and waitress and whatever, or for students to return from College and University to visit their favorite teachers. I have known many colleagues (myself as well) to have met former students on occasion, for coffee or lunch, even rounds of golf; and emails are common. Connections happen. In some way, human contact is a vital part of teaching, and the bonds made can be genuine, and lasting. That human touch. Everybody remembers a teacher or two they liked or disliked, admired or hated, someone who influenced their lives for better or worse. And while society does not condone the escalation of such contact, sometimes legally, sometimes ethically, and teachers always need to assess situations, appropriateness, power dynamics, and the rest, nevertheless, I would tell you that, at this very moment, there is not a secondary school in Canada, not one, in which some teacher and some student are not intimately involved. The Data-Child has matured younger. To revisit that old stereotype, the world of the pure and devout Catholic school girl no longer exists—it probably never did. Birth control is as readily available as jellybeans at the bulk store and sex is no longer the holy grail of a relationship or of our culture—wake up little Suzy, that starship has sailed. In the machinations of the world wide web, sex has been normalized; for most, coitus is simply a casual orgiastic feelie and then life moves on…with hockey scores to catch, selfies to send. And besides, beyond that, we live in a culture that celebrates youth and tries to make everyone deny the disease of aging. To be younger than young is the holy grail; sexuality, its chapel perilous. Having said that, there is no place for sexual predation, for grooming, in schools. Prosecute the guilty, yes, and then move on. And know there are far more important matters at hand. It's just that our world seems to be so shocked, so surprised that relationships, even sexual ones, sometimes occur in school situations, I think a broader, deeper understanding needs to be applied and not simply some narrow line of castigation or punishment. The Spanish Inquisition is over; we have burned enough witches.

▷ I have learned never to give advice—each of our lives is our own, unique, and what happens in one rarely applies to another. Try to keep quiet and listen to the comments and complaints of others, of students and colleagues; those individuals will often find their own path in the very process of expressing their thoughts. Long ago in ancient Athens, wise Socrates knew that so well.

▷ I have learned that all teachers can be effective teachers with hard work, researched lessons and attention to detail. I have also learned that the greatest teachers are those who seem to possess and emanate a kind of natural spirit, a font within; they can light a candle and it becomes a star.

▷ And I have learned, when all is said and done, that I follow a road outward bound, that I am forever nothing going nowhere…

…and by the time you read this, I may already have arrived.

Selected References

Note: I have not listed web-sites in these references; they tend to be ephemeral and erratic in nature; beyond that, they are generally easy to access anyway on the topic or reference of concern. And certainly, at this writing, many helpful research data-bases such as JSTOR, ERIC, Google Scholar, and others are available, and free (sort of!).

Aers, Lesley and N. Wheale. *Shakespeare in the Changing Curriculum*. London: Routledge, 1991.

Allen, David. *English Teaching Since 1965: How Much Growth?* Portsmouth: Heinemann, 1980.

Anders, Patricia, and B. Guzzetti. *Literature Instruction in the Content Areas*. Fort Worth: Harcourt, 1996.

Andersen, Neil. *Media Works*. Toronto: Oxford, 1989.

Anderson, Philip M. "The Past Is Now: Approaches to the Secondary School Literature Curriculum," *English Journal*, 75, 8 (December 1986), 19-22.

Aristotle. *The Basic Works of Aristotle*. ed. Richard McKeon. New York: Random House, 1941.

Arnold, Matthew. *Poetry and Criticism*. Boston: Houghton Mifflin, 1961.

Aronowitz, Stanley and H. Giroux. *Postmodern Education*. Minneapolis: University of Minnesota, 1991.

Atwell, Nancie. *In the Middle: New Understandings about Writing, Reading and Learning*. Toronto: Irwin/Heinemann, 2015.

Barlow, Maude and H-J. Robertson. *Class Warfare*. Toronto: Key Porter, 1994.

Barnouw, Erik. *Tube of Plenty*. New York: Oxford, 1990.

Barrell, Barrie and R. Hammett. *Advocating Change: Contemporary Issues in Subject English*. Toronto: Irwin, 2000.

Barrs, Myra, and A. Thomas. *The Reading Book*. Markham: Pembroke, 1993.

Bellanca, James and R. Gogarty. *Blueprints for Thinking in the Cooperative Classroom*. Palatine: Skylight, 1991.

Belanoff, Pat, "Over the Summer ... and Beyond ..." *English Quarterly*, 19, 4 (Winter 1986), 315-338.

Bennett, Barrie, and C. Rolheiser. *Beyond Monet*. Toronto: Bookation Inc., 2001.

Berthoff, Ann E. *The Sense of Learning*. Portsmouth: Heinemann, 1990.

Blake, William. *The Poetry and Prose of William Blake*. New York: Doubleday, 1970.

Bogdan, Deanne, "Literature, Values and Truth: Why We Could Lose the Censorship Debate," *English Quarterly, 20, 4 (Winter 1987), 273-284.*

—, "The Censorship of Literature Texts: A Case Study," in Nelms, B. *Literature in the Classroom: Readers, Texts and Contexts*. Urbana: National Council of Teachers, 1988, 235-248.

—. *Re-Educating the Imagination*. Portsmouth: Heinemann, 1992.

Booth, David. *Censorship Goes to School*. Markham: Pembroke, 1992.

Bradbury, Malcolm and J. McFarlane. *Modernism: 1890—1930*. London: Penguin, 1976.

Bradley, A. C. *Shakespearean Tragedy*. London: Macmillan, 1904.

Britton, James in Pradl, ed. *Prospect and Retrospect*. London: Boynton/Cook, 1982.

Brooker, Peter, and P. Widdington, ed. *A Practical Reader in Contemporary Literary Theory*. London: Prentice Hall, 1996.

Brown, Lloyd, "Polanyi's Theory of Knowing," *Canadian Journal of English Language Arts*, 11, 2 (1988), 5-19.

Carere, Sharon, ed. *Responding to Media Violence: Starting Points for Classroom Practice*. Toronto: Metropolitan Toronto School Board, 1997.

Carlyle, Thomas. *Sartor Resartus*. 1833. London: Oxford U. P., 2008.

Child, Philip, *et al*, ed. *Longer Poems for Upper School*. Toronto: Ryerson, 1952.

Clarke, Mark A. "Negotiating Agendas: Preliminary Considerations," *Language Arts,* 66, 4 (April 1989), 370-380.

—. "Some Cautionary Observations on Liberation Education," *Language Arts*, 67, 4 (April 1990), 388-398.

Coleridge, Samuel Taylor. *Biographia Literaria*. 1817. London: Dent, 1971.

Collie, Joanne and S. Slater. *Literature in the Language Classroom: A Resource Book of Ideas and Activities*. New York: Cambridge University, 1987.

Cook, David. *A History of Narrative Film*. New York: Norton, 2016.

Corcoran, Bill and E. Evans, eds. *Readers, Texts, Teachers*. London: Boynton/Cook, 1987.

Corcoran, Bill, "Spiders, Surgeons and Anxious Aliens: Three Classroom Allies," *English Journal*, 77, 1 (January 1988), 39-44.

Cox, Carole. *Teaching Language Arts*. Toronto: Allyn and Bacon, 1999.

Curtis, Bruce. *Stacking the Deck*. Toronto: Our Schools/Our Selves, 1992.

Dahl, Roald. *Matilda*. London: Puffin, 1988.

Deosaran, R. and E. Wright. *The Every Student Survey*, Research Service 138, Toronto Board of Education (Ontario), Research Dept. June 1976.

Dewey, John. *The School and Society (1902); The Child and the Curriculum (1915)*. Chicago: U. of Chicago P., 1990.

Diltz, Bert Case. *Pierian Spring*. Toronto: Clarke, Irwin & Company, 1946.

—-. *The Sense of Wonder*. Toronto: McClelland and Stewart, 1953.

—-. *Patterns of Surmise*. Toronto: Clarke, Irwin & Company, 1962.

—-. Sense or Nonsense. Toronto: McClelland and Stewart, 1972.

Dixon, John. *Growth Through English*. London: Oxford U., 1969.

Dodge, Diane and L. Colker. *The Creative Curriculum for Early Childhood* Washington: Teaching Strategies, 1992.

Dryden, Ken. *In School*. Toronto: M&S, 1995.

Duncan, Barry. *Mass Media and Popular Culture*. Toronto: Harcourt, 1988.

—-. *Mass Media and Popular Culture Ver. 2*. Toronto: Harcourt, 1996.

Durbin, William, "An Interview with John Dixon," *English Journal*, 76, 2 (Feb. 1987), 70-73.

Easthope, Antony. *What a Man's Gotta Do*. London: Routledge, 1990.

—-. *Literary into Cultural Studies*. London: Routledge, 1991.

Edelsky, Carole and S. Harman, "One More Critique of Reading Tests—With Two Differences," *English Education*, 20, 3 (October 1988), 157-191.

—-, *et al. Whole Language: What's the Difference?* Portsmouth: Heinemann, 1991.

Egan, Kieran. *Teaching as Story Telling: An Alternative Approach to Teaching and Curriculum in the Elementary School* (1986).

Eliot, T. S. *Collected Poems*. London: Faber and Faber, 1936.

Faludi, Susan. *Backlash: The Undeclared War Against American Women*. New York: Crown, 1991.

Farr, Marcia and H. Daniels. *Language Diversity and Writing Instruction*. Urbana: National Council of Teachers 1986.

Fish, Stanley, E. "Literature in the Reader: Affective Stylistics," in Tompkins, ed. *Reader Response Criticism* (1980), 70-100.

Fiske, John. *Understanding Popular Culture*. London: Routledge, 1989.

—-. *Reading the Popular*. London: Routledge, 1989.

Flesch, Rudolph. *Why Johnny Can't Read*. New York: Harper & Row, 1955.

Fountas, Irene, and G. S. Pinnell. *Guided Reading*. Portsmouth: Heinemann, 1996.

Froese, Victor, "Language Assessment: What We Do and What We Should Do," *Canadian Journal of English Language Arts*, 11, 1 (1988), 33-40.

Frye, Northrop. *Anatomy of Criticism*. Princeton: Princeton U. P., 1971.

—. *The Educated Imagination*. Toronto: Anansi, 1997.

—. *The Secular Scripture*. Boston: Harvard. P., 1978.

Fulwiler, Toby, "Journals across the Disciplines," in Newkirk, ed. *To Compose* (1986), 186-197.

—, ed. *The Journal Book*. London: Boynton/Cook, 1998.

Gardner, P.L. "The roots of technology and science: A philosophical and historical view." *International Journal of Technology and Design Education, 7* (1997), 13-20.

Gere, Anne, et al. *Language and Reflection: An Integrated Approach to Teaching English*. New Jersey: Prentice Hall, 1992.

Giannetti, Louis. *Understanding Movies*. Scarborough: Prentice Hall, 1996.

Giroux, Henry and R. Simon, eds. *Popular Culture: Schooling and Everyday Life*. Toronto: OISE Press, 1989.

Glasser, William. *Control Theory in the Classroom*. Toronto: Harpercollins, 1986.

—. *The Quality School*. Toronto: Harpercollins, 1990.

Golden Rule Books, The. Toronto: Copp Clark: Minister of Education, 1915.

Goodman, Kenneth, "Basal Readers: A Call for Action," *Language Arts*, 63, No. 4 (April 1986), 353-363.

—. *What's Whole in Whole Language?* New York: Rdr Books, 2005.

Goodman, Ken, *et al. The Whole Language Evaluation Book*. Portsmouth: Heinemann, 1990.

Graham, Neil and J. George. *Marking Sense: A Guide to Evaluation for Teachers of English*. Markham: Pembroke, 1992.

Grant, Janet. *The Writing Coach*. Markham: Pembroke, 1990.

Graves, Donald. *Writing: Teachers and Children at Work*. (1983).

—, "The Enemy is Orthodoxy," in Maguire and Pare, ed. *Patterns of Development*. London: NCTE, 1985, 153-163.

—. *Discover Your Own Literacy*. Portsmouth: Heinemann, 1990.

Greenblatt, Stephen and G. Gunn, eds. *Redrawing the Boundaries Transformation of English and American Literary Studies*. New York: MLA, 1992.

Gunning, Thomas. *Best Books for Building Literacy for Elementary School Children*. Toronto: Allyn and Bacon, 2000.

Gutteridge, Don. *Brave Season: Reading and the Language Arts in Grades Seven to Ten*. London: Althouse P., 1983.

—. *Incredible Journeys*. London: Althouse P., 1990.

—. *The Dimension of Delight: A Study of Children's Verse Writing, Ages 11-13*. London: Althouse P., 1988.

—, *Stubborn Pilgrimage: Resistance and Transformation in Ontario English Teaching—1960-1993*. Toronto: Our Schools/Our Selves, 1994.

—. *Teaching English*. Toronto: James Lorimer, 2000.

—. *The View from Darien: Essays on the Teaching of English*. Toronto: QuodSermo, 2023.

—. *O Frabjous Day! A Selection of Poems*. Selection and Introduction by Brian T. W. Way. Toronto: Wet Ink Books, 2023.

Hammett, Roberta and K. Sanford, eds. *Boys, Girls & the Myths of Literacies & Learning*. Toronto: CSPI, 2008.

Hannan, Elspeth. *Perspectives: Assessment and Evaluation*. Toronto: Harcourt, 1992.

Harker, John, "The Reading Connection: Facts, Skills and Literacy— What Is Reading For?" *Canadian Journal of English Language Arts*, 11, 2 (1988), 51-3.

Harper, Helen, "Literacy and the State: A Comparison of Hirsch, Rosenblatt and Giroux," *English Quarterly*, 22, 3-4 (1990), 169-179.

Harris, Joseph, "The Spectator as Theorist: Britton and the Functions of Writing," *English Education,* 20, 1 (February 1988), 41-50.

Harris, Muriel. *Teaching One-to-One: The Writing Conference*. (1986).

Hart, Andrew. *Understanding the Media: A Practical Guide*. London and New York: Routledge, 1991.

Henson, Kenneth. *Methods and Strategies for Teaching in Secondary and Middle Schools*. New York: Longman, 1993.

Hirsch, E.D. Jr. *Cultural Literacy: What Every American Needs to Know*. New York: Vintage, 1987.

Hollister, Bernard. *Mass Media Workbook*. Lincolnwood: National Textbook Co., 1991.

Hughes, Arthur. *Testing for English Teachers*. Cambridge: Cambridge U., 1989.

Jasper, Gigi, "Multiculturally Challenged," *English Journal*, 88, 2 (November 1998), 93-97.

Johnson, Ron and J. Bone. *Understanding the Film*. Lincolnwood: National Textbook Co., 2001.

Judy, Stephen, *Explorations in the Teaching of English*, 2nd. ed. New York: Dodd/Mead, 1981.

—— [Tchudi, Stephen], ed. *Language, Schooling and Society*. Portsmouth: Heinemann, 1985.

Karolides, Nicholas, M. Bald and D. Sova. *100 Banned Books*. New York: Checkmark, 1999.

Kerouac, Jack. *Scattered Poems*. San Francisco: City Lights, 1971.

Kidwell, P. A., Ackerberg-Hastings, A., & Roberts, D.L. *Tools of American Mathematics Teaching, 1800-2000*. Baltimore: Johns Hopkins U.P., 2008.

King, Marlene and J. Ranallo. *Teaching and Assessment Strategies for the Transition Age*. Vancouver: EduServ, 1993.

Kirby, Dan, T. Liner and D. Liner. *Inside Out: Developmental Strategies for Teaching Writing*. Portsmouth: Heinemann, 2003.

Kirschenbaum, Howard, S. Simon and R. Napier. *Wad-Ja-Get?* New York: Hart, 1971.

Knowlton, E. "The hand and the hammer: A brief critique of the Overhead projector." *Feminist Teacher,* 6(2), 21-23 (1992) 41.

Leggo, Carl. *Teaching to Wonder*. Vancouver: Pacific International, 1997.

Lightfoot, Martin and N. Martin, eds. *The Word for Teaching Is Learning: Essays for James Britton,* Portsmouth: Heinemann, 1988.

Livesley, Jack. *Media Scenes & Class Acts*. Markham: Pembroke, 1987.

——, *et al. Meet the Media*. Toronto: Globe, 1990.

Lloyd-Kolkin, Donna and K. Tyner. *Media & You: An Elementary Media Literacy Curriculum*. Englewood Cliffs: Educational Technology, 1991.

Lukens, Rebecca. *A Critical Handbook of Children's Literature*. New York: Longman, 1999.

Lusted, David. *The Media Studies Book*. London: Routledge, 1991.

Lynn, Steven, "A Passage into Critical Theory," *College English*, 52, 3 (March 1990), 258-271.

Maguire, Mary and A. Pare, eds. *Patterns of Development*. London, NCTE, 1985.

Making the Grade: Evaluating Student Progress. Scarborough: Prentice-Hall, 1987.

Marshall, Brenda. *Teaching the Postmodern*. London: Routledge, 1992.

Masterman, Len. *Teaching the Media*. London: Routledge, 1985.

McCrum, Robert, *et al. The Story of English*. London: Faber & Faber, 2011.

McCubbin, Rob. *Mediaprac: A Media Skills Book for Senior Students*. Melbourne: Longman, 1991.

McHale, Brian. *Constructing Postmodern*. London: Routledge, 1992.

McMahon, Barrie and R. Quin. *Stories and Stereotypes*. Melbourne: Longman, 1987.

McTeague, Frank. *Shared Reading*. Markham: Pembroke, 1992.

Media Literacy. Ministry of Education, Toronto, 1989.

Midwood, Dale, *et al. Assess for Success*. Toronto: OSSTF, 1993.

Miedzian, Myriam. *Boys Will Be Boys*. New York: Doubleday, 1991.

Milner, Joseph and L. Milner. *Bridging English*. New York: Macmillan, 1999.

Morris, Barbara S. "The Television Generation: Couch Potatoes or Informed Critics?" *English Journal*, 78, 8 (December 1989), 35-41.

——, "Why is George So Funny? Television Comedy, Trickster Heroism, and Cultural Studies," *English Journal*, 88, 4 (March 1999), 47-52.

Mottram, Eric. *Blood on the Nash Ambassador*. London: Hutchinson Radius, 1990.

Muldoon, Phyllis A. "Challenging Students to Think: Shaping Questions, Building Community," *English Journal*, 79, 4 (April 1990), 34-40.

Murray, Donald. *Shoptalk: Learning to Write with Writers*. Portsmouth: Heinemann, 1990.

Nachbar, Jack and K. Lause, ed. *Popular Culture: An Introductory Text*. Bowling Green: Bowling Green State University Popular Press, 1992.

Nagel, R., J. Trott, and B. T. W. Way. *Blueprint for Excellence: a design for effective schools*. Toronto: OSSTF, 1985.

Nelms, Ben F. ed. *Literature in the Classroom: Readers, Texts and Contexts*. Urbana: National Council of Teachers, 1988.

—-, "Sowing the Dragon's Seed: Introduction in the First Person," in Nelms, ed. *Literature in the Classroom*, Urbana: National Council of Teachers, 1988, 1-16.

Newman, Cardinal John Henry. *Apologia Pro Vita Sua and Other Writings*. London: Halcyon P., 2015.

Nikiforuk, Andrew. *School's Out*. Toronto: Mcfarlane, 1993.

Nodelman, Perry. *The Pleasures of Children's Literature*. White Plains: Longman, 1996.

Ohmann, Richard, "Literacy, Technology and Monopoly Capital," *College English*, 47, 7 (November 1985), 675-689.

Onore, Cynthia, "Whole Language, Whole School, Whole Community: Truths and Consequences," *English Education*, 31, 2 (January 1999), 150-168.

Ontario Public School Speller, The. Toronto: Copp Clark, 1914.

Ontario Readers Second Book, The. Toronto: T. Eaton Co., 1923.

Pace, Glenellen, "When Teachers Use Literature for Literacy Instruction: Ways That Constrain, Ways That Free," *Language Arts*, 68, 1 (Jan. 1991), 12-25.

Pantaleo, Sylvia, "Writing Responses to Literature: The Perspectives of Two Grade Four Students," English Quarterly, 30, 3/4 (1998), 28-41.

Parsons, Les. *Response Journals*. Markham: Pembroke, 1990.

—-. *Writing in the Real Classroom*. Markham: Pembroke, 1991.

—-. *Expanding Response Journals*. Markham: Pembroke, 1994.

Paterson, Shelley, "Evaluation and Teachers' Perception of Gender in Sixth-Grade Student Writing," *Research in the Teaching of English*, 33, 2 (November 1998), 181-208.

Peim, Nick. *Critical Theory and the English Teacher: Transforming the Subject.* London: Routledge, 1993.

Perrin, Robert, "'Barbie Doll' and 'GI Joe': Exploring Issues of Gender," *English Journal,* 88, 3 (January 1999), 83-85.

Plato. *The Collected Dialogues of Plato.* ed. Edith Hamilton and H. Cairns. New Jersey: Princeton U., 1961.

Phenix, Jo. *Spelling instruction that makes sense.* Markham: Pembroke, 1991.

Phinney, Margaret Y. *Reading with the Troubled Reader.* New York: Scholastic, 1988.

Pirie, Bruce. *Reshaping High School English.* Urbana: National Council of Teachers of English, 1997.

——. *Teenage Boys and High School English.* Portsmouth: Heinemann, 2002.

Pradl, Gordon M. "An Introduction," in Pradl, ed. *Prospect and Retrospect* London: Boynton/Cook, 1982, 1-6.

Press, Andrea. *Women Watching Television: Gender, Class and Generation in the American Television Experience.* Philadelphia: U of Philadelphia, 1991.

Probst, Robert. *Adolescent Literature: Response and Analysis.* New York: Merrill, 1984.

——. "Readers and Literary Texts," in Nelms, ed. *Literature in the Classroom.* Urbana: National Council of Teachers. 1988, 19-29

——. *Teaching Literature in Junior and Senior High School.* Portsmouth: Heinemann, 1988.

Proett, Jackie and K. Gill. *The Writing Process in Action: A Handbook for Teachers.* Urbana: National Council of Teachers, 1986.

Purves, Alan, T. Rogers and A. Soter. *How Porcupines Make Love III: Readers, Texts, Cultures in the Response-based Classroom.* White Plains: Longman, 1995.

Reiser, R.A. "A history of instructional design and technology: Part1: A history of instructional media." *Educational Technology Research and Development, 49*(1) (2001), 53-64.

Rich, Sharon. *Reading for Meaning.* Toronto: Nelson, 1998.

Richter, David. Ed. *Falling into Theory.* Boston: Bedford Books, 1994.

Rief, Linda. *Seeking Diversity: Language Arts with Adolescents.* Portsmouth: Heinemann, 1992.

Rissover, Fredric. *Mass Media and the Popular Arts.* Meramac: McGraw Hill, 1983.

Rodrigues, Raymond J. "Moving Away from Process-Writing Worship," *English Journal,* 74, 5 (September 1985), 24-27.

Rosenblatt, Louise M. "Language, Literature and Values," in Tchudi, ed. *Language, Schooling and Society.* Portsmouth: Heinemann, 1985, 64-80.

—-. *The Reader, the Text, and the Poem: The Transactional Theory of the Literary Work*. Carbondale: Southern Illinois P., 1994 (1978).

Rubin, Dorothy. *Teaching Elementary Language Arts*. Toronto: Allyn and Bacon, 2000.

Schrank, Jeffrey. *Understanding Mass Media*. Lincolnwood: National Textbook Company, 1986.

Shelley, Percy Bysshe. *Poetic Works*. London: Oxford U.P., 1970.

—-. *A Defense of Poetry*. 1821. New York: Bobbs-Merrill, 1965.

Slevin, James and A. Young, ed. *Critical Theory and the Teaching of Literature*. Urbana: National Council of Teachers, 1996.

Small, Robert, "Why I'll Never Teach Grammar Again," *English Education*, 17, 3 (October 1985), 174-8.

Smith, Frank. *Understanding Reading*. Toronto: Harcourt, 1978.

—-. *Writing and the Writer*. Toronto: Harcourt, 1982.

—-. *Reading Without Nonsense*. Toronto: Teachers College P., 2006.

—-. *Joining the Literacy Club: Further Essays into Education*. Portsmouth: Heinemann, 1987.

Stephens, Diane. *Research on Whole Language*. New York: R. C. Owen, 1991.

Stevenson, Chris. *Teaching Ten to Fourteen Year Olds*. New York: Longman, 1992.

Stewart, Sandy. *From Coast To Coast: A Personal History of Radio in Canada*. Toronto: CBC Enterprises, 1985.

—-. *Here's Looking At Us: A Personal History of Television in Canada*. Toronto: CBC Enterprises, 1986.

Strayed, Cheryl. *tiny beautiful things. advice on love and life from dear sugar*. New York: Viking, 2012.

Szuchewycz, Bohdan and J. Sloniowski, ed. *Canadian Communications: Issues in Contemporary Media and Culture*. Scarborough: Prentice Hall, 1999.

Tompkins, Jane P. ed. *Reader-Response Criticism: From Formalism to Post-Structuralism*. Baltimore: Johns Hopkins, 1981.

Way, Brian T. W. *Print Preview*. Toronto: Pearson, 2005.

—-. *Passages to Literature: a series of teaching guides*. London: Althouse P.: 2000-2010.

—-. *redirection*. Brighton: Hidden Brook P., 2015.

—-. *The Prince of Leroy*. Brighton: Hidden Brook P. 2018.

—-. *County Time*. Wellington: County Magazine, 2019.

—-. *american mankillers*. Picton: Printcraft, 2022.

—. *Perilous Journey in the Prose Fiction of Don Gutteridge.* Toronto: QuodSermo, 2023.

—. *Heads or Tales.* Wellington: County Magazine, 2023.

—. *Somebody should've told Fred and other stories.* Toronto: Sure Print and Design, 2024.

—. *magic birds.* Toronto: Sure Print and Design, 2024.

—. *Orchard of the Gods.* Toronto: Sure Print and Design, 2025.

—. *Bee: a book for all ages.* In process…

—. *My True Love: A Christmas Carol.* In process…

Weber, Sandra, and C. Mitchell. *"That's funny, you don't look like a teacher"* London: Fulmer, 1995.

Weiler, Kathleen. *Women Teaching for Change: Gender, Class and Power.* South Hadley: Bergin & Garvey, 1988.

Weir, Kathleen, "Freedom and Responsibility," *English Journal,* 80, 3 (March 1991), 43-46.

Whitcomb, Elaine, "Opening the World of Reading with the Internet," *Media & Methods,* (March-April 1999), 8.

Yeats, W. B. *Collected Poems.* London: Macmillan, 1933.

ADDENDUM:

On Funerals

For illimitable reasons, the human ritual of burying the dead is a supreme sign of civilisation and, through millennia, has undergone many variations, many changes, including during our time. From the visible corpse, cold and painted, in a dim room resonant with the *Adagio for Strings*, resting on silky satin in an expensive coffer of polished mahogany, shaded by floral decorations with esoteric names, *Zion Sprays* and *Pillows of Eternity*, and a darkly-clad congregation listening to priestly words read from an old book, a cemetery journey looming, to now, sudden, distant fire, ashes in cold ceramic or metal urns, a celebration of life in a rented hall months after the passing, an animated revel in spaces filled with finger-foods and potato chips, a rolling montage of digital photos, rock 'n roll or rap that once moved and shook, and ill-prepared speeches, brief and saccharine. And so our culture has found a less formal way of affixing closure to a beloved complexity, of finalizing our recollection of some human who made a difference to us and our world. One an attempt to put the corpse to rest; the other, to keep the dead alive. But, whatever the visceral ceremony of the lost, new paint gilded to an old sacrament, still, the ritual remains, binding memory as a primeval signpost for the living and the dead, a sacred wellspring of the imagination like a flame lit before a dark mirror, a flickering glimpse of what we were, who we are and where our destiny may reside, an altar, an offering, that quintessential possibility when love and time are contained and held like a holy stone in the palm of our hand.